Essential Law for Marketers

PRAISE FOR *ESSENTIAL LAW FOR MARKETERS*

This book is not only relevant, but easy to read and use. The focus on 'essential law' is unique in this field. No marketing practitioner working in Britain should be without this text. It is also comprehensive and up to date in the sense that it captures both traditional and rapidly expanding areas of marketing such as 'ambush' and 'cyber' marketing. A key to how successful a book is, is how often you find yourself using it. In this respect, the book will probably remain close at hand for easy access.

Dr Rafael Gomez, Interdisciplinary Institute of Management, London School of Economics

Few marketers have a full grasp of the law and legal matters rarely feature in marketing training. They will be grateful to Ardi Kolah for bringing English law into the marketing context in such a straightforward manner. An admirable introduction.

Professor Tim Ambler, London Business School

If you want an intelligent overview of the application of the law for marketers, then this is it. It should have been around years ago . . . .

Andrew Marsden, Category Director, Britvic Soft Drinks

Global brands are increasingly subject to a mass of laws and regulations and those charged with marketing and communications need to have a solid understanding of the law and how it applies in this context. *Essential Law for Marketers* is a seminal work on the subject. Agencies and clients can more effectively manage their marketing and communication activities by taking on board the information and lessons contained in this excellent book.

Raoul Pinnell, VP Global Brands & Communications, Shell International Petroleum Company

This book really is essential reading for all marketers and indeed for all general managers. It fills a major gap in the market and its many examples give a very practical guide to the intricacies of legal rights and responsibilities.

Sir Paul Judge, Judge Institute of Management, Cambridge University

Comprehensive, well written and easy to read. All the marketer ever needed to know about the legal and regulatory frameworks. A truly essential guide which I would recommend unreservedly.

Claire Watson, Director General, The Marketing Society

Brands and the value that they deliver are crucial for today's business. We have traditionally poorly understood the complex legal framework within which we operate. Ardi Kolah's legal knowledge and his insight into marketing strategy combine to set the industry standard. This book will appeal not just to marketers but to everyone involved in brand marketing and communication.

Ian Wright, Group Communications Director, Diageo plc

If you want to know the essentials of marketing law, then you'll find them here – an immensely valuable read....

Commodore Richard Leaman OBE,
Director of Communications, Royal Navy

Essential Law for Marketers is essential reading for all students and professionals of marketing. Packed with examples and written specifically for a marketing audience, it is the most comprehensive work on the subject and we're delighted to recommend it as an approved CIM text book to all our members.

Mike Detsiny, Chartered Institute of Marketing

I found it a clear and easy to use approach to marketing law – something I can pick up when I need it. As a small business it gives me the courage to make certain decisions without the immediate advice of a lawyer.

Cameron Leslie, Managing Director, Fabric

No marketer can afford to ignore the legislative context in which all businesses and organisations operate. *Essential Law for Marketers* is a timely and thorough guide to the current legislation that affects the practice of marketing – from data protection to defamation, advertising claims to licensing and sponsorship. Clear and concise, the book provides essential references and real-life examples to cover every marketing situation.

Tess Harris, Worshipful Company of Marketors

Understanding the law has become strategically important to the practice of modern communication, yet the majority of managers are poorly informed as to how the law can be used to protect and to promote corporate reputation and brand value. In this new book, Ardi Kolah presents the authoritative work on the subject, providing practical advice on how to integrate the communications power of the law into marketing and PR campaigns.

Chris Genasi, Director of Strategy, Weber Shandwick

This is an extremely useful book for any student of marketing. There is a very clear description of all the main legal issues which affect a marketer. The clarity of the writing will be a very pleasant surprise to anyone who previously has seen legal language as impenetrable. Legal points are illustrated by recent stories on marketing campaigns. We are necessarily affected by EU law and the book seamlessly moves across the various international legal systems. Also, it happens to be a very good book on marketing too. Many off-beat marketing tactics, e.g. Ambush marketing, are given a good factual explanation. I was surprised to find a legal book that I actually wanted to read. Students of CIM and CAM will find this a painless overview of a topic which could bring them grief. Thanks to this book, they are less likely to be caught out in a legal difficulty over marketing.

Jeremy Baker MBA (Harvard), London Guildhall University

Ardi Kolah has spent a lot of time studying the sponsorship scene from a variety of different angles. *Essential Law for Marketers* is required reading for anyone involved in sponsorship management and practice. The book succinctly explains the various laws and regulations which sponsors and property owners need to be aware of and the chapters on sponsorship and hospitality, as well as ambush marketing and data protection, take very complicated subjects and make these simple to comprehend.

Stephen Proctor, Founder, Sports Marketing Surveys

As marketing activities are increasingly subject to regulation and scrutiny, marketers must be fully cognisant of the law in relation to their profession. This knowledge reduces the risks to them and their company as they use multiple communications channels and analysis tools. Ardi Kolah's book provides both a guide and a reference which all marketers should have handy on their shelf.

Rob Wirszycz, Director, Momentum Capital and former D-G Computing Services & Software Association

It's a very good read. It's clear, simple and straightforward and you don't have to be a lawyer to understand it. The title sums it up – it's essential reading!

Richard Forbes-Robertson, CEO, Phosphorus

The convergence between law and public relations practice is getting closer particularly where statements and claims are now subject to both public scrutiny as well as legal challenge. Ardi Kolah is one of the industry's most accomplished public relations and marketing practitioners and has produced a well written and easy to understand guide to the law and I've no doubt the book will become the standard reference work on the subject.

Colin Farrington, Director General, Institute of Public Relations

Ignorance is no excuse – its every marketer's responsibility to understand how the law affects them. Covering everything from cookies to copyright; data protection to defamation and lobbying to libel, *Essential Law for Marketers* is a unique and comprehensive reference of all these areas. If you want to avoid visits from trading standards, brushes with the Advertising Standards Authority, litigation or worse... you must read this book.

Ian Hunter, Marketing Director, Fujitsu Services

This book is a definitive guide, for busy marketers, of the potential minefield of legal issues that they must navigate during the course of performing their job.

Paul van Barthold, Managing Director, BLM Media

Ardi Kolah's *Essential Law for Marketers* has been written with the legal virgin in mind and that includes a surprising number of advertising practitioners who should at least have a basic knowledge of the laws governing their business. This book is full of practical tips and suggestions that will also be relevant to the seasoned campaign director and is sure to prove essential reading for anyone in the advertising industry who needs to get up to speed with this complex area.

Claire Beale, Deputy Editor, *Campaign*

When building a business the last distraction you want is the legal implications of managing and promoting your brands. Few agencies are always on top of the type of detail you need to know about to stay on the right side of the law and ensure you don't damage the brand. I've often ended meetings with the phrase 'We need to check this with the lawyer', who then tells us the obvious – if only we had bothered to understand the basics of the law. This book is an essential guide to law, written for the marketer and is both interesting to read (amazingly) and has the right level of detail.

Charles Fallon, partner, Strategy & Investment Partners LLP and former Director, Saatchi & Saatchi Advertising UK

Essential Law for Marketers is a timely reminder to business communicators that the law can be both an ally and an adversary. Journalists, too, are no strangers to the complexities posed by the need to protect their intellectual property and copyright rights. Indeed, as freelancing and short-term contracts become the norm for writers of all descriptions, so the need for a comprehensive overview of the legal issues relating to trade marks, 'passing off', defamation and advertising becomes all the more relevant. *Essential Law for Marketers* reminds us also that, with the advent of the internet and other electronic media, the issues of territoriality and ownership are increasingly blurred. With its readable style and lively use of business examples, *Essential Law for Marketers* should find a home in the bookcase of all practitioners of the black arts of business communications.

Andy Smith, President, Chartered Institute of Journalists

Ardi Kolah has captured many of the substantial legal issues that marketers could face as regulation and compliance standards increase. This book offers clear explanations of relevant law, with examples and practical advice for maintaining marketing momentum . . . .

Professor Merlin Stone and Bryan Foss, IBM Financial Services Sector

I have known Ardi Kolah since he was an outstanding post graduate law student here at University College London. On the basis of that contact I am sure that *Essential Law for Marketers* is an exceptional book in terms of its content and clarity of writing. It is important that such a book be read by all law students who are interested in working within the creative industries and those who need a robust introduction to the way in which law has influenced this important sector.

Professor Jeffrey Jowell QC, Dean of the Faculty of Laws, University College London

For Zara

Essential Law for Marketers

A Kolah BA LLM FIPR FCIM FRSA Chartered Marketer

BUTTERWORTH
HEINEMANN

OXFORD   AMSTERDAM   BOSTON   LONDON   NEW YORK   PARIS
SAN DIEGO   SAN FRANCISCO   SINGAPORE   SYDNEY   TOKYO

Butterworth-Heinemann
An imprint of Elsevier Science
Linacre House, Jordan Hill, Oxford OX2 8DP
225 Wildwood Avenue, Woburn, MA 01801-2041

First published 2002

All references to English law in this book are as of May 2002

**The information contained in this book is for general purposes only. If you wish to obtain specific
legal advice or information, then seek the assistance of a suitably qualified lawyer who specialises
in your area(s) of concern**

British Library Cataloguing in Publication Data
A catalogue record for this book in available from the British Library

Library of Congress Cataloguing in Publication Data
A catalogue record for this book is available from the Library of Congress

ISBN 0 7506 5500 3

For information on all Butterworth-Heinemann publications
visit our web site at www.bh.com

Typeset by Keyword Typesetting Services Ltd, Wallington, Surrey
Printed and bound in Great Britain by MPG Books Ltd, Bodmin, Cornwall

CONTENTS

FOREWORD

I have known and worked with Ardi Kolah for a number of years and have found no one with such an in-depth understanding of the legal side of marketing.

In today's highly litigious society, knowledge of what is permissible in marketing is essential, even more so given the complex regulatory framework in which organisations operate today.

This book is well written, easy to understand and is a must for any truly professional marketer.

Professor Malcolm McDonald
Cranfield School of Management
May 2002

ABOUT THE AUTHOR

Ardi Kolah BA, LLM, FIPR, FCIM, FRSA chartered marketer is a leading practitioner in sponsorship, marketing and public relations with over 13 years' business consultancy experience.

He studied law at Kingston University, Surrey where he specialised in intellectual property law in his final year and holds a Master of Laws degree from University College and King's College, London. He taught at Westminster School before joining the BBC to work in network TV and radio as well as BBC World Service. From there he went on to hold senior positions with Andersen Consulting (Accenture), CMG plc and the Imperial Cancer Research Fund (Cancer Research UK).

He is also the holder of several national awards in marketing and public relations in the UK, is the managing director of Maverick UK and SponsorCalc, a Director of the Institute of Public Relations, a Fellow of the Chartered Institute of Marketing, and a Fellow of the Royal Society of Arts. He was admitted as a Liveryman of the Worshipful Company of Marketors in 2002.

He is the author of several leading works on sponsorship including *Maximising the Value of Sports Sponsorship, Measuring Successful Sponsorship* (published by FT Media), *How to Develop an Effective Sponsorship Programme, How to Develop Effective Hospitality Programmes, How to Develop Effective Naming Rights Strategies* and *Maximising Revenues from Licensing and Merchandising* (published by the SportBusiness Group), *The Global Market for Sponsorship* (published by Screen Digest), *Principles of Ethnic Marketing* and *Improving the Performance of Sponsorship* (published by Butterworth-Heinemann).

He is a visiting lecturer at Leeds Metropolitan University, an External Examiner for London Guildhall University, a regular commentator in the national press, radio and TV on marketing, branding, public relations and sponsorship issues, and chairs a substantial number of conferences every year.

He lives with his wife and daughter in S.W. London.

The author welcomes and appreciates feedback from his readers.

(Tel) Maverick UK +44 207 542 8110 or (e-mail) akolah@maverick-uk.com

ACKNOWLEDGMENTS

I would like to thank the following contributors for their invaluable input, contributions, suggestions and advice in the writing of this book:

Richard King, head of chambers, 5 Paper Buildings (Chapters 2–4); Angela Hall, barrister-at-law, 5 Paper Buildings (Chapters 2–4); Henry Ward, barrister-at-law, 8 New Square (Chapters 5 and 6); Mark O'Shea, partner, Rawlison Butler (Chapters 7 and 11); Kay Miles, solicitor, Rawlinson Butler; Keith Mathieson, partner, Reynolds Porter Chamberlain (Chapter 8); Andy Korman, partner, Hammond Suddards Edge (Chapters 16 and 17); Benedicte Ferragu, solicitor, Hammond Suddards Edge (Chapters 16 and 17); Chris Protheroe, director of sport, Copyright Promotions Licensing Group (Chapter 11); Andrew Skipper, partner, Lovells (Chapter 13); Marissa Parry, partner, Denton Wilde Sapte (Chapter 9); John Enser, partner, Olswang (Chapters 5, 10, 12 and 16), Louise Quinn, solicitor, Olswang (Chapters 5, 10, 12 and 16); Michael Burrell, chairman, Westminster Strategy (Chapter 14); and Nigel O'Connor, head of policy, Institute of Public Relations (Chapter 14).

Special thanks to Stuart Evans, partner, Rawlison Butler who worked tirelessly as the consultant legal editor and made an invaluable contribution to the robustness of this book.

Also special thanks to Stephen Groom and all his colleagues in the Br@ndlegal team at Osborne Clarke, who kindly allowed me to make use of the numerous case reports and valuable insights in their website (www.marketinglaw.co.uk) to help the book come alive for marketers, and to Alexandra Denison and her team at Berwin Leighton Paisner, who double checked all the case references and statute laws for the web site.

Finally, a special word of thanks to Tim Goodfellow, my publisher at Butterworth-Heinemann, for having the foresight to commission this book and for his fantastic enthusiasm, encouragement and support which made this all possible.

The British Codes of Advertising and Sales Promotion appears on the web site http://www.bh.com/companions/0750655003 by kind permission of the Advertising Standards Authority.

The law as stated as it applies to England and Wales is correct as of May 2002.

Ardi Kolah
Bloomsbury, London

1

INTRODUCTION

WHY DO I NEED TO KNOW WHAT THE LAW IS?

Knowing your legal obligations as well as your rights as a marketer is fundamental. No other profession – doctors, lawyers, architects, engineers, surveyors, teachers – is so poorly served in understanding the legal ramifications of its work in an easy and accessible way.

I hope this book demystifies the essential law for marketers and does 'what it says on the cover'.

Why should we, as professional marketers, be any different from any of the other professions mentioned above?

Ignorance of the law is a very dangerous state of affairs as it can lead to an infringement of someone else's intellectual property rights, an expensive lawsuit, a cancelled marketing campaign, damage to reputation that could take years to repair, and potentially a downturn in profits and share price. In extreme cases, it could even lead to insolvency and prison.

It is important that marketers refresh and update their understanding of the law, as changes in the law affect marketing best practice in many different ways.

A basic understanding of marketing law is essential if expensive legal battles are to be avoided. For example, when low cost airline Ryanair obtained confirmation from the courts in 2001 to continue with its British Airways comparative advertising campaign, marketers were left with a much clearer picture of just how far they could go when it comes to trumping the competition.

Most marketers have a hunch that the more they know the better, but at the same time, they are tempted to think it is possible to get by with the bare minimum. If you want to be aware of the key issues faced by marketers in the course of their daily business, rather than become a legal anorak, then this book is for you!

Whether at the pinnacle of your career as the director of marketing for a global FMCG brand, a senior marketer with over 10 years' experience, a marketing consultant with your own agency working with a small number of clients or new to the marketing profession, I hope this book will help to answer some of the basic and not so basic questions that as marketers we face daily.

A special web site to accompany this book can be found at http://www.bh.com/companions/0750655003.

HOW DO I USE THIS BOOK?

I suggest that you skim read the book cover to cover for the first time, stopping to pause at the chapters that interest you most. You will find that the examples of the legal points covered in the chapters are stories that help you to remember the points made a little bit easier. You will find these in boxes throughout the book.

Having skim read the book for the first time, go back and give the book a second, more thorough reading, but this time concentrate on the 'spine' chapters, i.e. Chapters 2–8. These are the core, non-industry specific chapters which give you the basic legal principles which underpin what follows in Chapters 9–17.

Your understanding of the book will be far greater if the spine chapters are mastered.

Write notes in the margins if you want to that will help you increase the sense of the topic the next time you need to consult the book.

APPLICATION OF THE LAW

The practice of law is much more difficult and more complex than learning the theory in the safety of the classroom.

As marketers, we need to understand and appreciate that an issue such as ambush marketing and the laws applicable to sponsorship may well have relevance to a marketing contract.

Likewise, an advertising and labelling issue may well have at its root a trademark infringement or a product liability claim.

As a marketer working in-house for a large corporation or partnership, many legal issues may present themselves throughout any given year.

There may be a dispute with a landlord over rent reviews or a difficult decision to be made in respect of selecting certain employees for redundancy.

Whilst acknowledging that marketers may face such issues given the financial and management burdens they have to bear, I have tried to elicit what I consider would be *essential* laws pertaining to their key functions, rather than everything you would ever need to know.

In doing this, no two individuals' notions of what is essential would be the same – if there are other legal areas to explore we can deal with these in further editions of this book. Your feedback is therefore important.

What is clear is that I can only skim the surface by giving you a solid grounding. For example, books on contract law will often amount to two volumes – even the law of agency merits a volume on its own! Likewise, employment law, which is only touched upon in this book, would fill a major space on your bookshelf.

For the purpose of this book, I do not think it is essential to know about employment law but we may revisit this in the future.

LAW AS IT APPLIES IN ENGLAND AND WALES

This book covers English law and how it applies to England and Wales only. Scotland is a separate jurisdiction with its own laws and whilst there should be a reasonable correlation between English and Scottish law, I am not covering the latter at any stage and separate advice from a Scottish lawyer will be needed if a marketer has issues across the border.

There is not, and never has been, any concept of 'UK law'.

European Union (EU) law has to a considerable degree been incorporated into English law, e.g. the anti-competitive provisions of the Treaty of Rome. Recently the European Convention on Human Rights has been enshrined in the Human Rights Act 1998 and appeals on intellectual property rights matters have been scheduled for hearing in Strasbourg.

Again, whilst EU is a highly specialised area, with relevance to marketers in England and Wales, I have concentrated only on the essential law as it applies to the subject areas outlined.

All references to English law in this book are as of May 2002.

Can I also draw your attention to the fact that the information contained in this book is for general purposes only. It does not aim to provide legal advice on any area. If you wish to obtain specific legal advice or information, then seek the assistance of a suitably qualified lawyer who specialises in your area(s) of concern.

2
MAKING AGREEMENTS

In this chapter:

- The anatomy of a contract in marketing
- The types of contracts commonly used in the marketing profession
- Pitfalls to watch for hidden in contracts
- How to avoid legal difficulties before they arise
- Checklist

Other useful chapters:

- Chapter 3: Making statements
- Chapter 4: Liability for defective products
- Chapter 5: Intellectual property rights
- Chapter 9: Advertising and labelling
- Chapter 11: Licensing and merchandising
- Chapter 17: Ambush marketing

INTRODUCTION

Contracts are based on agreement. The law of contract is the branch of law that determines when a promise or a set of promises are legally binding and enforceable.

A contract is made when two or more parties each promise to the other that they will do something (or refrain from doing something). In marketing, the archetypal situation is where the marketing agency says to the client: 'I will do X for you in return for £Y', to which the client replies: 'I agree' (which spelt out means: 'If you do X for me I will pay you £Y').

When the marketer makes an offer, which the client accepts (the offer could equally be made by the client, with acceptance by the marketer), the marketer has promised to do X and the client has promised to pay £Y.

A marketer, whether working in-house as a director or manager of marketing or within a marketing agency or as a marketing consultant, will need to enter into legal relations with a range of individuals and organisations.

The figure illustrates not only the stages in reaching an agreement, but also where issues such as performance, breach of contract and remedies fit within the overall flow of interaction between the parties.

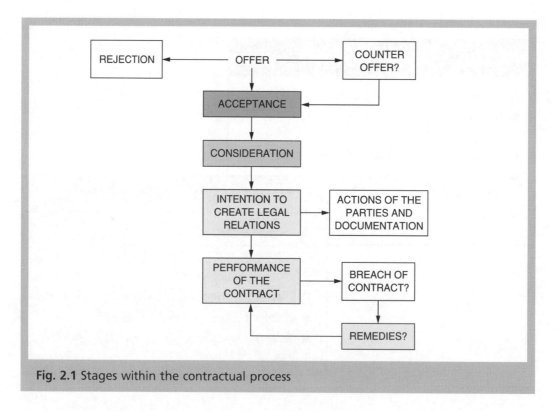

Fig. 2.1 Stages within the contractual process

A legal contract sits at the heart of the marketing process – whether it is for the artistic direction for the latest TV commercial, the design of a web site, a contract for public relations services or the provision of corporate hospitality at a major sporting event.

The contract can be written, oral or a combination of both. It should crystallise the intentions of the parties in a way that is recognised in law and is an instrument upon which both parties can rely should there be a dispute as to what is to be performed under contract.

Not all marketing activities are necessarily done under the terms of a contract. For example, when canvassers talk to the public about what they think about the latest detergent product or how many times they wash their hair every week – there is no contract created here between the public and the interviewers.

However, under the rules of the Market Research Society (MRS), the research company has agreed to comply with the MRS code of conduct as a condition of its membership.

This code is part of the contract that the company has entered into as a condition of its membership and breach of the code could result, in extreme cases, in expulsion of the company from the MRS for breach of that contract.

ANATOMY OF A CONTRACT IN MARKETING

Simple contract – offer and acceptance

A contract is made when two or more parties each promise to the other that they will do something or refrain from doing something.

POINT OF LAW

For example, a design consultancy offers to create a brand identity for a new product to be launched later in the year and the director of marketing at the client company agrees to go ahead with this proposal and pay the design consultancy on a retainer basis £6000 per month.

In this straightforward example, the design consultancy has made an offer to the marketing director of the client company which he accepts.

It could easily work the other way and the client could have given the instruction to the design consultancy to create the brand identity for the new product.

Fundamentally, the design consultancy has agreed to create a new brand identity based on a brief supplied by the marketing director and the marketing director has agreed to pay the consultancy on a monthly retainer basis.

Provided that money (known as 'consideration' in legal jargon) is discussed and agreed, then the two parties are legally bound and the price fixed.

However, life is not always so straightforward and the evidence of a contract may well be found in a combination of both oral and written statements or it can be found in the conduct of the parties to one another.

From a practical perspective, marketers should always ensure that whatever is agreed is written down in detail within the context of a contract.

For example, if the marketing agency thinks commission is 30% of gross profits and the client thinks it is 20% of net profits, then this could give rise to a legal dispute. In such cases, it is the word of one party against the other if there is an absence of a signed agreement. If the parties wrote down what they had agreed there would have been no (or at least less!) room for dispute.

The counter offer

In the above example, the design agency may have said that it wanted to charge a one-off fee of £150 000 and the marketing director may have originally said that he wanted to pay the consultancy a retainer of £6000 a month instead of a one-off fee.

The counter offer of £6000 per month operates to reject the original offer made by the design consultancy.

It is now open to the design consultancy to either accept or reject this counter offer by the marketing director or propose a new offer, e.g. to work for a lower fee, say £120 000, or to propose a higher retainer, say £10 000 per month.

It could also reinstate its original offer to do the work for £150 000.

This process of negotiation continues until agreement is reached. Once agreement is reached (as it did for £6000 per month), any variation to that agreement can only be made with the consent of both parties to the agreement.

Frequently there is a complex interrelationship of promises made by both parties. Often that complex interrelationship will be developed following extensive negotiation between the parties, with each possibly imposing some new condition(s).

The contract is only made when the parties have agreed with each other about all that they have been negotiating. Even then, there may not be a legally binding contract if it is clear from their negotiations that they are not going to treat their agreement as legally binding *unless* they both sign a formal written contract.

An offer or counter offer that has lapsed, e.g. because the time stipulated for acceptance has expired ('I need your answer by the end of this week'), or that has been rejected, e.g. by making a counter offer, cannot later be accepted *unless* it is re-stated by the person making it.

In some cases an offer (or counter offer) can be accepted by the actions or conduct of the parties.

If the parties enter into negotiations, but there is no outward assent to all the terms discussed by both parties, there will be no contract.

It sometimes happens that following such negotiations, one or both parties *behave* as though there is a concluded contract between them.

For example, commencing the work contemplated in the negotiation or by paying an advance fee, and the other party accepts that performance as though rendered under a contract.

In such circumstances there is almost certainly a contract, but determining its terms can be difficult.

An approach frequently applied is that the party tendering performance (the design agency) and acceptance of such performance (by the marketing director) is treated by the courts that in fact agreement has taken place.

'Consideration'

Any promise to do an act in exchange for another promise can constitute consideration. The promise to pay money can be only *one* of a number of promises that amount to consideration. The promise to pay money is, however, a *typical* consideration.

In law, 'consideration' is required for a contract to be enforceable. It will usually not be difficult to identify the consideration element required for a binding contract to come into existence.

Action of the parties

There are three important circumstances to take into account irrespective of whether or not there has been consideration present.

1. A gratuitous promise – one for which there is no promise or performance in return – is not enforceable in law.

For example, a simple promise to manage the public relations for a client where there has been no agreement to accept and pay for this service, would not normally give rise to a contract in law and could not be enforced by the person to whom it was made.

2. It is not possible to claim payment for a performance rendered gratuitously – one for which no request was made.

For example, the public relations agency without prior authorisation, activates a public relations programme and then seeks payment for it. The client would have no contractual liability to pay.

3. A promise to vary the terms of a contract will be unenforceable if there is absence of any promise or performance of the contract.

POINT OF LAW

For example, a public relations agency writes a letter to its client (with whom there is an existing contractual relationship) submitting its standard terms and conditions, stating that these are the new terms of the contract. In such circumstances, the terms are not enforceable as part of the contract.

The courts frequently have to determine whether the promises that parties have made to one another have been broken.

Often the issue that the courts have to decide is what the parties agreed in the first place before the marketing activity took place.

In doing so, the first question is always: is there a document signed by both parties or a series of documents signed by each of them that can be said to be the contract between them?

If there is, the court will stop there and determine from such document or documents what was agreed.

It will not admit evidence of what the parties said to one another or what they intended to agree, although it will admit evidence as to the background to the transaction in order to determine what intention the parties had when they created the documents.

Where there is no such evidence, the court will look at such documents as did come into existence at the time when the parties made their contract and will hear evidence from the parties as to what they said to one another at the time.

Often the parties' recollection is different and the court's task is therefore the difficult one of determining which (if any!) of the witnesses has a more accurate and credible recollection of what was said and agreed.

INSIGHT

Predicting the outcome of such proceedings is uncertain. Marketers should always ensure that the contract is in writing and is signed by all parties or, at the very least, that there is contemporaneous documentary evidence of what the parties agreed.

Usually only the parties to a contract can enforce the terms of a contract against one another (known as 'privity of contract').

This has the result that a third party who suffers loss as a result of a breach of contract cannot recover that loss itself because it was not a party to the contract.

In the above situation, *except in special circumstances*, the person who is a party to the contract cannot recover damages for the loss suffered by the third party because she or he was not party to the contract.

The effect of these principles has been mitigated for contracts made after May 2000 by the **Contracts (Rights of Third Parties) Act 1999 (CRTPA)**.

The 1999 Act (which is similar to laws in the US) provides a right of action to a third party that may not have been a signatory to a contract.

POINT OF LAW

For example, if a client commissions an advertising agency to create and execute a TV and poster advertising campaign, the advertising agency will usually contract directly with a media buying agency to buy the media for the campaign. In most cases the client will not be a signatory in these negotiations and the media buying agency will contract with the advertising agency. However, if the contract is entered into post May 2000, it will be covered by the CRTPA.

Under the CRPTA, such a contract will have been made for the benefit of the client.

The client will be able to recover damages against the media buying agency if the contract expressly states that the contract is made for the client's benefit or if it does not appear from the contract that the parties did not intend the provisions of the contract to be enforceable by the client.

Prior to 2000, a client would have had to rely on the *law of agency* in order to claim damages for breach of such a contract – the advertising agency in the above example would be acting as agent for the disclosed principal (the client) and thereby giving the client a right to sue under the contract even though it has not actually signed it.

However, since advertising agencies and other marketing businesses traditionally contract as principals, this way of recovering benefits apparently due to them under their agencies' contracts with others had not been open to brand owners until CRTPA.

Mistake

Occasionally marketing contracts can be void for mistake. This can occur where both parties are mistaken or (less often) where only one party is mistaken.

Where both parties are mistaken about a fundamental matter to do with the contract ('mutual mistake'), the result may be that there is no contract at all and the parties need to re-negotiate from scratch. In a marketing context, this could arise where both the parties to a contract for the sale and purchase of goods and marketing services are mistaken about whether the subject matter of the contract exists or not.

POINT OF LAW

For example, a client books hospitality facilities at a major agricultural trade show thinking that it was in April but in fact it was in February. Because only the client is mistaken about the date of the event, there is no mutual mistake and the contract is enforceable.

If one party is mistaken about something to do with the contract, the contract is usually unaffected and the parties must perform it in accordance with the agreement.

There is a limited exception to this rule which applies if one party knows that the other is mistaken about some essential matter to do with the contract but nevertheless stands by and allows the other to enter into the contract in such mistaken belief.

A party who engages in sharp practice in this way runs the risk that the court will permit the mistaken party to avoid the contract and treat it as having no effect, without risk of financial penalty or obligation under the contract.

The terms of a contract

The terms of the contract are the promises that the parties have made to one another or, putting it another way, the things that the parties have agreed to do (or agreed not to do). Such terms may be expressed or they may be implied from the other terms that have been agreed. They may also be implied by law.

If the contract is in writing, the express terms will be the terms that are written down.

How much the parties have written down usually depends upon how much they have thought about how the marketing contract they have made is to be performed and what could go wrong.

Where parties have given thorough consideration to what is going to happen and what could go wrong, they will often seek to provide for these matters in the marketing contract.

Frequently the contract will be made by reference to a detailed specification provided by the marketer in response to the requirements that the client has stated.

INSIGHT

For example, a sports sponsorship contract is a detailed document that sets out the rights, obligations, duties and responsibilities and typically includes:

- Details of sponsor (brand owner)
- Details of the property owner (rights holder)
- Commencement date
- Exclusivity
- Term
- Consideration
- Option to renew
- First right of refusal
- Details of the property being sponsored
- Category of sponsorship
- Territory that the sponsorship takes place within
- Rights holder's objectives
- Sponsor's (brand owner's) objectives
- Evaluation criteria

- Governing law and dispute resolution mechanism
- Intellectual property rights
- Termination events
- Insurance

Business terms and conditions

It is customary for any type of business or organisation to provide its products or services on similar terms on each occasion that it contracts with another party.

Accordingly, standard written 'Terms and Conditions' or 'Terms of Business' should be incorporated into every contract entered into.

It is advisable to have such terms and conditions properly drawn up to reflect the way in which the company or organisation actually does business, and it is essential that such terms and conditions are specifically incorporated as terms of every contract that is made.

In the context of a marketing agency and its client, the client should be provided with a copy of the terms and conditions *before* the contract is executed and where the contract is in writing or is evidenced in writing that the pre-contractual documents produced should state that any contract is made subject to the marketing agency's terms and conditions.

POINT OF LAW

For example, the design consultancy commences work on the new brand and submits its first invoice which states that all invoices that are outstanding after 60 days carry a late payment penalty of 10% of the invoice value.

The design consultancy cannot rely on this term unless it was brought to the attention of the marketing director before he entered into the contract.

Simply a reference to the terms and conditions, without actually providing a copy to the client, may be sufficient to cover the design consultancy, but clearly the marketing director could always ask to see these terms and conditions and these must then be immediately supplied.

If the terms and conditions contain any provision which is unduly onerous, e.g. a right to increase the contract price in defined circumstances or an exclusion of liability, the courts will usually say that if insufficient has been done to draw that term to the attention of the client, it does not form any part of the contract.

Within a marketing context, for example, the creation of a new web site by an external agency, a very common source of complaint involves the intellectual property (IP) clauses and what types of IP rights are transferred to the client for work undertaken and what stays with the supplier. For further discussion on this, see Chapter 5.

'Battle of the forms'

In many contracts, the terms and conditions often state that 'only these terms will apply'.

For example, if an exchange of correspondence indicates that the client company wants to incorporate its own terms and conditions into the contract, then the marketing agency must exercise great care to ensure that agreement is reached as to *which t*erms apply.

This will be a matter for negotiation. Where an oversight occurs, the court has to determine which of two (usually) mutually inconsistent documents the parties intended should apply – a situation described rather dramatically by lawyers as the 'battle of forms'.

In the absence of any other factors that demonstrate the intentions of the parties to the contract, the courts usually apply a strict 'offer and acceptance' analysis of the formation of the contract.

POINT OF LAW

For example, the marketing agency offers to contract on its own terms and conditions. The client purports to accept the offer, but says it does so subject to its own terms and conditions. The agency proceeds to provide services under the contract. In these circumstances the client's contractual terms apply. The client's purported acceptance was in fact a *counter offer*, which the agency accepted by its conduct when it performed the contract. In essence, the agency tacitly agrees because it continued to work and delivered under this contract and the client's terms were the 'last in time'.

Standard terms and conditions of business tend to be very one-sided and to favour the party who seeks to have them included in the contract. In the marketing profession, the balance may favour the marketing agency if it can get the client to agree to its terms and conditions.

As a result of the imbalance of bargaining power, the courts tend to construe such terms strictly *against* the party that has put them forward.

Also Parliament has determined that certain terms are unenforceable.

POINT OF LAW

For example, it is impossible to exclude liability for death or personal injury resulting from negligence and any term that seeks to do so is unenforceable. Also any exclusion or limitation of liability for negligence or any exclusion or limitation of liability contained in standard terms and conditions of business is subject to a requirement of reasonableness.

Test of 'reasonableness'

Reasonableness is determined by reference to all the circumstances which were or ought reasonably to have been known to the parties at the time when the contract was made.

This includes:

- Strength of the bargaining position of the parties

- Whether the client received an inducement to agree to the term

- In the case of limitation of liability – the resources that the brand owner might be expected to have to meet the liability

- Whether or not the brand owner can obtain insurance against liability for the loss suffered by the other contracting party

- The cost of such insurance

If the term relied upon is capable of excluding liability in circumstances that are unreasonable it will be unenforceable even though its application in the particular case concerned is not unreasonable.

Terms that provide that the client cannot set off its damage against fees payable to the marketing agency must also satisfy the requirement of reasonableness.

It is impossible to generalise about whether a particular term will be held to satisfy the requirement of reasonableness.

All the circumstances of the particular case must be considered.

POINT OF LAW

For example, exclusion of liability for loss by the client of profit which is alleged to result from failure of performance by the marketing agency is not unreasonable, provided that this does not result from a blanket exclusion of liability or totally negate the expectations that the client has from the contract.

Similarly, limitation of liability to the contract price payable under the contract could be regarded as a reasonable allocation of the financial consequences of non-performance or improper performance, especially where both parties know that the marketing agency has a small capital base.

Matters left unsaid

In the context of the marketing agency and the client, both parties often do not expressly agree all matters that will arise during the performance of the contract. Often terms as important as the fee to be charged or the time within which the services are to be performed are not expressly agreed!

In such situations, which ought to be avoided, the law attributes to the parties an intention to be reasonable – which is not a great state of affairs, for example, if the parties disagree over what is reasonable or not.

Thus, if the price for the job has not been expressly agreed, a reasonable price must be paid. This is determined by reference to evidence from a marketing expert witness as to the reasonable length of time that the work should have taken and the reasonable rate at which charge should be made.

This obligation to pay a reasonable price frequently arises where, during the course of performance of a fixed price project, extra work is ordered for which no agreement is made as to the price to be paid.

Similarly, if the overall time for performance of the work is not agreed, it is implied that the work will be done within a reasonable time having regard to all the circumstances.

Terms are also implied as to the quality of the services provided. It is implied that the work will be carried out with *reasonable skill and care*, which in the case of a marketer means with the *skill, competence and diligence to be expected of a marketer holding itself out as having the skill, competence and diligence of a professional marketer.*

Where the client has stated that it wants the work done to satisfy a particular purpose and relies upon the marketer to provide work to satisfy that purpose, a term will be implied that the work done by the marketer will be *reasonably fit for the purpose concerned.*

The test used by the courts in deciding whether a term should be implied into the contract is: *whether it is necessary, having regard to the terms of the contract as a whole, to imply the term in order to make the contract workable.*

POINT OF LAW

For example, in order for the marketing agency to perform the services agreed, it is necessary for the client to do something in advance and the contract does not expressly provide for the client to do it, the court will imply that the client will do this because otherwise the contract cannot be performed.

On the other hand, if some preliminary work has to be carried out that it is not necessary for the client to do and the marketing contract does not expressly provide for the client or the marketer to do it, it will *not* be implied that the client will do the work.

The guiding principle for whether a term will be implied is therefore whether it is *necessary* to enable the contract to be carried through, not whether it is reasonable that the term should be implied.

A situation sometimes arises where it is clear that some term must be implied to make the contract work, but there is more than one possible term that can be implied.

Here the court will imply the term that is the *most reasonable* as between the parties in the circumstances. The reasonable term is, however, only being implied because of the necessity of implying a term.

As the next case illustrates, the courts will imply a term into a contract that a marketing agency will not put the client into a situation where it could potentially be in breach of copyright. This could be relevant with respect to web designers where there may be a contract offered or where they have simply agreed terms over the telephone.

Antiquesportfolio.com-v-Rodney Fitch & Co. (2000)

The defendant marketer (Rodney Fitch) was a web site designer contracted to design a web site which was to sell antiques on-line. The client discovered that the designer had included in the site tiny icons and banners using images of antiques which were copied from photographs in a well-known antiques encyclopaedia.

The contract between the client and the marketer was silent about copyright but the client sued for return of all monies paid to the designer for the design of the web site on grounds of an *alleged breach of an implied term in the contract obliging the designer to supply a site which did not infringe a third party's copyright.*

The Chancery Court agreed with the client and emphasised that there was a general duty also implied into the marketing contract that a marketer was to use reasonable care and skill – a term which is implied by statute into all English law-governed contracts for the supply of services.

In this case, using reasonable care and skill meant that the marketer had an obligation not knowingly to use material that infringed a third party's rights without warning the client of this.

As the above points demonstrate, leaving matters for a court to decide is too risky and each party should spell out in detail what is expected under the contract.

Performance under the contract

A contract is performed when each party carries out its obligations in accordance with the terms of the contract.

It follows that in determining whether a party has performed its obligations under the marketing contract, it is necessary to determine by interpretation of the contract what that party agreed to do and then to determine whether the person has done what was agreed.

INSIGHT

This is a major area of disputes and could be avoided in most cases by the creation of a watertight contract.

It is not open to a marketing agency, for example, to say that it has not done what was agreed, but that what it has done is just as good as or even better than expected or requested by the client *unless* there has been prior agreement to vary the contract to provide for such substitute performance.

Estoppel

In the above example, it may be possible for the client to 'estopped' from saying that it did not agree to the substitute performance by the agency.

'Estoppel' arises when:

■ A party represents to the other (by words or conduct) that it will accept a substitute performance

■ The other party (the marketer) acts to its detriment in reliance on that representation

■ It is inequitable for the first party to insist on performance strictly in accordance with the terms of the contract

Time for performance

An issue that frequently arises in connection with performance is the time when obligations should be performed. Unless the parties have agreed something different (which is frequently the case) payment becomes due when the marketing services have been delivered (prior demand by delivery of an invoice is strictly unnecessary, but is expected in the marketing profession).

Late payments

If payment is late, interest is payable in accordance with the express terms of the contract.

If there are no such terms and the contract is a typical marketing contract, interest is payable:

■ Where the date of payment is agreed in the contract, from the agreed date for payment

■ Where the payment is an advance payment, from the day upon which the supplier's obligation is performed

■ Where the debt is a fixed sum agreed in the contract, 30 days from the performance of the obligation to which the debt relates

■ Where the amount payable is not a fixed sum agreed in the contract, from the date when notice of the amount of the debt is given to the paying party

Other contractual obligations

In the case of other contractual obligations, performance by the marketing agency or the client must be carried out within the agreed time for performance.

Where the parties do not specify a time for performance, it is *implied* by the courts that the parties will perform their obligations within *a reasonable time*.

What is a reasonable time must be determined in the light of the circumstances that prevail after the contract has been entered into but it is an imprecise science.

In many instances, there can be protracted delay in delivering what has been agreed under the contract *provided* that the matters causing the delay were beyond the control of the party who has to perform under the contract and that party has not acted negligently or unreasonably.

POINT OF LAW

For example, where the marketer knows that it was on deadline and decided to see another client it would not have acted reasonably in such circumstances as it should have arranged the new appointment for another time.

However, where a marketer is waiting for an action by the client and this is delayed, it will be reasonable for the marketer not to perform under the contract until the client has done what was agreed.

Where 'time is of the essence'

In marketing, it is more than likely that *time is of the essence*, i.e. that there will undoubtedly be a deadline for certain marketing activities to have taken place within an agreed timescale, whereby failure to comply will render the performance of no value.

POINT OF LAW

For example, the promotion of the new Harry Potter movie, the launch of the new BMW 3 Series, and Mitre's licensing and merchandising programme to coincide with start of the 2002 FIFA World Cup Korea/Japan^{TM} are all time-sensitive marketing activities.

The question here is whether the client can discharge the marketing contract (or vice versa) when an important deadline has been missed?

This depends on two important factors:

1. What the parties have said in the contract
2. The surrounding circumstances to the marketing contract

If marketing services are to be performed in connection with an event due to take place on a specific date, the parties may provide for a time for performance, which if not complied with, will render the performance of no value.

In such circumstances, *time will be of the essence*. On the other hand, time is *not* likely to be of the essence where the date for rendering performance is not time sensitive or critical.

Even where time is *not* of the essence, it is still a breach of contract not to perform within the time stipulated, or within a reasonable time if no time is stipulated.

In such situations, the other party cannot elect to treat the contract as terminated once such time has passed, although subject to a term of the contract excluding liability the client can recover damages for any loss sustained as a result of the delay by the marketer.

Once the time for performance has passed, the client can serve a notice on the marketing agency, stating that if performance is not rendered by a stipulated date he will treat the marketing contract as terminated.

From the client's perspective, it is prudent to be generous in stipulating such a time, as termination of the contract in reliance on too short a period can put the innocent party in breach of contract.

Use of subcontractors to perform under the marketing contract

It is very common within the marketing profession that a company will contract out its marketing to a third party who in turn subcontracts elements of this work to specialist service providers, such as a technical copywriter or sponsorship and hospitality agency.

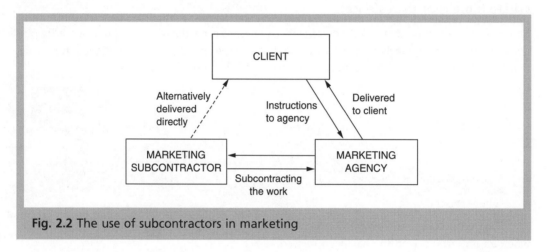

Fig. 2.2 The use of subcontractors in marketing

In the main, there should not be a problem here *unless* the contract expressly or impliedly provides that the marketing agency (and not a subcontractor) must perform and deliver those services.

POINT OF LAW

For example, media training is one area where the actual individual to carry out and perform the media training is vital to the quality of that media training being delivered.

Where subcontracting is permissible, then the marketing agency is still responsible for the quality of the work delivered by the agent or subcontractor.

In the absence of a contract term excluding any liability for the performance of agents or subcontractors, the marketing agency is liable for the failure of such agents or subcontractors to perform properly.

Illegality

For example, where a company deliberately attempts to mislead the public as to the safety of its new product, particularly in relation to children or pharmaceuticals (see Chapter 16), such acts will be illegal or against public policy or involve the commission of a civil wrong. Contracts that may be entered into in the furtherance of such acts are unenforceable and if an agency undertakes to assist a company in carrying out such acts it cannot then demand payment at a later date should the client refuse to pay.

It also does not matter that the parties are unaware that the act to be performed is illegal or against public policy. The position is the same where the contract is capable of being performed in a lawful manner, but both parties intend that it will be performed in a way that is illegal or against public policy.

The position is different where one party in the course of its performance under the marketing contract commits an unlawful or immoral act if this was *not* the intention or purpose of the parties when the contract was made.

It is obviously unlawful for the marketing agency to agree to use this material once aware that the client did not have any lawful right to it!

Ignorance of the law and ignorance of the facts

It is essential to distinguish between ignorance of the law and ignorance of facts that mean that the law will be broken.

This issue arises in marketing particularly where:

- Acts can only be carried out with a licence or permission
- Where the mechanism through which the act is to be carried out does not comply with a regulatory or statutory requirement

Ignorance of facts making contract unlawful

Often one of the parties to the marketing agreement will be unaware of the facts that make the performance of the other party unlawful.

POINT OF LAW

For example, the sports clothing manufacturer (licensee) is relying on the sports governing body (licensor) that it has the right to use a set of trademarks that the manufacturer wants to use on garments and other licensed merchandise.

In the above example, the manufacturer assumes that the sports governing body is acting within its legal rights and does not have any reason to believe otherwise.

In these circumstances, should the manufacturer proceed to produce merchandise only later to discover that in fact the governing body had some but not all intellectual property rights to the trade marks used on the merchandise (e.g. it did not have the right to use individual players' names, only the team name), the manufacturer could have a right of action against the governing body for any claims brought against it for trademark infringement brought by individual players.

The manufacturer (as the innocent party) could enforce the contract in relation to payments made under it, claim damages for breach of contract against the governing body but the governing body cannot rely on the marketing contract if it knew at the time when the contract was made that it did not have the licences and intended that the contract be performed in an unlawful way.

Ignorance of the law

Illegality includes acting in breach of regulations that are backed by criminal sanctions even where the marketer is unaware that the proposed activity is illegal.

Both in-house and external marketers must therefore be aware of the regulatory matters that affect them and must not make contracts that involve them in acting in breach of such regulations.

Termination

Contracts can come to an end in a number of different ways:

Natural end to the contract

The usual way is that both parties perform the contract in accordance with its terms. Once they have done so, the contract is at an end.

By agreement

In addition, the parties can agree at any time to end their obligations to one another.

Where the contract allows a party to terminate on certain conditions

A contract may also be brought to an end, either automatically or (more usually) at the election of one party, where the contract itself so provides.

It is common in contracts in marketing to provide that either party can terminate the contract if the other party passes a resolution to wind itself up or if some formal act of insolvency takes place. For example, presentation of petition is required for both winding up and for administration.

Significant breaches that go to the heart of the marketing contract

Marketing contracts commonly provide for termination in the event of a serious breach of contract by either party.

Usually such clauses distinguish between breaches and provide for the immediate right to terminate in relation to breaches that are fundamental to the contract, but for termination following a failure to remedy breaches within a set period after notice for less serious breaches.

In practical terms, the most significant question in relation to termination concerns the circumstances in which a contract can be terminated because of a breach by the other party.

Exceptional circumstances – not an automatic right to terminate

Not all breaches give rise to a right to terminate the contract. Most breaches do not give a right to terminate the marketing contract.

In general marketing practice, the right to immediately terminate *only* arises where:

▩ The contract provides for such a right in respect of the breach concerned (as discussed above)

▩ The term that is broken is a condition of the contract

▩ The failure of performance is such that it amounts to a repudiation of the contract

Conditions

In the context of a marketing contract that does not involve the supply of goods, such as branded merchandise or to which the supply of goods is only incidental, the question of whether a particular term is a condition of the contract depends upon whether the parties have expressly or impliedly agreed it to be a condition.

In the case of express agreement, it would be usual to find an express statement in the contract that breach of the term gives rise to a right to treat the agreement as terminated, although this result might derive simply from an express statement that the term is to be a 'condition'.

However, the use of 'condition' to describe a term does not necessarily lead to the conclusion that its breach gives the other party a right to treat the contract as terminated if in the context of the contract as a whole it is unlikely that the parties so intended.

What amounts to repudiation where the term breached is not a condition?

Repudiation of a marketing contract can arise where:

▩ One party shows by its words or actions that it does not intend to be bound by the terms of the contract

▩ One party commits a breach that goes to the root of the contract

▩ One party commits a breach that deprives the other party of substantially the whole of the performance that it expected under the contract

Although these legal tests are helpful, it is still very difficult in practice to generalise as to what circumstances constitute the repudiation of a marketing contract and it is dependent on the particular set of circumstances surrounding the marketing agreement.

It is clear that an outright refusal by either party to carry out their obligations or refusal to perform except in a manner inconsistent with the terms of the contract amounts to a repudiation.

Repudiation also occurs where because of a breach of contract by one party it becomes impossible for the contract to be performed in accordance with its terms and conditions.

For example, a retained PR agency organises a media interview with the BBC's consumer affairs investigative *Watchdog* TV programme for its client CEO believing that he would gain 'positive PR' coverage by agreeing to appear on the show.

The PR agency fails to evaluate the so-called 'media opportunity' or to provide media training or advice in order to prepare the CEO for the interview.

The result is that the client's disgruntled customers' complaints about the safety of the client's new 'child friendly washing machine' are put to the CEO on camera without warning and catching him completely off-guard – although *Watchdog's* producers have evidence that these allegations were faxed to the PR agency 2 weeks before the recording of the interview.

The item is broadcast, leading to more complaints from the public, removal of washing machines from all stores in the UK and a free fall in the manufacturer's share price.

The CEO of the client company finds it impossible to work with the PR agency given the damage to the company's reputation as a result of the agency's incredible lack of judgment and the CEO personally fires the PR agency.

Non-payment or delayed payment

Non-payment or delayed payment of an instalment of the fees payable for marketing services does not normally constitute a repudiation of the contract *unless* it demonstrates an intention not to pay for or an inability to pay for services to be provided in the future.

Contrary to popular belief, nor does non-payment or delayed payment by the client justify suspension of performance under the marketing contract until payment is made.

Significance of breach of condition or other reputiatory breach

The significance of whether a condition of a contract has been broken or whether there has been a breach of contract amounting to a repudiation is that the innocent party can elect to bring the contract to an end.

Election to terminate the marketing contract

If the innocent party so elects, neither party is thereafter under any obligation to the other in respect of future performance, although unperformed obligations due for performance before the repudiation, e.g. an accrued obligation to pay fees for services rendered, can still be enforced by the marketing agency.

The innocent party can also claim damages for breach of contract immediately despite the fact that the time for performance of the other party's obligations has not yet arisen.

In many cases the principal benefit to the innocent party is a commercial one of being able to get out of a contractual relationship that is not working well. Many marketing agencies would rather work on more satisfying and profitable accounts for other clients than stagger along in a relationship that is not working.

Election to affirm the marketing contract

Alternatively a marketer can elect to affirm the marketing contract. If it does so, the contract is not terminated and both parties must continue to perform the contract according to its terms and conditions.

The marketer (the innocent party in this example) cannot afterwards rely upon the same breach as justifying termination of the contract in the future, although it can of course elect to treat the contract as terminated as a result of a subsequent breach which also constitutes repudiation of the marketing agreement.

What amounts to termination or affirmation of the marketing contract?

This can be done in words or by conduct but must be communicated in some way to the other party. Refusal to provide further marketing services – which can be communicated by not supplying work that the other party expects to be supplied and thus knows that the work is not being done – can be sufficient.

Once a contract is at an end, neither party is under an obligation to perform further actions under it and the obligations can only be revived by a new agreement.

In the example of the marketing agency and the client, if the agency affirms the contract, it must perform according to its terms even though the other party may not be doing so.

Frustration of a contract

Frustration occurs where due to no fault of either party a contractual obligation cannot be performed because of some event which is outside their control renders the performance of the contract wholly different from what was undertaken by the contract.

Some marketing contracts may attempt to cover 'frustrating events' and what happens in such situations.

What amounts to a frustrating event?

Frustration of a marketing contract is highly unusual, but might occur as a result of new legislation (e.g. on tobacco, see Chapter 16) where the performance of the obligations of the parties becomes illegal or otherwise impossible.

In the context of contracts in marketing, frustration might also occur where an event in respect of which the marketing services are being carried out is cancelled, although much will depend on the terms of the contract and the precise obligation that is being undertaken.

POINT OF LAW

For example, corporate hospitality at the Cheltenham Festival 2001 and Ryder Cup 2001 had to be cancelled as a result of foot and mouth outbreak and the attacks on the World Trade Center and the Pentagon in 2001 respectively.

An unforeseen event that prevents performance for an abnormal period of time may also give rise to frustration.

The fact that an event causes a significant increase in the cost of performance is not sufficient to produce frustration. If the event is caused by one of the parties, then frustration cannot apply and the marketing contract remains in force.

Result of frustration of the contract in marketing

The effect of frustration is to discharge the contract automatically and bring the obligations of the parties in relation to future performance to an end.

For example, if the marketing director of a large corporate has paid anything under the contract he/she can recover the fees paid, subject to the party to whom the payment was made being able to deduct the amount of expenses that might have been incurred.

As could be highly likely in marketing, if the marketing consultant has conferred on the client a valuable benefit, e.g. a marketing strategy and plan, it can recover in respect of such fees an amount that the court considers just not exceeding the value of the benefit conferred.

If this should become the subject of litigation, the court may take into account, in deciding what amount should be paid, all of the circumstances surrounding the contract and its frustration. The marketing consultant will need to show to the court's satisfaction:

- The amount of expenses incurred before discharge of the marketing contract
- The value of the benefit conferred
- The effect on the benefit conferred of the circumstances giving rise to the frustration and that such circumstances have not rendered the benefit of no value

Remedies

Where the client has refused to pay a fee due under the marketing contract, the marketer is entitled to claim that fee and a court will give judgment for that sum upon it being proved to be due.

The marketer will not, however, be able to obtain judgment:

- If the contract has not been performed and so the sum claimed is not due
- Although the contract has been performed, if the work has been done in breach of contract so that the client has obtained *no* benefit from it or has suffered damage as a result of the breach

Assessment of damages

The damages awarded in consequence of a breach of contract are assessed by a court as the sum that is necessary to put the innocent party in the position it would have been in if the marketing contract had been performed.

Case where the client unjustifiably cancels the marketing contract

In the case where the client unjustifiably cancels a marketing contract, the marketer will usually be able to recover the fee expected to be paid on completion of the work less any costs that have been saved as a result of the cancellation of the contract.

Case where the client justifiably cancels the marketing contract

Where the marketer has delivered a poor standard of work or as in the case of the *Watchdog* TV example (above) has fallen below acceptable standards for the PR industry, then the marketer will be in breach of contract with the client, which will justify termination.

As a result, the client will usually also be able to recover a sum that puts it in the position it would have been in if the work had been done well.

For example, if the client acts to its detriment and as a result suffers economic loss.

However, establishing such a claim is often difficult because of four further principles:

1. The injured party must prove that the profits that would have been made. This is extremely difficult as it involves showing what would have happened in certain circumstances (known as 'causation').

2. The injured party must prove that the loss is caused by the breach and that there is a causal connection between the two events. There are often many reasons why profits are not as high as expected, and proving the link between the poor marketing and low profits is often impossible.

3. It must be within the reasonable contemplation of the parties at the time when the marketing contract is made that loss of the type sustained will be a result of the breach. It is therefore essential for the client to show that the marketer was aware at the time when the contract was made of the likely consequences of the breach.

4. Mitigation of loss. The injured party must take all reasonable steps to reduce or avoid the effect of a breach of contract, e.g. by getting another marketer to carry out the marketing campaign instead. If it does so, the cost of the substitute performance will usually be recoverable as damages against the original marketer.

Specific performance and injunctions

In the context of the marketing agency and its client, the court may order the marketer or client to fulfil their obligations under a marketing contract.

Where this involves ordering the performance of a specific act, the remedy is known in law as 'specific performance'.

A court may order the marketer or client not to do some act that would amount to a breach of contract. In law, this is known as an 'injunction'.

The court usually only orders specific performance or an injunction where damages are not an adequate remedy for the actual or proposed breach of the marketing contract.

The court will *not* order specific performance of a contract for personal marketing services, such as acting as the client's PR advisor.

It follows from these two principles that remedies of specific performance and injunction are likely to be *unusual in relation to personal marketing contracts*.

An injunction will, however, be a very useful remedy where one party has threatened to act in a way that it has expressly agreed not to act.

ENFORCING CLAIMS

Litigation

The most obvious method of enforcing a claim is to issue court proceedings. In a straightforward case, where it can be shown that there is no reasonable prospect of the claim being successfully defended, court proceedings can be quick and effective.

POINT OF LAW

For example, a recruitment company CEO hires a marketing and PR consultant to help advise on how to build the brand as well as gain positive media coverage for the new company.

Instructions are agreed in person and in e-mail correspondence and any additional work over and above 2 days' consulting work per month is approved in advance. The PR and marketing consultant lines up interviews for the CEO to appear on radio programmes but the news agenda overtakes the booking for the interviews and these do not happen.

The CEO refuses to pay the consultant for the additional time input on the account. In addition, the client denies that fees are owed and after an exchange of correspondence through the consultant's lawyers, proceedings are issued.

The court decides that the marketing consultant has acted in strict accordance with its instructions and the recruitment company is ordered to pay the full outstanding fees, plus interest and costs.

In many cases, the dispute between the parties is genuine and proper analysis of the position is complex with right and wrong on both sides. In these circumstances court proceedings can be expensive and slow and destructive of the commercial relationship between the parties. In such circumstances an alternative means of resolving the dispute can be advantageous.

Alternative Dispute Resolution

There are a number of alternatives to litigation through the courts. The most common are arbitration and mediation.

Arbitration

The parties agree to submit their dispute to an independent person (who may be a person with experience in marketing and need not be a lawyer, although lawyers are frequently appointed).

The decision of the arbitrator is binding on the parties and there is only a limited right of appeal to the courts on a point of law and then only with permission from the court.

Parties frequently provide for arbitration in their contracts in marketing and where they do, the court will stop any court proceedings brought by one of the parties and refer them to an arbitrator if the other party asks it to do so.

If the marketer has agreed to arbitration as a way of settling the dispute with a client and the ruling is not to the satisfaction of either party, then further legal action is unlikely to change the result.

Before signing a contract which includes an arbitration clause, all parties should be satisfied that this is how they wish any contractual dispute to be settled.

Some commentators point to the pitfalls of seeking justice through the use of an arbitrator. For example, some arbitrators are better than others and if the arbitrator is not up to the task, the losing party could feel that its rights have been denied.

Whilst on the surface appearing to be an attractive alternative dispute mechanism, arbitration is not necessarily a 'quick fix'. For example, it could take a long time and cause delays if the selection of the arbitrator has not been adequately provided for within the terms of the contract.

Instead, the parties might want to consider mediation as a form of dispute resolution avoiding both litigation and arbitration.

Mediation

Mediation is different to litigation and arbitration in that it is a consensual process.

The role of the mediator is to facilitate agreement between the parties, not to impose a solution on them. The mediator does not impose any sort of 'judgment' but just attempts to bring the parties to a consensual settlement they are both happy to sign up to.

It can happen within weeks, lasts no more than 1 day and if this does not resolve matters, the parties can litigate, safe in the knowledge that nothing said in the course of the mediation can be mentioned in court.

If, despite the mediator's best efforts, the parties are unable to reach agreement, they can seek resolution through the court or arbitration.

Early mediation of a dispute can bring substantial benefit. It can avoid the cost of the whole or part of court or arbitration proceedings (both in management time and lawyers' costs).

It can produce finality (by agreement) before the dispute has become a festering sore between the parties, thereby preserving a business and working relationship which could otherwise be destroyed by the risk of litigation.

Another advantage is that it can produce an agreement that leads to an outcome that is not possible for a court or an arbitrator to order, e.g. the completion of a direct marketing campaign or a personal service delivered to the client.

In the light of these benefits it is now common in the marketing profession for parties to agree to submit disputes to mediation after they have arisen. It is also becoming increasingly common for the parties to provide in their contract that they will attempt to mediate before taking court or arbitration proceedings.

English law

Should the contract be found to be governed by a law of a country other than England and Wales, an English court will assume that such law is the same as the law of England and Wales *unless* the principles of the other law are proved by expert evidence.

Often the application of a foreign law does not produce a different result to the application of English law and issues relating to the correct law to be applied are irrelevant.

CHECKLIST

All marketing contracts should set out as fully and clearly as possible the obligations that each party is to perform, as this chapter has illustrated.

These will usually include provisions as to the following:

- The work to be performed by reference to a detailed specification where appropriate
- The fees to be paid
- The right to charge for marketing work not covered in the original specification and the basis upon which such charges will be made
- How and when the fees are to be paid, and the payment of interest where payment is made late
- The time within which the work is to be carried out and whether the time stated is a contractual obligation or simply a target
- Whether performance can be rendered through an agent or subcontractor and the consequences if such agent or subcontractor fails to perform adequately
- The time within which any preliminary work to be done by the client is to be carried out and the consequences of the client's failure to do such work
- The standard of performance that is to be expected of the marketer
- The consequences of any failure of performance, with exclusion of liability where appropriate
- Limitation of liability for damage arising from failure of performance
- Any necessary stipulation as to confidentiality of information passing between the parties
- Intellectual property rights in the material produced in performance of the contract
- The circumstances in which the contract can be terminated
- The law applicable to the contract
- Mediation and/or arbitration provisions

In the context of the marketing agency and client relationship, marketing consultants frequently want to contract on similar terms with all clients.

In these circumstances it is possible to print the terms to be applied in a standard format as conditions of the contract which are incorporated by reference into all contracts.

However, all contracts are unique so it is prudent to check and double check that standard provisions apply. Where this is in doubt, seek legal advice.

3
MAKING STATEMENTS

In this chapter:

- Distinction between liability in contract and tort
- The key elements of liability in tort
- Negligent mis-statements
- Misrepresentation (including deceit)
- Malicious falsehood
- Slander of goods and title
- Defamation
- Checklist

Other useful chapters:

- Chapter 2: Making agreements
- Chapter 4: Liability for defective products
- Chapter 5: Intellectual property rights
- Chapter 8: Defamation
- Chapter 9: Advertising and labelling

INTRODUCTION

When making statements to potential buyers or clients, the marketer must be aware that the law places a duty to take care that such statements are true and a breach of this duty may lead to a claim in tort (which means a harm done to another party) against the marketer.

As marketers we are sometimes encouraged to take risks in the name of innovative and creative marketing or simply under pressure of time and business.

We are under constant pressure to get our voices heard above the noise of the market and that of our competitors.

Differentiation between brands has become so blurred that consumers are actually *tuning out* messages as they receive them. Consumers have become more cynical of marketing over the years and (paradoxically) at the same time they have become much more media literate.

This presents both an opportunity as well as a threat for marketers as media and audiences become ever more fragmented.

As Chapters 9 and 17 demonstrate, marketers have become much more aggressive in what they say and how they say it – even to the point where they risk damaging their own reputation and that of the brand they pledge allegiance to. Comparative advertising is an example of this trend (see Chapter 9).

DEFINITION OF TORTIOUS LIABILITY

POINT OF LAW

Liability in tort arises where the marketer breaches a duty imposed by law (as opposed to obligations set out in a contract). Such a breach entitles the claimant (anyone who has suffered as a result of the breach) to bring an action for damages to compensate for the loss and/or injury suffered.

Tortious liability includes:

- Deceit
- Negligence (including mis-statements and misrepresentations)
- Defamation (slander and libel)
- Trade libel
- Malicious falsehood
- Breach of statutory duty (e.g. breach of the marketer's obligations under Consumer Protection Act 1987)

These different heads of tort are all relevant to the marketer's obligations and potential liabilities to both the client (if the marketer is an advertising agency) and consumer (if the marketer is a brand owner).

Although there may be some overlapping in potential claims by the claimant (e.g. defamation and malicious falsehood) it is essential for a marketer to be aware of the potential pitfalls in relation to one claim rather than another (e.g. the availability of contributory negligence defence in a negligence claim) and the elements required to prove a claim in tort.

INSIGHT

In the examples given in this chapter the word 'marketer' must be taken to include the manufacturer or supplier who is putting the product on the market. A professional marketer would not be liable in contract to those who purchase goods or services, but (at most) mis-statements about the product which cause loss.

DISTINCTION BETWEEN CONTRACT AND TORT

A contractual claim is based upon the rights and obligations determined by reference to the express or implied terms of the contract (see Chapter 2). A claim in tort, on the other hand, relies upon duties placed upon the marketer by law.

Where the claimant has entered into a contract with a marketer, it may have the right to pursue a remedy in both contract and tort.

Importance of distinguishing between how damages are measured

Where this is the case, the claimant is entitled to choose to pursue an action under both or select one of the two. The choice will often depend upon the damages recoverable.

POINT OF LAW

For example, a self-employed builder reads an editorial placed by a marketer promising 'Look like Arnie Schwarzenegger in just 7 days' which promotes a vitamin supplement product and little else. The builder sends off for more information and receives a sales pack and order form, both of which repeat the claims prominently and guarantee success. The builder sends off for the product and after taking it for 7 days there is no difference in muscle tone. In fact, the pills make him so sick that he needs to seek medical assistance and is off work for a week as a result.

In the above example, if the claimant is successful, damages will be awarded to compensate the claimant for the loss suffered as a result of the marketer failing to perform, or failing to perform properly, an obligation under the contract.

Therefore, damages in contract put the claimant in the position that he would have been in, *had the contract been performed in accordance with its terms.*

Damages in tort, however, seek to place the claimant in the position that it would have been in *had he never suffered the wrongful conduct of the marketer*. In this case, compensation for the pain and suffering as a consequence of taking the pills and the loss of earnings as a result of being off sick for a week.

The above example may seem far-fetched, but in fact these type of claims are very common, particularly in the US and Canada. As discussed later in this chapter, public authorities are quick to clamp down hard on marketers that try to make statements or claims that are not defendable.

LAW IN ACTION

Wrigley Canada (2000)

Since 1996 the chewing gum marketer has been fighting for the right to promote its *EXTRA* gum as having cavity fighting properties. The Canada Radio-Television and Telecommunications Commission rejected a TV script making this claim and discussions with Health Canada led to the TV advertisement wording being amended:

New dental studies prove chewing Sugar Free EXTRA after a sugary snack can actually reduce the acids that cause cavities.

Despite this, a competitor manufacturer complained and on reviewing the wording the authorities took the view that the words constituted a drug claim which was not acceptable for a food product.

Wrigley decided to establish the position once and for all by seeking a declaration from the Federal Court in Canada. The action failed and the Court agreed with Health Canada's assessment.

This means that while *EXTRA* packs continue to state 'Won't cause cavities', the TV claim could not be broadcast.

Remedies in contract not available in tort

The claimant may wish to seek a remedy other than damages:

- *Specific performance* – the marketer (brand owner) must deliver the product or service as promised

- *Rescission* – the contract is deemed never to have been entered into, each party returns what they have received from the contract and therefore no claims can be made against the consumer by the marketer for non-payment of goods or services

- *Restitution* – the consumer is put exactly in the same position he was in before he entered the contract (similar to the usual remedy in tort)

These remedies are only available in contract and before commencing a legal action the consumer should consider whether there are any financial benefits of pursuing one form of relief above another.

Scope of liability

In choosing whether to commence an action in tort or contract against a marketer, the claimant will need to assess the scope of the marketer's liability under each head.

A claimant may find that a claim in tort will allow it to recover for loss *outside* of those recoverable according to the marketer's obligations under the contract.

Contributory negligence

Although not relevant to the choice between contract and tort, in a claim for breach of an absolute obligation under a contract, the marketer cannot rely on the principle of 'contributory negligence' to reduce the quantum of damages awarded.

Where the consumer claims in tort alone, however (or contract, but where the consumer could have brought a separate action in tort), it is open to the marketer to allege that the consumer has contributed to its own loss, thereby reducing the level of damages compensating the claimant.

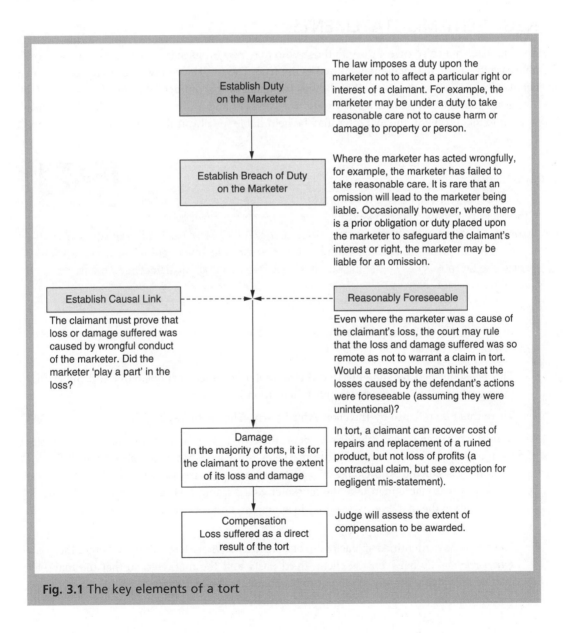

Fig. 3.1 The key elements of a tort

For example, the marketer advises use of the printing process, but says to the client that it should go to the printers to check that everything is to its satisfaction. The client agrees to go, but cannot do so at the last minute. He tells the marketer to go ahead anyway. If the client had gone it would have found that the process was unsuitable for what he wanted. In this case the client was also negligent about its own interests and this could reduce the liability of the marketer by a percentage assessed as equitable by the court.

NEGLIGENT MIS-STATEMENTS

The marketer may also owe a duty to those who may rely on its statements to exercise reasonable care to ensure that statements it makes are true. The marketer may owe such a duty to its client (in addition to any duties that it owes by virtue of its contract with the client).

If the marketer makes such a *negligent mis-statement* and a third person or the client relies upon it to its detriment, the marketer may be held liable for physical or economic loss suffered as a result.

For example, the marketer gives written advice to the client on a competition and promotion scheme, and this is relied on by the client who then invests £1 million in the promotion only to have the Office of Fair Trading investigate and then stop the promotion as it fails to comply with consumer protection legislation. The marketer may also be liable to any other investor if a 'special relationship' exists between the marketer and that investor.

In order for liability for negligent mis-statement to arise, there must be a *special relationship* between the two parties:

■ This is established by showing that the marketer assumed responsibility and the client/ third party trusted the marketer and relied upon its advice.

■ There must be reliance by the client/third party. This is an issue of fact.

■ It must have been reasonable for the client/third party to rely upon the marketer. In order for the reliance to be reasonable, the marketer must have assumed the responsibility for imparting its skill and knowledge on a particular area of marketing. This is an objective test – would a reasonable man take the marketer as assuming this responsibility? Reasonable reliance upon the marketer is required in statement and service cases, in order to establish the special relationship.

■ The courts have identified six factors to be considered when determining whether there is a *special relationship* between the client/third party and the marketer, so that the marketer may be held liable for any negligent mis-statement. The factors are:

1. The purpose of making the statement

2. The purpose of communicating the statement

3. The relationship between the marketer, client and any third party that is relevant

4. The size of the class to which the client/third party belongs

5. The state of knowledge (not intention) of the marketer

6. The reliance which is reasonable in the circumstances and the knowledge of that reliance by the marketer.

Damages

Damages will be awarded using a similar approach as with other tortious liabilities – putting the client/third party in the position that it would have been in had the tort never occurred.

The client/third party is entitled to recover for any economic loss suffered as a result of the reliance on the mis-statement, which may be the only loss suffered.

The loss sustained must, however, be both a *reasonably foreseeable* consequence of the marketer's breach of duty and a loss that the marketer had a *duty* to prevent the client/third party incurring.

The damages suffered may be reduced by a proportion to take account of contributory negligence in case where the negligence of the client/third party has been a factor in causing the loss.

Statements made 'without responsibility'

The marketer is able to protect itself from any action for negligent mis-statement where it makes the statement 'without responsibility'. This is because the marketer has made a statement with the intention that the client will not or should not rely upon it.

> **POINT OF LAW**
>
> For example, the marketer is a licensing agent for a major sports federation and says that it is very likely that it can strike a deal with a major software publisher in order to produce an interactive football game for the new Microsoft XBOX platform but adds that while it will do its best during negotiations to advise on the ability of the software publisher to produce a quality game it will not be responsible for the performance or effectiveness of the product in fact produced.

Disclaimers of liability

In the situation where a marketer uses a disclaimer to avoid liability, in doing so it makes a statement *without taking responsibility* as to its truth (there is no assumption of responsibility). See also Chapter 2.

POINT OF LAW

For example, when a marketer enters into a contract to provide advice to a client, it is possible for it to disclaim responsibility for a negligent statement or service provided. If there would normally be a duty owed by the marketer to a client (which would ordinarily be the case), the courts will look at the contract between the parties to determine the validity of any disclaimer.

A marketer cannot exclude liability for death or personal injury. In other cases, the disclaimer will only be valid where it would be *fair and reasonable* to exclude liability in the circumstances. The courts will consider whether the parties were on an equal footing when entering into the agreement and the skill involved in giving the advice.

These are relevant considerations because the courts will wish to determine how easy it would have been for the claimant to approach another marketer either instead of the defendant, or in order to seek a second opinion.

Clearly, it would be economic nonsense for the claimant to pay a significant sum to the marketer, only then to approach another marketer of the defendant's size for similar advice.

These issues raise the question of who (from the parties) should bear the loss resulting from negligent advice.

It may be that it would be most appropriate for the marketer to have adequate professional indemnity insurance and distribute the cost of this amongst all its clients rather than allowing the claimant to bear the burden of any negligence.

MISREPRESENTATION

Statements made before entering into a contract

Prior to entering into a contract (as discussed in Chapter 2), one party may make statements during negotiations to induce the other party to enter into the contract or for the purpose of establishing the facts on the basis of which the contract is made.

Sometimes such statements are made orally and sometimes they are made in writing. Such statements are known as *representations*.

If a statement about an existing fact is not true or if a person does not hold a belief, opinion or intention about which he makes a statement, the statement is known as a *misrepresentation*.

A misrepresentation of a past and existing fact includes where:

1. The marketer makes reference to a statement made by a third party

2. Conduct (express or implied) by the marketer which makes the client believe a certain state of affairs is true

3. The marketer makes a partial disclosure which is in fact true, but which induces the client into assuming that something else is true, when it is false

4. If the marketer states that it has an opinion or an intention that it does not in fact have

LAW IN ACTION

For example, in 1997 Bristol-based mail order health product specialist **Natural Woman** received a media pack from an up-market magazine **Executive Woman** that claimed it had an 85 000 circulation and 30 000 subscribers.

Relying on this information, the company placed a full-page advertisement for £1000 and bought in product to meet anticipated demand. After the magazine was published the advertiser did not receive a single enquiry which started alarm bells ringing. On checking with other advertisers, they discovered that the poor media response was shared with others.

Natural Woman attempted to question the magazine's publishers about its circulation figures and lack of response but was stone walled. The company decided not to pay for the advertisement and so the publishers issued a claim for the outstanding invoice.

At court, the media pack was read in light of the admission by the publishers that the highest ever print run for the magazine had been 35,000 and their subscriber database was no greater than 4000.

Given that was the case, the court ruled the publishers had misrepresented the magazine's circulation figures and subscriber levels, and dismissed the £1000 claim.

As this story illustrates, if a client buys advertising on the strength of circulation claims that turn out to be false, then this is a clear case of a misrepresentation to induce a party to enter into a contract under the **Misrepresentation Act 1967**.

As the next case illustrates, representations can also arise from conduct of the parties.

LAW IN ACTION

Aprilia World-v-Spice Girls Ltd (2002)

In May 1998, Spice Girls Limited (SGL), entered into a contract with Aprilia World Service BV (AWS) whereby AWS would sponsor the Spice Girls European Tour in exchange for royalties and endorsement rights in relation to a motor scooter named 'Spice Sonic'. It was envisaged that such rights would be of value until March 1999. The Spice Girls were described as 'currently comprising' five members.

Negotiations took place prior to the agreement and the parties commenced performance of the contract under non-binding heads of agreement before the formal agreement was made.

In that period all five Spice Girls took part in photo shoots and a commercial shoot knowing that AWS intended to market the Spice Sonic bearing images of all them. In correspondence the Spice Girls' agent also underlined the band's commitment to making the sponsorship deal work.

Before the commercial was made (and thus before the parties entered into the formal contract), Geri Halliwell informed the other members and management of her intention to leave the group at the end of September 1999. SGL did not inform AWS.

Following the split, SGL made a claim for unpaid royalties and AWS counterclaimed for the loss arising from the misrepresentation that none of the group had an existing intention to leave.

In January 2002, the Court of Appeal held that SGL had represented expressly and by conduct that none of the group had an existing intention to leave and that AWS would not have entered into the contract had it known that and had suffered loss as a result. It was accepted, however, that AWS could not recover costs incurred before the formal contract was made and the claim was limited to the cost of providing certain motor cycles to the Spice Girls under the contract. Claims for loss of profit were not recoverable because such loss had been incurred by AWS' parent company, not AWS itself.

Representations

Representations are typically statements about existing facts. They may also be statements about the belief, opinion or intention of the maker where what is said amounts to a statement of fact about the belief, opinion or intention held by the maker.

POINT OF LAW

For example, an account director says to a client that they believe if the client places its Christmas advertising promotion with the agency it will be done on time. As a result, in reliance on this, the client places an order for Christmas products for its store which it pays for in advance with its supplier, who arranges a special delivery in time for the Christmas promotion. The account director in fact did not know whether the promotion could be completed or not when they said they believed it could.

The contract is entered into by the client and 5 days later the client telephones the agency to see the art work for the promotion.

The account director tells the client that the artwork has been done for the advertisement when in fact it is still waiting to be done. The client asks to see this in the hour and the account director goes 'missing'. Another 4 hours later, the client speaks to the managing director of the advertising agency and discovers that there was never any hope of the work being done before Christmas. The client misses the deadline for running the Christmas sales promotion and loses business as a result.

Where misrepresentation is implied

Although defective products are dealt with in Chapter 4, it is important to highlight an area relating to dangerous products and misrepresentations.

Where a product is manufactured, packaged and sold, there is an implied representation of safety where, to the knowledge of the marketer, it cannot be safely used in the way that it knows it is likely to be used by the consumer.

In addition, the party that places a particular product in the hands of another is legally bound to warn that person of any known defect or danger.

A mere non-disclosure is not deemed to be a representation as to the non-existence of the defects. In this case, and where the knowledge of both parties is equal, it is reasonable for the marketer to expect the client to investigate whether there are any defects.

INSIGHT

See also Chapter 9 for more information on Advertising and Labelling and Chapter 4 on Liability for Defective Products.

Trade puffs

'Trade puffs' are not actionable as a misrepresentation. However, there is a fine dividing line between a mere trade puff and a misrepresentation, so marketers must take extreme care when preparing advertisements or product launches.

POINT OF LAW

For example, it would be a mere puff to say that a new CD-ROM product is 'state of the art', but promising that a product will do something, when it does not ('is the fastest on the market'), may lead to an action for misrepresentation, if the claimant relies upon the statement.

Self-commendation

Another widely used tactic of marketers is that of self-commendation. Like trade puffs, self-commendation is not actionable. The same limits as for trade puffs must be borne in mind, along with the issues of self-commendation through comparisons with competitors (see Chapter 9).

POINT OF LAW

For example, the marketing of a music CD as 'The Best 80s Dance Music in the World – Ever!' would qualify as a self-commendation and would not be actionable as a misrepresentation.

DECEIT

The claimant may go further than simply showing that a representation was untrue. It may also allege that the maker was fraudulent or deceitful. In such cases, the claimant must show that:

1. The marketer's representation was false
2. The marketer knew it was false when it was made, or it was made recklessly, not caring whether it was true or false

3. The marketer intended to deceive the client

4. The client was induced into a transaction

5. The client has suffered loss as a result

It follows that to be liable in deceit, not only must the marketer have no honest belief in the truth of its statement; it must also *intend* the client to act upon that misrepresentation.

However, if the marketer does intend its statement to be acted upon, it can be liable not only to the person to whom the statement was made but also to a third person if the marketer intended that the contents of that misrepresentation be passed to such third person.

INSIGHT

Thus a client may bring an action against the marketer for a misrepresentation made to a third party where the marketer intended that the contents of that misrepresentation were to be passed on.

An exclusion clause in a contract will not usually apply to liability that arises in cases of deceit.

Claims in deceit are not limited to cases where the parties enter into a contract with one another (although this is usually the case). They can arise where the person to whom the statement is made acts on the statement by entering into a transaction with another person (or refrains from doing something that he otherwise would have done) and suffers loss as a result.

In practice, it is difficult to found an action in deceit and such an action should not be commenced without reliable admissible evidence to support this serious allegation.

Further, in the example of the account director stating the work could be done in time when, in fact, the account director did not believe this, deceit could be proven but in practice, such blatant behaviour amongst professional marketers will be rare ('honesty really is the best policy').

Moreover it is often possible to succeed in an action for negligent mis-statement or mis-representation without having to allege deceit.

Representations true when made but later discovered by the maker to be false

Where a marketer makes a statement believing it to be true, but later discovers that it is false, it is placed under an obligation to inform the client of the falsehood *before* the client enters into any transaction (there is no such duty after the client enters into the transaction).

If the marketer fails to tell the client, it will be liable for misrepresentation.

INSIGHT

In the above example, if the account director believed that the work could be done by Christmas, but before receiving the order found out that it could not, the account director would be under an obligation to tell the client before accepting the order.

If the account director did not the agency would be liable for misrepresentation.

The same principle appears to be the case where the representation may have been true ('we can deliver to your timescale') when it was originally made, but later the same statement ('we can deliver to your timescale') becomes false due to a change in circumstances of which the marketer becomes aware.

Exclusion of liability for misrepresentation

It is possible to exclude liability for misrepresentation (unless the misrepresentation is made deceitfully) by a suitably worded condition in the contract between the parties.

Any such condition must, however, satisfy the requirement of *reasonableness*.

INSIGHT

For example, a statement that reads:

While every practical effort has been made to ensure that any statement of fact made prior to signature of in this agreement is true and accurate, and the (agency) is not responsible for any misrepresentations made by parties outside the signatories any of its representatives prior to the making of to this agreement unless such misrepresentation was made or confirmed in writing.

It is common for contracts to provide that the parties acknowledge that they have not entered into the contract in reliance on any oral statement made by the other party during negotiations except where such statement has been confirmed in writing and/or words to the effect of 'this is the entire agreement between the parties and no prior representations are incorporated' (the so called integration clause).

Such clauses are usually treated as being reasonable by the courts when made in the context of a commercial agreement.

Rescission

Where a party to a contract can establish that a misrepresentation has been made, it is entitled to 'rescind' the contract, i.e. treat the contract as though it had never been entered into.

Usually this gives the client the right to receive back any performance that it has given, e.g. the repayment of money that was paid to the marketer who made the representation, and the client ceases to be under any legal obligation to render any further performance under the contract.

From the client's perspective, if it acts in such a way as to lead the marketer to believe that it is not going to rescind the contract, then it loses this right to rescind the contract.

Damages

The client will be able to recover damages to recompense it for any loss that it has suffered as a result of entering into the contract in reliance on a misrepresentation *unless* the marketer can show that it believed that the misrepresentation was true and it had reasonable grounds for that belief.

Although it is common for a person to establish that he/she believed a matter to be true (cases of deceitful representation are quite rare), it is often difficult to show that there were reasonable grounds for a belief. Often reasonable care in investigating facts would have established the true position and so the managing director of the advertising agency in the above example should have known better.

Damage suffered must result from the misrepresentation. In order to recover damages from the marketer the client must be able to show that it acted to its detriment as a result of entering into the transaction it has suffered *actual loss or damage*. The misrepresentation need not be the sole inducement but it must have materially contributed to the decision to act in the manner that resulted in the loss.

In cases of deceit

Damages awarded for fraudulent misrepresentation are assessed on the basis to put the client in the position that it would have been in had the deceit never have taken place.

The claimant is also entitled to consequential losses arising from the deceit, provided that such losses flow directly from the misrepresentation. It is not necessary to show that the loss sustained was a reasonably foreseeable consequence of the loss.

For example, if the client sustained loss of profits these are recoverable under this head. It is also possible that the client may be awarded *aggravated damages*, compensating it for damage to its reputation with its own customers and injured feelings (if different) as a result of the deceit committed by the marketer.

In such cases, the defence of contributory negligence is not open to the marketer.

In cases of negligent misrepresentations inducing a party to enter into a contract

The client is entitled to the same damages as for negligent mis-statement (above), save that deceit rules on remoteness apply, meaning that the marketer will be liable for losses arising from the misrepresentation, even where the losses were not reasonably foreseeable when the misrepresentation was made.

This may increase the level of damages beyond those recoverable under a claim for negligent mis-statement. The defence of contributory negligence applies.

MALICIOUS FALSEHOOD ('TRADE LIBEL')

A claimant may commence an action for any written or oral falsehood if such a statement is made maliciously. This is the case even where the statement is not defamatory and would not ordinarily lead to a claim (see Chapter 8 and analysis of what constitutes malice).

In order to succeed in an action for malicious falsehood, it is essential that:

▓ The statement made was false

▓ That it was published to at least one person other than the claimant

■   The statement was made maliciously

■   The claimant is likely to suffer financial loss

Malice

Clearly, it is essential that the claimant prove malice. Without this element, however, there may continue to be a claim for falsehood, e.g. in defamation (see below).

In order to fulfil this requirement, the claimant needs to be able to show that the defendant either knew that the statement was false or that the defendant lacked an honest belief in its truth. Further, the courts tend also to require that the defendant had a dishonest motive for making the statement.

Malicious falsehood is a claim often made in comparative advertising cases (see below). There may also be a trademark infringement action (see Chapter 5), but where advertising is claimed to be false (see below and Chapter 9), malicious falsehood or 'trade libel' as it is often called, is also alleged.

LAW IN ACTION

Hello!-v-OK! magazine (1999)

In 1998, celebrity gossip magazine *OK!* sent a mail shot to marketers and trade magazines for the advertising industry showing a graph matching *OK!* magazine's sales performance in the last quarter against its main rival *Hello!*

Publishers for *Hello!* claimed the figures were inaccurate, underestimating *Hello!* weekly sales figures by 40 000, and sued for malicious falsehood and infringement of the *Hello!* registered trademarks.

On the eve of the trial in November 1999, a settlement was reached, whereby *OK!* agreed to pay *Hello!* damages and costs.

Although the case was settled, to succeed in an action for malicious falsehood *Hello!* would have had to go one step further by satisfying the court that *OK!* was malicious, or at the very least reckless as to the truth or falsity of what it was claiming when it quoted the allegedly false circulation figures – by no means an easy thing to prove.

The outcome may have been very different if the claims had been made under the **Comparative Advertising Regulations 2000** and the **EU Injunctions for the Protection of Consumers' Interests Directive 2001** (see below and Chapter 9).

The courts have indicated that they regard claims for malicious falsehood as in the same category as fraud when it comes to drafting of the pleadings (legal documents) that set out the claimant's case.

INSIGHT

In cases where lawyers are instructed to take action against a marketer
under a breach of advertising regulations involving *comparative advertising* (see Chapter 9),
they should not add in a claim for *malicious falsehood* just for good measure *unless* there is
reasonably credible admissible evidence establishing a *prima facie* (on the face of the facts)
case for malicious falsehood.

A mere comparison between two competitors' goods, causing loss to the claimant, is not
actionable. This is the case, even where the comparison is misleading.

Therefore, where the defendant states that its goods are superior to that of another marketer, even if untrue and causing damage to the other, this will not lead to a cause of action
against it *without* the element of malice.

**POINT OF
LAW**

For example, an advertisement including what was purported to be the
results from a scientific test comparing the quality of the claimant's and
defendant's products was alleged to be a malicious falsehood. The defendant had defended
the action on the basis that it was merely a self-commendation. It was held, however, that the
use of the scientific reports was enough to give a reasonable man the impression that a serious
claim was being made in relation to the claimant's product.

Any damages awarded under this heading will represent the claimant's economic loss
resulting from the statement.

The use of a claimant's trademark

Often in comparative advertising, it will be necessary to use the claimant's trademark (see
Chapter 5) in order to identify the claimant and make the comparison between the claimant's
and defendant's products. Use of trademarks in this way is permitted, provided that the
defendant does not take 'unfair advantage of, or be detrimental to, the distinctive character
or reputation of the trademark'.

Where a trademark is to be used in this way, the potential defendant must ensure that it
acts in line with honest practices; otherwise it may be at risk of a claim for either malicious
falsehood or infringement of the registered trademark.

SLANDER OF GOODS AND TITLE

Statements and claims may become actionable where the marketer publishes a comparison
which a sensible person would understand to be a claim that the competitor's goods or services
are in some way defective.

For example, if a statement said: 'Buying a Ford Mondeo car means that you're increasing your chances of being badly hurt in an accident. Choose a Volvo instead'.

In this example, Ford could bring an action against Volvo for slander. This of course this is a made up example and indeed there is no truth whatsoever in such a statement (in fact Volvo are owned by Ford!).

Volvo does not have to prove financial damage where it has been shown that the statement was intended to cause pecuniary loss and was either:

1. Published in a permanent form; or

2. was made in respect to the competitor's trade, office, profession or business held or carried on by the competitor at the time the statement was made; or

3. the claimant is *likely* to suffer financial loss.

In all other cases, to succeed in a claim, the claimant must prove the *actual* loss suffered as a direct result of the statement.

The loss may be temporary (e.g. a drop in the number of new car registrations) or a permanent loss of custom or customers.

DEFAMATION

This is covered in more detail in Chapter 8.

Defamation
Material is defamatory if it lowers the standing or damages the reputation of the aggrieved person in the estimation of right-thinking people generally.
For example, an advertisement which makes derogatory statements about an individual or a competitor brand owner may give rise to a defamation action.

It may be that the words taken in a particular context would have a defamatory meaning even though on their face the words do not appear defamatory.

Tolley-v-Fry (1931)

Tolley was an amateur golfer and his image was used to promote a chocolate bar produced by Fry that had not sought his consent. It was important for Tolley that he retained his amateur golf status in order to continue to compete in golf competitions, and therefore consenting to take part in advertising would have implied that he had relinquished his amateur status and had turned professional by accepting sponsorship contrary to amateur rules.

Tolley sued the marketer and was successful in showing that the advertisement was defamatory.

In any action for defamation, the claimant must first show that the statement complained of refers to him, although it is not necessary for the statement to include the claimant's name.

The claimant may also sue where a class of people are defamed (a group to which he belongs), provided he would be recognised as part of that group and his reputation would therefore be affected.

There are two types of defamation:

- Libel is usually written or broadcast – the defamatory statement is in some permanent form – and usually applies to advertisements

- Slander is usually verbal

POINT OF LAW

Libel

Libel is the permanent form of defamation. It is most often written or broadcast and usually applies to advertisements. A claimant is not limited to bringing an action against the original author of the defamatory statement; an action may be brought against editors or publishers and can be brought for each publication of the words.

A defence is available for defendants who merely caused or contributed to a statement being published, that they took reasonable care in publishing the statement and had no reason to believe that the statement was defamatory.

Where the slander causes special damage, the claimant is entitled to recover damages for the temporary loss suffered as a result of the slander.

POINT OF LAW

Slander

Slander is a non-permanent form of defamation, through spoken words or gestures. The general rule is that slander is only actionable where there has been special damage suffered as a result of the defendant's words. This is subject to four exceptions: imputing a criminal offence, imputing disease, imputing unchastity of a woman and slander of a person in their profession, trade or employment.

Who can sue?

An individual, partnership or company can sue for defamation (libel or slander) and a person or company outside the UK can bring an action for defamation, but *only* if it can prove that it has a reputation within the UK and the material in question has been published in the UK.

Local authorities, trade unions, most other unincorporated associations, political parties, and central and local government bodies *cannot* sue for defamation, although individual officers and members can, if they can be identified with sufficient certainty as being the subject of the defamation.

A defamation action can only be brought if the defamatory words have been published to someone other than the person bringing the action.

Who can be sued?

Potentially, anyone participating in the publication of defamatory material is liable; this includes the client, the marketer and the publisher or broadcaster.

Defences to an action for defamation

If a claimant proves that there was a defamatory statement, the marketer has a number of defences that it is able to rely on in order to avoid liability:

- *Justification* – the statement being true, the marketer was justified in publishing it
- *Absolute privilege* – particular statements which are judicial, parliamentary or official are protected by law on the basis that litigation and official business cannot be carried on without testing or alleging flaws in the characters of other individuals
- *Qualified privilege* – where the marketer has a legal, social or moral duty to make the statement and the receiver has a similar duty to receive it (e.g. correspondence between a marketer and its lawyers)
- *Fair comment* – where a statement is a criticism by a marketer is made about an issue already in the public domain and it is made without malice, the statement will not be defamatory

> **INSIGHT**
>
> Although it may be tempting to rely on the 'fair comment' defence, marketers should be extremely wary of doing so (see Chapter 8).

CHECKLIST

- Marketers must ensure that all statements used in marketing are true
- Untrue, false or deceptive statements can lead to an award of damages for the claimant
- Marketers must avoid negligent mis-statements

- Marketers owe a duty of care to the client for any advice given

- Marketers must be careful in the way in which business is conducted

- Marketers should re-consider making a partial disclosure which is in fact true, but which induces the client into assuming that something else is true, when it is false

- Marketers must inform the client of any change in circumstances, where the marketer has already made a representation as to the circumstances and no contract has yet been entered into

- Marketers can exclude liability for misrepresentation; however, the term in any contract will still need to pass the reasonableness test

4

LIABILITY FOR DEFECTIVE PRODUCTS

In this chapter:

- Definition of a defective product
- Claims in contract and tort
- Legal status of warnings
- Consumer Protection Act 1987
- Defences to the Consumer Protection Act 1987
- Checklist

Other useful chapters:

- Chapter 2: Making agreements
- Chapter 3: Making statements
- Chapter 9: Advertising and labelling
- Chapter 13: Promotions and incentives
- Chapter 16: Niche marketing

INTRODUCTION

When manufacturing, marketing and selling a product to consumers, care must be taken to ensure that the product is safe. This may be through checking that the product is free from any defect that may cause damage, or through clearly labelling the product so that the consumer is aware of any risks or special instructions.

Failure to do so may lead to actions in contract, tort or criminal law.

Where a marketer is not involved in any area of manufacture or supply, it will be rare for an action to be brought against it. Where the manufacturer is involved in the manufacture or distribution of the product or labels, it will be at risk of liability in this area.

DEFINITION OF 'DEFECTIVE PRODUCT'

If a claimant alleges that she has purchased a 'defective product', there are two possible complaints that the defendant manufacturer or supplier may be faced with:

- The claimant may allege that the product is dangerous
- The alleged defect may be that the product was purchased for a particular purpose and it simply does not work, or fails to work correctly

---

INSIGHT

'Products' in this area has been given a wide interpretation by the courts, e.g. food/drink, vehicles, machinery and chemicals. It is likely, therefore, that provided the claimant can point to some form of 'goods', as opposed to services, she will be able to allege product liability.

In determining whether a product is defective, the courts will take into account all of the circumstances involved in the provision and use of the product.

For example, this will include its marketing and advertising as a product may not *prima facie* be defective, but where it is advertised as being safe for a particular purpose when it is not, the product will be held to be defective.

A claim in contract

Where the claimant alleges that the product does not work properly, it is likely that the claim against the defendant will be in contract (see Chapter 2).

Such a claim will require the interpretation of the defendant's obligations under the terms of the contract. This is because there may be express terms of an agreement between the claimant and defendant concerning the purpose and standard of the product. If not, the law will imply into the contract terms that the product be of satisfactory quality and is appropriate for the user, so that it be reasonably fit for any purpose made known to the supplier.

Damages awarded will include economic loss suffered by the claimant as a result of the defect.

A claim in negligence

> **POINT OF LAW**
>
> For example, the claimant enters a café and purchases a bottle of ginger beer. Unfortunately, the bottle contains a decomposing snail, which poisons the claimant. Despite having no claim in contract, the claimant is entitled to bring an action in negligence against the manufacturer who is deemed to owe a duty of care to its consumers.

MANUFACTURE AND DESIGN DEFECTS

Most claims are for manufacture defects. In these cases, unless the manufacturer can show that the defect was not reasonably foreseeable or avoidable, it will be negligent.

On the other hand, the claim may be for a defect at a stage prior to manufacture. In these cases, it is essential that the claimant can show that the risk of damage ought to have been foreseen at the time that the product left the defendant's control.

Further, there may be justification defences on the part of the manufacturer or designer, on the basis that the social benefit of marketing the product outweighs the level of danger to a potential claimant; for example, a common medicine that has serious side effects to some takers.

Who can sue?

At common law, anyone who suffers loss and damage, either through personal injury or to property, is entitled to sue. This means that there is no restriction to the person who purchased the item – a mere bystander may sue.

There may, however, be some exceptions for reasons of public policy, e.g. a thief may not be able to sue for loss as a result of a stolen defective product.

Who can be sued?

At common law, the classes of defendants range from negligent manufacturers to negligent designers, installers, erectors and those involved in distribution. Thus, a wholesaler must take reasonable care to ensure that the products it distributes are safe.

WARNINGS AND FAILURE TO WARN

The adequacy of warnings and instructions may make all the difference as to whether a product is defective and/or the defendant is liable.

Where there was no warning provided on a product, the test is whether it was reasonable to require the manufacturer to provide a warning in the circumstances.

Issues of causation and remoteness are relevant in determining whether the product should have contained a warning, or whether the warning was appropriate. If there should have been a warning and the manufacturer failed to place one on the label, or the warning was inappropriate, the product will be deemed defective.

In order to determine whether a warning should have been provided by the manufacturer, the test for the court (as in ordinary negligence claims) is:

At the time of production, was there a foreseeable risk of the damage suffered by the claimant?

If so, any lack of warning, or an inappropriate warning, will make the product defective.

Where the defendant fails to include a warning on the product, but provides details of the warning to an intermediary, that may be a defence to a claim.

For example, the manufacturer of tyres will distribute these products with a warning to dealers that the tyres are not suitable for certain makes of cars.

It would then be for the intermediary to show that it was reasonable not to warn customers in the circumstances.

Ignoring warnings or instructions

Damage may be caused by the product, but through non-observance of a warning or the instructions.

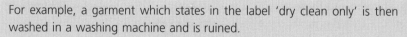

For example, a garment which states in the label 'dry clean only' is then washed in a washing machine and is ruined.

Generally, the defendant will *not* be liable where damage has been caused to the product as in the dry cleaning example above, or where the claimant uses the product for an illegitimate use or one that is substantially different from the use intended by the manufacturer.

However, if it is foreseeable that misuse will take place and will lead to harmful results, a duty may be placed upon the defendant manufacturer to warn the user of the product.

POINT OF LAW

For example, where there is a risk that the product will come into the hands of children.

INTERMEDIATE EXAMINATION

When a claimant brings an action, it will be essential for the defendant to consider its role in supplying that particular product to a consumer.

The courts have distinguished defendants who manufacture a product intended to reach a consumer, without any 'intermediate examination' of the product and those which will be inspected, before use by the consumer.

If the defendant is aware that *in all probability* the product will be subject to intermediate examination to determine any inherent safety risks and warn potential consumers, the manufacturer may be deemed as being too remote to be liable. The most appropriate defendant in this case would be the intermediate examiner.

Where there is no such likelihood of an intermediate examination, the manufacturer will be the most likely defendant.

It does not matter in these cases whether an intermediate examination did take place; if the manufacturer did not consider it probable that an examination would take place, it will be liable. It would be appropriate for the claimant to make the examiner a co-defendant to the action.

Where it is the claimant who discovers the defect, but continues to use it, she may cause there to be a 'break' in causation as her continued use disentitles her from blaming another for the damage suffered.

This is because the law relating to defective products has been developed to protect the consumer from hidden defects, which may cause damage and personal injury.

Further, in all cases of defective products claims, it is open to the defendant to raise the issue of *contributory negligence*.

DAMAGES

In an action at common law, an award of damages will be limited to physical damage only, for example, personal injury and *damage to property other than the defective product*.

Financial loss, as with most other torts, is irrecoverable under this head (see Chapter 3).

'Property other than the defective product' has led to some difficulty in the law, as it is often difficult to determine what is other than that of the defective product.

POINT OF LAW

For example, what if a tyre (on a vehicle) is defective. Can the claimant claim for the damage to the vehicle, as a separate item of property to the tyre?

Where the claimant gained the items of property as *a whole* (e.g. the manufacturer or some predecessor in title to the claimant fitted the defective product), the courts will take a common sense approach and assess whether the product was an integral part of the property.

Where the defective product was *fitted or added by the claimant* (or someone else), the claimant is entitled to sue for the damaged property.

POINT OF LAW

Therefore, if the tyre was fitted to the car, which was then purchased by the claimant, as a matter of principle it seems that there should be no claim for the damage to the vehicle as a whole.

LAW IN ACTION

The court might shy away from this unsatisfactory conclusion, however, and in one case a judge in the Court of Appeal tentatively gave the failure of a defective tyre on a car as an example of a case where there would be a claim in respect of damage to the vehicle.

The judge also thought that there would be a claim for damage to wine in a bottle caused by a defective cork. The case actually under consideration was a claim for damage to the contents of pails that had been bought in bulk in circumstances where the pails were defective and caused damage to the contents. The court did not need to decide the point – and accordingly did not do so.

Where the claimant is abnormally sensitive and suffers personal injury as a result of a defect, the defendant manufacturer's liability will depend upon how reasonable it is for the manufacturer to have protected against such risks to the claimant.

INSIGHT

For example, it is accepted that some claimants are allergic to particular products, for example, tea tree oil shampoo. However, it may be unreasonable to expect that a defendant manufacturer will warn of *all* risks against all potential purchasers or users of the shampoo product.

The general rule here is that where the claimant is already likely to be aware of an allergy, the claimant is not entitled to bring an action. However, in cases where it would be unlikely that the claimant would know of the allergy or increased sensitivity (often in the case of drugs) there will be a duty on the defendant to warn of such risks.

LIABILITY WITHOUT FAULT – THE CONSUMER PROTECTION ACT 1987

Following a number of famous complaints (such as the Thalidomide babies cases in the 1960s) it became clear that the normal negligence principles did not go far enough to protect claimants as it was often difficult to prove fault.

In an ever-increasing global market, there have been difficulties in relation to the duties owed by importers, rather than manufacturers of products.

Where a claimant has suffered from a defective product supplied after 1 March 1988, it may bring an action under the Consumer Protection Act 1987 (Part I).

A benefit to this action, as opposed to an action in negligence, is that there are clear categories of potential defendants against whom to bring an action.

The claimant does *not* have to prove fault on the part of the defendant.

The claimant simply has to show that there was a defect. It is then for the defendant to defend the action, with reference to one of the statutory defences (see below).

INSIGHT

Again, the claimant has the option of proceeding under both causes of action (negligence and under the Consumer Protection Act 1987), with a claim in negligence requiring the proof of fault.

In either case, it is first necessary to show that there is a defective product and in both areas, the same principles apply.

Who can sue?

It appears that the Consumer Protection Act 1987 (Part I) has not altered the scope of potential claimants. Although the 1987 Act suggests that only those with 'an interest in the property' may bring an action under the 1987 Act, it is likely that this would be held to mean anyone who has suffered as a result of the defect.

Who can be sued?

The Consumer Protection Act 1987 (Part I) provides four clear categories of potential defendants:

1. Producers (which includes manufacturers, abstractors (such as miners) and those who carry out a particular process (e.g. a drier of fresh food)

2. Those who hold themselves out as producers (e.g. by putting their trademark on the product)

3. Importers

4. Suppliers

DEFENCES, PARTICULAR TO A CLAIM UNDER THE CONSUMER PROTECTION ACT 1987 (PART I)

Warnings

It may be that using the principles on warnings and labelling above, the defendant may be able to show that the product ought not to be termed as 'defective'.

Development risks

This defence is used most frequently in relation to drug manufacture (see also Chapter 16).

It relies upon the principle that if, at the time of manufacture, the scientific knowledge was such that the defendant would not have been able to discover the defect, then it should *not* be liable.

Clearly, however, where the defect would have been discovered had further tests been carried out at the time, the defendant manufacturer of pharmaceutical products, for example, would be unable to use this defence.

Uncirculated products

In order to succeed under the Consumer Protection Act 1987 (Part I), it is essential that the claimant came to suffer the damage, following supply by another.

INSIGHT

Therefore, a claimant employee of the manufacturer may not be able to claim under the 1987 Act. The burden is upon the defendant manufacturer to show that the product had not been circulated at the time of the damage.

Subsequent defects

The defect must have existed before it left the particular defendant and it is for the defendant to show that it only existed *after* that time.

Non-profit activities

If a supplier did not supply the defective product in the course of business, then it cannot be liable. Producers have a further obligation in that they must show that it was not in the course of business *and* also that there was no view to make a profit in its supply.

Compliance with a legal requirement

If the defect is attributable to an Act of Parliament or a European Community obligation, the defendant has a valid defence to an action brought under the Consumer Protection Act 1987.

Again, as with the above defences, it is for the defendant to show that the defect was due to a legal obligation.

CRIMINAL OFFENCE

Added to the contractual and tortious duties placed upon the defendant as stated above, the Secretary of State lays down safety regulations from time to time.

Failure to comply with such regulations in the course of business may lead to prosecution for a criminal offence (along with a civil action for a breach of statutory duty). It is also a criminal offence to supply dangerous goods.

CHECKLIST

- What duties does the marketer have under any relevant contract?
- Is the product one in respect of which there is strict liability for defects under the Consumer Protection Act?
- Has reasonable care been taken to ensure that the product has no manufacturing or design defects?
- Is the labelling of the product adequate?
- Is there anything of which consumers should be warned?
- Is the product going to be examined by someone else before it reaches the consumer?

5

INTELLECTUAL PROPERTY RIGHTS

In this chapter:

- What is intellectual property?
- Difference between copyright, trademarks and the tort of passing off
- Trademarks
- Comparative advertising and trademarks
- Tort of passing off
- Personality or image rights
- Patents
- The issue of trade secrets
- Design right
- Checklist

Other useful chapters:

INTRODUCTION

Like any business dealing with creativity, the marketing profession depends on a set of principles established both in law and by way of mutual respect that enables those involved to receive proper recognition and reward for their input.

Prominent among these rules is the attribution to copyright (see Chapter 6), trademarks, the law of passing off and patent law (this chapter).

As media channels proliferate and the storage and transmission of content in digital forms grows, the issue of copyright protection and that of trademarks and passing off becomes ever more complicated.

Just as Chapter 6 provides an introduction to copyright, so this chapter is unable to do more than sketch the outlines of trademark, passing off and patent law that can help marketers stop competitors from exploiting the marketing campaign.

Chapter 11 continues the discussion on how trademark laws and passing off are applied in the context of protecting a licensing and merchandising programme.

The principles are once again relatively straightforward and yet in practice the subject is one of vast complexity.

Nearly every trademark case is decided on the given facts in that case, and it is rare that previous cases can assist to any great degree when a new mark is the subject.

The same applies to passing off and patent cases are almost entirely decided on the evidence in each case.

Of high importance to marketers is the issue of branding. All new products and services need to be branded. It is therefore essential that marketers not only pick the right name but also protect it from being exploited by third parties.

The creation of a brand name can be undertaken by a variety of specialist marketers. For example, advertising agencies have departments that can do the job, as do a select number of marketing consultancies as well as a few companies that specialise in this area of intellectual property rights (IPRs).

As discussed in Chapter 6, every piece of marketing or advertising adds to the value of a product, service or a company and yet this intangible asset is very often beyond the scope of copyright protection, as illustrated by the example of 'Exxon', a made-up word held not to constitute a literary work.

For protection of this type of IP, brand owners can use trademarks and the law of passing off.

For example, trademark exploitation and protection is an essential part of the revenue stream for all professional sports teams and clubs in the UK.

In the UK as elsewhere in Europe, trademarks are held and marketed by individual sports teams without a single body overseeing trademark portfolios. As a result there is a risk of inconsistencies in registration and enforcement as well as lost marketing opportunities.

Position in the UK market	Brand name
1	Coca-Cola
2	Walkers
3	Nescafe
4	Stella Artois
5	Muller
6	Persil
7	Andrex
8	Robinsons
9	KitKat
10	Pepsi
11	Carling
12	Pampers
13	Cadburys Dairy Milk
14	Ariel
15	Ribena
16	Whiskas
17	Walls Ice Cream
18	Heinz Canned Soup
19	Lucozade
20	Heinz Baked Beans
21	Felix
22	PG Tips
23	Pringles
24	Flora
25	McCain Chips
26	Huggies
27	Bold
28	Colgate
29	Bell's 8 Year
30	Tetley
31	Bird's Eye Frozen Poultry
32	Mars Bars
33	Budweiser
34	Lurpak
35	Chum
36	Dairylea
37	Foster's
38	Comfort
39	Ernst & Julio Gallo
40	Smirnoff Red Label
41	Mr Kipling
42	Sunny Delight
43	Velvet
44	The Famous Grouse
45	Tropicana
46	Jacob's Creek
47	Bird's Eye Frozen Readymeals
48	Bird's Eye Frozen Veg
49	Kleenex Facial
50	Celebrations

Fig. 5.1 The UK's top selling brands in 2001 [source: AC Nielsen/Marketing (2001)]

By contrast, with the availability of the **Community Trademark** (see Chapter 11) covering the European Union (EU) with a single registration, a league such as the National Basketball Association (NBA) which has registered its various teams' marks and logos with the individual home countries can now take advantage of a broader registration that will expand its protection and at the same time open the doors to new marketing opportunities.

As discussed in Chapter 11, under the **Paris Convention**, trademark holders can take out registrations in Japan, Mexico and the US in order to extend the marketing net and policing and enforcement efforts can be streamlined and focused.

This goes some way towards a unified licensing programme although not on the same structured basis as in the US. Such an approach helps to create a strong market position, with strong trademarks.

With the appropriate trademark registration and licensing plan, authorised merchandise bearing the trademarks of football teams such as Manchester United, Real Madrid or Bayern Munich could find themselves in San Francisco or equally Red Square in Moscow without fear of unlawful exploitation (see Chapter 11 for further discussion on licensing and merchandising).

WHAT IS IP?

IP is the umbrella term used to describe a bundle of different legal rights that typically include patents, trademarks, copyrights, personality rights and the like.

The property is 'intellectual' because unlike other types of property which consists of physical objects or assets, IP consists of abstracts – marks, logos, colours, slogans, expressions, processes, designs – intangible assets that cannot be adequately protected by purely physical means.

The essence of IP is that it is the purely legal rights over the properties which are the real boundary markers, beyond which competitors can be prevented from encroaching.

It is therefore necessary to understand, in respect of each separate category of IP, what exactly those rights are, how they come into existence and how they can be enforced and the limitations of such rights.

Trademarks

The European Court of Justice has observed that the essential function of a trademark is '*to guarantee the identity of the origin of the marked product to the consumer or end user by enabling him, without any possibility of confusion, to distinguish the product or service from others which have another origin*'.

A trademark which through careful management, skilful promotion and wide use comes in the *minds of consumers* to embrace a particular set of *values and attributes* both tangible and intangible (this chapter). Trademarks can be registered or unregistered. For the latter, see the tort of passing off.

Copyright

Copyright is the most international protection of IP rights and does not require formal registration. Copyright does not protect ideas underlying a work but protects the *form in which it has been expressed*.

Copyright is *the right to prevent a work being copied without the copyright owner's consent. Copyright also protects against a work being issued to the public, performed, shown or played in public, broadcast or adapted*.

In essence, a marketer - such as an advertiser - cannot use someone else's protected work and someone else cannot use the advertiser's protected work, without permission.

To do so will infringe copyright and open up an action to stop the marketer, withdraw the marketing campaign and even deliver up profits made as a result of the breach of copyright.

Copyright subsists only in specified list of types of work—literary, dramatic, musical and artistic (Chapter 6).

Passing Off

The tort of passing off protects the whole business, not simply the trademark, but the burden of proof is high—a right of action arises where one trader makes a *false representation to the public which damages goodwill in which the public hold another trader's goods and services*. This could be done innocently or by chance rather than being a deliberate act. Taking action under passing off can be more costly than relying on a registered trademark action. With unregistered trademarks, the marketer will need to establish to the satisfaction of the court that a *reputation* and *status* of the unregistered trademark actually exists *and* that the status of the unregistered mark which is claimed to be *infringed* needs to be proved (this chapter).

Fig. 5.2 Difference between copyright, trademarks and passing off

TRADEMARKS

The point of a trademark is that it provides the consumer, whether that be the public or trade buyers, with a way of knowing who it is that is responsible for producing goods or services.

INSIGHT

By seeing a trademark, consumers can infer certain things about the goods or service, because the mark tells them who is responsible for them. That inference may be one of very high quality or low cost.

For example, a trademark like 'Rolls-Royce' has the inference of high quality, whereas 'EasyJet' has the inference of low cost. Whatever the particular strengths of a brand which an undertaking strives to reinforce or build through marketing, the trademark becomes an indicator of that strength.

Certain goods will be sold under a variety of trademarks. For example, 'Ford' is a trademark, as well as its sub-brands such as 'Fiesta' and 'Mondeo'.

What is a trademark?

The **Trademarks Act 1994 Section 1(1)** defines a trademark as:

Any sign capable of being represented graphically which is capable of distinguishing goods or services of one undertaking from those of other undertakings. A trademark may, in particular, consist of words (including personal names), designs, letters, numerals, or the shape of goods or their packaging.

Certain types of sign are expressly envisaged by the 1994 Act. In particular, words, designs, letters, numerals or shapes can be trademarks.

A challenge for marketers is what can be registered graphically.

INSIGHT

For example, a colour can be represented graphically, so too can a piece of music. Certain sounds that are not capable of being represented in normal musical form as notes on a stave may yet be represented as onomatopoeic words (e.g. 'clippity clop').

It may be possible to represent a taste or a smell graphically, whether in words or by some sort of standardised scientific means, and there is nothing in the 1994 Act on the face of it which suggests that these would be unacceptable.

It should be noted that shapes are also acceptable as marks. It is easy to see how a shape can be represented graphically, whether in words or pictures, and there are many goods which are associated with very distinctive shapes, e.g. the shape of the Coca-Cola bottle and the leaping jaguar on the bonnet of a Jaguar XJ6.

Capable of distinguishing

A trademark must be capable of distinguishing the goods and services of one brand owner from the goods and services of another.

This is a key issue for marketers and has led to a certain amount of confusion amongst those seeking to interpret it, and has also generated some rather confused case law in the UK.

It would appear that marketers will need to satisfy a fairly low test: that the sign is not incapable of distinguishing the goods or services of different undertakings.

Philips Electronics-v-Remington Consumer Products Ltd (1999)

In this case the court had to decide whether the shape of the head of an electric razor could be a trademark.

In deciding the question, the court drew the analogy of welded mesh to try and illustrate the issue. Where the product was welded mesh, 'WELDED MESH' could not constitute a trademark since it could not distinguish one make of welded mesh from another. The judge suggested on the other hand that a mark 'WELDMESH' was different enough from the product for it to be capable of distinguishing that particular make.

In this action, Philips failed to argue that the 'Philishave' head constituted a trademark although it could challenge copycat products under patent law if the device had been registered as a patent.

Registration of trademarks

Until a trademark is registered, it has no protection other than passing off, if it has sufficient reputation (see below). In order to protect a brand, the marketer must decide which class of goods it wants to use the mark on and then register the mark for that class of goods.

For example, in 1994 promotions and incentives company **Red Letter Days (RLD)** created a product called 'Experience Vouchers' that could be redeemed for exhilarating experiences such as driving around a racing circuit, white water rafting, going for a trip in an air balloon or even a day out at the races. These vouchers could be bought by clients looking to provide hospitality to their own customers and staff. However, RLD did not register 'Experience Vouchers' as a trademark until 2001 and had relied on the tort of passing off to protect its product from imitation by competitor marketers.

An activity voucher supplier called **Exhilaration** was unaware of the registered trademark and went ahead and printed a 2002 corporate brochure referring to 'Experience Vouchers'.

One week after production it received a warning letter from lawyers acting for RLD saying that it had infringed RLD's trademark and threatening legal action unless Exhilaration handed over all the offending material to RLD for destruction.

Exhilaration claimed it had no choice but to agree to send all its brochures for destruction at a cost of £15 000. The alternative would have been to contest the action in court and even if it had been successful, its legal bills alone would have been in the order of £25 000. If it failed in its defence it would have faced paying both sides' costs in the order of £75 000, so it made the decision to comply on commercial grounds.

The Register of Trademarks is divided into 42 different categories of goods and services called 'classes'. An application for a trademark must specify which class or classes of goods the registration is to cover. It is important not to seek too wide a specification of goods as this may endanger the validity of the registration.

Fees for registration

At the time of going to press (2002), total Registry fees and professional charges for a UK trademark application relating to one class of goods or services will be in the region of £1000. This estimate is based on the application proceeding through to registration without any major objections being raised by either the Registry or third parties which will increase costs.

On average, the time from application to registration in the UK should be between 8 months and 2 years and the costs are staggered throughout this period.

Absolute grounds of refusal to register a trademark

The so-called 'absolute grounds of refusal' prevent marks being registered regardless of the presence or absence of other marks that may be on the Trademarks Register.

POINT OF LAW

Under **Section 3(1) of the 1994 Act**, the following will be refused registration:

a) signs which do not satisfy the requirements of Section 1(1)

b) trademarks which are devoid of any distinctive character

c) trademarks which consist exclusively of signs or indications which may serve, in trade, to designate the kind, quality, quantity, intended purpose, value, geographical origin, the time of production of goods or of rendering of services, or other characteristics of goods and services

d) trademarks which consist exclusively of signs or indications which have become customary in the current language or in the bona fide and established practices of the trade

This is qualified by the fact that marks may still be registered if they have acquired distinctiveness by virtue of their use prior to application.

'Distinctive' and 'capable of distinguishing'

The difference between distinctive and capable of distinguishing may seem arbitrary and it has produced some convoluted case law.

From a marketers' perspective, there are *two ways* of achieving distinctiveness:

- A made-up word and so inherently distinctive (such as Kodak)

- A mark which is not inherently distinctive but becomes distinctive by use (such as Radio Rentals – now re-branded Box Clever)

The following are all marks which all marketers have the legitimate right to use as they simply describe some aspect of their goods and therefore it is not in the public interest to restrict the use of such descriptive words:

- 'Premier' (quality)
- 'Bath cleaner' (purpose)
- '$1' (price)
- 'Welsh' (geographical origin)
- '24 hour' (time of service)

In addition, marketers will have applications for marks refused if they simply try to register ordinary words as marks merely by attaching an 'e' prefix to denote electronic commerce.

INSIGHT

The Trademarks Registry gives the example of 'e-florist'. The letter 'e' as a prefix has become customary in the trade of Internet business to signify a business which is conducted 'on-line' to some extent. Equally, the prefix 'm', signifying similar trade via 'WAP' mobile phone communication may offend in this way.

However, there could be occasions where ordinary words are capable of trademark registration if the description is obviously one that could not apply to the goods, e.g. 'South Pole' for bananas.

Section 3(2) of the 1994 Act excludes shape marks where:

- The shape is a result of the nature of the goods
- The shape of goods necessary to achieve a technical result
- Where the shape gives substantial value to the goods

This means that in most cases only relatively capricious shapes will be registrable.

LAW IN ACTION

Triomed (Proprietary) Ltd-v-Beecham Group plc (2001)

In this case, the lozenge shape for an easy to swallow pill was held by the court not to be registrable.

Section 3(3) of the 1994 Act excludes the registration of marks that are *contrary to public policy or morality, and marks that may deceive the public*. This can cause problems for marketers in determining what is contrary to public policy or decency as to whether the mark is capable of being registered.

POINT OF LAW

For example, whilst French Connection's 'FCUK' with its obvious sexual connotations is registered as a UK trademark, the sign 'BOLLOX' has been refused in an application for a European Community trademark.

Also excluded are specially protected emblems such as national flags and the Royal Coat of Arms.

Other marks that would be refused registration include:

- Marks whose use would be illegal (e.g. of a paramilitary organisation or terrorist group)
- Marks registered in bad faith (e.g. registering a trademark which is the name of a newly formed company with no intention of doing anything other than selling it to that company subsequently)

In respect of the practice of registering domain names for an improper purpose, see also Chapter 15.

Relative grounds for refusal

Section 5 of the 1994 Act sets out the relative grounds for refusal of a mark. These grounds depend on other marks that are already registered, and are aimed to prevent confusion between marks.

POINT OF LAW

Section 5 of the Trademarks Act 1994 provides:

(1) a trademark shall not be registered if it is identical with an earlier trademark and the goods or services for which the trademark is applied for are identical with the goods and services for which the earlier trademark is protected.

(2) a trademark shall not be registered if because

a. it is identical with an earlier trademark and is to be registered for goods and services similar for which the earlier trademark is protected, or

b. it is similar to an earlier trademark and is to be registered for goods or services identical with or similar to those for which the earlier trademark is protected,

there exists a likelihood of confusion on the part of the public, which includes the likelihood of association with the earlier trademark.

(3) A trademark which

a. is identical with or similar to an earlier trademark, and

b. is to be registered for goods or services which are not similar to those for which the earlier trademark is protected,

> *shall not be registered if, or to the extent that, the earlier trademark has a reputation in the*
> *United Kingdom and the use of the later mark without due cause would take unfair*
> *advantage of, or be detrimental to, the distinctive character or repute of the earlier*
> *trademark.*

This section envisages three basic scenarios.
The first is that the mark and the goods or services are the same in both cases.

POINT OF LAW

For example, Ace Automobiles would not be able to register AA for their own breakdown service.

The second is that the goods and services are similar, and there is a likelihood of confusion on the part of the public.

POINT OF LAW

For example, Virgin could not register Virgin Coke because of the confusion and previous registration of the word Coke by the Coca-Cola Company. Whilst the word cola is a generic term and is therefore capable of use (Virgin Cola), it cannot itself be registered as a trademark. Virgin of course is capable of trademark protection.

The third scenario (albeit a contractual dispute) is where a similar mark, although used in relation to different goods, would cause damage to the earlier registered trademark.

LAW IN ACTION

The Worldwide Fund for Nature (formerly World Wildlife Fund)-v-The World Wrestling Federation Entertainment Inc. (2002)

In 1994 the World Wildlife Fund (as it was then called) came to an agreement with the World Wrestling Federation. The Fund, which by that time had been using the 'WWF' initials for some considerable time, had been increasingly concerned about the Federation's use of the same initials and had started proceedings which were designed to stop the practice altogether.

A compromise agreement was reached in 1994. As part of the deal, the Federation agreed not to use the 'WWF' initials anywhere outside the US. Even in the US, it agreed to refer to itself as 'WWF' orally and for the purposes of sports events and advertisements. However, as the Federation became one of the hottest properties in the licensing market in the world, it was inevitable that 'WWF' began to take on a new meaning amongst the public and was more synonymous with wrestling than conserving the habitat of endangered species.

The Fund attempted to enforce the compromise Agreement in the UK Courts in 2001 and the penalty for non-compliance would be fines or, in serious cases, terms of imprisonment for its directors. The Federation defended on the basis that the 1994 agreement was an unacceptable restraint of trade and as such should not be enforced by the courts.

The Divisional Court held that unless the Federation could show that the restraint agreed in 1994 'went beyond any reasonably arguable scope of protection of the intellectual property rights in issue', then it could not try to rescind the agreement it had entered seven years ago.

As it had not shown this to be the case, the defence failed and the Fund got its injunction. This decision has now been upheld by the Court of Appeal in 2002.

Other exclusions to the ability to register a trademark include:

- Marks which have become part of ordinary language or trade and are synonymous with the products or service in general rather than in relation to one particular product (e.g. Hoover would not now be registrable)

- Marks whose use would constitute passing off

Exceptions to the above rule:

- Marks that would otherwise offend against the section are however allowable with the consent of the registered proprietor of the earlier mark

- Where it can be shown by the marketer applicant that there has been honest concurrent use of the two marks

A brand owner is permitted to use the symbol ^{TM} to denote that an application for a full trademark registration is pending. On receipt of the trademark certificate on registration, the brand owner should use ® to denote registration of that mark.

For guidelines to the proper use of a trademark, see Chapter 11.

Infringement of trademarks

This section reflects the provisions of **Section 5 of the 1994 Act** and effectively means that if a sign could not be registered because of an earlier registered mark, its use would infringe the registered mark.

POINT OF LAW

Section 10 of the 1994 Act relates to infringement and provides:

(1) A person infringes a registered trademark if he uses in the course of business a sign which is identical with the trademark in relation to goods or services which are identical with those for which it is registered.

(2) A person infringes a registered trademark if he uses in the course of trade a sign where because

   a. the sign is identical with the trademark and is used in relation to goods and services similar for those for which the earlier trademark is registered, or

   b. the sign is similar to the trademark and is used in relation to goods or services identical with or similar to those for which the earlier trademark is registered,

there exists a likelihood of confusion on the part of the public, which includes the likelihood of association with the trademark.

(3) A person infringes a registered trademark if he uses in the course of trade a sign which

   a. is identical with or similar to the trademark, and

   b. is to be used in relation to goods or services which are not similar to those for which the earlier trademark is protected,

where the trademark has a reputation in the United Kingdom and the use of the sign, being without due cause, takes unfair advantage of, or be detrimental to, the distinctive character or repute of the trademark.

Use in the course of trade includes fixing the sign to goods, packaging and business papers (including invoices). It also includes selling, offering, exposing for sale, or putting on the market goods or services under the sign, and importing or exporting under the sign.

However, as the case below illustrates, the courts try to take a sensible view when a trademark may appear within the legitimate commercial activities of another marketer.

LAW IN ACTION

Trebor Bassett-v-The Football Association

The well-known sweet manufacturer produced a series of cigarette cards for insertion into its packets of candy cigarettes, bearing pictures of the members of the England football team. The footballers were shown wearing the England kit which bore the 'Three Lions' crest. The FA threatened to bring an action for trademark infringement against Trebor Bassett. Trebor Bassett sued for unjustified threats and the FA counterclaimed for trademark infringement.

The court held that the fortuitous appearance of the logo on the players' shirts could not be use of the sign as a trademark with respect to the cards, any more than a newspaper report of an England match accompanied by a photograph of a player wearing the strip was use of the logo in respect of sales of newspapers. Accordingly the court held that there was no infringement of trademark and the FA threat was unjustified.

Section 10(6) of the 1994 Act provides that a marketer is perfectly entitled to use the sign for the purpose of identifying goods or services as those of the registered proprietor or a licensee, unless such use is 'otherwise than in accordance with honest practices in industrial or commercial matters if the use without due cause takes unfair advantage of, or is detrimental to, the distinctive character or repute of the trademark'.

Use of a trademark on the Internet

Use of a mark on a web site advertising goods constitutes use for the purposes of trademark infringement (see also Chapter 15).

Provided that such use is in the UK, or that the web site is directed at the UK market, unlicensed use can constitute an infringement. Of course, if the site is advertising the proprietor's goods, then that will be allowable insofar as it is in accordance with honest business practices, as the following case illustrates.

LAW IN
ACTION

Euromarket Designs-v-Crate & Barrel (2000)

Dublin-based brand owner Crate & Barrel (C & B) placed an advertisement in a UK-based estate agent's magazine with an Irish circulation. The advertisement carried an international telephone number and a web site address. The web site, accessible from the UK and elsewhere, naturally carried the Crate & Barrel name.

US-based Euromarket Designs (EMD) had built up a successful chain of homeware and furniture stores in the US and had registered Crate & Barrel as a trademark in the UK.

Neither brand owner did any material trade in the UK, but EMD sued C & B for trademark infringement and applied for summary judgment (where there is no case to answer so the defendant immediately loses).

The issue at the heart of the proceedings was whether there was material use of the trademark 'Crate & Barrel' by C & B in the UK, and whether the EMD registration of 'Crate & Barrel' was invalid on the grounds of non-use.

The Chancery Court held it unlikely that the web site could on its own amount to such use as it related only to the shop in Ireland and did not actively seek customers in the UK or for that matter elsewhere.

Regarding the estate agency magazine advertisement, despite the international telephone number and the UK circulation, the Court took into account its likely purpose and effect and concluded that this was not material use in the UK.

The court held that C & B would have a *reasonable prospect of running successfully a defence available to those using their own name in good faith and of persuading the court at trial that the EMD registration of Crate & Barrel was invalid on grounds of lack of use by EMD in the UK.*

The application for summary judgment was therefore dismissed. This did not mean that EMD would lose at trial, simply that C & B had a reasonable prospect of defending the case at trial.

This is not the first UK judgment in which a robust view has been taken by the courts as to whether use of a brand name on a web site is material use for the purposes of the Trademarks Act 1994 when the site is not specifically directed at the UK.

In full proceedings, marketers that take action for trademark infringement are entitled to disclosure of all documents held by the other side which that party intends to rely on.

With regard to the above case, EMD would be looking for evidence of commercial activities that did take place in the UK, e.g. sales invoices over the relevant period to see if any mail order sales were made to UK residents which might have been driven by the press insertion.

If it could be substantiated to the court's satisfaction that trading took place in the UK, then it may have grounds for a successful action for trademark infringement.

As for the 'own name' defence argued in the C & B case, this sounds superficially fair, though hardly encouraging for marketers relying on trademark searches before launching a new brand.

In other jurisdictions it is very common for marketers to carry out 'common law' searches such as trade and telephone directories, the Internet and other sources likely to reveal use of brand names which, though they might not be registered trademarks, could still, because of rules such as that relating to 'own name' use, cause a new product launch serious difficulties.

The courts have recently taken the view that the use of a name on a web site does not necessarily amount to usage of a trademark as the next case illustrates.

LAW IN ACTION

1-800 FLOWERS Inc.-v-Phonenames Ltd (2001)

A US based florist service, 1-800 FLOWERS, sought trademark protection in the UK and took action against the registered trademark owner of 0800-FLOWERS. The original trademark application failed and the Court of Appeal upheld this decision, on the grounds that the name was not sufficiently capable of distinguishing the US florist service and would be likely to lead to confusion.

The Court of Appeal held that the marketer's use of its name on its web site www.1800flowers.com was not sufficient to establish 'use' of the trademark in the UK.

Usage required *some active step in that area (UK) on the part of the user that goes beyond providing facilities that enable others to bring the mark into the area.*

In a separate case, the courts have shown reluctance to always find in favour of a brand owner that may have a common name but where there is virtually no risk of confusion should an element of this name be used by another marketer.

McDonald's Corporation-v-McChina (2001)

In the early '90s Mr Yuen opened his first restaurants under the names McChina Stir Fried and McChina Wok Away. In 1992 he applied to register 'McChina' as a trademark in the UK in respect of Chinese style food and restaurant services.

Predictably, the McDonald's Corporation opposed the trademark registration. It argued that Mr Yuen's use of the mark McChina would cause confusion and deception and it produced survey evidence suggesting a third of those exposed to the 'McChina' name would believe it was linked to the famous US monolith.

McDonald's won on the first round but lost on appeal at the Chancery Division which allowed Mr Yuen's trademark application to go forward to registration.

Marketers should approach the issue of survey evidence with caution. The court held that the survey evidence was flawed and that there was sufficient difference between the second syllables of McDonald's and McChina so that there was no real risk of confusion or deception.

Comparative advertising and trademarks

This is a brief discussion as the subject of comparative advertising is discussed in more detail in Chapter 9.

Before the 1994 Trademarks Act, the use of a competitor's trademark in a comparative advertising context would have constituted a trademark infringement.

INSIGHT

For example, an advertisement saying that 'Daz' washing powder scored five points in a recent test, compared to Persil's three points, would have infringed Persil's trademark.

This is addressed by **Section 10(6) of the Trademarks Act 1994,** so that comparative advertising does not infringe trademark use *unless it is not in accordance with honest business practices.*

As discussed in Chapter 9, in a recent court appearance, British Airways unsuccessfully sued Ryanair for, amongst other things, trademark infringement for an advertisement consisting of a table comparing Ryanair's prices to British Airways' prices.

Defences to trademark infringement

A brand owner will not infringe a trademark in the use of its own name and address. It is also not infringement to use the type of marks that are descriptive of the goods or services concerned *provided* that such use is in accordance with honest practices. These are the same types of marks which are not allowable under Section 3 of the 1994 Trademarks Act.

Mercury Communications Ltd-v-Mercury Interactive (1995)

The telecommunications giant Mercury Communications had registered the trademark Mercury for 'computer programs' under Class 42 of the Trademarks Act 1994.

Mercury Interactive was the UK subsidiary and distributor of a US software house and marketed programs in the UK under the names 'Mercury' or 'Mercury Interactive' under the parent name Mercury Interactive Corporation; and under the UK company's name Mercury Interactive (UK) Ltd.

In each case the word Mercury generally appeared in significantly larger type face than the other words.

Mercury Communications took action for infringement of its registered trademark but the court rejected its claim, on the basis that Mercury Interactive and its parent company could establish that it was generally known as Mercury and therefore likely to have a complete defence to an action for trademark infringement.

Non-use of a trademark

If the registered proprietor of a trademark does not use that mark in relation to the goods for which it is registered, that mark is liable to be struck off the register (see Euromarket Designs-v-Crate & Barrel above).

POINT OF LAW

The mark will be revoked if the mark has not been used for a continuous period of 5 years. The mark can be partially revoked if the mark is registered for a broad range of goods or services, but has only been used in relation to a few of those goods.

This can cause problems for even the largest of corporations, as the case below illustrates.

LAW IN ACTION

McDonald's Corporation-v-Joburgers (Unreported)

In South Africa, the McDonald's name and the 'golden arches', two of the world's most famous trademarks, went unused because of the apartheid system for a period of many years. When apartheid ended and McDonald's sought to re-establish its rights, it found that a burger chain in Johannesburg aptly named 'Joburgers' was using its marks.

McDonald's applied for an injunction but Joburgers successfully had McDonald's trademarks struck off the trademarks register for non-use. McDonald's subsequently won an appeal to have them reinstated on the basis that the marks were well-known foreign marks, but the lesson for marketers is nonetheless a sobering one.

Exhaustion of rights

One trademark issue that has recently found itself in the media is that of exhaustion of rights. The principle of exhaustion is that once a brand owner has put goods on the market in the EU under a trademark, those goods are free for anybody to sell. Parallel importation, e.g. of cheaper European medicines into the UK, cannot in normal circumstances be prevented by trademark proceedings unless the condition of the goods has somehow changed.

For a discussion on parallel imports and exhaustion of rights, see Chapter 11 on protecting a licensing and merchandising programme.

Remedies for trademark infringement

The remedies available for trademark infringement are essentially the same as those outlined in Chapter 6 in relation to copyright.

Marketers can sue for damages or an account of profits, delivery-up and an injunction.

INSIGHT

In many such actions, the opposite side will often respond to any action with a counterclaim for revocation of the trademark. It should be borne in mind by potential claimants that if the mark is vulnerable to an attack (e.g. it is fairly descriptive), the upshot of the action may be not only that no damages for infringement are awarded, but also that costs could also be awarded against the claimant and it could also lose its mark.

The same applies to patents, which are discussed briefly below.

Another reason for brand owners to be cautious about bringing either trademark or patent actions is that making groundless threats is itself actionable. In other words, if a threat is made to a potential defendant that proceedings may be brought, it is important that that threat is made on solid legal and factual foundations.

TORT OF PASSING OFF

There is also a full discussion on passing off in Chapter 11.

What is passing off?

Passing off protects any aspect of the presentation of a brand owner's products or service that distinguishes these products or services from a competitor's and helps the brand owner sell the product or service. In other words, passing off protects a brand owner's goodwill in its business.

The law of passing off is intended (amongst other things) to prevent consumers being misled into believing that goods or businesses are those of someone else.

Advertisements which falsely suggest that one brand owner's goods or services have a connection or association with another's business may give rise to a passing off action if this could cause damage to the innocent brand owner.

Examples of passing off include use of another's trade name, trademark or the 'get up' of its product and can include copying the underlying theme or idea of a well-known advertising campaign.

For example, a 'spoof' advertisement for Boddingtons' beer that used the Walls Ice Cream TV commercial setting for its product *Cornetto* (gondola in Venice set in a romantic setting with the main character eating an ice cream rather than drinking a pint of beer) could have caused problems for Boddingtons had Walls Ice Cream not seen the funny side to the campaign, on the basis of 'imitation is flattery'.

Common law (evolved by case law rather than as set down by statute law) affords marketers some protection of the value of their brands, even in the absence of trademark registration.

The law preventing 'passing off' provides this right. Very often, an action in trademark infringement and passing off will run side by side.

As with many common law rights, the premise of passing off is a simple one. The House of Lords in a famous passing off case involving the 'Jif' plastic lemon summarised the statement of law of passing off in one sentence: 'No man may pass off his goods as those of another'.

To succeed, a claimant will need to show:

- A reputation or goodwill acquired in the goods, name, mark or symbol
- A false representation has been made (whether intentional or not) leading consumers to think that the goods are those of the claimant
- Damage to the claimant

For example, a marketer of bubble gum will succeed in a passing off action against a competitor sweet marketer if it can show that aspects of its branding, packaging or advertising have been so extensively used in the marketplace that they have become distinctive of its brand of bubble gum, if such branding, packaging or advertising is used by that competitor in such a way as to give rise to a misrepresentation that the products or businesses are in some way connected.

In any of the above circumstances, the claimant must show that the actions of the competitor sweet marketer are likely to lead or have led to significant damage.

A distinction should be drawn between mere confusion and deception. Although a customer may be confused between two brands or companies, or not know the difference between them, no deception as required to show passing off occurs *unless* the customer is led to suppose that the defendant's product is that of the claimant.

> POINT OF LAW
>
> For example, marketers must be careful not to choose too descriptive names for their products or services.
>
> The more descriptive the name that a marketer chooses, the more likely it is that there will be other similar names used and the less will be needed to tell them apart.
>
> For example, 'Office Cleaning Services' and 'Office Cleaning Association' have been held by the courts to be different enough not to constitute passing off.

In essence, a misrepresentation can be any aspect of the goods/services in question, its presentation and/or packaging which can be shown to mislead the consumer into thinking they are getting such goods or services from one marketer when in fact it is another.

Evidence

It is essential that marketers obtain actual evidence of confusion among the public in passing off cases unless the facts speak for themselves (*res ipsa loquitur*) and the judge can make an order without hearing evidence (see Arsenal FC case below).

In such cases where evidence is required, witnesses may be required to testify as to confusion. However, a useful form of evidence for the court to consider are market surveys carried out by an independent market research organisation that can demonstrate misrepresentation because members of the public believe the goods of one brand owner are associated with another.

Marketers must adhere to high standards of fairness in the conduct of survey evidence:

- Methodology – the survey must be done fairly and by a method such that a representative cross section of the public is interviewed
- The sample must be statistically relevant
- Exact answers must be recorded in full (rather than pre-coded boxes)
- No leading/suggestive questions must be asked
- Interviewee should not be directed into a field of speculation upon which they would not otherwise have embarked
- Questions should be unambiguous and factually realistic (e.g. the question: 'who do you think made this?' has been specifically criticised for not being a question the consumer would normally ask herself/himself)

The defendant's lawyers must be shown:

- The number of surveys carried out

▦ The methodology and sample size of all surveys carried out

▦ All of the interviewees' answers

The weight given to a survey can be increased very substantially by supporting it with evidence from interviewers, independent witnesses of the interview techniques and in particular any interviewees who are willing to give evidence.

Members of the public can be unpredictable as witnesses, but their very independence tends to lend additional conviction to their evidence, and completely unsolicited evidence carries even greater weight.

Types of passing off

If an advertisement alleges that a product has been endorsed by a famous personality or company and their consent has not been obtained, then this may amount to passing off.

It may also amount to a malicious falsehood, a misrepresentation and, in limited circumstances, a defamatory statement (see Chapter 8).

There are a number of different types of activity which can be described, and be actionable, as passing off:

▦ Most common passing off is where a marketer is attempting to pass off its goods as another's

▦ Where the goods are in fact the claimant's goods, but are sold as being of a certain quality when they are not, for example where an old model or second hand product is sold as a new model

▦ 'Class' passing off – where a marketer sells goods alleged to be a certain quality of goods (e.g. whisky, which has strict controls in its manufacture, or Champagne), when in fact the goods do not fulfil the strict legal requirements of the class

▦ 'Reverse passing off' – the claimant marketer's goods are in fact those of the defendant (e.g. sending out a catalogue, ostensibly of one's own goods, when in fact the catalogue contains pictures of somebody else's goods)

INSIGHT

Passing off does not protect a mark or style absolutely – it protects a
marketer using that mark from confusing or deceptive use of that mark by someone else.
In theory anyone can use another's unregistered mark as long as no one is led to think that the
goods sold by the first marketer under the mark are those of the second marketer.

Damages

'Damage is likely to be suffered' – the brand owner does not need to show actual damage in order to succeed in an action for passing off. However, it will need to show that *damage is likely to be suffered*.

There does not need to be any intention to cause damage to the reputation of the brand owner – and in the majority of passing off cases the defendant rarely has intended to cause damage.

Quantification of damages

Damage is therefore typically caused by a party attempting to trade off the superior quality or reputation of particular goods. This can be quantified as:

- Direct loss of sales
- Degradation of the reputation of goods/services (by association with the defendant's inferior products)
- Loss of exclusivity or distinctiveness
- Loss of licensing and merchandising opportunities

Where the misrepresentation is so serious as to amount to fraud (dishonesty), then the courts tend to assume that damage has been or will be caused. However, in the majority of passing off cases some form of evidence of damage is required.

Locus standi (the right to bring an action)

In order to bring an action in passing off, a brand owner must normally be in business and have a favourable reputation in England and Wales, either as a business as a whole or in respect of particular goods/services. It is highly *unlikely* that start up businesses will satisfy this test as the necessary goodwill will not as yet have been established.

However, advance advertising on a sufficient scale may create a reputation before actual trading has started. Alternatively, the trading arm of an organisation that already has a reputation or the merchandising outlet for a sports celebrity may be able to sue from day one.

Trading situation

To be liable in passing off, the defendant must be in trade as well. There is no need for the brand owner to be competing in the same field of business – but the closer the two are to each other, the easier the case will be to prove.

Remedies

The remedies available are the same as those for a registered trademark infringement action:

- Injunction preventing further infringement
- Monetary damages
- Account of profits
- Delivery-up or destruction

Search and seizure orders (see Chapter 11) are less easy to obtain in respect of unregistered trademarks than registered ones, since there is a less clear cut right being infringed at the outset.

CURRENT UNCERTAINTY SURROUNDING UK TRADEMARK AND PASSING OFF LAWS

The value of trademark protection and the application of the common law of passing off have recently been thrown into question as a result of the High Court ruling in a recent football club 'rip off' case.

Arsenal FC-v-Matthew Reed (2001)

Arsenal Football Club is the proprietor of a number of registered trademarks including the words 'Arsenal' and the famous cannon logo. Arsenal applies these trademarks to a wide range of official club merchandise.

Matthew Reed is a trader in unofficial Arsenal merchandise which is branded with trademarks that are identical or similar to Arsenal's registered trademarks.

Following a history of disputes between Arsenal and Reed that went back 30 years, Arsenal eventually sued Reed in the High Court for passing off and trademark infringement (they had originally added copyright infringement to the action but dropped this before trial – which could have been a critical mistake).

Notwithstanding the fact that Reed was selling scarves and hats that featured logos and words that were identical to Arsenal's registered trademarks, the judge rejected Arsenal's claim that Reed's sales of unofficial Arsenal-branded merchandise constituted passing off.

The question of whether or not infringement of Arsenal's trademarks had taken place was left unresolved.

Essentially the decision casts grave doubts over the ability of football clubs (and other sports bodies) to prevent unlicensed sales of fan-targeted merchandise which features their trademarks.

The implications of the judgment could cost soccer clubs significant amounts of lost revenue in relation to merchandise sales by 'unofficial' traders.

It may also have an impact on the amount of money that official licensees of football clubs and sports event rights holders are willing to pay for merchandising licences.

Although it is likely the ruling will be reversed on appeal when it is heard by the **European Court of Justice** in 2002, the case has led to an urgent re-examination of the application of UK trademark and passing off laws as well as a review of how best trademark owners can protect their IPRs in light of the judgment.

Analysis of this judgment

The key issue in Arsenal's passing-off argument was the allegation that Reed's goods caused confusion among the relevant sector of the market – fans were deceived into thinking the merchandise was 'official'.

This allegation was rejected by the judge, partly because of a *lack of evidence* that Reed's use of Arsenal's trademarks did actually cause the necessary confusion (this is one of the tests – see above).

Some of the comments in the judgment are particularly worrying for marketers.

The judge, Mr Justice Laddie, said:

I find it difficult to believe that any significant number of customers wanting to purchase licensed goods could reasonably think that Reed was selling them ... It seems to me that the use of the Arsenal signs on Reed's products carries no message of trade origin.

Justice Laddie stressed that the *failure to provide evidence of confusion* was a key issue and therefore the case can be distinguished on its facts in this respect rather than becoming a 'counterfeiters' charter'.

The judge said that had Arsenal used a mock-up stall filled with various official and unofficial merchandise to find out the perception of the fans, or carried out market research of the 240 000 fans on its database, the club might have provided sufficient evidence to support the case of a likelihood of confusion.

Justice Laddie concluded that Arsenal's argument that fans believed there was a trademark connection between Arsenal and Reed (which was necessary to establish passing off) *failed for lack of evidence that Reed misled the public about the origin of the products.*

Further, the court held that Reed was merely using the Arsenal trademarks as a 'badge of allegiance' rather than as a trademark denoting a source of trade origin.

Unresolved issue

The judge went on to say that the question of whether Reed's 'non-trademark' use constituted an infringement remained *unresolved*, stating that this area of the law is unsettled and would need to be clarified by referral to the European Court of Justice.

From a marketer's perspective, until the judgment from the European Court of Justice expected in 2002, trademark infringement is going to be hard to prove.

Even though the case can be distinguished on its facts, it does provide an argument for cottage industry style merchandisers that will try to fit their own circumstances around the facts of the Arsenal case and claim that what they are doing does not fall within trademark use and is outside the reaches of trademark legislation.

If the European Court of Justice finds there is no infringement if the use of the trademark is perceived as a badge of support, loyalty or affiliation, then the business of selling not only football merchandise but any merchandise aimed at fans, whether in the television, film or music industries, will be hugely affected.

PERSONALITY RIGHTS

Today's pop stars, movie stars and athletes are some of the most recognisable faces on the planet. In sport, many personalities earn more money from licensing and merchandising and their personality rights than they do from competing or playing for a club.

For example, the world's most expensive football player, England captain
and Manchester United striker David Beckham could be worth as much as £40 million a year in
terms of sponsorship and licensing deals should he perform well before a global audience of 4
billion people in the FIFA World Cup Korea/Japan 2002™.

Personality or image rights of a football player

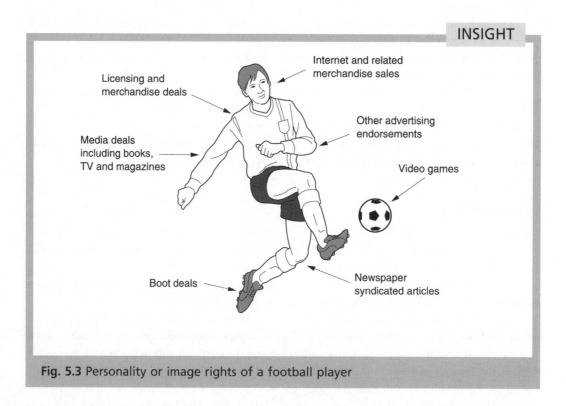

INSIGHT

Internet and related
merchandise sales

Licensing and
merchandise deals

Other advertising
endorsements

Media deals
including books,
TV and magazines

Video games

Boot deals

Newspaper
syndicated articles

Fig. 5.3 Personality or image rights of a football player

The right to exclusively control the commercial use of a name, image and other identifying
characteristics such as a voice, likeness and nickname is therefore very valuable.

Marketers (licensees) are prepared to pay vast sums of money to obtain the endorsement of a famous personality (licensor) in order to bask in the jet stream of public goodwill
and media publicity that it hopes will translate into increased sales for its products or
services.

For example, hair products marketer Brylcreem and fashion accessories
marketer Police pay Beckham £1 million a year, respectively, for the use of his image rights
in their marketing campaigns for hair products and sunglasses.

However, the legal protection of these highly prized personality rights is a complex issue, and is not helped by the lack of clarity and certainty of the law in England and Wales which is at variance with the legal protections offered in the US and other jurisdictions.

At the time of writing and for some time to come there is no clearly defined right of personality/publicity in the UK of the type that exists in other jurisdictions, e.g. in the US.

'Personality or image rights' in the UK is therefore a descriptive term of a
bundle of legal rights that are protected by a number of statutory and common law provisions,
none of which are specifically designed to protect against unauthorised use of a personality's
image.

In order to successfully exploit the personality as a commodity in its own right, it is essential that enforceable IPRs are identified and protected.

The main test, established under common law by Justice Laddie in the Elvis case (below) is: 'Personalities can only complain if the reproduction or use of their likeness results in infringement of some recognised legal right which she/he does own'.

The 'recognised legal right' referred to in the above definition is to be found in the following areas of law:

- Trademarks Act 1994
- Copyright, Design and Patents Act 1988
- Tort of Passing Off
- Defamation
- The Trade Descriptions Act 1968
- British Code of Advertising Practice
- Control of misleading advertisements regulations
- The Human Rights Act 1998
- Data Protection Act 1998
- EU Data Protection Directive (95/46/EC)

The acquisition and enforcement of so-called 'personality rights' has had a chequered history in the UK, with the courts never quite embracing the concept wholeheartedly.

For example, the decisions regarding the Princess of Wales Memorial Fund in relation to trademarks and dolls, and the Elvis trademarks case, bear this out.

Diana Memorial Fund (1999)

The trustees of the Diana Memorial Fund were unsuccessful in the action to prevent the Franklin Mint making and selling a commemorative Diana doll of the late Princess of Wales.

The essential problem is that the late Princess of Wales has long been part of the public domain. Whilst the Diana Memorial Fund may be able to protect its own trademark that features Diana's signature represented in her favourite colour and use this on a range of official merchandise, there is little prospect that it will ever be successful in preventing others exploiting her image and personality.

Elvis Presley Enterprises (1999)

Elvis Presley Enterprises was defeated in its efforts to prevent a trader (named 'Elvisly Yours') selling soap bearing the name of the late rock and roll legend.

Somewhat memorably, Mr Justice Laddie said that the consumer does not 'give a toss' whether a bar of soap bearing Elvis' image was produced with the sanction of his estate or not. Apparently, all that the man in the street wants is a bar of soap with Elvis' image appearing on it.

As these two decisions indicate, the courts are extremely wary of granting monopoly rights over personalities. Central to these decisions is the fact that Elvis and indeed the Princess of Wales have long been in the public domain.

Whilst Elvis Presley was alive he of course made considerable sums from his successful music career. At the time, merchandising formed a far less important role than it does today. The earlier refusal by the courts to accept the exclusivity of personality rights is illustrated by the **ABBA decision**, where the pop group encountered the refusal of the court to prevent unauthorised exploitation of their image and name.

In the case of the late Princess of Wales, whilst she was undoubtedly one of the most photographed women of her time, she did not herself exploit her image for her own commercial ends.

If the Princess of Wales had done so whilst she were alive and sought to prevent the sale of, for example, a commemorative mug, then in the absence of any defamatory innuendo, as she had no goodwill to protect, and in the absence of a trademark registration, she would have been unsuccessful.

Contractual protection

Every personality has a name, facial and other physical or style characteristics such as unshaven appearance, shaven head, and even the clothes and accessories they are famous for wearing. Personalities also have signatures and nickname logos associated with them.

INSIGHT

For example, world champion Formula 1 driver Michael Schumacher has a range of merchandise that uses his nickname 'Schumi'.

In sport, personalities also have biographical information and statistical data that form part of what is known as their 'Player Indicia'.

Player Indicia

In such instances, the existence of the contract for the use of the 'Player Indicia' is for the benefit of the marketer – the rights holder (personality) having made a contractually enforceable obligation not to use her or his 'image rights' for the benefit of another competitor marketer.

In the situation where a competitor marketer manufactures counterfeit products bearing the personality's likeness or image, the sports personality or its licensee will need to convince the court that it can recognise any legal right in the Player Indicia in question, whether under advertising, IP laws or otherwise (see also Chapter 11).

The existence of a contract may not *prima facie* result in the 'image rights' being protected as SFX, the international sports and management agency recently discovered.

LAW IN ACTION

SFX and Elite Sports Group (2001)

In November 2001, a dispute arose as to the title to the image rights of David Beckham on Manchester United football shirts. SFX, which represents Beckham, claimed that the star's image rights, which include shirts he has autographed, are an integral part of its contractual negotiations with Manchester United and therefore the star is entitled to additional payments as a result of the sales of the autographed shirts.

However, Elite Sports Group holds an official merchandising licence from the club and has been selling the autographed shirts for £275 ($358) a piece and no additional royalties have flowed to Beckham or his agent.

According to SFX, those image rights belong to Beckham and SFX, not Manchester United or Elite Sports Group. There was still further confusion as one official at the club admitted that the merchandise licence for Elite Sports Group only extended to action photographs of players that had been autographed and not other types of merchandise.

This story serves to illustrate an important point. Such confusion will continue to occur so long as the Football Association Premier League (FAPL) and Football Association (FA) Playing Contracts remain silent on the issue of players' personality and image rights.

POINT OF LAW

The rules of the FAPL set out in the FA Premier League handbook (1999/2000) states:

> *Particulars of any Image Contract Payment in respect of the Player should be set out in the contract with his club.*

As a result, a vast majority of football playing contracts have a short addendum by which the player grants to his employer (the club) a non-exclusive right to use his image or likeness on the club's promotional material whether that be through on-line and TV media or by appearing on merchandise.

POINT OF LAW

An 'Image Contract' is defined by the FAPL as:

> *Any contract whereby a Player transfers to any person, firm, partnership, company, corporation or other legal entity ('the transferee') the right to exploit his image or reputation either in relation to football or non-footballing activities and 'Image Contract Payment' means any payment made or liability incurred by or on behalf of a club to a transferee in order to acquire that right.*

In consideration for this, the player is ascribed an undefined amount as part of his remuneration package.

The boundaries to such activities appear to be in contention with respect to the above dispute.

The contractual situation can be still further complicated with the practice carried out by many football clubs where a players' pool collects and shares out extra revenue from the players' charges and appearances, photographs, and other promotional work undertaken on behalf of the club.

Whether the exclusive or non-exclusive basis for the exploitation of a player's image rights are granted to the club or team, this continues to be a source of confusion for both licensor and licensee.

However, taxation law is helping the players' cause. The ruling by the **Inland Revenue Special Commissioners** in the Denis Bergkamp and David Platt cases acknowledged for tax purposes at least that image rights could effectively be capital assets, notwithstanding that English law does not specifically recognise that such rights exist.

LAW IN ACTION

Sports Club plc-v-Inspector of Taxes (2000)

The Inland Revenue Special Commissioners took the view that promotional agreements fell outside a normal contract of service of a football star, and held that payments to footballers under such agreements concerning promotion, publicity, marketing and advertising were not taxable under Schedule E as payments or benefits in kind nor were they subject to PAYE.

Arsenal's football stars Dennis Bergkamp and David Platt separately contracted in 1995 to allow Arsenal to use the rights in their respective images for £1.5 million each.

Arsenal made payments under these arrangements directly to the players' offshore companies which owned their image rights. This allowed the players to avoid tax in relation to such payments.

If it continues to be held that promotional agreements, such as those relating to image rights, are genuine commercial agreements, then it is arguable that they can be separated from and considered distinct from the employment contract, as is the case for tax.

So although players can benefit from the tax loophole, such agreements could be used against them if they should move to another club or team under their existing contract as the original club would still hold the rights to their image.

Trademark protections

Trademarks are one of the most useful forms of protecting IPRs granted to marketers under Player Indicia contracts.

It is possible, in certain circumstances, to register Player Indicia as trademarks, domain names and Internet keywords (see also Chapter 15).

POINT OF LAW

For example, Formula 1 racing driver Damon Hill secured protection for the image of his eyes looking out from the visor of his racing crash helmet.

A practical issue that needs to be addressed very early on by the personality is what is actually going to be registered as a trademark and therefore can be licensed to a marketer?

It would be impossible and impractical to protect by registration all the different combinations and series of images that would be needed to secure a monopoly, and the cost of duplicating such protection in all the relevant markets would be staggering.

Registering nicknames and logos as trademarks may be an easier route than trying to protect facial images or names.

For example, Beckham has filed a Community Trademark application for a range of trademark classes covering products such as sunglasses, bags, football shirts and hair lotions!

However, the extent to which such trademark rights are practically enforceable is debateable.

Soon after the **Trademarks Act 1994** appeared on the statute books there was a rush of sports stars, agents and merchandising companies controlled by sports stars registering their names, nicknames and images as trademarks.

Football personalities such as Paul Gascoigne, Ryan Giggs, Eric Cantona and Alan Shearer have all obtained registrations for symbols which identify them whether these are their names, names and numbers (such as 'Giggs 11'), signatures, nicknames, caricatures or in some cases photographs of their faces.

However, as the judgments in the Elvis and Princess Diana cases illustrate, alongside recent statements made by the Trademarks Registry, there must now be a serious question mark over the validity and enforceability of some of these registrations, and the willingness of the Patents Office to allow similar applications to be registered in the future.

It does not follow that because the image, name or likeness of a sports personality is undoubtedly famous it is therefore necessarily distinctive in a trademark sense.

Further problems may arise if the use of the name in question was merely as one of a large number of names – the product manufacturer would no doubt argue that the names were being used in a descriptive rather than a trademark sense.

According to the English courts, the determining factor is the effect the registration of a sports personality trademark has in the minds of consumers.

INSIGHT

For example, if the trademark has the effect of bringing to mind the name or image of the sports star, then the fame of the sports star in question could be seen as a potential barrier to the likelihood of registering the symbol as a trademark.

Therefore, in order to achieve protection, the trademark must quite clearly be a badge of origin.

The personality has to be able to show that the mark will serve to identify her or his goods and is a badge of origin. If the sign functions as an indication of trade source, e.g. people buy the goods upon seeing the mark because they know that it comes from or is endorsed by the personality, then the mark is far more likely to be registrable and enforceable.

It is also a double edge sword. If the applicant is somewhat tardy in applying for registration, then the task of securing a future trademark registration might turn out to be more difficult if goods of the type that form the subject of the application are being sold and indeed have been sold in large numbers by competitor marketers.

Either way, personalities face a very difficult ride in the courts should they wish to take legal action in enforcing their trademark rights.

Personalities with 'personality rights' for sale can undertake the following proactive steps in order to bring themselves within the protection of the Trademarks Act 1994:

▨ Selection of non-descriptive, highly distinctive brands upon which to base a merchandise campaign – nicknames, logos and stylised marks are more likely to be validly registered and enforceable than descriptive names and portraits.

▨ Selection and registration of an appropriate brand should be registered as a trademark at the earliest possible stage in a personality's career. This will help defeat any presumption that on the part of the Trademarks Registry that fame equals non-distinctiveness.

▨ The brand selected by the personality should be used in relation to all merchandise endorsed or produced on the personality's behalf and marketed in such a way by the licensee marketer as to link the brand in the minds of the buying public with only those goods and services endorsed by the personality.

▨ The brand should become part of the package of assets that the personality carries with her throughout her career.

As discussed earlier in this chapter, where such marks are registered, it is relatively straightforward for the personality to take action for infringement against the unlawful use of its registered marks.

The situation is very different if a similar mark is used or if an identical mark is used in relation to similar goods of a competitor marketer.

In such instances, the personality will have to prove that there is the likelihood of confusion on the part of the public and this is much more difficult to prove under trademark law.

As already discussed above, UK judges will need to take a lot of convincing before they find that there is a presumption on the part of the public that where they see signs relating to a personality they would assume that the star has endorsed the product or service.

Copyright and designs

Copyright is particularly weak when it comes to protecting personality or image rights.

A person in the public domain is photographed almost every day, if not many times a day by a wide variety of people. In the absence of a right of privacy, the only way that an individual may control the use of photographs is to control the copyright in them.

With regard to designs, an integral part of merchandising campaigns is the sale of dolls and the like.

LAW IN ACTION

As long ago as 1941 in the Popeye case **(King Features Syndicate Inc.-v-O & M Kleeman)** producing a three-dimensional reproduction of a two-dimensional drawing was held to be copyright infringement.

More particularly, it is possible to register a doll or three-dimensional representation of a personality as a registered design under the **Registered Designs Act 1949**.

There are obvious advantages in so doing and the proprietor of it obtains the right to sue any person who without its permission makes, sells, imports or hires or offers to do any of these activities in connection with the product.

It also gives rights against anybody who makes anything for enabling the article to be manufactured as well as any article that bears the registered design or a design very similar to it.

Copying is not required. It is also possible to prevent the importation of articles that infringe design registration.

Tort of privacy

Unlike other jurisdictions such as the US, the UK does not have a tort of invasion of privacy serving to prevent the appropriation of a personality's name or likeness for a third party's benefit.

The British Code of Advertising and Sales Promotion

The **British Code of Advertising and Sales Promotion** (see also Chapters 9 and 13) includes within it a section on protecting privacy but it lacks any statutory force:

POINT OF LAW

Protection of privacy

13.1

Advertisers should not unfairly portray or refer to people in an adverse or offensive way. Advertisers are urged to obtain written permission before:

    a. referring to or portraying members of the public or their identifiable possessions; the use of crowd scenes or general public locations may be acceptable without permission

    b. referring to people with a public profile; references that accurately reflect the contents of books, articles or films may be acceptable without permission

    c. implying any personal approval of the advertised product; advertisers should recognise that those who do not wish to be associated with the product may have a legal claim.

13.2

Prior permission may not be needed when the advertisement contains nothing that is inconsistent with the position or views of the person featured.

13.3

References to anyone who is deceased should be handled with particular care to avoid causing offence or distress.

13.4

Members of the Royal Family should not normally be shown or mentioned in advertisements without their prior permission. Incidental references unconnected with the advertised product, or references to material such as books, articles or films about members of the Royal Family, may be acceptable.

13.5

The Royal Arms and Emblems should be used only with the prior permission of the Lord Chamberlain's office. References to Royal Warrants should be checked with the Royal Warrant Holders' Association.

Defamation

It can be defamatory to assert that a person has endorsed a product or service when this is not true (see Chapter 8).

The House of Lords decision in **Tolley-v-Fry & Sons Ltd (1931)** enshrined the principle and involved a well-known amateur golfer. A caricature of him appeared on one of the defendant's adverts for a chocolate bar.

Tolley objected on the basis that there was an innuendo that he had allowed his name to be used in return for gain – a position that was diametrically opposed to his status as a respected amateur golfer.

In the absence of defamation, merely using a personality's name or image for promotional purposes would not of itself amount to defamation. However, in some cases, the marketing of a product bearing the name of a well-known personality without authority, whilst not being defamatory, may amount to passing off.

The conduct of a particular trader may amount to the tort of interference with a subsisting contract.

In personality endorsement agreements, the parties to such a contract will have substantial mutual obligations between the personality and the manufacturer whose products or services are being endorsed.

In the case of sports personalities, the exclusive use of a particular brand of equipment may be essential to the relationship. The well-publicised, yet unauthorised association of that particular personality with another brand of cricket bat, for example, may result in a contract between the personality and its chosen partner being terminated.

The Human Rights Act 1998

The **Human Rights Act 1998** does contain the right to privacy, and according to some lawyers this could be used to protect personality rights and image misuse although this has yet to be tried in the English courts (see also Chapter 8).

The Act incorporates into UK domestic law most of the rights and freedoms found in **the European Convention on Human Rights (ECHR)**.

POINT OF LAW

Article 8 of the ECHR – Right to Respect for Private and Family Life:

1. *Everyone has the right to respect for his private and family life, his home and his correspondence.*

2. *There shall be no interference by a public authority with the exercise of this right except such as is in accordance with the law and is necessary in a democratic society in the interest of national security, public safety or the economic well-being of the country, for the prevention of disorder or crime, for the protection of health or morals, or for the protection of the rights and freedoms of others.*

In the UK, IPRs are struggling to keep up with commercial practice and there have been arguments made for a personality right to be introduced that would protect merchandising rights.

However, statutory protection for personality rights could not be open ended as this would be unworkable.

INSIGHT

For example, it would be an impossible situation were such a right was used to stifle legitimate activity like the filming, reporting, photographing, publishing and broadcasting of everyday events whether sporting or otherwise.

If it is accepted that personality rights are like other IPRs, then there is an argument that they should not be treated differently and that these rights should be included within the scope of the **Trademarks Act 1994.**

Used in the usual way on goods or in connection with services, there is no reason why a mark should not be protected. Any trademark that is already in the public domain cannot be registered without proof of distinctiveness, and there is no reason why personality rights should be an exception to this.

Protection must be sought quickly though. In terms of infringement, if there is no confusion or the likelihood of this, there is no reason why a trademark associated with a personality should in the final analysis be treated differently from other marks.

PATENTS

It is unlikely that marketers reading this book are likely to be exposed to patent law to any great degree, beyond deciding how best to exploit the inventiveness of a new product.

Nonetheless, the law is relatively simple (although the subject matter rarely is, almost by definition), and so it is worth setting out the basic principles here for completeness of this chapter.

It is governed largely by the **Patents Act 1977**, although there are some procedural provisions relating to patents in the **Copyright, Designs and Patents Act 1988**.

What are patents for?

Patent protection arose from letters patent, a royal monopoly granted to merchants giving them exclusive rights to a product.

It is now used to safeguard invention although it is a question of balance.

On the one hand, it is important to the technical advancement of society that marketers invest time, labour and money into technological improvement.

INSIGHT

A good example of this is in the pharmaceutical industry, which is striving continually to produce better drugs in the fight against disease. The problem is that developing a new drug can take millions, or billions of pounds and the end result is very often a product which can be reproduced at very little cost. If that final product (or the process by which a product is made) did not receive protection, there would be no motivation to research, since the money that had been invested would be almost entirely wasted.

The flip side is that the drug will be much more expensive, since the investment costs will be reflected in the price of the new drug.

Patents have an additional benefit to the public, which is that a patent (the invention) becomes a matter of public record and so is available for all to see.

That means that it is open to other marketers to try and 'engineer round' the patent, changing it sufficiently not to infringe, whilst retaining some of the invention's benefits.

This in itself should have the result that it becomes part of the store of knowledge that resides in the public domain rather than in some dusty research laboratory and stimulates competition and therefore advances science.

Requirements for the registration of a patent

There are three fundamental requirements for a product or process to be capable of achieving a patent:

1. It must be novel

2. It must involve an inventive step

3. It must be capable of industrial application

Novelty

In order to be patentable, an invention must be novel. This means that it must not form part of 'the state of the art' at the application's priority date.

Inventive step and obviousness

It is not possible to patent something which is obvious. In order to decide whether or not something is obvious, the marketer must consider the following:

▪ What is the inventive concept embodied in the patent?

▪ What would the 'man skilled in the art' have known at the time of the application? The skilled man is considered to be a non-inventive man who is used to working in the relevant field. He is imbued with the 'common general knowledge' of that field.

▪ What steps are required to get from the common general knowledge or existing products or processes, to the patent?

▪ Would those steps be obvious to the skilled man?

Industrial application

Patents are only available for inventions which are capable of industrial application.

This has a fairly wide interpretation that includes agriculture, but there are a number of exceptions.

Things that cannot be patented include discoveries, scientific theories and mathematical methods, aesthetic creations, schemes, rules and methods for performing mental acts, playing games (e.g. a way of completing the Rubik's cube), or doing business, computer programs or presentations of information.

Methods for medical treatments are also excluded for policy reasons.

Duration

Patent protection lasts for 20 years from the date of filing.

Infringement of patents

Patents set out in great detail what is covered by the registration. Any subsequent product which includes each of the features disclosed, will infringe that patent.

INSIGHT

Furthermore, the patent will be given a purposive construction, so that if the patent discloses an angle of 10° for a component, an angle of 9.5° in the alleged infringing device will not escape *unless* the function of the device is materially affected by the change or it was clear that the patent envisaged a greater degree of precision.

The acts that constitute infringement are extensive.

Making, disposing of or offering to dispose of, use, importing or keeping a product, infringes, and using a process or offering it for use where the user knows (or it would be obvious to a reasonable person) that use without consent would be an infringement also infringes.

For a process:

... it is an infringement to dispose of, offer to dispose of, use or import any product obtained directly by means of the process or keep any such product whether for disposal or otherwise. It is also an infringement to supply or offer to supply the means relating to an essential part of the invention for putting the invention into effect, when the person supplying knows (or it would be obvious to the reasonable person) that those means are suitable for putting, and are intended to put the invention into effect in the UK.

In the following case, the Court held open the possibility of an injunction being granted to interrupt use of a brand if products it has been used on have been shown to infringe a third party's rights.

LAW IN ACTION

Dyson-v-Hoover (2001)

Inventor Dyson sued Hoover for infringement of its revolutionary no bag cleaner, despite that Dyson's patent had just 1 year to run.

The court granted an injunction to Dyson on the following grounds:

- Hoover was prevented from using the VORTEX brand name for 6 months on any vacuum cleaner, even if it did not infringe Dyson's patent (goodwill in the VORTEX brand had been illegitimately acquired on a product that infringed Dyson's patent)
- Hoover was prevented from entering the market with its VORTEX competitor product after the expiry of Dyson's patent ('accelerated re-entry' on the back of development and marketing work in relation to a product that infringed Dyson's patent).

If this so-called 'brand infection' principle holds good for patent infringement, then the courts may start to apply the same reasoning if the product infringes other marketers' rights, such as the rights protected by passing off, copyright or design (see Chapters 6 and 13).

Exceptions to infringement of a patent

Just as with copyright, there are a number of things which marketers can do with a patent, including anything done privately for non-commercial purposes, and experimenting with the subject matter of the patent.

The issue of trade secrets

Many marketers do not patent their processes, but choose instead to keep their workings entirely secret.

LAW IN ACTION

Two famous examples are the recipes of **Coca-Cola** and **Kentucky Fried Chicken**.

The disadvantage of such an approach is that a marketer may be susceptible to 'reverse engineering', whereby the ingredients, the process or how a product works is determined from the end product. Nonetheless, keeping trade secrets rather than putting the information into the public domain through a patent may be more commercially expedient.

The need for a patent or the effective secrecy of key information are but two of the safeguards available. In addition, a marketer should rely on the duty of confidentiality that will be express or implied into the contracts for staff and all agencies involved in the business of the marketer that is of a sensitive and confidential nature.

Further protections are available to the marketer in the form of restrictive covenants in its employment contracts, which if properly drafted and enforceable will prevent employees, or teams of employees, from stealing ideas, campaigns, fellow employees and clients.

Action for breach of confidence is also open to individuals, although clearly there is less likely to be substantial damage than if trade secrets are divulged.

One famous recent example was the action brought by **Michael Douglas**, **Catherine Zeta Jones** and *OK!* magazine against *Hello!* magazine for printing photographs of the couple's wedding.

For further discussion, see Chapter 8.

Practicalities

Litigation is nearly always expensive, particularly in the field of patents, where expert evidence is nearly always required and litigation is extremely protracted. However, the value of these rights can be vast to a company.

INSIGHT

The amount of money that **Coca-Cola** has spent establishing the reputation of a brand that can be seen in every corner of the globe, from Nepalese villages many days walk from the nearest road, to the centre of Manhattan, New York is not an insignificant sum. Without protection, it is worthless.

As marketers responsible for establishing exactly that sort of reputation, whether or not on a similar scale, it is therefore vital to understand the fundamentals of the protection mechanisms available.

DESIGN RIGHT

It is unlikely that marketers will be concerned with the protection of such rights, although clearly the exploitation of designs may be a high priority.

Designs fall into three categories:

■ Registered designs

■ Unregistered designs

■ Designs protected by copyright.

There is a great deal of overlap between the three areas, all with differing scope and periods of protection.

Unregistered design

Under the **Copyright, Designs and Patents Act 1988**, there may subsist an unregistered design right in articles of a given shape and configuration. This right is referred to in the 1988 Act simply as design right. Like copyright, no formalities are required.

Section 213 of the **1988 Act** provides:

(2) *In this part 'design' means the design of any aspect of the shape or configuration (whether internal or external) of the whole or part of an article.*

No right subsists in designs which are 'commonplace', that is to say designs which are trite, trivial or hackneyed.

No right subsists in methods or principles of construction; aspects of design which are dictated by the need to fit or match other designs (for example the part of a three pin plug which has to fit into a wall socket); or surface decorations.

Infringement consists of making something exactly or substantially to the design.

Unregistered design right lasts for only 10 years.

Registered designs

It is possible for a design to be registered under the **Registered Designs Act 1949** (as amended).

Section 1(1) of the **Registered Design Rights Act 1949** provides:

(1) *In this Act, 'design' means features of shape, configuration, pattern or ornament applied to an article by any industrial process, being features which in the finished article appeal to and are judged by the eye, but does not include*

a. *A method or principle of construction or*

b. *Features of shape or configuration of an article which:*

i. *Are dictated solely by the function which the article has to perform, or*

ii. *Are dependent on the appearance of another article of which the article is intended by the author of the design to form an integral part.*

Designs under the 1949 Act must also fulfil a requirement of novelty akin to that for patents, which requirement has been amended by the **Registered Design Regulations 2001.**

According to the provisions of **Section 7** of the **1949 Act**, infringement of registered design right is by making or importing articles for sale or hire or for use in trade or selling, hiring or offering or exposing for sale of hire articles in respect of which the design is registered and to which that design or a design not substantially different from it has been applied.

Rights subsisting under the Act last for 25 years.

Designs which are protected by copyright

Certain articles may still be protected by copyright. In particular, design drawings of artistic works, e.g. sketches made in preparation for a sculpture, will attract copyright and future copies of either the sculpture or the drawing will infringe that copyright in the drawing.

Another example are buildings, which are 'artistic works'. Copying of buildings will therefore infringe copyright. Given the much longer period of subsistence of copyright (for which see Chapter 6), it is preferable to utilise copyright rather than design right if both are available. In practice, many proceedings will rely on both.

CHECKLIST

- Marketers must consider boundaries, territories, and categories for the protection of the marketing campaign
- Do not seek to register a trademark under too many classes
- Consider Community Trademark registration as a way of protecting the marketing campaign
- Weigh up the relative strengths and weaknesses of copyright, trademarks and passing off protections – remember that litigation is risky, expensive and time consuming
- Words, designs, letters, numerals, shapes and smells can all be protected
- Avoid too descriptive or ordinary language – this will not stop competitors from ripping off the marketing campaign
- Consider what is within acceptable boundaries of taste and decency when considering a new product or service launch
- Always keep meticulous notes and records of the marketing campaign – from conception to inception and execution – as the legal burden of proof for establishing IPRs and evidence of behaviour of the parties is high
- Do not rely on legal searches, e.g. the Trademarks Register, but also carry out common law searches for companies and brands in telephone directories and the Internet in order to avoid difficulties with 'own name' use
- Only use comparative advertising with extreme care (see Chapter 9)

- Beware that once IPRs have been established they need to be used – failure to do so may allow a competitor to rip off the marketing campaign as a trademark could be removed from the Trademarks Register for non-use

- Beware use of independent market research evidence in passing off actions – get independent statements from interviewers; independent witnesses of the interview techniques and in particular names and addresses of any interviewees who are willing to give evidence

- It may be preferable to try to protect the marketing campaign under 'clear cut' trademarks law rather than the law of passing off

- Look for protections in the form of patents, trade secrets and key restrictive covenants within the marketing team to protect the integrity of the campaign

6
COPYRIGHT

In this chapter:

- Nature of copyright protection
- Where copyright protection can assist in the protection of a marketing campaign
- Limitations on the use of copyright protection
- Marketing best practice
- Checklist

Other useful chapters:

INTRODUCTION

Modern marketing campaigns are extremely sophisticated given that they cross geographical borders, category territories, target markets, global audiences and jurisdictions. This raises a host of highly challenging legal marketing issues when considering how best to protect the integrity of an integrated marketing campaign.

For example, a brand name, logo or slogan can be protected by a range of legal instruments including registered (and unregistered) trademarks, copyright and the law of 'passing off'. Laws relating to design rights, defamation and malicious falsehood can also be used to protect a brand, a brand's packaging (its 'get up') or the shape and design of a branded product.

The rights holder, such as an FMCG brand owner, a major retailer, a publisher of interactive software, a fashion designer, a sports governing body, a football club, a movie studio or a recording artist will need to consider a variety of legal protections in order to safeguard the most valuable assets of any marketing inventory – the Intellectual Property Rights (IPRs).

In order to exploit the full range of sales and marketing opportunities open to the rights holder, IPRs must be secured before the marketing campaign has commenced.

As the following diagram illustrates, there are a wide variety of channels to market and many require copyright protection and enforcement in order to safeguard the integrity of the planned marketing campaign. Without such protections and enforcement, the rights holder faces the threat not only to the marketing campaign from competitors and illegal trading activities but risks damage to its present and future sales and ultimately its profits could suffer.

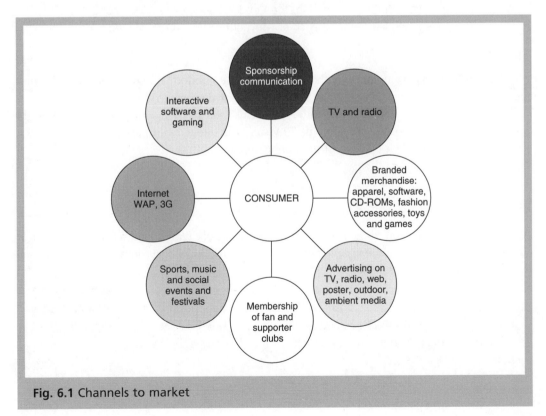

Fig. 6.1 Channels to market

Although the principles of copyright and other IPRs covered in this book are relatively straightforward, it is very easy to misunderstand how they apply in a marketing context as the following example illustrates.

Voodoo Lounge Bar, Leicester Square, London (2001)

To 'tart an' up its happy hour menus, trendy bar Voodoo Lounge in London's Leicester Square used a tartan design and also coined the phrase to describe its menu as 'Voodoo Lounge Essential Mix'. As anyone who listens to BBC Radio 1 on a Friday night will tell you, 'Essential Selection' and 'Essential Mix' are more to do with top DJ Pete Tong than a burger and fries.

Within days the Voodoo Lounge heard from Pete Tong's lawyers who claimed that 'Essential Mix' was Pete Tong's trademark and the Voodoo Lounge's use of the words on their menu card was detrimental to his character, given the club's association with dance music.

This letter was quickly followed by another – this time from the lawyers acting for English clothing brand Burberrys. They claimed the tartan design used on the menu cards constituted an infringement of Burberrys' copyright.

Given the media interest and not wanting to alienate either clubbers or fashion conscious Americans who favour Burberrys' clothing, the Voodoo Lounge agreed to change the menu cards without admitting liability for breach of copyright or trademark infringement.

Although we may sympathise with the owners of the Voodoo Lounge, the story underlines the need for caution when devising any name, phrase or design.

Even subconscious copying can cause problems (see below) and given that copyright protection lasts the life of the creator plus 70 years, it is dangerous to assume that because it has been around a while it belongs in the public domain!

WHAT IS COPYRIGHT?

As the name suggests, copyright is *the right to prevent a work being copied without the copyright owner's consent. Copyright can also protect against a work being issued to the public, performed, shown or played in public, broadcast or adapted.*

In essence, a marketer – such as an advertiser – cannot use someone else's copyrighted work and someone else cannot use the advertiser's copyrighted work, without permission.

To do so will infringe the copyright and open up an action to stop the marketer, prevent the marketing campaign and even deliver up profits made as a result of the breach of copyright.

Licence and assignment of copyright

The copyright owner can grant a licence or assign to another person the right to use the work. There may be several parallel copyrights in one work. For example, in the case of music (see below) there is copyright in the music score, words and recording of the music, respectively, and the consent of all the copyright owners must be obtained.

Origins of copyright protection

Copyright originally stemmed from the rights of printers to publish books. From this simple commercial monopoly, a wide umbrella of protection for all sorts of different works has developed over the years.

Harmonisation of copyright laws across the European Union (EU)

On 10 December 1997, the **European Commission** adopted a proposal for a Directive to harmonise copyright and related rights in the 'Information Society'. The Commission's aim is to establish a level playing field in the EU for products and services containing IPRs, and also to provide copyright owners with improved protection. The **proposed Directive** (which has not come into force) places particular emphasis on new media products and services, including those delivered on physical media (such as CD-ROM and DVD) and those delivered on-line and by the Internet.

The proposed Directive would harmonise certain aspects of the copyright laws of Member States; in particular, the rights of reproduction, communication to the public and distribution. In addition, it would harmonise the legal protection of anti-copying systems and information for managing rights.

How would the proposed EU Directive on copyright affect marketers?

The harmonisation of the above rights would not require any substantial changes to copyright law in the UK. However, there are several points of interest relating to the application of these rights in a digital environment:

- The right of reproduction is very broad and is intended to cover any form of reproduction, both on-line and off-line. Accordingly, the uploading and downloading of a work in a digital form and the storage of a work in the memory of a computer would be an infringement of this right.

- The right of communication to the public makes it clear that making a work available by means of any form of on-line distribution service, including an 'on-demand' distribution service, would be an infringement of this right.

- The right of communication to the public makes it clear that doing so, will not exhaust this right in respect of that work. Although this is considered to be the position under UK copyright law, it would certainly be helpful to clarify this point.

The right of distribution makes it clear that the first sale or other transfer of ownership of a work outside the Community would not exhaust the rights of the copyright owner in respect of that work within the Community. The proposed Directive would therefore expressly exclude the application of international exhaustion.

Exceptions

The **proposed EU Directive on Copyright** also provides for a number of exceptions to the reproduction right and the communication right. Some are obligatory (Member States would be required to implement them) and others are optional for Member States.

The most important of these exceptions being proposed are:

- The obligatory exception to the reproduction right that would exclude certain acts of reproduction that are dictated by technology. These are therefore considered to be incidental to the use of a work, rather than having any separate economic significance. For example, this would cover the creation of certain 'cache' copies that arise during transmission over the Internet.

- A further optional exception to the reproduction right that would allow establishments accessible to the public to reproduce works where this is not done for direct or indirect economic or commercial advantage.

- If the UK were to implement all of the exceptions set out in the proposed EU Directive, then substantial modifications to copyright law in the UK law would be required.

This has not happened as yet, so the law on copyright as it affects marketers in the UK is governed by the **Copyright, Designs and Patents Act 1988** (see below).

No agreement as to harmonisation (at time of writing)

Copyright owners and their associations have criticised the proposed EU Directive because of the number and scope of the exceptions. In particular, rights holders oppose the exception that would allow copying for private purposes, on the basis that this right has traditionally been abused. In addition, rights holders argue that the exception in respect of temporary copying would enable on-line service providers to avoid liability, even if they know that their networks are being used to carry works that have been copied illegally and have the technical means to remedy it.

Copyright owners and their associations have also pointed out that the provisions relating to the protection of technical measures is limited. In particular, they point out that these provisions only provide protection against technical devices that provide access to a work, and not against technical devices that permit the unauthorised use of a work.

In addition, they are concerned that these provisions do not make it clear whether circumventing devices can legitimately be marketed when they have legitimate purposes.

This is a particular cause for concern for copyright owners since they are acutely aware of the problems that tape to tape copiers and devices for making so called back-up copies of computer software have caused in the music and the software industries respectively.

As the Commission recognises, the interests in this are 'divergent and often conflicting'. In addition, the stakes are very high. Accordingly, the lobbying looks set to continue well into 2002.

COPYRIGHT, DESIGNS AND PATENTS ACT 1988

Current copyright law in the UK is governed by the **Copyright, Designs and Patents Act 1988** and protection under the Act may be attached to literary, dramatic and musical works, databases, artistic works, sound recordings, films, broadcasts, cable programmes and typographical arrangements, as well as designs.

Copyright law is based on two sound commercial principles:

- That the labour that goes into any given piece of work is valueless *unless* it can be adequately protected
- The avoidance of infringing others' IPRs

Not only is there an understandable stigma attached to being labelled a plagiarist within the marketing profession, but also the financial consequences of directly copying a competitor's marketing campaign and 'stealing' its IP assets can be severe.

Credibility and reputation with consumers, who the marketer is trying to influence in the first place, can be lost and will be hard to rebuild, if the marketer is publicly condemned for 'sharp practice' and unfair or anti-competitive behaviour.

Is all work protected by copyright?

Contrary to popular belief shared amongst some marketers, there is no copyright in an idea, no matter how original or unique the marketing idea may be.

This is why marketers need to be extremely careful about discussing proposed marketing campaigns in the open before they have actually launched.

POINT OF LAW

For example, in idle chatter with a marketing journalist a marketer lets slip about a proposed campaign for a new product and in the same week a news item appears in *Marketing Week* before the campaign breaks. The story runs the risk of ruining best laid marketing plans and gives competitors an 'early warning' signal to run a 'spoiler' campaign on similar or even identical lines. In such a situation, there is no recourse to a legal remedy for the marketer for any loss or damage that it may have suffered as a result of the competitor's similar or identical marketing campaign.

Copyright protection will not apply to other situations such as a discussion with friends on the competition entry to compose a new radio jingle, the ideas for a new TV commercial shared with colleagues in an advertising agency or a new marketing concept such as 'brandcasting' unless these are fixed, whether by a sketch, in writing or recorded in some form. This does not have to be done by the originator of the idea but can be done by a third party.

In another respect, copyright protection can be further limited to protecting only the *form* in which the idea is reproduced.

> **POINT OF LAW**
>
> For example, a newspaper editor who writes an editorial expressing an opinion does not gain a monopoly in that opinion. She simply gains a monopoly of the combination of words used to express her opinion.

As the above point illustrates, there are limits to how far the law will recognise the copyright in the work to be protected.

> **POINT OF LAW**
>
> For example, it would be possible to write a book that takes the ideas of another book and expresses them in a slightly different way. Essentially what has been taken is nothing more than the ideas of the first book, and yet clearly there could be an infringement of the copyright if 'substantial' parts of the original book were reproduced in whole without the permission of the author (see Infringement of Copyright below).

How does a copyright come into existence?

This is governed by statutory conditions under the 1988 Act:

1. The author is a British citizen, an individual domiciled or resident in the UK or a body incorporated under the law of part of the UK

   or

2. The work was first published in the UK

These are not the precise stipulations, for which see the 1988 Act which is set out on the *Essential Law for Marketers* web site which can be found at http://www.bh.com/companions/0750655003.

Provided either of these conditions can be satisfied and that the work is recorded in some way (as discussed above) there are no other formalities to be complied with. No application forms to fill in and no fee to be paid.

Use of the copyright symbol

Best practice in the marketing profession is to use the standard copyright notice '© [name of copyright owner] [year of first publication]'. This is helpful as it creates a legal presumption that the named individual or company is the copyright owner and notifies the public that a work is protected by copyright (but see warning below).

However, in the UK it is not essential to include the © symbol as copyright arises automatically and there is no registration system (compared with trademarks, see Chapter 5).

Marketers should not presume that by placing a © symbol on their work affords any greater degree of protection. This symbol has no impact on the subsistence of copyright in a work, but merely gives rise to a presumption that the name corresponds to the owner of the copyright in that work, until the contrary is proved.

Who owns the copyright?

The first copyright owner is generally the creator of the work. The main exception is where the work is made in the course of employment, when the employer is the first copyright owner.

If a marketer uses a freelancer, e.g. a freelance designer, then the position is slightly different to that of an employee.

Freelance contributors retain copyright ownership *unless* their contracts state otherwise. Ownership of copyright can be assigned or the right to use copyright works can be licensed.

How long does copyright last?

The duration of a copyright varies depending on the nature of the work in question.

Literary, dramatic, musical or artistic works

Literary, dramatic, musical or artistic works are protected until 70 years after the end of the calendar year in which the author dies. This a very long period particularly by comparison to other IPRs (see Chapter 5).

If the author is unknown, the period will last 70 years from the time the work was made or the time that the work was first (legitimately) made public.

Sound recordings

In sound recordings, protection lasts for 50 years from the end of the calendar year in which it was made, unless in that time it is released to the public (whether by publication, performance or broadcast) in that period, in which case it is entitled to protection for 50 years from the end of the calendar year in which it was released.

Films

Films are protected for 70 years from the end of the calendar year in which the last known living member dies out of the set consisting of the principal director, the author of the screenplay, the author of the dialogue or the composer of the music specially created for and used in the film.

If the identity of all of the above is unknown, then the period runs from the film's creation or release, whichever was the later.

Broadcasts and cable programmes

Broadcasts and cable programmes are protected for 50 years from their delivery as a programme.

Typographical arrangements of published editions

Typographical arrangements of published editions are only protected for 25 years from the end of the calendar year in which they were published.

Who has title to the copyright work?

In order to show infringement of copyright, it is necessary to show title in the work. One might assume that there is an author who creates the work and thereafter is entitled to copyright. It is not always so straightforward.

Copyright, as already mentioned, is an IPR. As such it can be sold, transferred, assigned and licensed. It can also be inherited, which is clearly important given that most copyrights substantially outlast the author.

Further complications may arise when work is done for another.

> **POINT OF LAW**
>
> The 1988 Act stipulates that when an employee creates a literary, dramatic, musical or artistic work, or a film in the contract of his employment, his employer is the first owner of any copyright in the work subject to any agreement to the contrary.

When a work is commissioned, that work will initially subsist in the creator, rather than the commissioner in most circumstances. However, if a marketer commissions a glossy product brochure from a designer, there must be at the very least a licence to use it for its own business purposes.

Categories protected by Copyright, Designs and Patents Act 1988

- Original works
- Literary works
- Dramatic works
- Musical works
- Artistic works
- Sound recordings
- Films
- Broadcasts
- Cable programmes

Original works

Simple creation of a work is not quite enough to attract copyright, since otherwise each subsequent copy of any given work would also attract copyright protection.

The work must also be original and this is usually taken to mean 'not copied from a copyright work'. It certainly does not mean 'unique' or 'ingenious' although of course if the marketing is iconoclastic it does help the brand!

POINT OF
·LAW

For example, if two marketers were to produce two identical treatments for the launch of a new soft drink without any reference to each treatment or any other work, both would attract copyright, since they were not copied.

However, there are degrees of originality that the marketer needs to be aware of.

INSIGHT

For example, the idea of a tragedy of star-crossed lovers for a coffee TV commercial is a theme that has long since passed into the collective consciousness – as has the rest of Shakespeare's *Romeo and Juliet!*

However, a contemporary writer or director might substantially build on a similar basis with elaborate and detailed additions. Whilst copyright may subsist in the final expression of the combination of ideas, those that were copied from *Romeo and Juliet* or its successors would not be original.

Literary works

This is the most familiar form of copyright aimed at protecting books, articles, poems, layout and even some advertising copy – although some examples of the latter would not probably win awards as a form of 'literary work'!

The word 'literary' is therefore not used in its normal sense, but is used to define written or printed matter and could also apply to mundane material such as tables and compilations (other than databases), computer programs and preparatory design material for such programs.

Such works need not even be immediately understandable, in the sense that it may be encoded, or take the form of a computer program which has a string of numbers and letters that may seem meaningless.

However, as the following story illustrates, the work must have meaning rather than consist of a rambling stream of consciousness.

POINT OF
LAW

An advertising creative, starved of creativity, decides to take a long lunch break with a few friends. After drinking himself insensible, he decides to carry out an experiment in order to see if anything could be gained from the jottings he made whilst intoxicated. Surprisingly, nothing could and copyright could not subsist in the 'work'!

There is no concept of 'literary merit' inherent in copyright protection. An advertising copywriter enjoys the same rights as a Booker Prize winner.

The issue is when does a piece of work become a literary work? Is a strap line sufficient or even a new brand name for a product?

A copyright work must be the result of a *substantial amount of skill and/or labour on the part of the author*. A name or title cannot usually be protected by copyright, as they are generally not substantial enough to satisfy the requirement that they should be 'literary works'.

Advertising slogans and catchphrases generally also fall into the same category as names or titles, although in exceptional cases a long slogan may attract copyright protection if it is particularly distinctive and it can be shown that it was clearly the result of the application of considerable creative talent. Alternatively, trademark rights may offer some protection (see Chapter 5).

As discussed above, *de minimis* works will not attract copyright protection as the following two examples illustrate.

> ### LAW IN ACTION
>
> In the case **Exxon Corp-v-Exxon Insurance Consultants International Ltd (1981)** copyright was held not to subsist in the made-up name of the well-known oil giant 'Exxon'.
>
> In the 1928 case of **Sinanide-v-La Maison Cosmeo**, the slogan 'beauty is a social necessity, not a luxury' and some variations on the theme was held by the court to be too trivial to attract copyright protection.

However, a written advertisement containing even a few lines of text may well attract protection, as may a written script for a television or film advertisement.

An expression that is often used in deciding what is worth protecting is 'what is worth copying is prima facie worth protecting'.

Although there is certain logic to this proposition, care must be taken in applying it to all situations. In the Exxon example, the word 'Exxon' was worth copying for the famous brand association, not the copyright.

Exxon is still capable of being protected under trademark protection rather than copyright and cases in which the marketer is attempting to protect the brand value rather than the creativity in the brand name is discussed in detail in Chapter 5.

Copyright also subsists in the layout of literary work, should the layout require a substantial input of skill or labour.

> ### POINT OF LAW
>
> For example, the format of a web site or an advertising poster may be of paramount importance to somebody trying to attract custom or achieve some other aim, whether or not commercial. In such a case, the actual words used may be of almost secondary importance. The protection afforded to layout provides a remedy in the event of piracy of such a format.

Dramatic works

A 'dramatic work' as envisaged by the 1988 Act is closer to the commonplace interpretation of the words. The Act explicitly includes works of dance or mime, but gives no further guidance.

It has been suggested that there must be some set choreography or plan to a work for it to be protectable under copyright law.

INSIGHT

From the marketers' perspective, the issue is unlikely to arise unless there has been a special show arranged to help launch a product and part of the show may involve some form of choreographed performance either by actors or dancers which would then be protected under copyright.

Musical works

In the UK, the composition (music), the lyrics and the recording of a music track are protected by copyright as a musical work, literary work and sound recording respectively.

The copyright owner of such works has the exclusive right to do and to authorise various acts in the copyright work – known as 'restricted acts' (see below).

Music can be an ideal tool for brand repositioning – musical taste is often seen as a barometer for lifestyle and outlook – but the flipside is that getting it wrong can alienate potential customers.

POINT OF LAW

For example, in 2001, *The Times* gave away a Björk CD-ROM in an attempt to move away from its perceived image as being slightly stuffy and attract more trendy readers, who might be expected to prefer *The Guardian* or *The Independent*.

Marketers like to use music within marketing communications because it is a very powerful, emotional tool.

INSIGHT

For example, mundane events, such as a new product launch at an engineering trade show can be transformed by the ingenious use of music and moving images to create excitement and anticipation and fun.

Brand owners use music in a wide variety of ways to promote their brands which goes beyond picking the music for their TV ads.

Music has a long history as a promotional tool, from Michael Jackson's ill-fated Pepsi tie-in – the singer was burned in 1983 when his hair caught fire during filming for a Pepsi promotional video – and Weetabix 'Top Trax' tape giveaways in the 1980s, through Beverley Craven's

Tampax-sponsored tour in 1993, to Pepsi's more successful tie-ins with the Spice Girls and Robbie Williams, and the Levi's-initiated European music tour, headlined by US rappers OutKast to promote Levi's Engineered Jeans product range.

As a result, radio and TV commercials have become an art form in their own right and have been responsible for launching the careers of many pop artists.

INSIGHT

For example, pop group Babylon Zoo enjoyed short-lived success with the chart hit *Spaceman* after the track was used as the music for the Levi's 501s jeans TV and film advertisements in the late 1990s.

Restricted acts (covers all protected works, not just music)

'Restricted acts' include reproducing musical works and synchronising sound recordings with the visual images of a TV or cinema advertisement. The marketer must therefore obtain the permission of the copyright owner to include a track in an advertisement.

The copyright in a musical work and the copyright in a sound recording do not co-exist in parallel.

Copyright in musical works lasts for the life of the composer plus 70 years, while copyright in a sound recording lasts for 50 years from release.

The difference is important as it means that use of a new recording by a composer long dead (e.g. Beethoven) will still require consent from the owner of the sound recording even though the composition is out of copyright.

Conversely, use of a sound recording over 50 years old composed by the performer of the track may also require consent as the composition may not yet be out of copyright.

Even if the original sound recording is out of copyright, use of a new digital re-master may create a new 50-year period of copyright. Similarly, a new arrangement of a musical work will itself be a new copyright work.

A marketer should check carefully that both the composition and the sound recording are in fact out of copyright before assuming that the track is in the public domain and may be freely used.

Even where the composer and the performer of the track is the same person, the owner of the copyright in the musical work is usually different to the owner of the copyright in the sound recording.

Ownership of musical works

Composers often assign or grant an exclusive licence to music publishing companies of all the rights in a composition whereby the publishing company will collect income on the composer's behalf.

The copyright in a sound recording will in most cases be owned either by the record company under its recording contract with the artist, or (if the artist is not signed) by the artist.

Collecting authorities

The **Mechanical Copyright Protection Society Limited (MCPS)** and the **Performing Right Society (PRS)** handle the rights to make a recording of and broadcast musical works, respectively.

For sound recordings, **Phonographic Performance Limited (PPL)** is the collecting society for both making a reproduction and broadcasting in the UK.

In most cases, MCPS and PPL will not be authorised to grant a licence for reproduction of music in advertisements on behalf of their members and marketers will normally have to deal direct with the artist's publishing and record company.

Obtaining a licence for the use of a musical work

When clearing the use of existing tracks in advertisements the marketer must either obtain a licence from either the relevant collecting society or, as in most cases, the actual copyright owner. This can be a long and tortuous process without any guarantee of success and therefore the marketer will require expert copyright agency assistance.

The marketer can obtain contact details of the copyright owner from MCPS and PPL but should double check these details as the collecting societies' records may not necessarily be correct or up-to-date.

Payment of licence fees for musical works

Each licence is dealt with on a case-by-case basis and fees depend on many factors, including media, territory and duration of the campaign.

INSIGHT

For example, the use of a well-known music track or performer, such as Moby, on a TV commercial will be more expensive than using an unknown composer or performer for the same commercial.

Licence fees can range from a few hundred to hundreds of thousands of pounds so marketers must not get carried away by trying to sign up David Bowie for their latest advertising campaign unless there is budget. Even then, David Bowie is unlikely to agree to have his music used in this way!

Practical considerations for the use of musical works

The marketer should ensure that the music licence sets out in detail the advertisement in which the music is to be used, the method, area and period of transmission of the advert (which should cover the entire duration of the campaign) and an option for a stipulated fee to use the music for a further period or in additional media in case the campaign is extended.

The licensed recording should also be clearly identified as there may be different versions and/or re-mixes of the song.

The marketer should also take into account that the licence will normally provide that the track may not be altered or parodied and a separate licence will be required to broadcast the advertisement on TV.

In the UK, broadcasting music in public is a 'restricted act' for which permission is needed from the copyright owner. As virtually all broadcasters in the UK have a form of blanket licence from PPL and PRS, the marketer will not normally have to get involved in this aspect for clearance purposes.

If the marketer decides to short cut the entire music clearing process by not obtaining a licence for the use of a musical work, then it runs the substantial risk that the marketing campaign could be pulled within 24 hours and a claim for substantial damages from the copyright owner not to mention the negative publicity could quickly follow.

INSIGHT

A marketer may also find that negotiating licence fees after the start of the marketing campaign may prove to be a lot more expensive as a result!

If the track used in the TV commercial contains any uncleared samples of music, the copyright owner of the music samples could claim copyright infringement by the marketer and seek damages.

INSIGHT

A warranty from the owner of copyright in the principal material that it owns all the relevant rights is all very well, but even if this is backed by an indemnity, it can still be a major hassle handling the claim by the owner of the rights in the sample and recovering any claims under the indemnity signed by the owner of the copyright in the principal material, which is worth no more than the asset value of the owner itself.

A marketer could also face a claim from a copyright owner if the licensor does not own all of the rights granted to the marketer under the licence or if the licensor has limited authority.

POINT OF LAW

For example, it may be that the licensor is not authorised to grant a licence for a re-recording of the original song for the TV advertisement without the copyright owner's consent.

As a result, the marketer's licence may be *invalid* if the copyright owner has not consented to use of the song in the advertisement.

Artistic works

Artistic works as envisaged by the 1988 Act are not restricted to 'works of art'.

From a marketing perspective, photographs which are used extensively throughout all forms of marketing communications fall under the description of artistic works.

Other forms of artistic works include:

- Graphic works

- Sculptures or collages

- Architectural works (buildings and models for buildings)

- Works of artistic craftsmanship

Graphic works

Graphic works include paintings, drawings, diagrams, maps, charts and plans, engravings, etchings, woodcuts, lithographs, and similar works.

Maps and directions to places of interest, offices and events are used extensively through-out marketing communications. However, maps are also subject to the 1988 Act and as such are classified as artistic works.

For example, marketers should think twice before copying a map and including it with tickets to a corporate hospitality event with little thought as to the owner of the IP in that map, as the experience of the AA demonstrates.

AA-v-Ordnance Survey (OS) (2001)

After years of legal arguments, the AA and OS finally settled their copyright dispute in 2001 over alleged infringement of copyright in maps. The AA agreed to pay £20m in respect of over 500 different AA atlases, town maps and fold-out maps.

The AA denied infringing copyright in the maps, but OS argued that detailed analysis of the AA maps revealed slavish copying of stylistic features in OS originals such as the width of roads in each map. The large settlement sum resulted from a combination of the OS tariff and over 300 million copies which AA printed of the offending maps over the period in question.

One of the commonest myths in marketing is the belief that maps are somehow in the public domain and free to all to copy at will.

Clearly the AA were not guilty of such an attitude in this case, but checks should always be run and suitable licences organised where appropriate, whenever maps are likely to be included in marketing materials.

Even 'modified' maps could still amount to an infringement of copyright. Marketers are best advised to obtain a licence for the use of a map to be absolutely sure of not running the risk of copyright infringement and a substantial claim for damages as a result.

Sound recordings

Sound recordings are relatively straightforward, being recordings of sounds, or recordings of reproductions of other copyright works, provided that they are not recordings of existing sound recordings or films.

The medium is unimportant. Marketers must always be slightly careful with sound recordings because so many other copyrights may subsist in the work.

INSIGHT

For example, if beer brand **Tennents**, sponsor of the popular **'T in the Park'** concerts, decided to transmit a recording of one of its concerts, it would need to clear copyright with the artists concerned. In addition, there would be copyright in the musical score, the words and other sound effects within the concert. Permission to copy the recording of the live performance may therefore not prevent infringement of other IPRs.

Films

Many famous films have spawned a series of famous TV commercials.

POINT OF LAW

For example, a scene with Steve McQueen in the 1960s cult classic *Bullit* was re-worked for the launch of Ford's new sports car Puma in the 1990s.

This did not amount to an infringement of copyright as Ford worked with the producers and copyright owners of *Bullit* to make it appear that Steve McQueen was driving the *Puma* motorcar (and therefore obtained a licence for use).

But had Ford decided to 'reconstruct' a famous car chase based loosely on the film *The Italian Job* (starring Michael Caine) it is a moot point whether it would have infringed film copyright in the movie – it would amount to a question of degree.

Whether or not there may be copyright infringement, marketers should be wary about potential actions for passing off their goods through associations with movies.

Broadcasts and satellite TV

There are a number of other IPs in which copyright can subsist. Amongst them are broadcasts (along with certain safeguards in the case of certain satellite broadcasts) and cable programmes.

Published editions

One important protection under copyright law is granted to the typographical arrangement of published editions.

Spoken word

There is copyright in the spoken word, but only once it has been recorded in a permanent form. In addition, the work must qualify for protection by being original and it must not be a copy. In addition, for an action of breach of copyright of the spoken word a 'substantial' part of the work must have been copied.

There are also a number of exclusions from liability, e.g. where there is incidental inclusion of the work or its use is in the public interest (see below).

RESTRICTED ACTS AND INFRINGEMENT OF COPYRIGHT

Rights

Having established title in the work, **Section 16 of the 1988 Act** gives the copyright owner the exclusive right to:

- Copy the work
- Issue copies of the work to the public
- Perform, show or play the work to the public
- To broadcast the work, or show it via cable
- To adapt the work, or do the acts set out above in relation to an adaptation of the work

Infringement of copyright

Any person who is not the copyright owner who does any of the above acts or authorises someone else to do them without the licence of the copyright owner will be in breach of copyright.

It is not a defence to copying for a marketer to claim that it has not broken copyright law simply because a third party printer under its instructions did the actual copying.

The infringing acts breach copyright law if they are done in relation to the work, or any substantial part of it. They are also infringing acts whether they are done directly or indirectly by the offending party.

Substantial part

Prohibited acts infringe copyright if they are done in relation to the work *or a substantial part of it*.

Much of copyright litigation is spent arguing whether or not a piece of a work that has been taken constitutes a substantial part of the copyright work.

A common mistake made in marketing is that this has something to do with the proportion of the work that has been copied. It is not about quantity but rather about the circumstances under which a copy has been made.

Just because only one page out of a book of several thousand pages has been copied does not mean that a 'substantial part' in this sense has not been taken.

Neither does it have anything to do with the quantity taken.

A tiny fragment of a painting that is less than a few centimetres square may constitute a 'substantial part'. More pertinent is what skill and labour was needed or utilised in the creation of the work.

If a work or a part of it is copied verbatim or exactly, the test will normally be fulfilled. The principal difficulties arise in situations where the copy is similar but not identical to the work alleged to have been copied.

An example might be a table of information (a compilation, so attracting literary copyright), which is reproduced with the same information but in a completely different order (ignoring any database rights that might subsist for the purpose of the example).

The issue of whether or not a substantial part of the table has been copied depends on the nature of the information.

If the skill and labour was in collecting the information, then a substantial part has been taken.

If however the information was freely available, but the value of the table and the difficulty in its compilation was in ordering that information in a given way, a substantial part of it would not have been taken since that order is not present in the copy.

Direct or indirect copying

It is irrelevant for the purposes of the 1988 Act whether the act of copying is done directly or indirectly, or whether any intervening copy infringes. In other words, a photograph of a copyright painting is an infringement of the copyright in the painting, but a photograph of the photograph is also an infringement of the painting.

The fact that the first photograph was taken by the artist and copyright owner, and so did not constitute an infringement, does not prevent the subsequent photograph being an infringement of the painting itself.

Copying

In order to infringe a copyright by copying, the 'infringing' work must be copied directly or indirectly from the copyright work. Although this sounds utterly self-evident, it may of course be the case that both pieces of work, and the relevant parts of them, have been copied from the same entirely different source, alternatively both works, though identical, have been derived completely independently.

POINT OF LAW

Copying of a literary, dramatic, musical or artistic work means reproducing the work, or a substantial part of the work *in any material form*.

This is a very broad prohibition. The recital of a poem is a material reproduction of the poem.

A mimed version of a play would be a material reproduction of a dramatic performance, although not the literary work that is the play's script.

The 1988 Act specifically provides that making a copy of a three-dimensional work from a two-dimensional artistic work, and vice versa, is an infringement.

This, in combination with the direct or indirect provision, means that it is an infringement of copyright in a painting to paint a picture of a three-dimensional rendering of the painting. Merchandising relies on this broad prohibition.

INSIGHT

For example, a model of the character Harry Potter from the film *Harry Potter and the Philosopher's Stone* or a tea mug with a picture of Harry Potter may be material reproductions of various copyrights in that film, including literary copyright, artistic copyright, or even dramatic copyright.

Copying in relation to literary, dramatic, musical or artistic works includes storing the work in any medium by electronic means. This not only means that storing images on computer constitutes an infringement, but has an important impact in respect of the Internet.

POINT OF LAW

For example, on visits to a web site, images, formats and text are often stored, temporarily or permanently, on the PC or Mac of the marketer. This may be an infringement of any copyright works on that site, for which the browser is liable.

Copying news clippings

There are two types of copyright in any newspaper article (excluding any copyright in photographs):

- Copyright in the literary content (protecting the skill and labour of the author)
- Copyright in 'the typographical arrangement of published editions'

The latter is a species of copyright that has its roots in the days of metal linotype and printing presses, protecting the skill and labour of the typesetter.

Many marketers need to keep track of news coverage that is generated about their own and their competitors' organisations within the international, national, regional and local news media and subscribing to a news clippings service is usually the most economical way in which to achieve this.

The **Newspaper Licensing Authority (NLA)** and the **Copyright Licensing Agency (CLA)** collectively represent the vast majority of newspaper, journal and magazine publishers in the UK.

Their task is to police the unauthorised photocopying, downloading and analogue or electronic distribution of their members' material and to encourage those who wish to distribute press or magazine cuttings within organisations to take out CLA or NLA licences.

These licences allow such use of published material on a controlled, annual basis in return for a fee.

NLA has traditionally relied on typographical copyright infringement to prove breach of copyright because ownership of the typographical copyright is easier to prove as this invariably will be owned by the publishing company employing the typesetters.

However, the law until July 2001 was unclear as to whether marketers that then copy and distribute these news clippings throughout the organisation are in breach of typographical copyright under the 1988 Act.

LAW IN ACTION

Newspaper Licensing Agency-v-Marks & Spencer plc (2001)

Marks & Spencer plc marketing department refused to take out an NLA licence in respect of the 500 000 or so copies of newspaper articles that it photocopied and distributed internally each year, with the assistance of a press cutting agency.

The NLA sued Marks & Spencer for copyright infringement and won first time round, but Marks & Spencer appealed and the Court of Appeal, along with the House of Lords, took a different view.

The House of Lords held that typographical copyright protected only the arrangement of the newspaper as a whole – in other words, the way in which all the multifarious articles in a newspaper are put together on the pages – and not the arrangement of a single article.

This got the marketers off the hook, as the copies distributed were of individual articles and there was no evidence that sufficient numbers of articles from any single issue of a newspaper had been taken to amount to a 'substantial part' of the issue as a whole.

The NLA are now threatening new proceedings against Marks & Spencer on the basis of breach of literary copyright, so multiple photocopiers of published material without CLA or NLA licences should not sound the all clear as yet.

'Fair dealing' defence

At the Court of Appeal, the judges, whilst holding in favour of the marketers, threw out a defence under 'fair dealing'.

What is 'fair dealing'?

Fair dealing is a concept which has never been fully defined in law and does not in itself give specific permission to copy. It is acceptable as a defence only if the act of copying does not unfairly deprive copyright owners of revenue or other benefits. For example, the copying of a single line of text may be deemed unfair if this is the key to the plot of a book.

What is a reasonable proportion?

1. One article in a single issue of a periodical or set of conference proceedings.

2. An extract from a book amounting to 5% of the whole or a complete chapter.

3. A whole poem or short story from a collection, provided the item is not more than 10 pages.

4. Do not copy sheet music at all.

5. Do nothing which could prevent you from signing, if required, a declaration to the effect that:

   ■ You have not previously obtained a copy of the same material.

   ■ You will only use the copy for research and private study and will not supply a copy to another person.

   ■ To the best of your knowledge, no other person with whom you work or study has or intends to make, at about the same time, a copy of substantially the same material for the same purpose.

   ■ You understand that you may be liable for infringement of copyright if the copy you make does not conform to these requirements.

Infringement of copyright rests with the person making the copy, *not* with the providers of the equipment.

Electronic copying

The fair dealing concept applied to books, journals and other printed materials has evolved over time. There is no generally accepted principle of fair dealing in relation to information on the Internet or other electronic sources.

Marks & Spencer had argued that even if it had copied a substantial part of the typographical copyright, the defence of fair dealing for the purpose of reporting current events should apply. The Court of Appeal held this could not apply to copying within a commercial organisation for commercial reasons.

Given that the **House of Lords** found in favour of the marketers and therefore there was no infringement of typographical copyright, they remained silent on this point, so the reasoning by the Court of Appeal may stand.

This is not good news for marketers as it has often been thought that 'reporting current events' was a good fall-back position for multiple commercial copiers to take.

POINT OF LAW

For example, had the marketers at Marks & Spencer cut out of *The Times* a whole page article into the health benefits of organic foods (which mentioned Marks & Spencer's range of organic vegetable ranges) and then commissioned a design agency to produce a national poster campaign that reproduced the entire one page article alongside the slogan 'Britain's leading organic grocer' then the design company would be liable for secondary infringement of copyright.

Secondary infringement

Secondary infringements constitute an infringement of copyright if the person or persons doing those acts *knows or has reason to believe* that the articles concerned are infringing copies of a copyright work.

These are:

- Importing an infringing copy otherwise than for personal and domestic use
- Possessing or dealing with an infringing copy in the course of business, selling, hiring, or offering or exposing for sale or hire of such a copy, exhibiting in public or distributing such a copy, or distributing such a copy otherwise than in the course of business to such an extent as to affect prejudicially the owner of the copyright
- Providing the means to make an infringing copy
- Permitting premises to be used for the purpose of an infringing performance
- Providing apparatus for an infringing performance of sound recording, showing films or receiving visual images or sounds conveyed by electronic means

Permitted acts

Copyright is necessarily a balance between the rights of copyright owners and the rights of the public to make use of available works. As a result, there are a number of exceptions or 'permitted acts' to the prohibitions contained in the 1988 Act.

POINT OF LAW

If a marketer was studying for a CIM Diploma or to become a chartered marketer, then photocopying articles from books and newspapers for private study purposes only (private use, education or archive use) would be a permitted act.

It is also not infringement to include copyright material incidentally.

For example, if a marketer was directing a new Christmas sales TV advertisement for a client in the middle of Oxford Street in London, there would almost certainly be a large number of different copyright works in the background, from bus timetables and advertising posters to artwork displayed in shop windows.

By reason of the fact that a reproduction in any material form constitutes an infringement of those works, it would be virtually impossible for the TV commercial director to avoid infringing these copyrights. It would be almost impossible to avoid including any copyright work within the field of vision and it may require a Herculean effort to track down a vast array of copyright owners in order to obtain a licence.

Another important exception is that relating to designs. Before the 1988 Act, a design drawing, being an artistic work, was infringed by a three-dimensional representation of that work. In other words, a desk, if it was copied from a picture of that design of desk, would infringe the copyright in the design drawing.

Under the 1988 Act, it is not an infringement of copyright in a design drawing to make anything other than an artistic work to the design.

LICENSING

Another useful way for a marketer to protect the integrity of the marketing campaign is to take out a licence for the use of copyright materials.

Licence or permission from the copyright owner potentially removes a barrier to use which would otherwise not be permitted under the 1988 Act.

Licences may be exclusive, so that the licensee is the only entity entitled to do the acts, or a licence may be non-exclusive, allowing a number of licensees to use the copyright material in their marketing.

For example, FIFA granted licences to a variety of brand owners for the use of its logo for the 2002 FIFA World Cup Korea/Japan™ and some of these were on a non-exclusive basis, allowing competitor brands to also use the trademarks. However, FIFA does try to prevent clashes between competing marketers by providing licences on a territorial rather than category basis.

Remedies

If there has been an infringement of a copyright, the copyright owner or an exclusive licensee (but not non-exclusive licensees) may sue for a remedy.

Interim relief

Where the copyright owner is suffering serious ongoing damage, it may be appropriate to apply for interim relief. This will normally take the form of an injunction preventing the acts complained of.

POINT OF LAW

For example, where a marketer has obviously copied the 'get up', colours and design of a soft drink that infringes copyright of a competitor brand, then an interim injunction could be obtained to get the supermarket to remove the offending item from its shelves. In this example, there would also probably be an action in respect of infringement of trademarks and passing off (see Chapter 5).

In order to obtain an interim injunction, the marketer must first show that there is a serious case to be answered.

Assuming that there is, the court will then consider whether or not the damage that the marketer is suffering or is likely to suffer (if the acts are merely threatened) before the trial could be compensated by damages paid by the defendant at trial.

If money would adequately compensate for the damage, no injunction will be granted. The court will then consider whether or not, should the action continue to trial and the marketer then lost, the marketer would be able to recompense the defendant for any damage suffered as a result of the grant of the injunction.

If the marketer could do so, the court will finally consider the balance of convenience, i.e. which side is the likeliest to suffer the least injustice by the potential grant of the injunction.

If the balance of convenience is decided in favour of the claimant, an injunction will be granted *until trial*.

Other orders, such as an order allowing the search and seizure of infringing articles and/or evidence of infringement, or an order freezing an infringer's assets may also be granted under particular circumstances at the discretion of the court.

POINT OF LAW

For example, this frequently occurs when a marketer fears that there has been a breach of its copyright and other IPRs and calls in the HM Customs & Excise and Trading Standards officers to make an inspection on a factory producing counterfeit merchandise and other products.

All such remedies are costly for the marketer in the short term and potentially costly for the infringing defendant in the long term.

Remedies at trial

At trial, should copyright infringement be shown, the marketer may obtain a number of remedies for any damage suffered as a result of the infringement.

Injunctive relief

Injunctive relief, preventing the acts complained of being done by the defendant, can be ordered, the breaching of which constitutes a contempt of court, with very serious consequences for the defendant.

Damages

Damages can be obtained in two ways:

▓ The marketer deciding whether to seek compensation for the damage actually suffered or

▓ Whether to recover the profits that the defendant has obtained by the infringement of the marketer's copyright (but not both)

If the marketer decides to pursue the latter remedy (commonly referred to by lawyers as an account of profits), the defendant must account for all profits that have been made as a result of the copyright infringement.

> **POINT OF LAW**
>
> For example, if a defendant has copied 10 000 books in their entirety and sold them at a profit of £10 000 then this is relatively straightforward. However, it is usually much more complex in licensing and merchandising cases involving, for example, interactive software products where a computer programmer has copied 10 lines of another program and included them in his program of 1000 lines, which has subsequently been sold at a profit of £1m.

The marketer is only entitled to profit *attributable to the infringement*. In the above example, depending on the relative importance of the material 10 lines of code, this could be hundreds of pounds if the benefit was insignificant or hundreds of thousands of pounds if those 10 lines of code were the fundamental basis on which the program operated.

Computation and assessment of damages

In both the examples (above), if the marketer was also selling the relevant books and would otherwise have made £10 000 profit, it would be entitled to £10 000 in damages.

If, however, the marketer was not selling them, then it might only be entitled to the *reasonable royalty which it would have been paid had a licence been obtained*. There might be a further question of damage to its future rights to sell the book.

'Flagrancy damages'

Additional damages may be awarded by the court if, knowing that the acts concerned were infringements, the defendant nonetheless carried out those acts (lawyers sometimes refer to this as 'flagrancy damages').

'Delivery-up'

The marketer may also obtain an order for 'delivery-up' of any infringing articles that the defendant has in its possession. This is particularly useful in cases of stopping illegal merchandise from flooding the market and affecting the legitimate sales of branded merchandise as well as affecting the market value for this product.

As with any litigation, a major proportion of the expense of a trial is the legal costs of that trial. At least in theory, the winner at trial will recover its legal costs from the other party, although in practice this is significantly less than 100% but can be a very significant sum.

For example, it would not be all that unusual for a trial to determine whether a claimant has a right to several hundred pounds in damages to cost tens of thousands of pounds in legal fees.

The point here is that the marketer needs to be watchful on the issue of costs but at the same time be seen to be protecting the integrity of a marketing campaign by being prepared to defend its reputation irrespective of whether the defendant has the means to pay compensation.

MARKETER/CLIENT RELATIONSHIP

As this chapter has demonstrated, infringing the work of another party is surprisingly easy, and to do so can result in very serious and costly consequences.

Litigation in order to protect IPRs that are the foundation of the integrity of a marketing campaign is a very expensive process and usually very time consuming.

The lost management hours spent dealing with a litigation claim is a substantial expense in itself. There is then the question of damages, which may be substantial, plus a marketer may become liable for the opposition's costs if they successfully defend the action.

Where the marketer is using, for example, an advertising or marketing agency, it is likely that the agency will have been responsible if there is any infringement of another's copyright in a given piece of work.

However, usually the marketer (and often this will be a very large and powerful brand owner) has authorised the making of that work and will also be liable for copyright infringement.

This could have further ramifications for both the marketer and its agency.

INSIGHT

For example, if the copyright owner sues the marketer, it is likely that a clause in the agency agreement to produce the work in the first place will be breached. On this basis, not only does the agency not get paid, but it may well become liable for any damages awarded against the marketer, along with any costs awarded and the marketer's own legal costs in defending the claim.

This situation could arise, for example, if a £2m television advertising campaign has to be pulled because of threatened or actual litigation for breach of copyright. The agency may well be liable for all associated legal costs and damages plus the costs of cancelling the TV campaign with the broadcaster.

The buck will stop with the agency so agencies need to ensure that they are adequately covered by indemnity insurance to cover such an outcome.

MORAL RIGHTS

In addition to commercial copyright, the author of say a marketing book or white paper on an aspect of customer relationship marketing may have certain additional rights, known as 'moral' rights under the 1988 Act.

What are moral rights?

There are four moral rights:

- The 'credit right' to be identified as author or director
- The 'integrity right' not to have the work subjected to derogatory treatment
- The right not to be falsely described as author or director
- The right to privacy in privately commissioned wedding or other domestic photographs and films

Moral rights only arise in respect of literary, dramatic, musical and artistic works and films.

INSIGHT

From a marketer's perspective, they will normally be asserted in relation to a marketing book, article or white paper written by the marketer.

The 'credit right' must be 'asserted' before the right can be infringed and moral rights do not apply at all in a number of instances.

Ownership and dealings

Moral rights are personal rights and cannot be transferred, assigned or licensed unlike other types of copyright but can be inherited. The 'author' of a work is the person who creates it or in the case of computer-generated works, the person who makes the arrangements for the work to be produced.

Joint authorship and ownership of copyright is permissible, if the work has been created in collaboration with others.

POINT OF LAW

Given that moral rights are personal, an advertising agency could not insist to have its name on every advertisement or poster site that carried its creative work even if it was the first owner of the copyright in material as a result of its employees producing it in the course of their employment.

It is standard practice that moral rights are waived in many copyright assignment contracts so that the assignee (brand owner, publisher, record company, sports governing body) is free to deal with the copyright in any way it may so wish.

Position with the employer

The first owner of the copyright is the creator, unless that person is an employee, in which case it is the employer – provided the work is created as a condition of employment. In such cases, the employee may be required to waive any moral rights pursuant to a contract of employment with the employer.

> **POINT OF LAW**
>
> For example, if a marketer working for IBM writes a book about CRM which uses data, statistics and case studies taken directly from IBM, and uses IBM's time to write the book, then the copyright in the book would belong to IBM unless there is a precise agreement to the contrary.

Duration of moral rights

The basic period of protection for copyright works where the author is within the Berne Convention expires at the end of the period of 70 years from the end of the calendar year in which the author dies.

The moral rights other than right to object to false attribution, also last until this point. The right to object to false attribution lasts only 20 years after the death of the falsely attributed 'author'.

What happens if someone's moral rights are infringed?

Provided that the moral rights apply, the author or director can sue and may be entitled to damages. The court has the power to grant an injunction preventing an infringing act. In the case of the right not to be subjected to derogatory treatment, the court may require an approved disclaimer to be made disassociating the author or director from the treatment of the work.

There is very little case law on moral rights and so it may be a lottery for the marketer to commence an action in order to assert its moral rights.

CHECKLIST

- Marketers should check that copyright in a proposed marketing activity (e.g. the shape of a new soft drink bottle) does not already exist or is protected by copyright
- Marketers should keep quiet about the launch of a new marketing campaign as the ideas used for the campaign are not protectable under copyright law
- Use of the © symbol is always helpful in all types of media where copyright protection is sought, but is not in itself a guarantee of protection

- Check that freelance contracts transfer or assign copyright to the marketer

- Keep a full diary note of all meetings, presentations, a full notebook of all sketches, drawings and all preparatory work for a proposed marketing campaign: this may be necessary as evidence in court of the substantial amount of skill and labour that has been expended in the creation of the marketing campaign

- Copying of a substantial part of another work is not just about volume but also about the quality of the material that is being copied

- A licence will be required to copy news cuttings from national, local and regional newspapers and magazines

- An interim injunction is probably the fastest way to stop a breach of copyright in an emergency situation; however, legal costs can quickly escalate, making a full-blown action prohibitively expensive

- Marketers should consider developing good working relationships with HM Customs and Excise and Trading Standards Offices that can carry out enforcement activities

- Marketers should consider employing forensic accounting services offered by the major accountancy practices in order to check that the appropriate copyright and other IPR royalties are being paid for the use of copyright material owned by the marketer

- Marketers should ensure that they have adequate professional indemnity insurance in case of legal actions taken against them, as well as insurance to take legal action in the protection of the integrity of the marketing campaign

7

DATA PROTECTION

In this chapter:

- Background to the EU Data Protection Directive (95/46/EC)
- Summary of key concepts used in the Data Protection Act 1998
- Notification rules under the Data Protection Act 1998
- Explanation of the full effects of the Data Protection Act 1998 on marketers with responsibilities for managing and using information recorded on a database
- Protection of the individual's rights with respect to personal information
- Checklist

Other useful chapters:

- Chapter 8: Defamation
- Chapter 9: Advertising and labelling
- Chapter 10: Broadcasting
- Chapter 13: Promotions and incentives
- Chapter 15: Cyber marketing

INTRODUCTION

Marketers seem to have been getting into hot water for a long time when it comes to the use of customer information.

For example, in the US, on-line marketer DoubleClick was served with 15 separate lawsuits totalling more than $1 billion in compensation for its failure to comply with data protection regulations.

The claims related to DoubleClick's use of 'cookies' (see Chapter 15) to track consumers' on-line activities without their knowledge, although DoubleClick denied the data collected identified any particular individual.

Nevertheless, it was an expensive lesson and DoubleClick was forced to pay compensation.

Other marketers in the US have fallen foul of consumer protection laws criminalising unfair and deceptive practices. For example, in some States this can amount to not having a data privacy policy on a web site, and thereby failing to tell consumers how the data would be collected, used and passed onto third parties.

In the UK, marketers have also been having a hard time. For example, in 2000 the **Data Protection Commissioner** (now known as the Information Commissioner) reported a record increase in the number of complaints over the misuse of personal data held by third parties, with 130 out of 145 organisations taken to court found to have illegally used or obtained data under the **Data Protection Act 1998.**

LAW IN ACTION

Thames Water Utilities and the Data Protection Commissioner (1999)

As a privatised water utility, Thames Water was keen to fully exploit the potential for making more profit and wanted to fully utilise its database of customer names and addresses, used up to that time only for providing water utility services and billing.

It therefore started to use customer details for the purposes of marketing non-water-related products.

After this came to the attention of the Data Protection Commissioner, Thames Water was informed that the practice was contrary to the first of the eight fundamental personal data protection principles of the **Data Protection Act 1998** (see below), requiring the fair and lawful obtaining and processing of personal data.

To avoid enforcement action by the Commissioner, Thames Water gave various undertakings. These effectively prevented it from:

■ Using data relating to its customers to market non-water utility-related services or goods available from either Thames Water or third parties

■ Transferring customer data to third parties for marketing purposes

The only way round these restrictions was for Thames Water to obtain its customers' express consent to such activities and this could not be implied from simple lack of response to a mailing indicating that recipients' details would be used for non-obvious activities unless they sent back an 'opt-out' reply.

Before starting out on or authorising a third party to start a marketing campaign promoting non-obvious products, Thames Water had to be in possession of documentary proof that every single recipient of the intended campaign had consented to this use being made of their data. This could be by way of a ticked 'opt-in' box or a blank 'opt-out' box.

As this case illustrates, a few years ago it was fast becoming clear that above all other consumer issues in the on-line environment, use of personal data and privacy generated the most concern, dismay, mistrust and uncertainty.

UK marketers had been collecting and using data for years in scant regard for even the most basic requirements of the data protection legislation, such as the need to register with the Data Protection Commissioner.

Now the game is up.

The **Data Protection Act 1998,** which came into full effect at the end of the first transitional period in October 2001, is not just another essential law for marketers – it is essential that *all marketers comply with it* if they use a database (electronic or manual) in direct marketing, and all other promotional, marketing and other activities.

The new Information Commissioner has more powers than the previous Data Protection Commissioner, and will have a stronger case for additional manpower and resources over the next few years in the pursuit of protecting the public and safeguarding individuals' rights to know what information about them is being held on a database or in any other relevant electronic or manual filing system.

POINT OF LAW

For example, under the **1998 Act**, all manual filing systems containing information on clients and prospects will need to be overhauled in order to comply with the 1998 Act and large marketers, such as power utilities, supermarkets and financial services companies, with huge databases will be directly affected.

Individual consumers – the target of most marketing campaigns – now have more access, control and redress over what information is stored about them by marketers.

Even though it is early days since the full implementation of the 1998 Act, unless marketers comply with *all* the regulations under the 1998 Act then it will be simply a matter of time before a letter arrives in the post from the **Information Commissioner** (currently Elizabeth France) threatening compliance – or much worse. So act now before it is too late!

'Spamming', e-mail marketing, 'cookies', fax marketing and Short Message Service (SMS) (mobile phones) marketing are dealt with separately in Chapter 15.

The 1998 Act affects *all* marketers reading this book. For example, a recent survey by leading law firm Osborne Clarke, based in London, showed that 93% of all marketers surveyed had been involved in e-mail marketing in the last 12 months and 71% had been involved with mobile text messaging marketing – a figure that is likely to increase to over 90% in 2002/03.

In addition, the survey showed that the two most important issues for marketers in 2002 are data protection and compliance with the Data Protection Act 1998.

Obtaining, holding, using and sharing information about customers and prospects is an essential element of the marketing mix.

However, from a public policy perspective, the rights and freedoms of individuals in society must be protected from unwanted interest and intrusion, including that from marketers!

Balanced against this is the freedom for marketers to go about their business communicating with existing customers and prospecting for new customers.

In the UK, this balance is achieved by the provisions contained in the Data Protection Act 1998.

INSIGHT

Provided marketers are aware of their obligations as *data controllers* and individuals' rights as data subjects (see below), this legislation does not necessarily prevent marketers from carrying out any type of marketing activity. Rather, it lays down the ground rules which must be observed and followed to the letter.

The aim of this chapter is to give an overview of the implications of this legislation and what marketers need to know and do in order to keep within the boundaries of the law.

The 1998 Act is complex and affects all marketers on an everyday basis whenever dealing with all types of information about individuals – whether as employees, as customers, or as prospective customers or otherwise.

Most of the provisions of the 1998 Act were brought into force on 1 March 2000 to comply with EU requirements. The 1998 Act is not entirely innovative as it replaces the previous Data Protection Act 1984 and although the new 1998 Act has the same aim which, broadly speaking, is to protect individuals' privacy and rights, it goes further with regard to the obligations of those dealing with information about individuals and the rights of those individuals. Given that the 1998 Act is very recent, there is limited case law in this area.

This is expected to change dramatically in 2002 when the Information Commissioner intends to take a tough line against high profile marketers that transgress the provisions of the 1998 Act and make these an example to other marketers in the profession.

INSIGHT

It is no longer possible to see data protection in isolation. Rather, it should be seen as part of a new regime of laws addressing privacy and the rights of the individual including the **Freedom of Information Act 2000**, the **Human Rights Act 1998**, the **Regulation of Investigatory Powers Act 2000** and the **Consumer Protection (Distance Selling) Regulations 2000** (see Chapter 13).

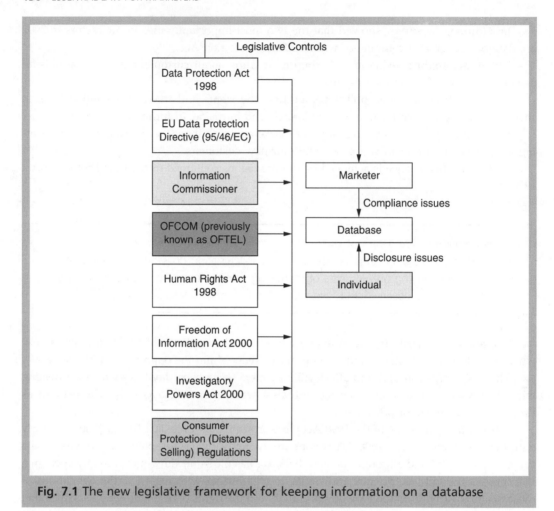

Fig. 7.1 The new legislative framework for keeping information on a database

EU DATA PROTECTION DIRECTIVE (95/46/EC)

This Directive has resulted in the introduction of conforming data protection laws throughout Europe and in the UK.

The **1998 Act** and **EU Directive** apply to personal data – data from which an individual (a *data subject)* can be identified.

POINT OF LAW

In the jargon of the Act, *data controllers* (including marketers) who determine the purpose and manner in which personal data about *data subjects* is to be processed are **regulated** by the Act.

Data processors (including marketers, their agencies and subcontractors) that process personal data on behalf of *data controllers* are **regulated to a lesser extent**.

From an image rights and right of privacy perspective (see Chapter 8), individuals have a legal right to know how a third party has obtained, recorded and holds personal data about themselves *provided* that such data is proscribed under the conditions set out in the Act. The 1998 Act also applies to the transmission and retrieval of such data.

Stricter rules apply to sensitive personal data including information as to an individual's racial origin, political opinion, religious belief, mental health or condition, sexual life or criminal record.

The rules are applied by an authority in each EU country. In the case of the UK, it is the Information Commissioner operating through the Information Commissioner's Office (**www.dataprotection.gov.uk**). This public body issues guidance about the application of the legislation to particular situations and is responsible for notifications and maintaining a register of data protection enforcement of the Act.

The 1998 Act and equivalent legislation in other EU countries sets out certain principles which apply to personal data:

- *It must be processed fairly and lawfully which will only be the case if certain conditions are met, including telling the data subject why they are subject to scrutiny and who the data controller is*

- *Personal data may only be processed if the data subject has consented or if the processing is necessary or another exemption applies*

  - *for the purpose of an existing contract (or entering into a new contract) with the data subject*

  - *to comply with a legal (as opposed to contractual) obligation*

  - *to protect the vital interests of the data subject*

  - *to carry out public functions*

  - *for the purpose of legitimate interests pursued by the data controller or by a third party to whom the data are disclosed*

POINT OF LAW

The **explicit consent** of the *data subject* is required for sensitive personal data to be processed (unless an exemption applies) and in all cases the data must be accurate, up to date and appropriate for the purpose for which they were processed.

Appropriate security measures must be taken by *data controllers* to ensure the security of their processing systems to include secure storage and transmission, technical and organisational measures against unauthorised processing or accidental destruction of personal data.

Personal data may only be transferred to a country outside the European Economic Area (EEA) provided there is an adequate level of protection for personal data.

As discussed below, the US has in this sense adequate data protection laws and, through the EU, has agreed 'safe harbour ' principles with the US whereby registered US companies in certain industries meeting certain requirements may be considered to comply with EU data protection laws.

KEY CONCEPTS USED IN THE DATA PROTECTION ACT 1998

Broadly speaking, the legislation covers all 'processing' of 'personal data' by 'data controllers'.

Key concepts

POINT OF LAW

Data

Information which is processed, or intended to be processed, automatically, or is recorded manually as part of a structured filing system, or is an 'accessible record', like a database of customers. The important point to be aware of is that it covers both computer records *and* certain manual records.

Personal data

Data which relate to a living individual who can be identified from the data and other information which is in the possession of, or is likely to come into the possession of, the data controller.

Sensitive personal data

A specified subset of personal data being more personal matters, for example, religious belief, sexual orientation, political affiliation, health matters, racial or ethnic origin, trades union membership, commission or alleged commission of any offence.

Data subject

A living individual who is the subject of personal data (includes minors).

Data controller

A person or entity who either alone or with other persons or entities determines the purposes for which, and the manner in which, any personal data are or are to be, processed.

Data processor

A person or entity other than an employee of the *data controller* who processes personal data on behalf of the *data controller*.

Processing

Obtaining, recording or holding personal data or carrying out any operation or set of operations on the personal data, for example, organising, retrieving, consulting, disclosing, transferring, combining, erasing (almost anything!)

Possession

Defined very widely – not necessarily that the personal data are in the physical control of the *data controller*.

As discussed in this chapter, it is therefore very difficult to envisage any action involving personal data that will not be regulated by the 1998 Act.

NOTIFICATION RULES UNDER THE DATA PROTECTION ACT 1998

The starting point for all marketers is whether notification to the Information Commissioner (previously known as the Data Protection Commissioner) of its processing of personal data is necessary.

The answer in 99.99% of all marketing cases is emphatically 'yes'!

If a marketer is required to notify and does not, it is a **criminal offence** and the penalty is now up to £5000 plus costs in the Magistrates' Courts and unlimited in the Higher Courts.

POINT OF LAW

All legal entities, whether individuals, firms or companies who process personal data about living individuals on a computer (whether about customers, employees or otherwise) or who employ someone else to do so on their behalf, are (subject to certain exceptions) required to notify.

For example, a parent company such as WPP or Omnicom cannot make one notification on behalf of it and its group companies. Every company in the group that processes personal data must have an individual registration *unless* it can rely upon an exemption.

Generally, the exemptions from notification are for:

- Individuals who process personal data for personal, family or household affairs (including recreational purposes)

- *Data controllers* who are only processing personal data for the maintenance of a public register

- *Data controllers* who do not process personal data on computer

- Some 'not for profit' organisations

- *Data controllers* who only process personal data for any one or all of the following purposes:

  - staff administration

  - accounts and records

  - advertising, marketing and public relations

POINT OF LAW

The last exemption only relates to marketing a marketer's own business. If the marketer is marketing a client's businesses or passes information on to other parties (even within the same group) then the exemption does not apply and the marketer will need to notify.

Even if a marketer might be exempt under one of the above headings, if it carries out one of a number of specific purposes, then the exemption does not apply and it is required to notify the Information Commissioner.

For example, this can include processing for legal services, debt administration and factoring, provision of financial services and advice and credit referencing. The exemption will not apply if a marketer processes personal data which have been processed by or obtained from a credit reference agency.

A marketer may need to defend its position to rely on an exemption in the criminal or civil courts and therefore should seek legal advice or check with the Information Commissioner's office before making a decision *not* to notify.

Marketing best practice is always to notify even if not strictly required to do so in order to avoid any doubts that the exemptions will apply. The current (2002) fee for notification is £35 per year.

Even if a marketer is exempt from notification, this does *not* exempt it from compliance with the other provisions of the 1998 Act and which it is legally obliged to observe.

POINT OF LAW

Where a marketer has registered, it must ensure that the registration is kept up to date as failure to notify the Information Commissioner of any changes is also a **criminal offence**.

EXPLANATION OF THE FULL EFFECTS OF THE DATA PROTECTION ACT 1998

The data protection principles provide the benchmark for compliance with a marketer's data protection obligations and, broadly speaking, all *personal data* must:

1. Be obtained and processed fairly and lawfully

2. Be obtained only for specified and lawful purposes

3. Be adequate, relevant and not excessive in relation to the purposes for which they are processed

4. Be accurate and kept up to date

5. Not be kept for longer than necessary

6. Be processed in accordance with the rights of the individual

7. Be kept under adequate security precautions to prevent loss, destruction or unauthorised disclosure

8. Not be transferred outside of the **European Economic Area (EEA)** *unless* the marketer is satisfied as to the level of security or another exemption applies.

All personal data must be obtained and processed fairly and lawfully

When collecting any personal information from individuals, marketers must ensure that they have a lawful reason for processing individuals' data and explain (preferably in writing) who it is, the purpose that is intended in processing this data and for whom the marketer may give this data to.

As a matter of best marketing practice, marketers should provide this information in advance as well as give the option to request that such data are not processed in this way.

POINT OF LAW

For example: 'Please tick the box if you DO NOT wish your details to be passed onto our other partners that have relevant offers and discounts to your needs'.

If the personal information is obtained from someone *other than* the *data subject* (or *data controller*) then *unless* it would involve *disproportionate effort* by the marketer or the marketer needs to comply with some *legal obligation*, it must provide the individual whose information it has with its name and details as to how it intends to process that individual's data.

POINT OF LAW

For example, a marketer receives information from a client detailing the names and addresses of its customers and prospects which the marketer then uses or intends to use for its own purposes and not solely as directed by its client.

In this situation, the marketer is the *data controller* of any of that information that is personal data.

Before obtaining that data or as soon as possible thereafter, a marketer must notify the individual that it has their data and what it intends to process them for, ensuring that those individuals at least have the right to 'opt-out' of any particular processing of their data if they wish.

Generally, in order to be deemed to be fairly processing personal data, marketers must meet certain conditions.

For example, if the personal data are 'sensitive' then the following conditions must be met:

- The individual must give their prior consent to the specific use the marketer wishes to put their data to

    or

- The use of their data must be necessary for certain specified purposes

'Specified purposes' include performing a contract to which the individual is a party or taking steps at the request of the individual with a view to entering into a contract.

POINT OF LAW

For example, the retailer of a washing machine requires the name, address, telephone details and hours when the customer is likely to be at home in time for the delivery of the washing machine. This information is entered into a centralised database that is accessible by the delivery department for the company as well as by the accounts payable department.

In such a situation, the only reason the retailer has the particular individual's data is for the sole purpose of performing a contract that it has entered into with the customer and as a result the retailer does not require specific consent to do this.

However, if the same data were used to try and sell breakdown insurance cover as part of a direct marketing campaign, then personal data would be being used for another purpose (selling an insurance policy) and therefore consent will be required.

Under the 1998 Act there are no specific requirements with regard to *how* the consent should be obtained, e.g. there are no provisions that it must be either unambiguous or in writing.

As already discussed in this chapter, it should be sufficient (other than for sensitive personal data) for the marketer to incorporate into the relevant documentation a request for the individual to tick a box if they do *not* want their personal data to be processed for any specified purposes.

POINT OF LAW

Marketers must give individuals an option to tick a box if they do not want the marketer to process their data for marketing purposes or to transfer their data to other parties or to transfer them outside of the EEA.

Marketers should also provide an address and/or telephone number that customers can contact if they would like to *opt-out at a later date*.

In the situation where a marketer receives personal information from a third party, e.g. a direct mail house, and this is being processed for the benefit of the marketer, then the direct mail house should ensure that individuals on the direct mail list are informed that their data may be passed on and that they are given the option *not* to have their data processed in this way.

If the direct mail house is also using these data to market itself and/or business associates, then it must ensure that the individuals on the list are made aware of this and are given the option to 'opt-out'.

With respect to sensitive personal data, the consent obtained has to be more explicit.

For example, a health club requires all applicants to complete a full and
frank questionnaire about their lifestyle, dietary, social, physical fitness as
well as declaring any illnesses suffered in the last 5 years including heart disease, diabetes,
other serious illnesses, sexually transmitted diseases and AIDS.

Under the 1998 Act this will be treated as sensitive personal data which will require explicit
consent for the health club to use.

As noted above, the individual must give their *explicit* consent for the obtaining and
specific use of their sensitive data or the processing must be necessary for certain specified
purposes.

These include the exercise or performance of any legal obligation (not contractual), the
protection of the vital interests of any person where the consent of the *data subject cannot be
reasonably obtained* or the protection of the vital interests of any third party *where the consent of the
data subject has been unreasonably withheld.*

It is **highly unlikely** that any of these exceptions will apply to marketers and therefore
consent to process sensitive personal data will always be required.

To obtain 'explicit' consent is more onerous than the consent required for processing other
personal data and in marketing practice, it is likely to mean that the individual concerned
specifically and positively consents.

In the health club example, the marketer must obtain the individual's *explicit*
consent to having and processing these data. At the time of the application
process to join the health club, the marketer (preferably in person) must explain the information that will be processed using these particular data and asking the individual to confirm *in
writing* that the health club may process these data for that purpose.

The marketer must then ensure that it does not use or transfer to any third party these data
for any other purpose. In such a situation, an *'opt-out'* box is unlikely to be sufficient for
sensitive personal data and the individual should be asked to *'opt-in'*.

All personal data must be obtained for specified and lawful purposes

Marketers are under a duty to only use any personal information obtained in accordance with
the purposes that have been notified to the Information Commissioner (if any), as advised to the
data subject **and** in accordance with any other relevant laws or obligations.

All personal data must be adequate, relevant and not excessive in relation to the purposes for which they are processed

Marketers should ensure that the information held about individuals is only what is absolutely
relevant. For example, the names and birth dates of the children of the individual is unlikely to

be relevant. If it is not relevant, marketers should not ask the question of the individual and marketers should not hold or process their data.

All personal data must be accurate

Marketers should ensure that all personal information held is kept accurate and up to date and active checks are made to ensure this.

All personal data must not be kept for longer than necessary

Marketers should ensure that there are suitable processes in place to ensure that any personal information that is no longer reasonably required is deleted securely. For example, with paper-based records, a shredding machine is very common within many marketing and public relations agencies, and is effective in destroying sensitive documentation no longer required.

All personal data must be processed in accordance with the rights of the individual

Subject to very limited exceptions (discussed above), all individuals are entitled to know what personal data the marketer is holding about them.

All personal data must be kept under adequate security precautions to prevent loss, destruction or unauthorised disclosure

Marketers must ensure adequate security for all personal information held and used, taking into account the nature of the data and the harm to the individual which could arise from their disclosure or loss. The level of security required may differ on a case by case basis.

Rudimentary security measures such as access and passwords on computer files and security locks on cupboards for paper based data will be a minimum standard.

> **POINT OF LAW**
>
> Computer legacy systems dating back to the 1970s and early 1980s could be potential time bombs as such systems will need to comply with the 1998 Act and therefore databases written in old computer language such as C, C++, UNIX and COBOL will need to be 'data cleaned' – kept up to date and compliant with the 1998 Act – a potentially expensive process for the marketer given that these computer languages are fast becoming redundant.

Marketers should also consider the physical security of their computer systems and other files and ensure that back-up copies are kept securely.

In addition, all staff should be clear as to who has access to what and for what purpose. For example, within the employee manual, misuse of personal data should feature as a disciplinary offence.

Access to data by other individuals should be very carefully considered to ensure that personal data are not disclosed to any unauthorised individuals without the individual's consent.

Also, if marketers outsource processing of any personal data to a third party ('data processor'), then it is a requirement of the 1998 Act that there is a *written* agreement in place with them and that they have sufficient security in place.

Third parties must be contractually obliged to *only* act on the marketer's specific instructions in relation to the data and to comply with this security principle of the 1998 Act.

Personal data cannot be transferred outside of the European Economic Area unless the marketer is satisfied as to the level of security or another exemption applies

Subject to certain specific circumstances, marketers may not transfer personal information outside of the EEA *without* the consent of the individual.

The Data Protection Act 1998 prohibits the transfer of personal information to countries outside the EEA which do not have adequate controls to protect the rights and freedoms of individuals in relation to the processing of their personal information. This applies whether between group companies or to suppliers, customers or other third parties.

There are *limited* exceptions where such transfers will be allowed, such as where the individual has given their consent or where the transfer is necessary for the conclusion of a contract, but in marketing practice the significance is likely to rest on whether there is 'adequate' protection in any particular case.

The 'transfer' of data in this respect includes disclosing information or making it available.

> **POINT OF LAW**
>
> Any information held on a web site could give rise to a transfer and, if this information is accessed by anyone (including members of the same group of companies) from a country outside the EEA, it will be an unauthorised transfer if that country does not have adequate data protection measures, unless an exception applies.

What is adequate protection?

There is no definitive definition, but it involves an assessment of the level of risk in any particular transfer and will not necessarily depend on specific legislation being in place in the relevant countries. The burden falls on the marketer, as *data controller*, to assess the adequacy in each case and regard must be had to:

- The nature of the personal data
- The country of origin of the data and their final destination
- The purposes for processing the data
- The laws, international obligations and any relevant codes of conduct or other rules of the destination country
- Any security measures taken

Whether there is 'adequate' protection in a particular case will depend on the specific circumstances of that case.

Switzerland, Hungary and Canada

The **European Commission** has the power to give 'safe harbour' clearance to countries on an individual basis and at the time of publication (2002) **Switzerland, Hungary and Canada** have been given such security clearance. Canada's clearance does not cover transfers to public bodies or private organisations for non-commercial purposes.

Hong Kong, Japan, New Zealand and Australia

The European Commission is expected to look at granting security clearances to **Hong Kong, Japan, New Zealand and Australia** in the future but nothing definitive has yet been published.

US

The **US** has always been an issue as far as data protection is concerned as many European marketers transact business with US corporations and in the course of which may need to transfer personal information to the US.

However, the US currently has no general data protection laws and with its freedom of information policy, appears unlikely to adopt one in the foreseeable future.

Because of this, the European Commission and the US Government finalised discussions in July 2000 on the development of 'safe harbour' principles.

Under this arrangement, the **US Department of Commerce** (with the assistance of the European Commission) has published 'safe harbour principles' which practically mirror the obligations under the **EU Data Protection Directive**.

In this connection, work is now proceeding to create a set of model terms for contracts between marketers transferring data across the Atlantic which will be recognised by the European Union as placing adequate obligations on the US marketer.

In addition, businesses in the US can self-certify with the US Department of Commerce undertaking to comply with such principles.

POINT OF LAW

Marketers can avoid legal difficulties in the transfer of personal data between the UK and the US by observing the following simple steps:

- Ensure that the transfer of personal data is only for the purposes of performing a contract. For example, if merchandise ordered on-line in the UK is manufactured in the US and it is clear that the products are to be delivered by post from the US to the UK, then it is essential that the customer's name and address is transferred to the US for that purpose. Providing the data are *only* used for this purpose, then this will be legal. Note that if the products are only held outside the EEA for the data controller's convenience and it is not *necessary* to do so, then this exemption could not be relied upon.

- Where merchandise is ordered on-line, the marketer's web site must clearly state where the customer places an order that the data may be transferred out of the UK to a country which does not have adequate data protection laws. Provided this is accompanied by an opportunity to *opt-out* of such transfer, this should be in conformity with the 1998 Act.

Marketers on both sides of the Atlantic should enter into a bilateral written contract which obliges the US marketer to deal with the data in a manner that is fully consistent with UK data protection legislation. The US marketer will be under a contractual obligation to keep the data secure, not to disclose them to third parties and to only use the data for purposes which would either have been obvious to the customer at the time that they input their data or which have been disclosed in advance at the point of collection of the data.

As previously discussed, intra-group transfers (transfers between group companies) of personal data out of the EEA are not exempt from '**Data Protection Principles**'. If sending and receiving marketers are separate companies, there will be a transfer of data for the purposes of these rules, regardless of whether the companies are in the same corporate group.

Data controllers in the EU are then entitled to presume that adequate protections are in place for personal data transferred to any US business that has signed up to the 'safe harbour' arrangements.

An up to date list of companies that have registered can be found on the US Department of Commerce web site **www.export.gov/safeharbor** and by linking to the Safe Harbor List.

Model contract terms

There are two forms of model contract terms approved by the **European Commission** (in June and December 2001 respectively) which can be used by EU marketers in their relations with countries outside of the EEA. The first can be used to transfer personal data to parties in countries outside of the EEA which have *not* been otherwise approved, to provide adequate protection for the personal information they wish to transfer. The second can be used to employ data processors based outside of the EEA.

These can be accessed on the Essential Law for Marketers web site at www.bh/com/companions/0750655003.

The clauses will provide protection for individuals by allowing them a direct right of action against the marketer in the EU and/or the recipient of the data.

The model contract terms will also provide EU marketers with the contractual rights to oversee and take action against their contracting third party and to require an indemnity in case of any violation of the personal information.

However, both the EU data controller and the recipient of the data are *equally liable* to the individual for any violation of their personal data and the individual may take action against either one or both of them. This right of action and the indemnity between the parties should also give comfort to the individual as they are an additional incentive for the recipient of the data to protect them.

PROTECTION OF THE INDIVIDUAL'S RIGHTS UNDER THE DATA PROTECTION ACT 1998

Individuals have a number of rights in relation to the personal data held about them and in general these include:

1. The right of access

2. Prevention of processing likely to cause damage or distress

3. Prevention of processing for the purposes of direct marketing

4. Rights in relation to automated decision taking

5. The right to take legal action for compensation if they suffer damage

6. The right to take action to rectify, block, erase or destroy inaccurate data

7. The right to make a request to the Information Commissioner for an assessment to be made as to whether any provision of the Data Protection Act 1998 has been contravened

Marketers are most likely to encounter the right of access and the right to prevent processing for direct marketing. It is important that all marketers know how to recognise a subject access request and realise that it must be dealt with promptly. The request does not need to mention the Data Protection Act 1998 specifically but procedures should be in place and be accessible to ensure requests are dealt with properly.

The right of access

Every day the Information Commissioner receives complaints from members of the public, often to do with their right to know what data are being held about them. It is therefore important that marketers deal with any requests for access promptly and correctly.

Generally, all individuals will have the right to see all of the data a marketer has about them.

The individual must make a written request and must enclose the necessary fee (this should only be what is reasonable to cover costs and this is currently not greater than £10).

The individual is then entitled to be told whether the marketer or someone on its behalf is processing their personal data and, if so, they are entitled to a description of the personal data, the purposes for which they are being used and those to whom they are or may be disclosed.

This information must be supplied in a permanent form by way of a copy, unless this is not possible, would involve disproportionate effort or the individual agrees otherwise.

If any of the information in the copy provided by the marketer is not intelligible without explanation, then the marketer should also give an explanation of that information and, subject to any other individuals' rights, the individual is also entitled to any information as to the source of their data.

Marketers must comply with any valid request *promptly* and *within 40 days of receipt of the request* or, if later, within 40 days of receipt of any further information it may require to satisfy itself as to the identify of the person making the request and to locate the information that person seeks and the fee.

In the normal course of business, a marketer need NOT respond to a request until:

- It receives the request in writing
- It receives the prescribed fee (£10)
- Until it has received further information that it requires and has requested in order to respond to the request

A marketer does NOT need to comply with the request if it has already complied with an identical or similar request by the same individual in the past, unless a reasonable interval has elapsed.

> POINT OF
> LAW
>
> The information that a marketer should give is all that which is contained in the personal data at the time the request is received, subject to any routine amendments.

Marketers must not make any special amendments or deletions which would not otherwise have been made and must not tamper with the information in order to make it acceptable to the individual.

An important consideration in complying with any such request is to consider whether in doing so there may be a risk of disclosure of data relating to another individual.

If this is likely, then the marketer is *only* required to disclose those particular data if the other individual has consented to the disclosure or if it is otherwise reasonable in all the circumstances to comply with the request without the consent of the other individual.

If the marketer is satisfied that the *data subject* will not be able to identify the other individual from the information then the marketer MUST provide the information.

Marketers must be wary of requests to disclose personal information received from a partner or spouse as it cannot ordinarily release this information unless and until it is satisfied that the other individual wishes such disclosure to be made and that they are happy for this disclosure to be made to the partner/spouse.

Ideally, marketers should insist on a written request directly from the individual and provide the information directly back to them to ensure that they are not contravening any of their rights.

However, marketers should be entitled to assume that a parent is entitled to make a request and receive information in relation to an offspring under the age of 16 years.

So what does a responsible marketer do when contemplating a promotion aimed at children that involves collecting their names and addresses, either on-line or off-line, and processing those data?

POINT OF
LAW

Where data relate to marketing to children

A key issue for marketers is the marketing to children (which is dealt with in more detail in Chapter 9 and Chapter 16).

Surprisingly, the **Data Protection Act 1998** says very little about it. For example, the 1998 Act does not stipulate any minimum age below which express consent of a responsible adult should be obtained before 'children's' data can be lawfully collected and used for marketing and selling purposes.

So does this mean that 5-year-olds can validly consent to the collection and use of their data on-line?

The only advice from the Information Commissioner is that marketers must bear in mind that proper informed consent is needed and that advantage should not be taken of children's naiveté.

It also recommends that if responsible adults are giving consent on behalf of minors, the adult should keep the child's interests paramount, not those of the adult.

And that is about it, apart from the law of contract (see Chapter 2) which makes it clear that under-16-year-olds cannot enter a legally binding contract.

As a starting point, marketers should bear in mind the contract law principle and make it clear that if any binding commitment to a loyalty scheme, prize promotion or product purchase is required, then the binding signature of a responsible adult will be required.

The marketer will also, particularly in an on-line environment, want to consider measures reasonably necessary to minimise the risk of deception/fraud.

The marketer should also observe the **Direct Marketing Association (DMA) Code of Practice for Commercial Communications to Children On-line**.

This is mirrored to a greater or lesser extent in the guidelines recently published as part of the Government's umbrella '**TrustUK**' on-line consumer protection code certification scheme.

The **DMA Code** recommends:

Children must not be eligible to participate in a promotion in which prizes such as, for example, holidays, pet animals, goods or cash are offered which may be likely to cause problems between parent and child, unless the rules require the written consent of a parent.

Unsolicited commercial e-mail communications must not be addressed to children without the verifiable and explicit prior consent of the parent/teacher.

The DMA Code also requires that web sites directed to children should require a child to give their age before any other personal information is requested. If the age is under 14, the child should be excluded from giving further personal information until the appropriate, verifiable and explicit consent has been given.

Personal information relating to other people, for example parents' ages and occupations, should not be collected from children, whilst a child's access to a web site should not be made contingent on the collection of personal information or entice a child to divulge personal information with the prospect of a special prize or other offer.

Notices requiring parental consent should be clear and written in language easily understood by children. They should be located at the point where the personal information is collected and include an explanation of the purposes for which the data are being collected.

For further discussion of the DMA Code of Practice as well as marketing to children, see Chapter 16.

Prevention of processing likely to cause damage or distress

An individual has the right to give the marketer written notice requiring it to cease or not begin using their personal data if it is causing or is likely to cause unwarranted damage or damage and distress.

However, this right is *not* available if the marketer is using their data with their consent or if it is necessary for the performance of a contract, to comply with a legal obligation (other than by contract) or to protect their vital interests.

If a marketer does receive such a request, it must reply *within 21 days* stating whether or not it has complied, or intends to comply, with their request and, if not, stating its reasons.

If an individual is not satisfied with its reasons for not complying, then in extreme cases the individual may seek a court order to enforce compliance, so it is important to at least respond to such requests even if the marketer does not believe it actually needs to accede to it.

Prevention of processing for the purposes of direct marketing

An individual may, at any time, by written notice require a marketer to cease or not begin processing their personal information for direct marketing purposes.

If a marketer receives such a request, it *must* comply and it should ensure that it has processes in place that no further marketing materials are sent to that individual.

Personal information in relation to automated decision taking

If a marketer uses an automatic means of processing personal information to make a decision about an individual which significantly affects them, e.g. whether they are entitled to apply for hire purchase or credit in order to purchase a product, then the individual is entitled to require that this is *not* the only basis on which the marketer makes the decision.

Individuals are also entitled to be told of the logic involved in taking those automated decisions. If the decision is made solely on automatic processing, the marketer must notify the individual as soon as reasonably practicable and, *within 21 days*, they may require the marketer to reconsider the decision or retake the decision on a different basis.

Taking action for compensation if they suffer damage

Any individual who suffers damage or damage and distress as a result of any contravention of the requirements of the 1998 Act by a *data controller* (marketer) is entitled to compensation if the marketer cannot prove that it had taken such care as was reasonable in all the circumstances.

Taking action to rectify, block, erase or destroy inaccurate data

An individual may, at any time, apply to the Court for an order requiring a data controller to rectify, block, erase or destroy any data relating to them that is inaccurate.

The marketer may then also be required to notify other parties to whom the data have been disclosed and may also be subject to a costs order. It is therefore even more important to ensure that all data held by a marketer are accurate and kept up to date.

CHECKLIST

- Marketers must adhere to the eight principles of data protection:

  1. Personal data shall be processed fairly and lawfully

  2. Personal data shall be obtained for one or more specified and lawful purposes only

  3. Personal data shall be adequate, relevant and not excessive in relation to the purposes for which they are processed

  4. Personal data shall be accurate and where necessary be kept up to date

  5. Personal data shall be kept for no longer than is necessary in relation to the purposes for which they are processed

  6. Personal data shall be processed in accordance with the rights of the data subject

  7. Appropriate technical and organisational measures shall be taken against unauthorised or unlawful processing and against accidental loss or destruction or damage to personal data

  8. Personal data shall not be transferred outside the European Economic Area (EEA) *unless* there is an adequate level of protection in relation to the processing of personal data or another exemption applies

- Marketers should carry out a data audit that should answer the following questions:

  1. What data do you hold?

  2. What format are they held in?

  3. Where are you transferring them?

  4. How do you process them?

  5. What procedures and processes do you have in place?

- Marketers should notify the Information Commissioner for all group companies (currently £35 annual fee). On-line notification is very straightforward and can be done on-line at www.dataprotection.gov.uk

- Marketers should establish a compliance programme and appoint data protection officers

- Marketers should establish a procedure for dealing with *data subject* access requests

- Clients, marketers and subcontractors should review marketing service agreement contracts and contracts with other third parties and incorporate either a simple data protection clause or a comprehensive data protection clause depending on the circumstances and nature of the relationship

CHAPTER 8

DEFAMATION

In this chapter:

- Definition of a defamatory statement
- Liability for repeating a defamatory statement someone else has made
- Defences
- The limits of fair comment
- 'Knocking copy' and defamation
- The tort of malicious falsehood
- Human Rights Act and freedom of expression
- Checklist

Other useful chapters:

- Chapter 3: Making statements
- Chapter 4: Liability for defective products
- Chapter 5: Intellectual property rights
- Chapter 9: Advertising and labelling
- Chapter 10: Broadcasting
- Chapter 14: Lobbying
- Chapter 15: Cyber marketing
- Chapter 16: Niche marketing

INTRODUCTION

It is important to understand the limits of freedom of expression in a marketing context. Marketers need to take particular care that their marketing activities do not fall foul of the laws of libel and malicious falsehood.

POINT OF LAW

For example, if an advertisement refers to a person or a company in dis-paraging terms, there is a risk that it may be libellous. Unchecked factual claims may, if false, also give rise to a claim for malicious falsehood.

Both the marketer and the publisher of an advertisement will run the risk of legal action if the advertisement is found to contain libellous statements. As damages in libel trials are usually set by juries and can be notoriously high, marketers should have all 'knocking copy' adver-tisements and marketing material reviewed by a lawyer prior to publication.

This is of particular importance as the assessment of damages may be influenced by the extent of publication. In the case of some advertising campaigns, publication may be wide-spread, leading to a potentially high award of damages.

Sometimes words and pictures make private matters public. This chapter discusses the extent to which individuals' rights to personal privacy may inhibit what a marketer can say and do.

DEFAMATION

Material is defamatory if it tends to harm the reputation of another person so as to lower him or her in the estimation of right-thinking people generally.

Therefore, an advertisement which makes derogatory statements about an individual or company may give rise to a defamation claim.

The term 'defamation' covers **libel** and **slander**. The distinction between the two is of little practical importance. Libel concerns the publication of defamatory material in non-transient form such as print and broadcast. Slander covers transient publications such as defamatory words spoken at a party, or during a meeting, seminar or conference.

Slander cases are rare principally because it is difficult to prove that particular words were spoken unless (unusually) a recording exists.

For this reason, this section deals with defamation as it relates to the law of libel.

Publication

No liability for defamation arises unless the defamatory words are published to *at least* one third party. Publication to the claimant alone, e.g. in a letter or e-mail, is *not* actionable.

A number of people may become liable for defamatory material because they have caused or contributed to its publication.

For example, where defamatory material appears in an advertisement on a web site, the following people may be held responsible:

■ The marketer

■ The advertising agency (where applicable)

■ The web site owner

■ The web site designer

■ The Internet Service Provider (ISP) whose server gives access to the site

Where a defamatory statement is included in a news release, the person defamed has potential claims against:

■ The author

■ The marketer (if different to the author)

■ The person issuing the news release

■ The printer

■ The distributor

■ All of the above

INSIGHT

It follows that a marketing professional or an advertising agency that issues
material on behalf of a client may itself be liable for the defamatory content of that material.
   If the client rather than the professional marketer is sued, the client may seek to join its professional adviser in the proceedings. If the professional marketer wishes to protect itself against such direct or indirect liability, it may wish to extract suitable contractual warranties and indemnities from the client (see Chapter 2) or take out suitable insurance cover.

Provided publication of the defamatory statement has taken place in the UK, an action for libel can be brought in the UK courts. There will be 'publication' in the UK if material on the Internet can be accessed from the UK, wherever it may have originated.

Publication of defamatory material may also give rise to claims for libel in other countries where publication takes place. In appropriate cases, marketers should consider taking advice from lawyers in those countries.

For further discussion on this issue, see Chapter 15.

Who can sue for libel?

Individuals and organisations can sue for libel, including companies, not-for-profit bodies, professional associations and charities.

LAW IN
ACTION

For example, fast food giant **McDonald's** famously sued two anti-
capitalism campaigners who circulated pamphlets containing colourful
and wide-ranging criticisms of its business and employment practices as well as its burgers
(the case was dubbed 'McLibel').

Retailer **Marks & Spencer** successfully sued Granada TV over false allegations that it sold
garments it knew had been manufactured by child labour.

However, the following *cannot* sue for libel:

- Dead people (if the claimant dies, his action dies with him and his estate cannot
  continue it)
- Public authorities such as government departments or local councils
- Political parties

INSIGHT

Marketers should take legal advice before making defamatory allegations
against public bodies such as local authorities. Although a local authority cannot sue for
defamation, the statement may by implication be defamatory of that local authority's chief
executive, who can sue for the damage to his reputation.

Reference

No-one can sue for libel unless the words either refer to them directly or would have been
understood to refer to them. As the next example illustrates, an individual may be taken to have
been referred to even without being named.

POINT OF
LAW

For example, **Deputy Prime Minister John Prescott** will be identifiable
whether he is referred to by name or as the Deputy Prime Minister, the
MP for Hull East or even as 'Two Jags' (his preferred mode of transport).

Perhaps less obviously, Prescott could be implicitly referred to in, say, a presentation which
criticised aspects of the government's transport policy if at the relevant time he had responsibility for that department's policy.

'Class libels' raise particular problems.

For example, an opinion piece in *FT Creative Business* that 'all marketers are corrupt' is not actionable by the 600,000 or so marketers in the UK (source: Chartered Institute of Marketing) as no individual marketer could maintain to the satisfaction of the court that *FT* readers would have understood that statement as a direct reference to one individual marketer.

In contrast, a suggestion or implication that cement manufacturers in the North of England are engaged in restrictive practices, could well be actionable if there are only a few such companies since each member of that 'class' could say it had been put under a 'cloud of suspicion'.

The meaning of words

The issue of meaning is central to the determination of whether material is defamatory.

In many cases the meaning of words is plain enough but language is often open to different interpretations. Reasonable people may sometimes read quite different meanings into the same words and words and pictures taken together may convey a very different impression than when considered in isolation of each other.

For example, a senior British Airways captain may be happy for his picture to be used in a promotion for the airline, but he will be less happy if his image is used to illustrate an external campaign highlighting the importance of training since that may wrongly imply that he is in need of training himself.

Marketers should also take particular care over the inappropriate use of library pictures in case of accidental defamation (also check that the right to use the picture has been secured – see Chapter 6).

For example, a library picture of a young girl should not, without her parents' consent, be used in connection with an advertisement for a children's charity since that might suggest that the parents were unable to look after her. In general, the subject's consent should be obtained before using any library picture of a real person in any form of commercial literature since the person may well object to the implication that he or she was willing to promote the product or service in question.

The careless use of words which also have slang meanings may result in unintended offence. 'Snort', 'toot', 'line' and 'joint' are all good old-fashioned English words which because of their association with illegal drugs may trap the unwary marketer into unintended libels.

Marketers should also be on guard against the 'hidden' meanings of words. Words which may look innocent at first reading, may convey a completely different meaning to readers who are in possession of other information.

POINT OF LAW

For example, to describe a javelin thrower as 'the Ben Johnson of field athletics' will convey to those who know that Ben Johnson was disqualified from the Olympic Games (for drug taking) a clear suggestion that the javelin thrower has taken performance enhancing drugs.

In the same way, describing someone as a regular visitor to a particular neighbourhood may be defamatory if it is known that the neighbourhood is the home of, say, a brothel, crack den or a clinic for the treatment of sexually transmitted diseases.

A marketer may be liable for defamation even it is doing no more than repeating what another marketer has said.

POINT OF LAW

For example, if car manufacturer A repeats the strap line from a comparative press advertisement by car manufacturer B that says 'C's cars are the least reliable cars made in the UK' it is not enough to show that B made such a claim. A would have to show that C's cars **are** the least reliable if it is successfully to defend a libel action by C.

Liability for defamation can be established irrespective of the marketer's intention. It is no defence to say 'I didn't mean to say that'. However well-intentioned the marketer may have been, it will be liable for any defamatory impression the words may be held to create.

Furthermore, prior publication by itself is no defence to a defamation action. The fact that something has been said or published before does not mean that it can be repeated with impunity (see further defences below).

What is a defamatory statement?

It is only defamatory statements which give rise to liability for defamation. Having established what words mean, the next step is to consider whether that meaning is defamatory.

The classic, but possibly unhelpful, legal definition of 'defamatory' mentioned at the beginning of this chapter is a publication which 'tends to harm the reputation of another person so as to lower him or her in the estimation of right thinking people generally'.

POINT OF LAW

A more useful guide for the marketer is to ask itself whether it would like these things to be said of itself. If not, the words are almost certainly defamatory.

In many cases it is obvious whether something is defamatory or not. For example, allegations of professional incompetence, dishonesty, criminality and immorality will clearly be defamatory.

However, statements which on the surface may appear defamatory may just be on the borderline, as the next case illustrates.

LAW IN ACTION

In the case of **Berkoff-v-Burchill (1996)**, the court had to decide whether acclaimed actor Steven Berkoff might have been defamed by acerbic jour-nalist Julie Burchill when she described him as hideous-looking.

Writing of a character called 'the Creature' in the film 'Frankenstein', Burchill wrote:

The Creature is made as a vessel for Waldman's brain, and rejected in disgust when it comes out scarred and primeval. It's a very new look for the Creature – no bolts in the neck or flat-top hairdo – and I think it works; it's a lot like Steven Berkoff, only marginally better-looking.

Two judges decided that the article was capable of being defamatory of Berkoff and decided that the question whether it was should be left to a jury to decide. Lord Justice Millett thought Berkoff's case should be dismissed: his proceedings were 'as frivolous as Ms Burchill's article'.

As the following cases illustrate, it is almost impossible to provide an exhaustive definition of what will be held to be defamatory as each case will be decided on its relevant facts.

LAW IN ACTION

Dolores O'Riordain, lead singer of the pop group the Cranberries, received substantial damages for false allegations that she had appeared on stage without her knickers.

Owner of Tottenham Hotspur football club and Amstrad entrepreneur **Sir Alan Sugar** received £100,000 for being called 'a miser'.

Actor **Martin Clunes,** star of BBC 1's hit sitcom *Men Behaving Badly*, received £1000 when former Prime Minister Margaret Thatcher's press secretary Sir Bernard Ingham described Clunes as a 'stupid, nasty, foul-mouthed, posturing juvenile with a limited command of the language'.

On the other hand, the heavyweight American soprano **Jessye Norman** had her libel action struck out on the ground that the words complained of were incapable of being defamatory.

Norman had sued *Classic CD* magazine for a profile that related to a story that she had got stuck in a revolving door. She was supposedly advised to turn sideways and had responded: 'Honey, I ain't got no sideways'. She denied making the remark, which she said exposed her to ridicule. Lord Justice Peter Gibson, as he threw the case out, praised her vocal talents but not her sense of humour.

The presumptions of falsity and damage

The law of libel makes two presumptions in favour of those complaining of defamation:

1. A defamatory statement is presumed to be false until the contrary is proven. This presumption has invariably proved useful to claimants and has on occasion encouraged unmeritorious claims to be brought in the expectation that the defendant will be unable to prove to the necessary legal standard and with properly admissible evidence that what was said was true.

2. Damage is presumed to have been caused by a defamatory statement. A claimant in a libel action need not prove any actual loss, financial or otherwise (though if such loss can be proved, for example, lost job opportunities, that loss can be claimed as well).

The parties to a libel action have a right to trial by jury and it is the jury's responsibility to award damages (this being unusual for a civil case today). It is frequently a matter of uncertainty what damages will be awarded in a libel action.

What can be guaranteed is that a libel complaint will be expensive to defend. All too often the damages paid to the claimant are dwarfed by the scale of the legal costs. Marketers finding themselves on the wrong side of litigation proceedings may employ a variety of tactics like a payment into court as a way of attempting to settle the action.

Brand owners should be aware of the time and costs involved in commencing a legal action against a competitor – it can be extremely disruptive and unless the victor is very fortunate, it is unlikely to recover all its legal costs in the action.

Defences to libel

There are three principal defences to libel:

Justification

'Justification' is the legal term for truth. A libel action will not succeed if the words complained of are true.

Note that the defendant must prove the truth of the specific allegation complained of and that there is limited opportunity for introducing 'similar fact' evidence.

POINT OF LAW

For example, a brand owner cannot justify an allegation that A stole money from B by proving that he (previously) stole money from C.

However, a plea of partial justification is sometimes permissible. In the **'McLibel' case** (above), the defendants satisfied the judge that some of what they had said was true, which served to reduce the damages awarded against them.

As long as the marketer can prove that what it has written or communicated is true, it will have a complete defence to any libel claim.

Fair comment

This protects the expression of opinion as opposed to allegations of a factual nature. The distinction between fact and comment is a crucial one in defamation.

For example, to say that disgraced Tory Minister Neil Hamilton accepted a bribe is a factual allegation; to say that an MP who accepts a bribe is a disgrace to Parliament is a comment.

Provided the facts on which the comment is based are true (or privileged – see below), fair comment is an almost invincible defence.

It will, however, be defeated if the claimant can show that the publisher was motivated by malice, which is discussed below.

It is not usually possible to turn an allegation of fact into an expression of opinion simply by the use of prefatory words such as 'in my view' or 'it seems to me'. The courts assess whether something is an expression of opinion – and thus susceptible to a defence of fair comment – not just by looking at the words used but by assessing whether it is capable of objective verification. If not, it is likely to be regarded as comment.

For example, in an article in the *Evening Standard* that appeared in 2001, the author Tom Bower wrote the following:

Revenge rather than self righteousness has motivated Richard Branson's latest bid to run Britain's Lottery.

Branson sued Bower for libel. Bower defended his article as fair comment. The court decided that the above remark was indeed a 'comment', not a statement of fact. The suggestion that Branson was motivated by revenge was a value judgment expressed on matters of public interest, not an objectively verifiable fact.

The courts do not make an assessment of whether a comment is objectively 'fair'. The law of defamation protects even the most pig-headed, prejudiced and absurd expressions of opinion.

In this regard, the expression 'fair comment' is indeed something of a misnomer: *unfair* comment is likely to be no more libellous than the most conscientious and balanced opinion piece in the most conservative broadsheet newspaper.

The key is that it is comment and not driven by malice (below).

Privilege

Statements made can be protected by privilege: absolute and qualified. No action lies in respect of a defamatory communication protected by **absolute privilege**.

However, a defence of **qualified privilege** will fail if the claimant can show that the defendant was motivated by malice.

Broadly speaking, privilege is a form of public interest defence: where it is in the public interest that a communication should be made, no action for defamation will lie at all (absolute privilege) or only where the claimant can establish that the communication was made maliciously (qualified privilege).

There are many circumstances in which the law recognises that freedom of speech is essential. In such cases, a person may make a statement under the protection of absolute privilege even if that statement turns out to be defamatory and untrue.

> POINT OF LAW
>
> For example, statements made in Parliament, fair, accurate and contemporaneous reports of court proceedings and reports of public bodies such as the Competition Commission are protected by **absolute privilege**.

On occasions which are not protected by absolute privilege, qualified privilege may still arise if a statement was fairly warranted by the occasion and it was not made maliciously (in the knowledge or belief it was untrue or out of some improper motive).

Many statements made by professionals and others in the course of business – for example, in correspondence with a client – are likely, if defamatory, to have been made on an occasion of **qualified privilege**.

Such an occasion arises where the person who makes a communication has an interest, or a duty, legal, social or moral, to make it to the person to whom it is made, and the person to whom it is so made has a corresponding interest or duty to receive it. This element of reciprocity is essential in order for the statement to enjoy the protection of qualified privilege.

The scope for successfully defending a defamatory publication on the ground of qualified privilege has been increased in recent years due to a landmark ruling by the House of Lords in 1999. In **Reynolds-v-Times Newspapers**, it was established that in certain circumstances the media may have a duty to communicate information even though that information may later turn out to be inaccurate.

However, it is unlikely that the law of qualified privilege will be of much relevance to communications of a commercial nature such as are the ordinary currency of marketing professionals.

In deciding whether it is legally safe to say something defamatory about a third party, the best advice is to seek to ensure that it is either true or fair comment.

If a marketer wishes to rely on a defence of privilege, it is best to seek specialist legal advice before publication.

Malice

A defence of fair comment or qualified privilege will be defeated if the claimant can show that the person making the communication acted out of malice.

Malice will be inferred in the following circumstances:

■ Where the defendant (the person responsible for the publication) has no honest belief in the truth of the statement complained of. This is exceptionally difficult to prove.

■ Where the defendant publishes an untrue statement with reckless disregard of its truth or falsity. Carelessness, impulsiveness and irrationality are not the same as indifference to the truth.

POINT OF LAW

For example, if a fast food company were to announce falsely that a rival's beef products were contaminated by BSE without taking proper steps to check its facts, it would almost certainly be held to have been reckless. The more serious the allegation is, the greater the responsibility to check that it is accurate.

■ Where the marketer making the statement uses the occasion of privilege for an improper purpose. For example, a defendant advertising agency cannot maintain it was acting pursuant to a duty (advancing its client's case), if the real reason for making the statement was to injure the claimant.

The House of Lords has said that juries should be 'slow' to draw such an inference, particularly when the defendant shows it had an honest belief in the truth of what it said.

Pleas of malice are commonly to be found in libel actions whenever defences of fair comment or qualified privilege are raised.

While it is certainly possible to imagine cases in which marketing professionals might make statements dishonestly, with reckless disregard for the truth, or for the dominant purpose of injuring a third party, such cases are in practice likely to be rare.

Other defences to libel

If someone's contribution to a defamatory communication is innocent in nature, e.g. if it has printed or distributed material without realising it was defamatory, it may have a defence if it can show:

■ That it was not the author, editor or publisher of the statement

■ That it had no reason to believe the publication was defamatory

■ That it took reasonable care in relation to the publication

It should be noted that this defence, contained in **Section 1 of the Defamation Act 1996**, is intended to assist 'secondary' publishers. It will not help those who were responsible, in whole or part, for the content of defamatory material. Nor will it assist those who acted in a careless manner towards the publication.

With respect to an Internet Service Provider (ISP), the courts will view the ISP as a 'secondary' publisher of defamatory statements. While it could therefore be the subject of an action for defamation, it would normally have a defence under Section 1 of the 1996 Act (see also Chapter 15).

It is beyond the scope of this chapter to give detailed consideration to other defences, which include limitation and offer of amends. In the event that a complaint of libel is received, legal advice should be sought at the earliest opportunity.

MALICIOUS FALSEHOOD

What is 'malicious falsehood'?

An action for the tort of malicious falsehood (sometimes known as 'trade libel', although it applies to individuals as well as businesses) may arise where an untrue statement has been made about the claimant.

For a claim to succeed, the claimant must show that an untrue statement has been made dishonestly or recklessly and it is or is likely to cause *financial loss*.

It is not necessary to prove that the words are defamatory; but it is necessary to show:

- The words were false

POINT OF LAW

For example, if an advertisement is misleading about a competitor marketer and can be shown to have been published maliciously – in other words recklessly as to its truth or falsity or for some improper motive – then it could constitute a malicious falsehood.

- The defendant marketer has acted maliciously
- The words are likely to cause financial loss

If this is the case, the marketer can expect to face a legal action to stop further use of the advertisement as well as an action for compensation.

Where a claimant may wish to bring an action for malicious falsehood

It is usually easier to sue for defamation than malicious falsehood because in such an action it is not usually necessary to prove malice or actual financial loss. But where a claimant is unable to sue for defamation because, for example, the words complained of are not defamatory, a malicious falsehood action may be the only legal avenue available.

How does the law of malicious falsehood affect comparative advertising?

The courts will not entertain legal proceedings based on advertising or marketing puffs, taking the view that such puffs are not intended to be taken seriously or to have any kind of serious legal effect.

Phrases such as 'lowest prices ever', 'sale of the century', 'knockdown prices', 'best ever performance' and 'the *only* way to travel by air' will be regarded as ordinary trade puffs and the law will not concern itself with them.

The law will, however, intervene where claims made about another's products or services

LAW IN ACTION

For example, in 2002 the High Court ordered **Comet** to withdraw certain promotional posters from outside its stores. The posters had falsely claimed that Comet's prices were lower than those offered by its competitor, **Currys**. The statements were clearly directed at Currys and were intended to be taken seriously and to cause financial damage to Currys. Moreover, the evidence before the court clearly demonstrated that Comet must have realised its allegations were false.

In a similar case, **British Airways** failed to establish a case of malicious falsehood. British Airways sued **Ryanair** for trademark infringement and malicious falsehood in respect of a comparative press advertisement Ryanair placed in 1999. The claim concerned two advertisements each comparing Ryanair fares to several European destinations with more expensive British Airways rates headed by 'Expensive BA.... DS!' and 'Expensive BA' respectively.

British Airways complained about the offensiveness of the headlines of the advertisements, and the unfairness of individual price and destination comparisons.

On the 'trade libel' point, Mr Justice Jacob held that while the advertisement might amount to vulgar abuse or may be taken as offensive, it did *not* amount to malicious falsehood as the substance of the advertisements was true. In fact Ryanair had failed to point out a further disadvantage of the BA fare in respect of the destination comparison of Dinard, namely that the traveller had to change planes. Not doing so could not make the advertisement dishonest.

The judge held that the average customer would not find the price comparison misleading and the fact that the airlines flew to different airports in one of the destinations used in the advertisement did not make the comparison unfair.

The judge's remark that 'the real reason BA does not like the advertising is precisely because it is true' confirms that it is perfectly acceptable to criticise a competitor marketer in advertising as long as the comparison is true.

go beyond self-commendation and are intended to be taken seriously. As the next two cases illustrate, the more detailed and damaging the allegations are, the less likely they are to be regarded as mere puffs.

For further discussion on comparative advertising, see Chapter 9.

THE IMPACT OF HUMAN RIGHTS LEGISLATION

Article 10 of the **European Convention on Human Rights (ECHR)**, now incorporated into UK law by the **Human Rights Act 1998**, contains the right to freedom of expression. However, that right is subject to 'such restrictions as are necessary in a democratic society' and that includes the law of libel.

While it is impossible to argue that the law of libel as a whole is incompatible with the right to freedom of expression, the courts do recognise the importance of freedom of expression and seek to apply the law accordingly.

The 1998 Act contains specific provisions aimed at ensuring that freedom of expression is given proper consideration by the courts.

Freedom of expression includes commercial speech such as advertising and promotion and where the law imposes unreasonable restraints on the exercise of such freedom arguments based on the ECHR may well be helpful and appropriate.

PRIVACY

The exercise of freedom of expression under **Article 10 of the ECHR** is also subject to 'the rights of others'. These rights include the right of privacy contained in **Article 8 of the Convention**.

Article 8 provides that everyone has 'the right to respect for his private and family life, his home and his correspondence'.

Any interference with that right must be 'necessary in a democratic society in the interests of national security, public safety or the economic well-being of the country, for the prevention of disorder or crime, for the protection of health or morals, or for the protection of the rights and freedoms of others'.

In relation to material which might infringe the privacy of individuals, for example a TV campaign featuring images of people going about their everyday business or a piece of direct mail containing pictures of celebrities used without their consent, two issues arise:

▪ Has anyone's privacy been infringed?

▪ Can any such infringements be justified?

It used to be said, at least until the **Human Rights Act 1998**, that there was no law of privacy in the UK. That is certainly no longer true, though it is true to say that the scope of the right to privacy in this country remains uncertain.

For example, the courts have not ruled on the extent to which a person has a right to protect his or her image. In Catherine Zeta Jones's case against *OK!* magazine, at least one of the three Court of Appeal judges did suggest that Ms Zeta Jones had a right to control the manner in which she was portrayed in the media.

Whether infringements of privacy can be justified is likely to depend on the nature and extent of the intrusion measured against the reason for the intrusion. Gross intrusions will have to be justified by the most compelling reasons of public interest. However, even more trivial intrusions will still require some justification beyond the mere exercise of freedom of expression. In practice, it is difficult to see that the courts will ever regard a purely commercial justification as sufficient to excuse any infringements of privacy, unless they are extremely trifling.

CHECKLIST

- Examine all marketing communications for unintended or hidden meanings. A marketer should consider whether the intended meaning could be misunderstood by reasonable people.

- A marketer should take care not to libel someone accidentally. Sweeping generalities may sometimes unintentionally reflect on particular individuals.

- A marketer should ensure that any pictures are accurately captioned and that they properly relate to the text they illustrate.

- A marketer should write what it means to say. If it does not wish to say something critical or defamatory of a third party, it should make it clear who it is it wishes to criticise and why.

- Can a marketer prove the truth of what it has written or broadcast? It is not enough to believe or even know that something is true. Libel law requires the marketer to prove it by means of admissible evidence.

- A marketer must have the necessary documentation and witnesses that are able and willing to back it up. In appropriate cases, a marketer should consider taking legal advice. Such advice is usually much cheaper at the pre-publication stage than after a complaint has been received.

- If a marketer intends merely to express an opinion, it should make sure that the language used is appropriate for that purpose. If its opinion might be misinterpreted as a statement of fact, it risks losing a defence of fair comment which would otherwise be available.

- If a marketer intends to rely on a defence of privilege, it should consider taking legal advice. The applicability of privilege in particular instances is a technical area of the law.

- If a marketer thinks its motives for writing something may be suspect, they almost certainly are! Don't do it!

- In promoting its own or a client's business, the marketer should consider whether it is necessary or effective to denigrate a competitor marketer. If it is, then it should concentrate on denigrating the product rather than the competitor.

- A marketer should ensure that its criticisms of a competitor marketer's products or services can be fully substantiated.

- A marketer should consider whether it is doing anything which might be regarded as an infringement of someone's privacy. If so, the marketer ought to consider alternatives. If there is no practical alternative, the marketer must satisfy itself that its infringement has a suitable justification.

9

ADVERTISING AND LABELLING

In this chapter:

- Types of advertising
- The advertising industry regulators
- General principles of advertising
- Misleading advertising
- Comparative advertising
- Ambient media
- Advertising and labelling of specific goods, services and causes
- Checklist

Other useful chapters:

INTRODUCTION

Advertising is one of the primary communication channels for any brand owner and is likely to command the lion's share of the marketing budget.

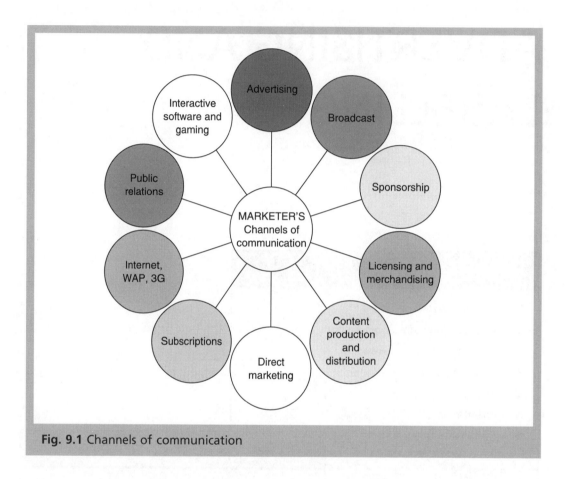

Fig. 9.1 Channels of communication

According to annual research by Propeller and Media Report Editorial, some of the best advertising campaigns in the UK cross the traditional boundary with editorial and end up making the news.

Given its pervasive nature (TV, radio, poster, cinema, billboards, Internet, WAP, mobile, ambient and print are just a few examples!), advertising is subject to a raft of statutory controls.

In fact, there are in excess of 170 statutes which directly affect the practice of advertising. In addition, there is a great deal of self-regulation within the marketing industry and specific advertising and labelling legislation as well as general legal principles. In both the legislation and the codes of the self-regulatory bodies which operate alongside the legislation, there are specific rules depending on the product being advertised and the medium.

Rank according to most media coverage (2001)	Marketer	Campaign
1	Marks & Spencer	Zoe Ball teamed up with Julian Clarey, Hugh Laurie, Sir Steve Redgrave and others to help Marks & Spencer retain its top-of-the-poll position for its campaign 'Exclusively for Everyone'
2	Coca-Cola	On-going brand activity and celebrity ads featuring pop idol Christine Aguilera
3	Tesco	Controversy over price claims
4	Sainsbury's	Jamie Oliver campaign
5	Pepsi	On-going brand activity including celebrity ads featuring pop idol Britney Spears
6	BT	BT Anytime
7	Labour Party	General Election campaign where William Hague was shown wearing Margaret Thatcher's hairdo
8 =	Conservative Party	General Election campaign that highlighted a string of 'broken' promises
8 =	Opium	Use of celebrity Sophie Dahl
10 =	French Connnection	FCUK – outrageously daring play on an expletive. So successful that others have tried to imitate the advertising
10 =	Guinness	On-going TV campaign
12	Walkers Crisps	Use of comedy involving popular former England football captain and now TV presenter Gary Lineker
13	Halifax	Campaign fronted by Halifax staff rather than actors
14	Royal Mail	Using the celebrity and glamour of Sir Elton John to promote what is a very unglamorous marketer

Fig. 9.2 Ads that make news [source: *Ads That Make News* (2001) compiled by Propeller and Media Report Editorial]

As a result of the vast amount of regulation and self-regulation, this chapter will discuss only the principal laws and self-regulatory codes that are relevant to marketers in the area of advertising and labelling.

TYPES OF ADVERTISING

Editorial advertising

The **British Codes of Advertising and Sales Promotion** (print advertising), and the **Independent Television Commission Code of Advertising Standards & Practice ('ITC Code')** and **Radio Authority Codes of Advertising Standards and Practice ('Radio Authority Code')** (broadcast advertising) all require that advertisements be clearly distinguishable as such and recognisably separate from programmes or editorial material (see also Chapter 10).

Product placement

The **ITC Code** and **Radio Authority Code** prohibit product placement and an independent television company was recently fined by the ITC for infringing this provision. Although there is no such restriction on films shown in UK cinemas, there is a question as to whether the broadcasting of films on UK television might, insofar as they contain placed products, infringe the ITC Code. No case is known of, however, where enforcement action has been taken against a UK TV station in this regard.

Subliminal advertising

This is prohibited by law as well as by the codes covering broadcast advertising (see also Chapter 10).

Outdoor advertising

This includes billboards, bus shelters and other physical media. Planning restrictions prevent the display of print advertising without the permission of the local authority responsible for town and country planning in the area in question.

There is no planning restriction, however, on the display of print advertising in an enclosed place such as a football ground or railway station, nor is there any planning control on the use of print advertising on vehicles such as buses and taxis and inside public buildings.

However, advertisements for the London Underground need to be cleared by the **Advertising Standards Authority (ASA)** and as the following two cases demonstrate, marketers face inconsistencies within the self-adjudication process.

LAW IN ACTION

Adult radio station **Heart 106.2** wanted to appeal to a late night adult audience and run 'Just another night' advertisements on the London Underground. The advertisement showed two clothed adults although the male is checking out the elastic of his female companion's top while she bears down on him in a passionate embrace.

London Underground Limited refused to carry the advertisement but allowed a similar campaign for a film entitled 'The Escort' which at first sight seemed even more raunchy. The copy on the advertisement read: 'I'll be your friend, I'll be your lover, but it's strictly by the hour' and the male looks at his watch while in close contact with the female.

Why the difference? The answer, according to the ASA which rejected complaints for the film was that apparently the naked couple shown close-up were at such an angle to each other it would have been physically impossible for them to be doing anything except embracing, whereas the Heart 106.2 advertisement was far more suggestive.

Apart from planning law restrictions, the law of trespass prevents the display of advertising on the walls of buildings or on fences without the consent of the owner.

There will be a trespass also if the advertisement over-hangs the property of another, or is distributed in a way which interferes with the property of another, e.g. by lifting a car windscreen wiper to put a hand-bill under it.

Trespass is a tort (civil wrong) for which the property owner may recover damages from the trespasser or obtain a court order or injunction preventing further trespass. Affixing posters to property without the owner's consent can also amount to the criminal offence of criminal damage.

Telephone canvassing

The **Consumer Protection (Distance Selling) Regulations 2000** which came into force in October 2000 give consumers confidence in purchasing goods and services where there is no face to face contact with the marketer, and ensure that all marketers operating distance selling schemes meet the basic requirements laid down in the Regulations.

Recently consumers have been known to enter new contracts for gas or electricity over the telephone without realising they have done so and in some cases without even knowing the identity of the new supplier. It is often the most vulnerable people who unwittingly find themselves with a new contract.

Under the Regulations consumers shopping for goods and services by telephone, mail order, fax, digital television and the Internet have the right to:

- Be told at the outset of the call the identity of the marketer, the purpose of the call and be given clear information about the goods or services offered

- To be sent written confirmation after making a purchase

- A cooling off period of seven working days to cancel any contract

- Protection against fraudulent use of credit cards

The **Office of Fair Trading (OFT)** and **Trading Standards Offices** have a duty to consider any complaint about a possible breach of the regulations. Where it is considered that a breach has occurred, the OFT has the power to apply for an injunction in the courts against the marketer in order to obtain compliance with the Regulations.

However, the OFT *cannot* take up an individual's dispute with a marketer nor can it obtain redress for the complainant.

The Regulations apply to almost all types of home shopping but there are exceptions:

■ Business to business contracts

■ Financial services

■ Auctions

■ Contracts for the sale of land

■ Automated vending machines or automated commercial premises

Some of the Regulations will *not* apply to:

■ Deliveries of food and beverages

■ Transport, accommodation, catering or leisure services provided on specific dates or within specified periods

■ Timeshare agreements

■ Package holidays

Gas and electricity marketers, such as npower®, have recently been told to clean up telephone canvassing practices or face action by the OFT. The consumer watchdog is increasingly concerned about the high pressure telephone canvassing methods used by a number of energy marketers attempting to get consumers to switch suppliers.

The Regulations ensure that consumers are protected from rogue telesales staff.

Direct mail advertising

The **Consumer Protection (Distance Selling) Regulations** provide a statutory right to opt-out of receiving such material. More recently transparency is also a requirement of the E-Commerce Directive in respect of providing name, address of marketer and clear prices.

In addition, the **Companies Act 1985** obliges a limited company to carry its place of registration, registered number and the address of its registered office on, amongst other things, any order form which it prints, for example in an advertisement. In some cases, the law requires that certain facts be made available to the customer before buying.

These requirements apply to advertisements inviting orders off the page as well as to the display of goods in retail premises.

Internet advertising

There is as yet no UK legislation that specifically governs advertising on the Internet as the E-Commerce Directive has not yet been implemented in the UK and the **European Union (EU) Sales Promotions Directive** is still at the Consultation Stage. Judicial and administrative decisions have held that ordinary principles apply but have yet to clarify fully the difficult issues of jurisdiction.

The self-regulatory advertising control system administered by the **Committee of Advertising Practice** and the **Advertising Standards Authority** is applied to advertising on the Internet placed by UK-based marketers who have by and large accepted ASA findings.

Use of the Internet by marketers in the UK as regards any processing of personal data falls under the **Data Protection Act 1998** and the jurisdiction of the Information Commissioner (see Chapter 15).

The **Direct Marketing Association (DMA)** has issued Codes for its members covering marketing in an E commerce context and marketers should regularly consult and respect the opt-out register, part of the DMA's e-mail preference service.

THE ADVERTISING REGULATORS

Television and radio advertising

The UK, as a EU Member State, is subject to a number of the **EU Broadcasting Directives**, which have been implemented largely by the **Broadcasting Act 1990**.

The ITC

The ITC was set up under the **Broadcasting Act 1990**. It is given the power by the government to control the content of all broadcasting on the licensed or independent television channels (e.g. those that carry advertising including cable and satellite) and its power extends to controls over the content of advertising.

It has published the **ITC Code** which all independent television companies must follow when accepting television commercials for broadcast. In practice, the Code is administered by the **Broadcast Advertising Clearance Centre (BACC)**, which pre-vets almost all UK broadcast advertising on behalf of the commercial television networks.

The ITC also publishes and enforces a **Code of Programme Sponsorship**, which 'sets standards and practice in the sponsoring of programmes and identifies the methods of sponsorship to be prohibited or to be prohibited in particular circumstances'.

All independent television companies are required to comply as a condition of their licence. For further discussion of the Code, see Chapter 10.

The Radio Authority

The Radio Authority was, like the ITC, set up under the auspices of the **Broadcasting Act 1990**, and it has exactly parallel powers. It also publishes the **Radio Authority Code** and a **Code on Programme Sponsorship** with which all radio advertising must comply.

The Radio Code is different in some details from the ITC Code and is administered by the **Radio Advertising Clearance Centre (RACC)** in the same way as the BACC, but in a radio advertising context. For further discussion of the Code, see Chapter 10.

The Broadcasting Standards Commission (BSC)

The BSC receives complaints from the public concerning 'unjust or unfair treatment or unwarranted infringement of privacy' on all UK TV networks including the BBC and is also concerned with:

> *... practices to be followed in connection with the portrayal of violence and practices to be followed in connection with the portrayal of sexual conduct and standards of taste and decency.*

While the BSC is not given specific authority to control advertising content on television or radio, its power is wide enough to apply to advertising. In principle this could bring them into conflict with the ITC and the Radio Authority, although to date this does not appear to have occurred.

Self-regulatory bodies can be divided broadly into two types: those which were established and given their powers by statute, principally for the broadcast media, and those that are purely voluntary organisations having no statutory authority, e.g. the Advertising Standards Authority (ASA) and the Committee of Advertising Practice (CAP).

The CAP

This is a committee composed of representatives from a wide range of bodies involved in advertising, including bodies representing media owners (such as the **Newspaper Society**), advertisers (such as the **Advertising Association**) and advertising agencies (such as the **Institute of Practitioners in Advertising**).

It publishes the **British Codes of Advertising and Sales Promotion (BCASP)** which governs most advertising in Britain (except television and radio advertising which are governed by the ITC and Radio Authority Codes mentioned above).

The CAP is a self-regulatory body without statutory powers, but its media members agree not to accept any advertising which contravenes the BCASP. Nevertheless, many advertisements and sales promotion schemes do get through the net and complaints are received by the CAP (or the ASA, see below). The consequences of a complaint of breach of the Codes are described below.

The ASA

The ASA was set up in 1962 to oversee the workings of the **CAP** and monitors advertisements on its own account and will, in appropriate circumstances, intervene to stop an advertisement which it considers contravenes the BCASP, even if no complaint has been received.

It is independent of both the government and the advertising industry and acts as a self-regulatory body for the advertising industry, overseeing *non-broadcast* advertisements in the UK.

It promotes 'legal, decent, honest *and* truthful' advertising by means of the BCASP. The Committee's members include representatives from the advertising, sales promotion and media businesses and responds to all complaints in respect of non-broadcast advertisements made to it in writing by mail or online at **www.asa.org.uk**.

The ASA works to ensure that its guidelines are adopted and adhered to by all those in the marketing profession, from publishers to advertising and sales promotion companies and its activities include investigating complaints. The full code is available on http://www/bh.com/companions/0750655003.

The ASA's remit covers advertisements in paid-for space on-line, including banner and pop-up advertisements, sales promotion anywhere on-line and commercial

The ASA Codes apply to the following non-broadcast media:

- Advertisements in newspapers, magazines, brochures, leaflets, circulars, mailings, fax transmissions, catalogues, follow-up literature and other electronic and printed material
- Posters and other promotional media in public places
- Cinema and video commercials
- Advertisements in non-broadcast electronic media
- Viewdata services
- Marketing databases containing consumers' personal information
- Sales promotions
- Advertisement promotions
- Advertisements and promotions covered by the Cigarette Code

e-mails. It does not cover general product information on home pages (see also Chapter 15).

If a marketer wants publicly to commit to keeping its on-line advertisements legal, decent, honest and truthful, it can join the *admark* scheme. This was set up by the Committee and is supported by the ASA.

The admark scheme

The admark scheme is an opt-in scheme that allows marketers to promote their support for legal, decent, honest and truthful advertising by:

- Displaying the admark icon on their 'paid for' advertisements
- Providing information about the scheme on their web sites

The admark scheme enables consumers to tell who has pledged to follow its rules and is dependent on a higher level of awareness amongst consumers than it enjoys at present (see **www.admark.org.uk**).

In the event of a complaint or a request for a (non-binding) pre-clearance, the Committee reviews the advertisement in question in the light of the **ASA Codes**.

Conformity with the ASA Codes is assessed according to the advertisement's probable impact when taken as a whole and in context. This will depend on the medium in which the advertisement appeared, the audience and their likely response, the nature of the product and any additional material distributed to consumers.

Alternatively the ASA may request media companies (e.g. publishers and poster site contractors) to invoke their standard terms of practice, which all include adherence to the ASA

POINT OF LAW

If the Committee finds the advertisement to be in breach of the ASA Codes it can request that the marketer withdraws the advertisement from all media. If the marketer fails to do so, regardless of any pending appeal it can be 'named and shamed' in the ASA's weekly report of its findings published on the ASA web site.

Codes.

As a consequence the media companies may refuse to publish further advertisements of the offending marketer until the situation is rectified.

It is advisable for marketers to address any concerns in advance of publication and pre-empt any potential problems (this is obligatory with respect to tobacco marketers – see Chapter 16).

This can be done by obtaining legal advice in respect of each proposed advertisement or alternatively it is possible to pre-clear advertisements with the ASA (further information is given in Chapter 10).

Independent Committee for the Supervision of Standards of Telephone Information Services (ICSTIS)

ICSTIS regulates the content and promotion of premium rate telephone services advertised in the UK and is responsible for setting and reviewing standards within the industry.

This is achieved through its **Codes of Practice** that can be found on its web site: **www.icstis.org.uk**.

It investigates public complaints, monitors services, recommends measures to achieve compliance with the Code and publishes information relating to its work.

If a marketer operates a premium rate service, it will be automatically bound by the ICSTIS Codes. Premium rate service providers are licensed by the UK regulator for the telecommunications industry (OFTEL) and under the terms of the licence the marketer undertakes to comply with the ICSTIS Code.

If such premium rate services are used in advertisements or sales promotions, they must comply with the ICSTIS Codes. For example, the marketer must ensure that the charge for calls to each service is clearly stated in all promotions. In addition prices must be noted in the form of a numerical price per minute, inclusive of VAT, or the total maximum cost to the consumer of the complete message or service.

In respect of promotional material involving premium rate services aimed at children, the ICSTIS Code provides that the material must state the maximum possible cost of the service and highlight that the service should only be used with the consent of the person responsible for paying the telephone bill.

GENERAL LEGAL PRINCIPLES

Is a marketer contractually bound to sell products/services at the price advertised?

In most cases a marketer is not contractually bound by its advertising.

As discussed in Chapter 2, one of the fundamental ingredients of a binding contract is the acceptance of an offer. The generally accepted view is that an advertisement amounts only to an 'invitation to treat', the 'offer' only occurring when the customer responds to the advertisement by identifying the product that they wish to purchase and proffering the purchase price.

The 'acceptance' occurs when the money is taken by the retailer and the purchase handed over. The rationale for this is that the marketer should not be obliged by contract to supply to every single respondent to its advertising, otherwise it would be placed in an invidious position were the advertising to be so successful that it ran out of stock!

Can advertisements ever be a contractual offer?

Not usually, but as ever with principles of law, there can be exceptions. For example, if the advertisement is worded in such a way as to suggest that the marketer does regard it as a contractual offer by which it is happy to be bound to all who respond to it, then it will be regarded as an offer.

> **LAW IN ACTION**
>
> In the 1891 **Carlill-v-Carbolic Smoke Ball case**, an advert stated that the sum of £100 reward would be paid to all who bought the smoke ball and still contracted flu. As earnest evidence of its commitment, Carbolic announced that the sum of £100 had been placed on deposit at an identified bank. Mrs Carlill saw the advertisement, bought the product, contracted flu and sued Carbolic for the £100.
>
> She won on the basis that the advertisement's content clearly showed an intention to be bound and should be regarded as in the nature of a contractual offer.

Are e-tail sites contractual offers rather than advertising?

There is danger of this. Therefore, as the marketers will want to retain control over the contracts, this is why most e-tail web site terms and conditions state clearly that a contract will not be regarded as formed until the ordered goods are dispatched or the marketer has e-mailed the customer to confirm that the product is in stock and is being shipped.

What about marketers who advertise but do not sell to the end user?

The marketer may not have a contract problem, but a misleading advertisement could lead to local authority Trading Standards Office taking an interest with a view to initiating a criminal prosecution for offences under:

■ Trade Descriptions Act 1968 (materially false product descriptions)

▨ Consumer Protection Act 1987 (misleading price indications)

▨ Food Safety Act 1990 (false descriptions relating to food)

to name but a few, while the ASA may become involved either through a complaint from a consumer or competitor marketer or intervening itself.

When devising an advertising campaign or formulating labelling of products, marketers should also bear in mind that there are various regulatory bodies which are relevant as they have their own additional rules or guidelines in respect of advertising for particular products, services or professions.

Professional Body	Type of Marketer
Association of British Pharmaceutical Industry	Medicinal product marketers
Law Society	Solicitors in England and Wales
British Herbal Medicine Association	Herbal remedies and health supplements marketers
Investment Management Regulatory Organisation	Investment and financial services marketers
Securities and Futures Authority	Financial products marketers
Financial Services Authority	Financial services marketers
Institute of Chartered Accountants	Chartered accountants marketers
Portman Group	Alcoholic drinks marketers

Fig. 9.3 Examples of industry-specific regulatory bodies

MISLEADING ADVERTISING

If a marketer creates an advertisement which is misleading it may be caught in a variety of legal traps. For example, the advertisement may infringe a registered trademark (see Chapter 5) or constitute a malicious falsehood (see Chapter 3).

If the advertisement is misleading as to the product advertised, then subject to a few exceptions, it is likely to be caught by the Control of Misleading Advertising Regulations 1988.

Control of Misleading Advertising Regulations 1988 (the Misleading Advertising Regulations)

An 'advertisement' is defined by the **Misleading Advertising Regulations** as:

... any form of representation which is made in connection with a trade, business, craft or profession in order to promote the supply or transfer of goods or services, immovable property, rights or obligations.

The Misleading Advertising Regulations do **not** apply to investment or other finance related advertisements (see Chapter 16).

Definition of a misleading advertisement

For the purposes of the **Misleading Advertising Regulations** an advertisement is misleading if in any way:

... it deceives or is likely to deceive the persons to whom it is addressed or whom it reaches and if, by reason of its deceptive nature, it is likely to affect their economic behaviour or, for those reasons, injures or is likely to injure a competitor of the person whose interests the advertisement seeks to promote.

LAW IN ACTION

Office of Fair Trading-v-Tobyard (1989)

In this case, the marketer made the following claims in its advertising of a slimming product:

- The product could result in permanent weight loss
- Success was guaranteed
- The product contained an ingredient which was a scientific breakthrough
- The product prevented fats entering the bloodstream
- The product enabled the user to lose a specific amount of weight in a specified time
- The product was 100% safe in all cases

All the above claims were found by the court to be misleading and likely to deceive the persons to whom it was addressed by making false claims for the product and was likely to induce those persons to buy the product.

The OFT

The OFT is required to consider complaints about misleading advertisements, other than those within commercial broadcasting (for which see Chapter 10).

The complainant will need to demonstrate to the OFT's satisfaction that other appropriate means of dealing with the complaint had failed to resolve the issue of the advertisement in question.

POINT OF LAW

For example, this would include complaining to a local Trading Standards Office or to a self-regulatory body such as the ASA. The OFT may then bring proceedings for an injunction to prevent publication or continued publication of the advertisement in question.

However, the most likely first steps taken by the OFT on upholding a complaint would be to seek assurances from the marketer that it will modify or not repeat an offending advertisement.

The threat of action by the OFT may also be enough to ensure compliance, as the next case demonstrates.

LAW IN ACTION

In November 2001, the **OFT** used its new powers to threaten applications to the court for immediate 'Stop Now' orders banning conduct contrary to consumer protection legislation.

Allied Carpets of Orpington, **Furnitureland** of Penge, **Fairway Furniture** of Plymouth and **Gregory & Porritts** of Bolton were all allegedly publishing misleading advertising by promoting supposedly illusory interest free credit or 0% finance deals.

The illusion arose because interest was in fact charged on the whole of the loan if a lump sum was not paid off in full at the end of the 1 year interest free period. All four marketers backed down before court action was taken and agreed to stop this form of advertising.

The **ITC** is under a similar duty to consider complaints about broadcast advertisements on commercial television and it may refuse to allow an advertisement to be broadcast which it considers to be misleading.

The Regulations place the **Radio Authority** under a similar duty to investigate in respect of misleading advertisements on commercial radio. It has the power to give directions including not to transmit the advertisement.

See Chapter 10 for further discussion of these Regulations.

Trade Descriptions Act 1968

A marketer may also be prosecuted under the **Trade Descriptions Act 1968** if the advertisement contains a false trade description.

The 1968 Act's primary purpose is to ensure truthful advertising and a trade description covers claims in respect of:

- Quantity of goods
- Size or gauge of goods
- How the goods were made or processed
- What the goods are made of
- The goods' fitness for purpose
- The goods' strength, performance, behaviour or accuracy
- Any other physical characteristics which the goods possess
- Where, when and by whom the goods were made

In relation to services this includes a description of the manner in which a service is provided.

The falsehoods in respect of both trade and services must be material in order to bring about a prosecution. As far as enforcement is concerned, local Trading Standards Offices are under a statutory duty to enforce the provisions of the 1968 Act which confers on them the power of entry, inspection and seizure of the marketer's property.

COMPARATIVE ADVERTISING

Comparative advertising, sometimes also known as 'knocking copy', is advertising which identifies a competitor. It can be direct or indirect, positive or negative.

POINT OF LAW

For example, direct comparative advertising is where an advertisement explicitly compares a product with another named product such as brand X batteries last three times longer than brand Y batteries.

Indirect comparative advertising is where only one product is specifically described but is said to be better than competing products.

POINT OF LAW

For example, an advertisement which states that brand X nappies are more absorbent than all other nappy brands on the market.

Positive comparative advertising aims to take advantage of the reputation of a competitor's product by identifying one product with the other.

A negative comparative advertisement, on the other hand, aims to alert the consumer to the differences between the two products in a way which casts a bad light on the competitor's product.

Promoting a product at the expense of a rival is becoming a fashionable advertising strategy in the UK and has its roots in the US. The right to freedom of speech enshrined in the US constitution gives marketers plenty of scope to talk about rivals in their advertising and many have been unable to resist the opportunity of casting their competitors in an unfavourable light.

POINT OF LAW

For example, IT giant **Oracle** frequently uses comparative advertising. Its campaigns frequently suggest that its software products run faster than those of **IBM**. According to Oracle, pre- and post-campaign research among its target audience suggests that if the message that Oracle is faster than IBM is repeated often enough, it will stick subliminally in the minds of its customers. Oracle frequently looks at IBM's web site, sees what it is claiming and uses it against it. Alternatively, Oracle will use an independent survey as a factual comparison for its products.

But direct and aggressive advertising is not exclusively a US preserve. In recent years, there has been a distinct rise in comparative advertising in the UK, and a corresponding increase in the legislative and regulatory provisions marketers planning comparative campaigns should be aware of.

The rules governing comparative advertising are vigorously enforced by the courts and this is one of the most litigious areas of marketing practice for many marketers.

The fact that there is no immunity from the regulations even if the comparative advertising is published by an entity other than the one offering competing goods or services means that everyone involved in comparative advertising will need to pay attention to the following:

POINT OF LAW

The main pieces of legislation that cover comparative advertising:

■ The Control of Misleading Advertisements (Amendment) Regulations 2000
■ EU Injunctions for the Protection of Consumers' Interests Directive (2001)
■ EU Misleading and Comparative Advertising Directive (2001)

The Codes

Broadcast media: television

In the UK broadcast and non-broadcast advertising are regulated by similar but separate regimes, although injured competitors in broadcast media have arguably quicker means of recourse than in the non-broadcast media.

In the case of broadcast advertising, all broadcasters licensed by the **ITC** must comply with the terms of their licence which will include provisions on advertising, and with the ITC Code of Advertising and Standards Practice.

Therefore all advertisements broadcast on terrestrial television, on non-domestic satellite services which operate from the UK but do not use broadcasting frequencies allocated to the UK, on cable and on public teletext services will have to comply with the Code's provisions on comparative advertising.

These prohibit advertising which directly or by implication unfairly attack or discredit other products, advertisers or advertisements. For the latest version of the code see **www.itc.org.uk**.

Note that on-line advertisements are not regulated by the ITC. The ITC does not vet advertisements prior to broadcast; instead advertisers and agencies may submit adverts to the **BACC** for advice prior to transmission about compliance with the ITC Codes.

For all advertisements except local ones, which may be cleared by the broadcaster, the BACC will scrutinise scripts prior to production of the video as well as partially completed videos and finished commercials.

Although submission to the BACC is voluntary and can never be regarded as a guarantee of legality, broadcasters will be reluctant to carry advertisements which have not been viewed by the BACC since non-compliance with the ITC Codes can result in fines and revocation of the licence to broadcast.

Companies and individuals can make complaints to the ITC about infringements of the Code. The ITC has a statutory duty to investigate all complaints. All 'complaints of substance' are listed in a monthly report where the assessment is reported along with the responsible agency. In addition to imposing penalties on the broadcaster, the ITC is able to forbid the broadcast of any advertisement in breach of the Code.

For further discussion, see Chapter 10.

Broadcast media: radio

The **Radio Authority** licenses and regulates all commercial radio services in the UK. One of the conditions of a Radio Authority licence is compliance with the **Radio Authority Advertising and Sponsorship Code**, the latest version of which can be found at **http://www.radioauthority.org.uk**.

The Code will apply to all adverts broadcast on national, local, cable, satellite and restricted services, on both analogue and digital platforms.

Examples of restricted services are special event radio and localised permanent services such as hospital and student radio. The Radio Authority requires that advertisements for products in one of the Code's 'special categories' and those for national transmission are submitted to the **RACC** for clearance.

Also when advertising copy is 6 months old or more it must be re-submitted to the RACC. The presence of an RACC clearance form does not guarantee transmission as the ultimate decision to accept a campaign rests with the broadcaster.

Consumers and companies may complain directly to the Radio Authority whose sanctions include broadcast apologies and/or corrections, fines and the shortening or revocation of licences.

For further discussion, see Chapter 10.

Non-broadcast media

Advertisements in newspapers, magazines, posters, brochures, leaflets, cinema and video cassettes must comply with the requirements of the **BCASP**.

The **ASA** supervises compliance with BCASP by monitoring a selection of advertisements and investigating complaints but it does not pre-vet them.

The **CAP**, which publishes the Codes, offers pre-publication advice to advertisers, agencies and media. The general principles of the BCASP relating to comparative advertising are that comparisons should be clear and fair and not selected in a way that would give competitors an artificial advantage.

Consumers and companies may complain to the ASA who will investigate the complaint if they decide it provides a case for investigation because it is within the scope of the ASA's work and it does not arise from a misunderstanding of the advertisement.

All complaints investigated appear in the *ASA Monthly Report*. The ASA can request a broadcaster to remove an offending advertisement but does not have the power to compel broadcasters to do so.

However, it is able to refer a case to the **Director-General of Fair Trading** who may apply for an injunction under the **Control of Misleading Advertisement Regulations 1998** (see below). In addition to this manufacturers and publishers will be reluctant to use advertisers who are frequently the subject of ASA reports.

The Control of Misleading Advertisements (Comparative Advertisements) (Amendment) Regulations 2000

The effect of **Directive 97/55EC on Comparative Advertising** was to harmonise EU law so that both indirect and direct comparative advertising are allowed in all EU Member States *subject* to certain conditions the advertisements have to satisfy in order to be legal.

The Control of Misleading Advertisement Regulations 1998, now amended by the Control of Misleading Advertisements (Comparative Advertisements) (Amendment) Regulations 2000, which came into force in April 2000, implement this Directive in the UK.

The amended Regulations define 'comparative advertising' as:

... any advertisement which, in any way, either explicitly or by implication, identifies a competitor or goods or services offered by a competitor.

Any advertisement falling within this definition caught will *automatically* be illegal **unless** it satisfies *all* the following requirements:

1. It is not misleading

2. It compares goods or services meeting the same needs or intended for the same purpose

3. It objectively compares one or more material, relevant, verifiable and representative features of those goods and services, which may include price

4. It does not create confusion in the market place between the marketer and a competitor or between the marketer's trademarks, trade names, other distinguishing marks, goods or services and those of a competitor

5. It does not discredit or denigrate the trademarks, trade names, other distinguishing marks, goods, services, activities or circumstances of a competitor

6. For products with designation of origin, it relates in each case to products with the same designation

7. It does not take unfair advantage of the reputation of a trademark, trade name or other distinguishing marks of a competitor or of the designation of origin of competing products

8. It does not present goods or services as imitations or replicas of goods or services bearing a protected trademark or trade name.

If the comparative advertisement promotes a 'special offer' then further rules apply:

Any comparison referring to a special offer shall indicate in a clear and unequivocal way the date on which the offer ends or, where appropriate, that the special offer is subject to the availability of goods and services, and, where the special offer has not yet begun, the date of the start of the period during which the special price or other specific conditions shall apply.

The Amendment Regulations do not provide a means by which one competitor can sue another over a comparative advertisement but they do provide a mechanism which one advertiser can use to threaten another with if the former does not desist in his comparative advertising campaign.

This is because it extends the provisions of the **1998 Regulations** which require the Director General of Fair Trading to consider complaints (other than frivolous or vexatious ones) about misleading advertisements to complaints concerning comparative advertisements.

This means that the Director General of Fair Trading must consider all complaints brought to him about advertisements other than broadcast advertisements (which are dealt with by the ITC and the Radio Authority).

If the Director General considers that all existing means of regulation have been exhausted (such as a complaint to the ASA) and considers the advertisement to be misleading he may apply to the court under the **Control of Misleading Advertisement Regulations 1998, Regulation 6** for an injunction.

If he does not do so, he must provide the complainant with the reason for not making such an application.

The court will take all interests into account, including the public interest, and if it considers the application to be misleading it will grant an injunction to prevent the continued publication of an advertisement.

The Trademarks Act 1994

Only the proprietor or a registered user of a trademark is entitled to reproduce it. However, comparative advertising in all media will often reproduce the trademark of a competitor. **Section 10(6) of the Trademarks Act 1994** provides that:

Nothing in the preceding provisions of this section should be construed as preventing the use of a registered trademark by any person for the purpose of identifying goods or services of those of the proprietor or a licensee.

However, this is qualified in order to prohibit detrimental use of the mark:

But any such use otherwise than in accordance with honest practices in industrial or commercial matters shall be treated as infringing the registered trademark if the use without due cause takes advantage of or is detrimental to the distinctive character or repute of the trademark.

Infringement of a competitor's trademark in comparative advertising could result in a claim for damages and/or a proportion of the defendant's profits, withdrawal of the offending advertisement and payment of the competitor's legal costs.

LAW IN ACTION

The first case to be decided under **Section 10(6)** of the **Trademarks Act 1994** was **Barclays Bank plc-v-RBS Advanta (1996)** which considered whether a table which compared the features of two credit cards side by side infringed the competitor's mark.

It was held that the test for infringement was an objective one and would not be satisfied unless a reasonable audience considered the use to be otherwise than in accordance with an honest practice and whether the use of the trademark gave the defendant some advantage or inflicted some harm on the repute of the mark which was more than minimal.

The judge, Mr Justice Laddie, held that it was unlikely that a reasonable reader would see the advertisement as dishonest.

Other recent cases in this area show that the courts have taken a robust approach to actions for trademark infringement in the context of comparative advertising.

LAW IN ACTION

For example, the High Court found in favour of **Ryanair** when it was unsuccessfully sued by **British Airways** in a high-profile legal battle over its comparative advertisement headlined 'Expensive BA . . . . DS', which contrasted the carriers' prices on certain European routes.

BA claimed the advertisement brought its brand into disrepute.

When ruling in favour of Ryanair, the judge, Mr Justice Jacob, called it 'immature' in bringing the action saying that the advertisement was no more than vulgar abuse.

Five years earlier, the same judge had dismissed as 'hopeless' a case brought by Vodafone against mobile phone rival Orange concerning the latter's comparative advertising.

LAW IN ACTION

In that case, the advertisement said 'On average, **Orange** users save £20 every month'.

The saving was expressly stated to be in comparison with **Vodafone's** 'equivalent tariffs'.

The claim for trademark infringement failed because the judge found that the statement made by Orange was true and not misleading.

Use of competitors' names in comparative advertising should always be referred to a lawyer before published, as opinions may vary between different judges as to what is fair and what is not.

Passing off

Comparative advertisements carry a risk that a consumer will identify or confuse one product with the product of a competitor. Where this results in damage to a product it could result in an action in tort for passing off. However, where a reasonable consumer would not be confused as to the origin of each product in a comparative advertisement, an action for passing off will not succeed.

Copyright

Advertisers engaging in comparative practices should be careful not to infringe copyright in the material they are using. There may be an artistic copyright in the artwork of a competitor product's container for example. This would be infringed by reproduction of that artwork without consent of the copyright owner.

Malicious falsehood ('trade libel')

A claim of this nature may be brought where a manufacturer of a product has made, in a comparative advertisement, a false statement in relation to a competitor which is (a) malicious and (b) has caused damage.

The following case is an example of a successful claim for trade libel.

LAW IN ACTION

Compaq Computer Corporation-v-Dell Computer Corporation Ltd (1992)

In this case Dell Computers were issued with an injunction to stop publishing advertisements which compared the price and features of various models of the two brands of computers in the form of a table with two columns which also contained pictures.

Beside the pictures was the wording 'Dell's new 386 desktop systems are basically the same as Compaq's. Yet Compaq's systems are, quite literally, thousands of pounds higher'.

Compaq based its claim on the fact that the advertisement was not comparing like for like; for example a 100MB computer was being compared in price to a 12MB computer.

The judge found that in these circumstances a statement that the two computers were 'basically the same' did constitute trade libel.

How the system works

The new comparative advertising rules do NOT give competitors the right to sue each other for 'knocking copy' that breaks the new Regulations.

POINT OF LAW

But if brand owner A is unhappy about competitor B's comparative advertising claims, these regulations give A an extra stick to beat B with by way of threats to report B to the OFT or consumer groups, unless B stops making the offending claims.

So far as legal proceedings are concerned, litigation can arise by way of applications to the court by the OFT so long as it is satisfied that all 'existing means' for regulating the comparative advertisement in question (e.g. in a printed or on-line advertising context, the ASA/CAP scheme) has been used and has failed to prevent continued use of the offending advertisement.

Broadcast advertising: a different regime

In the case of broadcast advertising, injunction applications are not necessary, since the ITC and the Radio Authority are the 'existing means' of regulation and if they are satisfied that an advertisement breaches the comparative advertising regulations they will simply order their licensees not to carry the advertising in question (for further discussion, see Chapter 10).

Who triggers the Regulations?

A competitor marketer or consumer may complain to the ASA, ITC or Radio Authority depending on the medium in which the comparative advertisement appears.

Alternatively they may go directly to the OFT – a tactical manoeuvre and one which may be useful in sending a warning shot carried out under the gaze of publicity in the media.

However, if they do this, the OFT will refer the matter back to the relevant regulatory body and will only consider applying to the court for an injunction if, despite adverse findings by the ASA for example, the marketer continues using the offending advertisement.

Since January 2001 when the **EU Injunctions for the Protection of Consumers' Interests Directive** was implemented across Europe, for the first time in the UK, organisations representing consumers, such as the Consumers' Association and any other bodies which meet the laid-down criteria, are able to apply to the court direct to enforce a range of consumer protection measures.

These measures have been introduced across the EU by way of Directives over the last 15 years and one of the Directives consumer associations are able to police is the **EU Misleading and Comparative Advertising Directive**.

In a sense, UK marketers now face a 'double whammy' with the less than delightful prospect of complying with the **Control of Misleading Advertising (Amendment) Regulations 2000** as well as attempting to avoid the attentions of eagle-eyed **consumer organisations** looking for an opportunity to justify their existence and use their brand new powers.

So what impact are the Regulations likely to have?

According to some commentators, these new Regulations will have a significant impact for marketers.

In the past, the OFT was constrained to apply for court injunctions in a small number of cases and predictably these powers were used only in respect of recidivist 'fringe' marketers advertising products such as hair restorers, slimming aids and get-rich-quick schemes.

However, increasingly the ASA in its findings in respect of 'knocking copy' has been taking on board the concepts of the **EU Misleading and Comparative Advertising Directive.**

The EU Directive provides that only products meeting the *same* needs can be compared.

Now that the **Control of Misleading Advertising (Amendment) Regulations 2000** are in force, marketers who are nimble enough to avoid these risks will still not be home and dry as they may be caught out by the 'same needs' provision (see below).

A departure from existing rules on comparative advertising

One of the reasons why the impact of the **Control of Misleading Advertising (Amendment) Regulations 2000** was minimal was that the definition of 'misleading' was little more than a re-articulation of existing rules, such as those contained in the ASA/CAP British Code of Advertising.

These new regulations, on the other hand, are in significant ways a material departure from the existing regulatory landscape.

Inconsistencies with pre-existing Codes?

Up until May 2000, existing ASA/CAP Print Advertising Code did not require in terms that 'only' goods or services 'meeting the same needs' or 'intended for the same purposes' could be compared.

Separately, neither the ITC Code nor for that matter the ASA/CAP Code required expressly that comparative advertisements must 'objectively compare one or more material, relevant, verifiable and representative features' of the products in question.

Similarly, there was no specific requirement contained in either of the Codes, or in any existing legislation, that if an advertisement referred to a special offer the advertisement had to, in all cases, in a clear and unequivocal way, indicate the date on which the special offer ended or, if the offer had not yet begun at the time the advertisement was published, give the date of the start of the offer.

The Regulations' requirement that if appropriate the offer should be expressed to be 'subject to availability' was also not necessarily an absolute rule under any existing Code or Regulation.

Can a marketer reproduce a competitor's trademark in the interests of vigorous competition?

The answer to this question depends on whether the competitor marketer's trademark is registered in the UK for the products that are featured in the comparative advertisement.

If this is the case, then there will be *prima facie* infringement of the trademark if the court is satisfied that it is being used 'otherwise than in accordance with honest practices in industrial or commercial matters' and this 'without due cause takes unfair advantage of or is detrimental to, the distinctive character or repute of the trademark'.

> **POINT OF LAW**
>
> In simple English, so long as the comparative advertisement is not significantly misleading the marketer should be within the law.

Effect on broadcast media?

For a discussion on how the Codes and Regulations affect broadcast media, see Chapter 10.

What legal risks does comparative advertising present for a marketer in the UK?

Apart from the extensive new rules introduced by way of the **Control of Misleading Advertisements (Amendment) Regulations 2000** (above) and the impact of the **EU Misleading and Comparative Advertising Directive**, the principal legal risks for a marketer are legal actions for:

- Trademark infringement
- Trade libel
- Passing off
- Trade Descriptions Act 1968 (false product descriptions)
- Consumer Protection Act 1967 (misleading price indications)
- Consumer Credit Act 1974 (misleading credit deal offers).

Are the Rules now open to interpretation since EU Misleading and Comparative Advertising Directive?

As the discussion below indicates, the application of the rules is likely to vary between Member States in the EU, which will immediately result in differing interpretations of the rules depending on the jurisdiction that the marketer is operating within.

The 'comparative advertising' definition

All advertising can be argued as being 'comparative' in nature in that it seeks to persuade the consumer to buy the advertised product or service in preference to another competitor and of course marketers need to comply strictly with the Control of Misleading Advertisements (Comparative Advertisements) (Amendments) Regulations 2000.

However, what is caught by the new Regulations will be 'any advertising which explicitly or by implication identifies a competitor or goods or services of the same kind offered by a competitor'.

A critical question for marketers is when does a comparative advertisement 'by implication' identify a competitor?

POINT OF
LAW

For example, if there are only a handful of sources for a particular product or
service and these are all fairly well-known to the prospective customer (e.g.
national supermarket chains, electricity suppliers or cable TV services).

Applying the same test as for defamation (see Chapter 8), it could be argued strongly that
any comparative claim in advertising in these sectors 'identified competitors by implication'
and was therefore caught by the Regulations.

Advertising that 'objectively compares one or more material relevant verifiable and representative features'

Precisely what a 'material' or 'relevant' feature is may very well vary depending on the
particular requirements of the consumer and the cultural differences across the European
Union.

INSIGHT

Given that the underlying purpose of these Regulations is to facilitate comparative advertising moving freely across the EU, there is concern as to whether regulators in
Spain, Germany and Sweden, for example, are going to take exactly the same view as to
precisely what this requirement means.

**Comparative advertisements must not 'discredit or denigrate' the trademarks, trade names,
other distinguishing marks, goods, services, activities or circumstances of a competitor**

This is potentially inconsistent with existing UK law in this area. The Regulations do not
state for example, as does Section 10(6) of the Trademarks Act 1994 in a similar context, that the
'discrediting' or 'denigrating' may be permissible unless it is 'without due cause'.

It is unclear whether this means that however accurate and capable of substantiation the
'knocking copy' might be, it will still fall foul of the Regulations?

This is unlikely to be the case and so the Regulation is subject to the *proviso* that if the
comparative advertisement is accurate and capable of substantiation *and* provided it does not
offend against the Regulations, a marketer cannot be found to have 'discredited' or 'deni-
grated' its competitor.

The twin threats of a potentially more restrictive regime for marketers that indulge in
comparative advertising practices and injunction applications by consumer groups should not
be taken lightly by marketers contemplating long-running comparative advertising campaigns.

All comparative claims and references to special offers in UK advertising must now be
checked carefully against the Regulations.

The dangers of different interpretations of the complex new rules are such that despite the
EU Directive's laudable ambitions, prudent and responsible marketers may consider it appropriate to seek legal advice in respect of planned comparative advertising campaigns.

INTELLECTUAL PROPERTY RIGHTS (IPRs)

As discussed in Chapters 5 and 6, marketers will protect the integrity of the marketing campaign through the enforcement of IPRs and therefore care must be taken not to infringe the rights of any third party. The most relevant IPRs are likely to be copyright and trademark material.

All third party copyright material used in an advertisement must be cleared by the marketer prior to publication and the necessary assignments or licences obtained.

INSIGHT

This is not always straightforward, especially in relation to the use of music.

For example, in respect of any soundtrack used, the marketer must ensure that the rights have been obtained from the appropriate rights holders in the music itself and in the sound recording of the music. Copyright is dealt with in more detail in Chapter 6.

As mentioned in Chapter 5, a trademark is any distinctive sign which can distinguish the goods and services of one marketer from those of another and can include words, logos and pictures. They represent the goodwill associated with a marketer and can be immensely valuable.

A competitor marketer's trademark may be used in certain limited circumstances for the purposes of comparative advertising (see above).

AMBIENT MEDIA

As the name suggests, ambient advertising refers to the limitless possibilities presented by advertising on any non-standard medium outside the home.

Examples include:

- Advertising on taxis, buses, tube trains, lorries
- Flyposting (which is illegal)
- On the backs of car park tickets
- On hanging straps in railway carriages
- On the sides of egg and milk cartons
- On a larger scale, it includes projecting images on the side of a building and slogans on the side of a hot air balloon.

The ASA Codes apply to posters and other promotional media in public places and so such advertisements must comply with these rules and the legal restrictions outlined (above). The ASA Codes also regulate the use of such marketing techniques such as leaflet dispensers and the use of audio material.

It is important for marketers to consider what (if any) special rules apply to advertising on the particular ambient medium to be used.

In addition to the ASA Codes there are specific regulations which may apply depending on the nature of the ambient medium used.

Flyposting

Flyposting is an offence under the **Control of Advertisements Regulations 1992** punishable by a maximum fine of £1000 per advertisement. If the ambient marketer then fails to remove the posters they can also be committing a criminal offence under the **Criminal Damage Act 1971**.

Although rap and hip hop groups with new singles, remixes and albums regularly feature as the subject of flyposting advertising alongside other 'hip' marketers such as house, garage and rave clubs and gigs by popular local bands corporate marketers have also tried hard to copy this 'underground' and 'viral' marketing approach in order to make their brands more interesting than they would otherwise appear to be.

LAW IN ACTION

For example, in June 2001, insurance company **Royal & Sun Alliance** launched the 'Where's Lucky?' flyposting campaign throughout central London for the launch of a consumer insurance product. Westminster City Council complained and gave the marketer 48 hours to remove the offending posters or face prosecution. However, the publicity stunt caught the attention of the national media with 11 stories in the national press.

Taxi advertising

Advertising on licensed London taxis is further regulated by the **London Cab Order 1934** which gives the Public Carriage Office the power to give directions as to the display of any advertising material outside and inside cabs.

These rules are currently embodied in the Consolidated Guidelines on Advertising on Licensed London Taxis. Approval involves two stages, provisional and final.

For advertising on the outside of cabs, these must be viewed with the full livery adorning the outside for inspection.

For advertising on the inside of the cab, there are rules which indicate which areas and surfaces may carry adverts.

POINT OF LAW

Also, nakedness within adverts is strictly regulated and advertisements which 'seek to involve the driver as an agent of the advertiser' are forbidden.

ADVERTISING AND LABELLING OF SPECIFIC GOODS, SERVICES AND CAUSES

As with advertising there is a plethora of legislation dealing with the labelling of products and much of this emanates from the European Union which aims to harmonise the application of labelling on products.

> **POINT OF LAW**
>
> For example, the Directive on pre-packaged liquids (**EU Directive 75/106**) requires the presence of an 'e' mark on packaging. A small 'e' at least 3 mm high should be placed in the same field of vision as the indication of the nominal volume of the contents. The 'e' mark is a certification that the package complies with a prescribed standard.

There are many areas where there is regulation, some covered below. Areas such as the advertising and labelling of medicines, tobacco and cosmetics have their own specific requirements.

> **POINT OF LAW**
>
> ■ There are many complex labelling regulations and rules
>
> ■ Some products have their own self-regulatory bodies and codes
>
> ■ Some labelling requirements are mandatory, others may be added by the marketer in order to assist the consumer and sell the product, e.g. labelling a food product as 'kosher'

Financial services/credit

The **Consumer Credit Act 1974** imposes a licensing system on the various kinds of businesses that collectively make up the credit industry. The 1974 Act applies to Great Britain and Northern Ireland and is administered by the OFT.

A business that is connected in any way to the provision of credit, hire or hire purchase facilities where the debtor or hirer is a non-corporate may need a licence. In particular a licence will generally be required if a business intends to lend money, offer HP terms, issue trading checks or credit cards or sell on credit.

Advertisements for any such credit services must also comply with the terms of the 1974 Act.

Section 46 of the **1974 Act** renders it an offence to convey information which in a material respect is false or misleading. More detailed requirements as to the content of credit advertising are contained in the **Consumer Credit (Advertisements) Regulations 1989**.

Broadly these Regulations apply to advertising in any form which relates to the provision of credit. However they do not apply to all forms of credit and careful reference must be made to these Regulations in each case.

For further discussion on the marketing of financial services products, see Chapter 16.

Financial services

Misleading statements

The **Financial Services and Markets Act 2000** makes it a criminal offence, punishable by up to 7 years' imprisonment, for any person who:

- Makes a statement, promise or forecast which he knows to be misleading, false or deceptive;
- Dishonestly conceals any material facts whether in connection with a statement, promise or forecast made by him or otherwise; or
- Recklessly makes (dishonestly or otherwise) a statement, promise or forecast which is misleading, false or deceptive.

The statement, promise or forecast should be made for the purpose of inducing (or being reckless as to whether it may induce) a person to enter into an agreement.

For example, an advertising agency could also be liable unless the agency proves that it reasonably believed that the material would not create an impression that was false or misleading.

Financial promotion

There is a separate offence of communicating a financial promotion in the course of business which has either not been approved by an authorised person or is not an exempt communication.

Although the term ' financial promotion' is not defined in the 2000 Act, the term refers to an invitation or inducement to engage in an investment activity.

POINT OF LAW

Again, an advertising agency could be liable unless it shows that it believed on reasonable grounds that the advertisement had been approved by an authorised person or was exempt from the restriction.

An exempt communication includes, for example, a company's annual accounts and directors' reports.

In addition, the **British Code of Advertising** and the **ITC, Radio Authority** and trade association carry detailed sections covering advertising for investments.

For further discussion on the marketing of financial services, see Chapter 16.

Investments

The **Financial Services Act 1986** makes it a criminal offence, punishable by up to 7 years' imprisonment, for any person to induce another person deliberately or recklessly to make an investment decision on the basis of a knowingly or recklessly made statement, promise or forecast which is misleading, false or deceptive or made through dishonest concealment of material facts.

POINT OF LAW

For example, an advertising agency could also be liable unless the agency proves that it reasonably believed that the material would not create an impression that was false or misleading.

There is a separate offence of issuing an investment advertisement which has not been approved by an authorised person.

POINT OF LAW

Again, an advertising agency could be liable unless it shows that it believed on reasonable grounds that the advertisement was approved by an authorised person or that the advertisement was permitted by **Section 58** of the **1986 Act**.

This exempts from the regulations certain materials such as annual reports of public companies.

In addition, **the British Code of Advertising** and the **ITC**, **Radio Authority** and trade association Codes carry detailed sections covering advertising for investments.

For further discussion on the marketing of financial services, see Chapter 16.

Automotive

The fuel consumption of passenger cars sold in the UK has to be determined by officially approved tests. If reference is made in advertising to a car's fuel consumption, the law requires that the results of all those tests be included in the advertisement. The **ITC Code** contains a Motor Cars and Driving section, whilst a 'Motoring' section now features in the new **Code of Advertising**.

Food stuffs

The advertising of food is controlled principally by the **Trade Descriptions Act 1968**, the **Food Act 1984** the **Food Labelling Regulations 1996** and the **Food Safety Act 1990**.

Food in this context includes:

- Drinks
- Substances of no nutritional value
- Chewing gum
- Articles used as ingredients in food preparation

Food in this context *excludes:*

- Live animals, birds or fish
- Animal food stuffs
- Controlled drugs
- Medicinal products

Under **Section 8** of the **Food Safety Act 1990** it is unlawful to advertise for sale for human consumption any food which fails to comply with food safety requirements.

> **POINT OF LAW**
>
> Examples of such non-compliance would be if the food is rendered injurious to health, is unfit for human consumption, or is contaminated, or that it would not be reasonable to expect it to be used for human consumption. Such food stuffs will be deemed harmful to everyone or to a substantial proportion of the community, such as children and elderly people.

Definition of advertisement under the Food Safety Act 1990
Section 53 of the **1990 Act** defines an 'advertisement' as:

> *... any notice, circular, label, wrapper, invoice or other document, and any public announcement made orally or by any means of transmitting light or sound.*

Section 15 of the **Food Safety Act 1990** provides that it is unlawful to publish, or be a party to the publication of, an advertisement which falsely describes any food or is likely to mislead as to the nature, substance or quality of the food.

A court would look at what an ordinary person would understand the meaning to be or whether an ordinary person would be misled. Advertisements have been found to be misleading due to what the advertiser has chosen to *omit* despite the actual content being truthful.

Under **Section 20** and **Section 21** of the **Food Safety Act 1990**, both the brand owner and the advertising agency must be able to prove that they took all reasonable precautions to avoid committing an offence. Any food advertised must comply with food safety requirements.

A publisher will have a defence if it can show that it received the advertisement in the course of business and had no reason to suspect that its publication would amount to an offence.

> **POINT OF LAW**
>
> A brand owner found guilty of an offence would be liable on indictment to a fine and/or imprisonment for a period not exceeding 2 years; or on summary conviction to a fine not exceeding the statutory maximum and/or imprisonment for a period not exceeding 6 months.

The Food Safety Act 1990 creates an offence of falsely describing food or giving it a label calculated to mislead as to the nature, substance or quality of the food.

The **Food Labelling Regulations 1996** control the use of particular names, descriptions and claims in relation to food, mainly in packaging and labelling but in some cases they have relevance to advertising.

The Regulations provide that subject to certain exceptions, all food ready for delivery to the ultimate consumer (or a catering establishment) should be marked or labelled with:

- The name of the food
- A list of ingredients
- Durability indication
- Special storage conditions or conditions of use
- Name and address of marketer (manufacturer/packer/seller)
- Place of origin (certain cases only)
- Instructions for use (certain cases only)
- Requirements about the manner of marking or labelling the food are set out.

If there is a claim about the presence or low content of a particular ingredient in a food, the label should provide an indication of the minimum or maximum percentage of that ingredient in the food.

POINT OF LAW

Labels cannot make claims that the food has tonic or medicinal purposes and there are also conditions that need to be met if claims about reduced or low energy value, protein, vitamins, minerals, cholesterol or nutrition are made.

Certain words and descriptions cannot be used in relation to foods.

POINT OF LAW

For example, the word 'milk' may not be used as the name of an ingredient where the ingredient is the milk of an animal other than a cow unless the word is accompanied by the name of the animal, and the use of the word as the name of the ingredient complies in all other respects with the Food Labelling Regulations.

There is certain nutritional information about food that needs to be included on the label even if no nutritional claims are being made about it.

Further provisions relate to food which is not pre-packed, food which is sold from vending machines, alcoholic drinks, food which includes raw milk, food packaged in gas so as to extend durability and food with sweeteners, added sugar or aspartame or polyols.

See also Chapter 16 for a discussion on the marketing of organic and genetically modified foods.

Dietary products

Misleading statements as to the fitness for purpose or performance of a dietary product create a risk of prosecution under the **Trade Descriptions Act 1968**, while the **Food Labelling Regulations 1996** require that the food must be capable of fulfilling any claim made.

Looking to industry self-regulation, the **BCASP**, the **ITC Code** and the **Radio Authority Code** carry extensive sections regulating the advertising of slimming or diet products.

Alcoholic beverages

There are no specific regulations dealing with the advertising of alcoholic beverages but the **BCASP**, and the **ITC Code and Radio Authority Code** lay down detailed guidelines for print, television and radio advertising of such products.

A volume alcohol content of 1.2% is the cut-off point for the applicability of most of the detailed guidelines of the Codes, although the **Radio Authority Code** provides that if a broadcaster considers that a significant purpose of an advertisement for a low alcoholic drink is to promote a sister brand of stronger alcoholic content or if the drink's low alcohol content is not stated in the advertisement, then all the detailed guidelines should be applicable regardless of whether the alcohol content is below or above the 1.2% level.

For further discussion on the marketing of alcoholic products, see Chapter 16.

White goods

There are no specific regulations dealing with the advertising of white goods (fridges, freezers, microwaves). However this is not the case in respect of their labelling.

The **Energy Information Regulations** apply to tumble driers (SI 1996 No 601), washing machines (SI 1996 No 600), refrigerators and freezers (SI 1994 No 3076), combined washer-driers (SI 1997 No 1624), dishwashers (SI 1999 No 1676) and lamps (SI 1999 No 517).

These Regulations have all been amended by **The Energy Information and Energy Efficiency (Miscellaneous Amendments) Regulations 2001**.

The scheme basically means that marketers of these white goods have to supply labels and tables of information ('information notices'), e.g. the energy consumption of the appliances, to the retailers of the goods and these labels must be attached to the appliance if the appliance is being displayed to consumers.

These requirements do not apply if distance selling is taking place. There are explanatory notes accompanying each of the Regulations which marketers should read if involved with marketing any of the items mentioned.

Apparel

Nightware

The **Nightwear (Safety) Regulations 1985** apply to nightwear including garments commonly worn as nightwear. The Nightwear Regulations apply to all marketers who supply nightwear and garments used for a similar purpose in the course of business, whether or not that business is one of dealing in nightwear.

> POINT OF LAW
>
> It is an offence to supply, offer to supply, agree to supply, expose for supply or possess for supply nightwear that is not in compliance with the Nightwear Regulations.

The Regulations state that all mail order advertisements for adults' nightwear, pyjamas, babies' garments and terry towelling robes should include either prescribed 'Keep Away From Fire' symbols or statements confirming compliance with the Flammability Standard set out below.

The Regulations depend on whether the nightwear is for:

- Babies (under 3 months old and having a chest measurement not exceeding 53 cm)
- Children (3–13 years old and having a chest measurement not exceeding 97 cm and a sleeve measurement not exceeding 69 cm)
- Adults

The Regulations provide that:

- Babies' nightwear must carry a permanent label showing whether or not it meets the **Flammability Standard** (British Standard BS5722)
- Children's nightdresses and dressing gowns must satisfy the Flammability Standard
- Pyjamas and cotton terry towelling robes for children do not have to meet the Flammability Standard but they must carry a permanent label showing whether or not they do so
- Adults' nightwear must carry a permanent label showing whether or not they meet the Flammability Standard (the Flammability Standard applies to the whole garment, including any labels)
- Nightwear which has been treated with flame retardant chemicals must carry the appropriate warning label about washing and suitability of washing agent
- Second-hand nightwear and nightwear intended for export are exempted from the provisions of the Nightwear Regulations

Footwear

There are no specific regulations dealing with the advertising of footware although there are detailed labelling regulations.

The **Footwear (Indication of Composition) Labelling Regulations 1995** apply to footwear sold or offered for sale to consumers.

The marketer (manufacturer), its agent in the EU or the party that first places footwear on the EU market has to ensure that the footwear complies with the labelling requirements in the Regulations.

The label should:

- Give information as to the material which constitutes at least 80% of the surface area of the upper, at least 80% of the surface area of the lining and sock and at least 80% of the volume of the outer sole; or

- If there is no such material, give information about the two main materials used in the composition of the footwear

The label should be affixed to at least one foot of each pair of shoes and this can be done by way of 'printing, sticking, embossing or use of an attached label; and shall be visible, securely attached and accessible'.

Marketers should not supply footwear unless it is labelled in accordance with the Regulations and non-compliance is an offence (Statutory Instrument SI 1995 No 2489).

However, certain types of footwear are excluded from the Regulations, including second-hand footwear and protective footwear.

Package holidays

The Package Travel, Package Holidays and Package Tours Regulations 1992 define a package holiday as the 'pre-arranged combination of at least two of the following components when sold or offered for sale at an inclusive price and when the service covers a period of more than 24 hours or includes overnight accommodation:

- Transport

- Accommodation

- Other tourist services not ancillary to transport or accommodation and accounting for a significant proportion of the package'

The Regulations provide that holiday brochures relating to packages must not be misleading and if it is then the marketer (tour operator or retailer) of the package holiday may be liable to compensate the consumer for loss suffered in consequence of the misleading description.

The Package Travel Regulations contain requirements for brochures for advertising package holidays which should be studied in detail by marketers if they operate in this area.

Toys

The ASA Codes deal specifically with advertisements and promotions aimed at children as it is recognised that the way in which children perceive and react to advertising is influenced by their age, experience and the context in which the message is delivered.

All of these factors are taken into consideration by the ASA when conducting a review. In particular, advertisements aimed at or featuring children should not exploit their credulity, loyalty, vulnerability or lack of experience.

All toys need to be appropriately labelled under the **Toys (Safety) Regulations 1995.**

Under the Regulations, toys are described as 'any product or material designed or clearly intended for use in play by children of less than 14 years of age' and the Regulations apply to all toys on sale in the UK and marketers who supply them.

'Supply' is defined in Regulation 3(1) as including offering to supply, agreeing to supply, exposing for supply and possessing for supply in the course of any business, not only a business dealing in toys.

The marketer (manufacturer or its authorised agent) must ensure that the toys satisfy certain legal requirements:

1. That the essential safety requirements in Annex C of the Toys Regulations have been complied with.

2. That the toy bears the CE mark which is a positive declaration that:

   - the toy satisfies the essential safety requirements;

   - that compliance with the essential safety requirements has been verified by use of the appropriate attestation procedures and that these have been correctly applied by an authorised person;

   - that the toys satisfy the requirements of all of the **New Approach Directives** *applicable.*

3. The CE mark must be visible, easily legible and in indelible form on either the toy or its packaging, the Regulations include stipulations about the style and size of the CE mark. It is an offence under the **Trade Descriptions Act 1968** to affix a CE mark to a product which is not the subject of legislation requiring the mark to be affixed.

4. That the toy bears the name and address of the person taking responsibility for the safety of the toy and where appropriate warnings and instructions for use (for details see Annex E of the Toys Regulations).

5. Information about the satisfaction of the safety requirements must be kept available for inspection by enforcement authorities.

It is an offence under the Regulations for a marketer (manufacturer, its authorised representative or an importer) to supply toys which do not satisfy the essential safety requirements or do not carry the CE mark or the name and address details or the other required information.

It is also an offence for a marketer to supply toys which would jeopardise the safety or health of users or third parties when used as intended or in a way that is foreseeable (e.g. bearing in mind the normal behaviour of children).

In addition, it is also an offence to supply toys which do not bear the CE mark or name and address details or other required information.

The company as well as individual directors can be prosecuted if the alleged offence was carried out with their consent. There is a defence of due diligence. Trading Standards Offices are responsible for enforcement. Upon summary conviction the marketer is liable to a fine not exceeding £5000 and/or a maximum prison sentence of 6 months.

For further discussion as to the marketing of products aimed at children, see Chapter 16.

Pharmaceutical products

In accordance with the **Medicines Act 1968** it is a criminal offence to issue a false or misleading advertisement for medicinal products and under **Medicines (Advertising) Regulations 1994** it is a criminal offence to advertise a medicinal product in respect of which there is no product licence or certificate of registration.

In addition, under the **Cancer Act 1939** it is an offence to take part in the publication of any advertisement which contains an offer to treat cancer, to claim that they have a cure for cancer or to give advice on treatment.

It should be noted that the definition of 'advertising' contained in the **1968 Act** is very broad:

advertisement includes every form of advertising, whether in a publication, or by the display of any notice, or by means of any catalogue, price list, letter (whether circular or addressed to a particular person) or other document or by words inscribed on any article, or by means of a photograph, film, sound recording, broadcast or cable programme, or in any other way, and any reference to the issue of an advertisement shall be construed accordingly.

The definition of advertisement does not require the material to be published by or on behalf of the drug supplier or manufacturer. However, it does require a product claim to be made in text.

'Advertisements' to the public of the following medicinal products are prohibited (subject to some exemptions, e.g. for approved vaccination campaigns):

- Products available on prescription only

- Products in respect of which a marketing authorisation has not been issued

It is an offence to publish prohibited advertisements. If the drugs mentioned are only available on prescription or are not licensed in the UK, publication of any advertisement in relation to these drugs would be an offence.

The 1968 Act requires that, subject to certain exemptions, all medicinal products receive a product licence before they can be marketed in the UK.

If a medicinal product is non-prescription and it has a marketing authorisation (that means it is licensed in the UK), then advertisements can be issued but they must comply with a list of rules as to, for example, production claims that can be made.

In addition, any medicinal products for which marketing authorisations have been issued may only be advertised with the consent of the holder of authorisation.

The following are examples of materials which make a product claim and are prohibited from advertisements:

- Material which suggests that the effects of taking the medicinal product are guaranteed, are unaccompanied by side effects or are better than, or equivalent to, those of another identifiable treatment or medicinal product

- Material which suggests that health can be enhanced by taking the medicinal product
- Material which suggests that health could be affected by not taking the medicinal product

If references to drugs are only to the components of the drugs, then provided that the components are not readily identifiable as something used in a particular drug which would effectively identify the particular drug, it is not necessary to have the consent of the marketing authorisation holder and it may be possible to discuss their effects in ways which, if they were drug brands, might be construed as 'advertisements'.

It is difficult to predict what material will and will not be acceptable. The relevant authority, the **Medicines Control Agency (MCA)** examines items about drugs on a case by case basis in the light of their policy guidelines and it is not easy to predict precisely their approach.

Indeed, the area of advertising of medicinal products is a grey area and the **1994 Regulations** concerning advertising of medicines have not been tested in court.

If the MCA did take offence over the material the sanctions available are a fine (for publisher and/or author) or a term of imprisonment (obviously the corporate author is not at risk here) or both. The MCA would not seek to prosecute without discussing the issue and attempting to compromise but they may insist on material being withdrawn if it does not comply with the 1994 Regulations.

It is possible to supply the MCA with text to obtain their view on whether it contravenes the 1994 Regulations; however, this would put the MCA on notice and give them the opportunity to amend the text. A copy of *What is a Medicinal Product* is available on their web site at **www.mca.gov.uk**.

It is important to establish which drugs are not licensed and which drugs are available on prescription only, as advertisements are prohibited in these cases. In the case of drugs which are non-prescription and are licensed, the consent of the marketing authorisation holder is required and compliance with specific rules in relation to the form and content of the advertisement is also required.

The **Medicine (Labelling and Advertising to the Public) Regulations 1978** impose requirements and restrictions on the advertising direct to the public of medicinal products for administration to human beings. They prohibit the advertising of medicinal products available on prescription only and cover content and form of advertisements.

The **Medicines (Advertising) Regulations 1994** implement **EU Directive 92/28/EC** and prohibit advertising for the prevention, treatment and diagnosis of certain diseases. The Regulations specifically prohibit certain advertising methods such as suggesting that health can be enhanced by taking the medicinal product or referring to a recommendation by scientists, health professionals or persons who are neither of these but who because of their celebrity status could encourage the consumption of medicinal products.

Advertising addressed to the medical and dental professions is covered by separate regulations whilst the **Association of the British Pharmaceutical Industry** has published a **Code of Practice** for the pharmaceutical industry covering promotions aimed at those professions.

Advertising for OTC proprietary medicines is governed by the **Code of Advertising Standards and Practice** of the **Proprietary Association of Great Britain (PAGB)**, which has been accepted and approved by the **Department of Health** and is operated by the industry, who have the PAGB adjudicate their advertising.

The **ITC Code** and **Radio Authority Code** and the **British Code of Advertising** all have special sections giving guidelines as to the making of health claims and the advertising of medicines and treatments.

For further discussion on pharmaceutical marketing, see Chapter 16.

Tobacco and cigarettes

The advertising of all tobacco products on television is prohibited by the **ITC Code**. Similarly advertisements for cigarettes, cigarette tobacco and papers (but not cigars and pipe tobacco) are prohibited on the radio by the **Radio Authority Advertising and Sponsorship Code**.

All other forms of advertising are permitted but are subject to very stringent restrictions and controls contained in the **Cigarette Code** which forms part of the BCASP which covers issues such as advertising expenditure, media selection, health warnings and promotions.

The Cigarette Code sets out a number of provisions and restrictions by which tobacco advertisers agree to abide in relation to the advertisement of cigarettes, hand-rolling tobacco, cigarette papers, filters and wrappings, special offers, competitions and other sales promotions as well as products displaying the colours, livery, insignia or name of a cigarette brand in a way that promotes smoking rather than these other related products.

As a general principle, advertisements for the above-mentioned tobacco products must not incite people to start smoking, glamorise smoking, make smoking appealing to children, nor suggest that smoking is safe, healthy, natural or popular.

All advertisements falling under the scope of the Cigarette Code must be submitted to the **CAP** for clearance prior to publication. The issue of a signed, dated and numbered certificate of clearance from CAP is mandatory in relation to all advertisements for cigarettes and hand-rolling tobacco.

For further discussion on tobacco and cigarette marketing, see Chapter 16.

Charities

The **Charities Act 1993** stipulates that where a registered charity has an annual income in excess of £5000, all advertisements should state that it is a registered charity. If this is not adhered to, anyone who issues or authorises the issue of a non-compliant advertisement will be guilty of an offence and liable to a fine of up to £1000.

The television and radio Codes require media owners to accept advertising requesting charitable donations only if they are satisfied as to the charitable status of that body.

Other provisions of the Codes covering broadcast charitable advertising require that marketers should handle with care and discretion matters likely to arouse strong emotion and they should respect the dignity of the people on whose behalf the appeal is being made.

Separately, regulations introduced pursuant to the **Charities Act 1993** govern situations where commercial businesses, in the course of carrying out their normal activities, undertake advertising, promotional or sales campaigns which involve making charitable contributions.

These require that the business has a written agreement with the charity concerned covering particular points. They require also that relevant marketing material carries information about, amongst other things, the proportion of the sale price going to charities and the identity of the recipients.

CHECKLIST

- Is the advertisement legal, decent, honest and truthful?

- Are there specific legislation or codes which deal with the product being advertised?

- Is the advertisement misleading as to the product or services marketed?

- Is there a comparison between competing marketers' products? If so, is it done in a way that is permitted?

- Does the advertisement contain any potentially defamatory material?

- Is the copyright cleared in respect of all aspects of the advertisement?

- Does the advertisement use any third party's trademarks?

- Is the product safe?

- If the advertisement is being sent to a database of people, is this in compliance with the Data Protection Act 1998?

- Is the advertising or labelling of products covered by specific regulations or codes?

- Does the advertising medium require adherence to specific regulations or rules?

- Is a premium rate telephone service used or mentioned?

- Is the advertisement aimed at children?

- If the advertisement is being broadcast, does it comply with the relevant codes?

10

BROADCASTING

In this chapter:

- The broadcast media framework
- The regulators of British television and radio
- Independent Television Commission (ITC) Code of Practice and regulations regarding product placement
- ITC Code on Programme Sponsorship
- Powers of Broadcasting Standards Council
- BBC Producers' Guidelines
- Powers of the Radio Authority
- Communications White Paper
- Interactive broadcast services
- Future of broadcasting
- Checklist

Other useful chapters:

- Chapter 3: Making statements
- Chapter 9: Advertising and labelling
- Chapter 12: Sponsorship and hospitality
- Chapter 14: Lobbying
- Chapter 16: Niche marketing

INTRODUCTION

In the beginning there was the British Broadcasting Corporation (BBC). From its creation in 1927, the BBC enjoyed a monopolistic position for nearly 30 years as the nation's principal radio and terrestrial TV broadcaster.

Radio enjoyed most of that supremacy as the principal broadcast medium at a time when the cost of a TV set was equivalent to a month's salary and in any event the BBC broadcast for just a few hours of TV a day.

It was not until 1953, with the Coronation of Queen Elizabeth II, that a full appreciation of TV's appeal and power was reached in a single day. There were only 2 million TV sets in the country at the time and yet 20 million people watched the Coronation Service taking place at Westminster Abbey. That was an average of ten viewers per TV set and accounted for 56% of the adult population. As a result of that one televised event, the future growth of TV was assured.

Then came the **Television Act 1955** and with it the dawn of commercial TV. Viewers now had an alternative to the BBC and marketers' advertising revenues would help to pay for the new service, which meant that marketers had for the first time some economic influence over what was being broadcast as broadcasters depended on audience viewing figures in order to charge for advertising air time (known as the 'rate card').

In today's multi-channel and multi-media environment, the advent of terrestrial commercial TV and its impact for those early marketers looks like a distant memory – for example, does anyone remember the Gibbs SR toothpaste commercial – the first TV commercial broadcast in the UK?

From the beginning, those members of the viewing public with access to both BBC and ITV showed a preference for ITV. A very small minority (6%) claimed to dislike the existence of advertisements on TV. A majority 53% claimed actively to like them and 86% said they were happy with them.

Alongside the growth and development of television, the advertising industry created memorable advertising campaigns to fit between the programmes, such as 'Beanz Meanz Heinz', 'For Mash, Get Smash', Katie and Oxo, Henry Cooper and Brut aftershave and 'I'd Like to Teach the World to Sing' (Coca-Cola).

Despite the fragmentation of media and with it the fragmentation of audiences – there are now many more channels for broadcasting a message such as commercial radio, mobile phones (SMS and WAP), Internet and broadband – terrestrial, cable, satellite TV is still overwhelmingly the medium of choice for marketers in reaching a mass market audience, although some commentators argue that sponsorship is a much more accurate and effective mass marketing tool (see Chapter 12).

Given the power of television, the medium is unique in having its own framework of complex legislation that has an impact on what can and cannot be broadcast.

THE REGULATORS OF BRITISH TELEVISION AND RADIO

There are a number of UK regulatory bodies responsible for supervising content of broadcasts and protecting the interests of the consumer:

- The **Independent Television Commission (ITC)**
- The **Broadcasting Standards Commission (BSC)**
- The **Radio Authority**

In the UK, these regulatory bodies review advertisements but legislation vests primary responsibility in the **ITC** and the **Radio Authority**, who in turn impose regulations and obligations on their licensees, the television and radio broadcasters.

The **Broadcasting Act 1990** imposes on the **ITC** and the **Radio Authority** the duty to draw up and periodically review codes governing standards and practice in advertising and in the sponsoring of programmes, and prescribing the advertisements and methods of advertising or sponsorship to be prohibited.

It is these codes with which the majority of this chapter is concerned. The codes are significant works in their own right such that only an essential outline is provided.

Other legislation imposes on the ITC and the Radio Authority a duty to consider any non-frivolous complaint that an advertisement is misleading or is a comparative advertisement outside of the scope of the rules governing such adverts.

Both the ITC and the Radio Authority also, as a matter of policy, consider and provide an individual response to every complaint they receive.

THE ITC

The ITC was established under the auspices of the **Broadcasting Acts of 1990 and 1996** to regulate all commercial television services by licensing and supervising programme and local delivery services (web site: **www.itc.org.uk**).

Role of the ITC

The ITC can apply sanctions to licensees who break the rules which range from requiring broadcast apologies and/or corrections to fines and ultimately to shortening or revocation of licences.

The **ITC's Code of Advertising Standards and Practice (CASP)** requires all broadcasters licensed by the ITC to vet all advertisements in advance of broadcast to ensure compliance with the Code. The vetting role is predominantly carried out by the **British Advertising Clearance Centre (BACC)** on behalf of licensees. The BACC reviews proposed TV commercials submitted to it by marketers. The system is self-regulatory and does not mean that the licensees guarantee that these TV commercials will be free from ITC sanctions (see below).

The ITC also constantly monitors output, and will intervene where it is appropriate for it to do so and not only where a complaint has been received.

Cable, satellite and digital licences are normally granted virtually on demand
provided that the ITC is satisfied that the prospective licensee is a fit and
proper person and is not disqualified by the 1990 Act from holding the licence and that the
television service concerned conforms to the consumer protection requirements of the ITC's
Codes on Programmes, Advertising Standards and Practice, Programme Sponsorship and the
Rules on the Amount and Scheduling of Advertising.

By virtue of the **1990** and **1996 Acts**, the ITC has the power to:

- Issue licences allowing commercial television companies to broadcast in and from the UK
  regardless of whether consumers receive the service via set top aerials, cable or satellite, or
  whether the format of the service is analogue or digital

- Regulate the provision of television services by ensuring that broadcasters adhere to the
  requirements of the ITC's published licences, codes and guidelines on programme content,
  advertising and sponsorship, together with technical performance.

Each licensee (broadcaster) is subject to the conditions of the licence which cover matters
that include standards of programmes and advertising.

The ITC's powers are coupled with an overriding duty to ensure that the television services
provided to viewers throughout the UK are as wide ranging as possible and maintain standards
of high quality and appeal to a range of tastes and interests.

At all times the ITC has a duty to ensure that a level playing field exists in the provision of
these services; part of this duty may involve the investigation of complaints which are regularly
published.

ITC's Codes of Practice

Television companies licensed by the ITC must comply with the letter and spirit of its
Programme Code with regard to programme content. Primarily the Code states that television
advertising should be 'legal, decent, honest and truthful'.

For example, under the **2001 Programme Code**, broadcasters must ensure
that advertisements and sponsorship idents (short commercials played just
before and just after the programme) comply with relevant ITC Codes of Practice which are
specific to television advertisements (the **ITC Code of Advertising Standards and Practice**
and the **ITC Rules on Amount and Scheduling of Advertising**) and **ITC Code of
Programme Sponsorship**.

Marketers need to observe these Codes very strictly and ensure that television advertising:

- Is not misleading
- Does not encourage or condone harmful behaviour
- Does not cause widespread or exceptional offence

POINT OF LAW

For example, if an advertisement purported to come from the Highways Agency and was extolling the virtues of a new side impact safety feature of the latest Ford family saloon, then this would be a breach of the ITC Code.

Equally, if an advertisement for a brand of vodka showed men in a bar drinking and then driving to a football match where they were seen chanting the strap line for the vodka in an aggressive way at rival supporters (of another brand), this would also be a breach of the ITC Code.

Advertisements must be clearly separated from TV programmes and restrictions are placed on their rate of recurrence and duration.

The responsibility of checking that advertising proposals comply with these Codes remains with the licensee (broadcasters such as Channel 4, Channel 5 or Sky One), although advice may be sought from the ITC where there is any doubt as to the interpretation of its rules on content control and time of transmission.

POINT OF LAW

In the interest of maintaining standards in connection with violence and decency certain programmes and advertisements may not be transmitted before the 9 pm watershed. For example, this would include women's products such as sanitary towels and advertisements for contraceptives.

The ITC Programme Code

The Programme Code as it relates to broadcasters sets out editorial standards which audiences are entitled to expect from commercial television services in the UK.

Its objectives are to ensure that requirements covering programme content which are covered in the Acts are satisfied. It has a wide ambit encompassing all licensed programme services and certain foreign satellite programmes included in local delivery services.

The principles of the **European Convention on Human Rights** have also been incorporated into the Programme Code.

Compliance with the Programme Code is a condition precedent to the grant of licences by the ITC to television operators.

The ITC monitors programme output on transmission to ensure compliance with the Programme Code and will take action when a complaint is made by a viewer or consumer or independently of a complaint where the ITC deems it to be necessary.

However, in the event that a complaint is received directly from the viewer to the broadcaster, the broadcaster is obliged to inform the ITC on how any such complaints are dealt with.

Regulations governing product placement

The ITC takes a strict view of product placement (**Section 8.3 of the Programme Code**) and does *not* allow it in the interests of editorial independence, e.g. the inclusion of a product within the programme in return for payment to the programme maker or broadcaster (or their representatives).

> POINT OF LAW
>
> The general rule is that a marketer may not pay for the inclusion of, or reference to, a product or service within a programme. This is called 'product placement' and is prohibited.

In order to circumnavigate this rule, marketers may be tempted to donate goods or services in the hope they will be featured in a programme and this will be completely legitimate provided *where their use is clearly justified editorially products or services may be acquired at no or less than full cost*.

The marketer is *not* allowed to attach a condition to the provision of the goods or services relating to the 'manner of its appearance in the programme' and at no time can the product be given 'undue prominence'.

> POINT OF LAW
>
> 'Undue prominence' may not be given to a commercial product or service, and it must be clear that no impression is created of external commercial influence on the editorial process. In no circumstances may the manner of appearance of a product be the subject of negotiation or agreement with the supplier. Branded products should not, as a general rule, be referred to in audio by brand name, or shown in close-up or from an angle which displays the branding to best advantage, or for any significant length of time.

Commercial products or services may not be given undue prominence (**Section 8.4 of the Programme Code**) in any programme; any and all references must be kept within the justifiable limits of editorial requirements.

> POINT OF LAW
>
> For example, a whole scene in a soap opera cannot be contrived in order that the product is shown continuously on camera where there is no artistic or dramatic reason for doing so.

Thus when considering whether the prominence of a particular product or service in a programme may be in breach of the Programme Code, consideration must be given to whether there could be a perception that the editorial process has been compromised by external commercial influences.

As the next case illustrates, where the Programme Code has been breached, the ITC may use sanctions against licence holders, including the imposition of a financial penalty or the revocation of a licence grant.

LAW IN ACTION

In July 2001, the ITC announced a financial penalty on licensee London Weekend Television (LWT) for breaches of the ITC Code of Programme Sponsorship in the series Clubavision.

The ITC found that the selection of clubs to appear in ITV's late night music programme Clubavision was influenced by the paying of fees and/or expenses to a promoter and this compromised the production company's editorial judgment. The ITC concluded that there had been a breach of **Section 15.1, 'Product Placement'**, of the ITC Code of Programme Sponsorship. A fine of £100 000 was considered appropriate, given the serious and long-running nature of the Code breach, and the importance the ITC places on protecting the editorial integrity of programmes from commercial influence.

Despite the constraints of the Programme Code, provided that marketers follow the rules closely, they could even get a credit on the programme *provided* a basic text acknowledgement lasting no more than 5 seconds is included within the end credits of the programme for the donated product and *only* where the identity of the product or service is not otherwise apparent from the programme itself.

ITC complaints procedures about programmes

Complaints about programmes can relate to matters such as accuracy, impartiality, language and sexual portrayal.

In the event that a complaint is made by a viewer in relation to television advertising and sponsorship, the ITC will investigate the complaint where it is deemed necessary.

ITC Code of Advertising Standards and Practice (CASP)

The **ITC CASP** as it relates to marketers prescribes certain conditions for broadcast advertising that must be met.

A fundamental principle under CASP is that advertising must be 'legal, decent, honest and truthful'.

POINT OF LAW

The main body of the **ITC CASP** deals with standards for advertisements on such matters as:

- The separation of advertisements and programmes
- The persons appearing in advertisements and programmes
- Captions and superimposed text
- Politics, industrial and public controversy
- Taste and offence
- Misleading viewers
- Prices and price claims
- Comparisons and denigration of others
- Unacceptable products or services such as the occult, betting tips, betting and gaming, guns and pornography

The standards are generally short and prescriptive, such as Rule 17 (Superstition) 'No advertisement may exploit the superstitious'.

There are then six appendices dealing specifically with:

- Advertising and Children
- Financial Advertising
- Medicines, Treatments, Health Claims, Nutrition and Dietary Supplements
- Charity Advertising
- Religious Advertising
- Statutes Affecting Television Advertising

The appendices are more detailed, but again largely compose of rules that must be complied with in respect of advertising of that nature.

There are also a series of **Guidance Notes**. Some of these are supplementary guidance to specific rules of the Code (such as that on Motorcars and Driving, intended to assist in the interpretation of Rule 21). Others, such as that dealing with on-screen text and sub-titling in advertisements are stand-alone and contain detailed technical requirements as well as general principles.

A recent addition to the Code is a Guidance Note on 'virtual' advertising, the alteration or addition to a broadcast signal of computer-generated advertising to replace pre-existing physical advertising.

The ITC produces a monthly *Television Advertising Complaints Report* detailing its decisions on complaints of substance in relation to the Code and also summarising all other complaints which it has received but which it feels require no further investigation. These reports are instructive to understand the manner in which the Code is applied and how complaints are considered by the ITC.

In January 2001, a TV commercial for **Van den Bergh Foods' Chicken Tonight Stir-In Paste** showed a woman sitting on a floor cushion with what appeared to be a ready to cook chicken on a cushion in front of her.

She was attempting to engage the chicken in her inexperienced attempts at meditation and was heard to say ' Om, dina Om' whilst sitar music played in the background.

The commercial ended with the woman chastising the chicken for its lack of participation: 'You can't just sit there with your legs crossed. You're going to have to chant as well'. Sixteen viewers, all with close links to the Hindu faith and some writing on behalf of large groups, said that they had been insulted and offended by the commercial which had ridiculed their religion and had used their sacred prayer to advertise a meat sauce when their faith forbade them from eating meat.

The BACC maintained that the advertiser was aware of the need to take care with the execution after the BACC had first considered the script.

However, the marketer, Van den Bergh Foods, expressed regret and disappointment at the offence it had caused. It said that thorough research had been undertaken prior to broadcast and that it had been taken by surprise by the complaints received but that it was sorry for the offence caused.

The marketer said that as soon as it had become aware of a problem it had removed the commercial from air and it assured the ITC that the advertising would not be transmitted again in its current form. Van den Bergh Foods told the ITC that it had considered the 'purely generic nature' of the chanting in the commercial to have been humorous based on the fact that the woman 'was clearly not an accomplished meditator' and that it had not been intended to convey any specific reference to meditation as a religious practice in the Hindu faith.

The ITC accepted that no offence had been intended but nevertheless concluded that the degree of offence caused made the advertising inappropriate for broadcast and it accepted the marketer's assurance that there would be no further transmissions.

Complaints about a TV commercial are given an initial assessment to gauge the urgency of the complaint, after which it is passed to case officers for further investigation.

In the first instance, the ITC directs enquiries initially to the broadcaster (licensee) carrying the advertisement, or to the **BACC** where it has cleared the TV commercial on behalf of the broadcaster.

Misleading advertisements

In the case of investigations into allegations of misleading advertisements under CASP, the ITC *has the power to consider a factual claim inaccurate if adequate evidence is not furnished to it* (see also Chapter 9).

Broadly, advertising will be misleading if it is likely to deceive those who see it and if consumers are likely to alter their economic behaviour as a result of the deception (by, for example, taking time to explore advertised offers or basing their purchasing decisions on the advertisement).

The ITC will look at the overall impression conveyed by the advertisement to a reasonable viewer.

INSIGHT

All important limitations and qualifications to an offer must be made clear in any advertisement. Absolute claims (e.g. 'best on the market', 'lowest prices guaranteed') must be backed up by clear evidence, and the marketer must be able to deliver on its promise.

Prices must include all non-optional extras, including taxes, duties and fees imposed on buyers, and the identity of an advertiser must be made apparent when advertising might otherwise be materially misleading (this may affect certain types of 'creeping' advertising campaigns).

LAW IN ACTION

In November 2001, a TV commercial for **BT Cellnet** (now O$_2$) stated: 'Now all BT Cellnet customers can use their mobiles abroad' and showed a man on a beach making a call to a friend at home in the UK and asking him to send him a text message. Superimposed text stated (amongst other things) 'Some service restrictions may apply on Pay and Go'.

Five complaints were received from viewers claiming that the advertising was misleading as they had understood that they could use their phones abroad as normal but had found that whilst abroad they could not receive calls or send text messages.

BT Cellnet explained that the advertisement had been designed to promote the use of its Pay and Go and Pay monthly packages by users abroad and had intended to introduce a full range of international services from 1 July 2001.

However, shortly before this date it had discovered that there were likely to be transmitter problems in some countries, lasting until August 2001, resulting in some users on the Pay and Go platform not being able to receive calls or send text messages.

As soon as it had become aware of the problem the marketer added the text referring to 'service restrictions' to the TV commercials. It argued that it was in any event correct to suggest that BT Cellnet customers could use their mobiles abroad. During the time the advertising had been on air all its customers had been able to use their phones in some capacity.

The BACC stated that it believed the text used had been adequate to alert viewers to the fact that certain restrictions on use were currently in place.

However, the ITC took a different view and judged that viewers were likely to have understood the reference to being able to use their phones abroad as implying that they could make use of the main functions as normal and in particular would be able to make and receive calls and send and receive text messages.

The ITC did not accept that the 'service restrictions' text had adequately alerted viewers to the nature and extent of those limitations. It therefore ruled that the advertising had been misleading and required that it not be re-shown in its current form.

If the result of an investigation is that the case officer decides that there are no or insufficient grounds for upholding a complaint, this is relayed to the complainant.

If the complainant is not satisfied with the initial findings the matter can then be referred to a more senior case officer.

In the instance that the complainant has a strong interest in the outcome of the investigation or is well informed about a disputed fact or technical difficulty, the ITC has the discretion to allow the complainant to comment on the provisional assessment *before* confirming a decision to dismiss a complaint.

Details of ITC decisions are published each month in the *Television Advertising Complaints Report* which reports on:

- Complaints that were upheld

- Those complaints that were not upheld but raise issues that the ITC wishes to give guidance on for the future

- Complaints about adverts that have a higher number of complaints than most

- Complaints which raise substantive issue of code interpretations which may be of wider interest to marketers and the public

Revised ITC CASP

The revised ITC CASP (currently under consultation at time of writing) is likely to move away from the subjective concept of 'taste and decency', and instead fleshes out in detail the types of advertisements which may 'cause serious or widespread offence against generally accepted moral, social or cultural standards'.

Whilst acknowledging that viewers can be offended by all manner of things, the ITC emphasises the need for advertising to reflect acceptable community standards in relation to the portrayal of death, injury, violence, religion, offensive language and the treatment of minorities, in particular. The ITC will not therefore intervene where advertising is simply criticised for not being in good taste unless the material contravenes prevailing community standards.

More specifically, whilst 'theatrical' violence, such as that common in action or adventure films, should generally be acceptable, together with violence which has a stylised cartoon or slapstick quality, adverts should not appear to condone people using violence or aggression to get their own way or depict violence in everyday situations involving ordinary people.

Depictions of tragic personal experiences such as death or injury should be carefully judged and advertisements should not contain harmful stereotypes, unless the advertisement seems generally acceptable to most members of the group in question as well as to the broader public.

Having said this, the use of humour may reduce the risk of offence in borderline cases and advertising which could be considered risqué may be carefully scheduled in programmes containing comparable material.

Protecting children

Children receive more detailed treatment in a new Section 10 of the Code, which should be considered for any advertising which is aimed at children, features children or which could harmfully influence children even if not of direct interest to them (children do not only want or buy 'children's products' so advertising for other product categories may need to be designed with that in mind).

Generally, advertisements must not contain material which could lead to physical, social, moral or psychological harm to children or younger teenagers, nor may they take advantage of children's inexperience or 'their natural credulity and sense of loyalty'.

Broadcasters should beware of 'harmful emulation' and should balance the realistic risk of the behaviour being encouraged against how serious the consequences could be if there was emulation.

Advertisements for 'expensive' toys, games and comparable children's products must include an indication of their price ('expensive' is currently defined as £25 or over).

Advertisements which offer to sell products or services by mail, telephone, e-mail or Internet should not be aimed at children. The Code has always contained scheduling restrictions relating to the broadcast of certain advertisements 'when large numbers of children are likely to be viewing'.

This rather vague guideline has now been replaced in the draft Code by detailed guidance on when potentially harmful or exploitative advertising should not be shown to children between certain specified ages (children are categorised into four age bands: under 4 years, 4–8 years, 9–12 years and young adult teenagers).

For further discussion on marketing to children, see Chapter 16.

ITC rulings

Final decisions on substance and wording are taken by the **ITC's Director of Advertising and Sponsorship** after considering comments on draft decisions from the advertising agency or marketer and the licensee or BACC.

Comments are usually accepted subject to receipt before the imposed deadline which will be faxed to the broadcaster (licensee) and relevant BACC Group Head to relay to the advertising agency or marketer (usually by the close of business on the seventh working day after the day of faxing).

An extension may be granted in relation to the deadline for the receipt of comments where the ITC does not propose to uphold the complaint.

If the complaint is to be upheld, extensions to the deadline will be granted if there are compelling and fully explained reasons for the requested extension.

If a marketer finds that its TV commercial is subject to investigation, the commercial cannot continue to be aired, which may mean that a launch campaign for a new product may need to be put back if the key marketing strategy for that launch depends on a nationwide TV campaign.

The ITC will usually insist that advertising is suspended until the complaint is resolved throughout the duration of an extended deadline for the receipt of comments, *unless* a good reason to the contrary can be established, e.g. where the marketer is able to outline a satisfactory defence to the disputed issue and can confirm the defence with certain outstanding details.

However, if no one wishes to comment on the draft decision the broadcaster/BACC must confirm a 'nil return'.

Appeals procedure

If a broadcaster or marketer wishes to make an appeal against the decision taken by the ITC, it should notify the ITC by the close of business on the third working day after receiving the confirmed decision. As soon as is reasonably practicable after notice a full written statement on the grounds of appeal should be sent to the **Chief Executive of the ITC** and certainly no later than the tenth working day after receipt of the decision being appealed.

Appeals by advertising agencies, marketers or licensees should be submitted by a director of the company concerned.

Further appeal to the full Commission of the ITC

A further appeal process is available to all parties that are not satisfied with the decision of the Chief Executive.

This consists of a further appeal to the **Chairman of the ITC** requesting that the matter be put before the full **Commission**. The deadlines for notification of appeal and submission of the statement of appeal are at the end of the third and tenth working days respectively after receiving the Chief Executive's decision to reject the first appeal.

The Chairman decides whether to allow a further appeal before the full Commission and if this is granted, the papers will be put before the Commission at the next most convenient meeting.

Appeals to the Chief Executive and Chairman do not form part of the standard decision making process on complaints and provide appellants with the opportunity for a retrospective review of decisions already taken.

The ITC has the right to suspend advertising *at any stage* during the investigation of a complaint pending resolution. This right may be exercised where the breach is clear and significant, or there are strong *prima facie* grounds for concern about a significant detriment to the public.

Marketers must be wary of abuse of the appeals procedure against complaints made about TV commercials. The ITC has the right to suspend advertising if it encounters obstruction or unjustified delay in the pursuit of its investigations.

ITC CODE ON PROGRAMME SPONSORSHIP (CPS)

In simple terms, programme sponsorship is the payment by a marketer to receive a credit associating it with a particular programme.

Broadcast sponsorship currently accounts for only about 2% of total advertising revenues in the UK and some commentators say that it is unlikely ever to account for more than 10% because there are a finite number of suitable TV programmes available for sponsorship.

However, given the relaxation of the ITC Code on TV sponsorship (see below) coupled with potentially more relaxations arising out of the up and coming EU review of the TV Advertising Directive there may well be more, not less, opportunities for TV sponsorship open to marketers and may well dent revenues generated from traditional TV advertising.

The **Television Without Frontiers directive** defines programme sponsorship as:

... any contribution made by a public or private undertaking not engaged in television broadcasting activities or in the production of audio-visual works to the financing of television programmes with a view to promoting its name, its trademark, its image, its activities or its products.

For a full discussion on other types of sponsorship, see Chapter 12.

Main objectives of the ITC CPS

The main objectives of the regulation of television sponsorship under the **ITC CPS** are to prevent the distortion of programmes for commercial reasons and maintain editorial integrity, as well as to sustain a degree of separation between advertising and sponsor credits, thereby prohibiting the use of credits as a mode of extending the time allowed for advertisements.

Therefore, in the interests of transparency, the placing of sponsors must be clearly identified at the beginning and/or end of the programme in order that viewers are not misled in connection with inadvertent endorsement of sponsored products.

For example, **Baileys** liquor sponsors *Sex and the City* on Channel 4's E4 and this is conveyed before the programme, as 'bumpers' before and after each commercial break and at the end of the programme.

The CPS should be construed in conjunction with the **ITC CASP**, the **ITC Rules on the Amount and Scheduling of Advertising (RASA)** and the **ITC Programme Code**.

Compliance with the CPS is a *mandatory* condition of an ITC licence; as such all broadcasters (licensees) should ensure that relevant employees and programme makers, including those from whom they commission programmes, understand its contents and significance.

Independent producers and other suppliers of programme material should seek guidance on specific proposals from the relevant licensee.

Sponsorship of programmes is allowed (except for news and current affairs programmes). However, this area is heavily regulated by the ITC under its **CPS**, but recent relaxations have opened up new opportunities for marketers (see below).

Sponsors of a particular programme can pay the provider for the receipt of a credit associating it with that programme.

However, the programme provider must be careful not to allow the sponsor to exert undue influence on the editorial content of programmes or indeed the scheduling of programmes.

For guidance on such matters, close reference should be made to the ITC's CPS published in Autumn 2000 which stipulates the degree to which a programme may credit particular sponsors.

Recent relaxation on the rules of sponsorship credits

In October 2000, the ITC published its new **CPS**.

Marketers are no longer prohibited from displaying their products within the credit sequences at the beginning and end of sponsored programmes or in 'break bumpers'.

The proviso is that the programme sponsorship must help to reflect the link between the sponsor and the programme.

What exactly does this mean? There are some good and not so good examples of programme sponsorship and it sometimes appears that satisfying this proviso is not very onerous for marketers.

POINT OF LAW

For example, is **Cadbury's** sponsorship of **Coronation Street** (ITV1) credits showing a whole street made of chocolate with chocolate characters a good link with the show? In order for it to be effective, the brand values of the programme and the brand values of the sponsor must be aligned in a way that makes sense for the audience.

Coronation Street and chocolate (in my view) is a tenuous link although Cadbury's positioning as 'The Nation's Favourite' probably saves them as *Coronation Street* is the nation's favourite soap.

Bailey's sponsorship of **Sex in the City** (Channel 4's E4) is better as Baileys has successfully re-positioned an old fashioned liqueur and infused it with a young attitude by promoting the drinking of it with ice as a sophisticated and sexy alternative to gin and tonic or vodka and tonic. This has been supported by print, poster and other media advertising.

One of the worst TV sponsorships was **Equitable Life** insurance company and US sitcom *Frasier* (Channel 4) where there was absolutely zero connection between the show and a boring financial services company.

Domino's Pizza and *The Simpsons* (Sky One) is perhaps the best example of TV sponsorship, aimed at a youth market. Domino's Pizza faced stiff competition from Pizza Hut and had a quarter of the advertising budget of the US giant and so could not compete in the TV advertising stakes. By tying up with *The Simpsons* and integrating this throughout its marketing (Bart Simpson even appeared on the lid of the pizza boxes) immediately gave Domino's Pizza a point of differentiation – making the product 'cool' for teenagers looking to eat pizza and watch The Simpsons. Further enhancements were made through interactive TV which meant that pizzas could be ordered through the TV.

Domino's Pizza built its brand and substantially increased its market share without spending millions of pounds in advertising unlike its rival Pizza Hut.

In theory, under the new regulations marketers are now free to provide contact details, allowing for the first time the inclusion of telephone numbers, web addresses and a representation of the marketer's product in such credits *provided* that these do not 'contain a direct exhortation to purchase the product' or make representations as to its 'attributes, benefits or price'.

The ITC's continuing concerns about distinguishing advertisements and sponsor credits are dealt with by rules which state that credits must *not* include any extract from advertising campaigns of the marketer in the last 3 years and must *not* be used explicitly to resolve promotions in other media, e.g. by containing numbers in a scratch card or other off air promotions.

INSIGHT

Another significant change is that for the first time it will be possible to sponsor business and financial programmes.

Although this general prohibition has gone, however, the rules will continue to operate so as to prevent sponsorship occurring where there is any potential influence on editorial content.

Accordingly, if any business or finance programme also falls into any of the categories of programme which are still restricted, such as news or current affairs programmes, then such programmes will be prohibited from seeking commercial sponsorship.

The **CASP** and **RASA** set out the rules concerning the separation of programmes from advertisements, detailing when it is acceptable to include programme footage in advertising.

They stipulate that if there is a close similarity between a programme's content and an advertisement (or similar business development activity) it may constitute grounds for regarding the programme as having an unacceptable promotional purpose.

POINT OF LAW

For example, a car manufacturer could not sponsor a consumer affairs programme that road tested various car marques against each other on performance and price because of the risk of confusing viewers that the car manufacturer had some influence over the result of the tests.

To maintain impartiality on the television, the ITC does not allow certain marketers to sponsor certain types of TV programme and broadcasters (licensees) are responsible for ensuring that these restrictions are adhered to.

Types of Programmes that *Cannot* be Sponsored	Nature of Marketer
All	Political bodies
All	Tobacco manufacturers (wether or not they sell other non-tobacco products or services)
Prevented from referring to prescription only brands in their credits	Pharmaceutical manufacturers
Not allowed to include coverage of horse or greyhound racing or the results thereof. However the new ITC Code of Advertising Standards and Practice is likely to lift the ban on advertising bookmakers	Bookmakers
Cannot sponsor games that are similar to the games played in bingo halls and casinos	Gaming companies

Fig. 10.1 Types of programmes that cannot be sponsored on TV

Enforcement

Under the **Broadcasting Act 1990**, the ITC can direct a broadcaster (licensee) to include a correction or apology (or both) in the form and at the time(s) it may determine where the licensee has failed to comply with any condition of the licence.

Such a direction may not be made unless the licensee has been given a reasonable opportunity to make representations to the ITC.

The ITC can also serve a notice on a licensee requiring payment of a penalty within a specified period or reduce the period during which the licence will be in force for a period not exceeding 2 years.

The maximum amount of any financial penalty depends on whether or not a penalty has previously been imposed during the licence period.

For example, if it is the broadcaster's first fine then the maximum penalty is 3% of its qualifying revenue for the last complete accounting period. If this is not the first time that the ITC code has been broken, then the maximum penalty increases to 5%.

GUIDANCE ON THE REGULATION OF INTERACTIVE TELEVISION SERVICES (iTV)

In February 2001, the ITC produced its first **Guidance Note to Broadcasters on the regulation of iTV**. This guidance is predominantly aimed at ITC licensees but is also of relevance to marketers.

iTV services are provided in the course of and as an adjunct to programming. They may be 'dedicated' services, accessed in their own right, such as electronic shopping malls or 'enhanced' services allowing background information to be provided on programmes or on advertised products as they are displayed on the screen, or allowing commercial material to be linked with programming through the click of an icon.

The guidance makes it clear that interactivity must not prejudice the fundamental principle of separation of programmes from advertising.

Accordingly, the ITC has proposed a 'light touch' regulatory regime to be put in place in respect of each of the forms of iTV services outlined above.

For 'dedicated interactive' services the regulation is minimal and from a marketer's perspective does not propose to set any standards of content. For 'enhanced' services the guidance is more specific.

POINT OF LAW

For example, interactive icons within editorial programming are not allowed to be branded and may not be used in a way that encourages undue prominence of products appearing in a programme.

ITC'S POSITION ON THE REGULATION OF THE INTERNET

The ITC's powers extend to television programmes on the Internet and to advertisements which contain still or moving pictures.

However, at the time of writing, the ITC are 'not seeking to apply these powers at present' to the Internet.

The ITC has reiterated that it does not intend to regulate the Internet however users get access to it, and therefore Internet-via-TV services where full web access is available via the TV un-moderated by broadcasters are currently excluded from the ITC's self-imposed remit.

For further discussion on cyber marketing, see Chapter 15.

ITC CODE FOR TEXT SERVICES

The **ITC Code for Text Services** primarily regulates teletext services. It limits permitted advertising on Public Teletext (the teletext services on Channels 3 and 4 (including S4C) to 35% of the total number of main pages offered.

The ITC Code for Text Services contains specific rules on sponsorship, sponsor credits, product placement and advertisements generally.

These seek to ensure the separation of advertising from editorial content through the use of dividing lines and different colours and from specific editorial content entirely (e.g. children's pages from alcoholic drinks advertisements).

Any sponsorship must be clearly acknowledged, without affording the sponsor editorial control, or permitting restricted or prohibited sponsors from becoming involved.

The ITC Code for Text Services is slightly more relaxed than that for broadcast services, e.g. betting tips and betting and gaming (including pools and bingo) advertisements are permitted, however generally it follows the established Codes.

The ITC issue warnings and fines to licensees who breach the ITC Code for Text Services and the licensees could ultimately have their licences revoked.

BACC

The BACC is funded by broadcasters in an effort to ensure the advertising they transmit complies with the ITC Codes. It also provides an advisory service to marketers on the interpretation of the Codes and offers a pre-transmission clearance service for advertising.

Marketers will be required to provide evidence supporting any claims made in their advertisements. Apart from the occasional advertisement destined only for discrete local broadcast, every television advertisement will be approved by BACC prior to broadcast to ensure that it is in line with the approved script.

Scripts submitted in the prescribed form can usually be cleared within two to three days. All final versions must be submitted on video. Viewings occur every morning, but two working days should be allowed for BACC to advise on approval.

Further information on BACC is available on its website **www.bacc.org.uk**.

Approval does not relate to the technical quality of the advertisement and nor does it usurp the right of rejection by individual broadcasters or guarantee that the ITC will not take action if the advertisement is found to breach any of the ITC Codes.

Notes of Guidance for marketers are available from the BACC. They reflect its interpretation of the **ITC Codes** which they supplement and expand. The Notes of Guidance are not exhaustive or definitive but they should be referred to by marketers in advance of any submission for approval in order to expedite the process and avoid obvious mistakes.

POWERS OF THE BSC

The BSC (which regulates broadcasters rather than marketers) was established under the Broadcasting Act 1996.

The Commission will consider complaints relating to:

- Unjust or unfair treatment in a programme
- Unwarranted infringement of privacy in, or in connection with the obtaining of material included in, a programme
- The portrayal of violence or sexual conduct in programmes
- Other matters of taste and decency

Fairness and infringement of privacy

The BSC has a number of duties which are covered by the ITC Programme Code. For example, this includes the portrayal in broadcasts of violence and sexual conduct and to matters of taste and decency generally.

The BSC considers complaints relating to *fairness* (unjust or unfair treatment or infringement of privacy) and *standards* (portrayal in broadcasts of violence and sexual conduct and to matters of taste and decency).

In considering 'unwarranted infringement of privacy' the key word is 'unwarranted'.

For example, secret recording may or may not be considered justified according to the circumstances. It is also possible that programme material gathered in a public place may be challenged on the grounds of infringement of privacy.

The way that programme makers act in gathering material may constitute breach of privacy even if the material is not transmitted (see also BBC's Producers' Guidelines below).

If complaints concern matters that are the subject of legal proceedings or if the BSC deems that the complaint would more appropriately be remedied by law it is not permitted to consider such complaints.

Where a complaint is considered by the BSC and there is a certain element of overlap between the functions of the ITC and the BSC, e.g. a copy of the complaint must be sent to the ITC and if the complaint is upheld, the BSC may require the ITC to direct the broadcaster (licensee) to publish a summary of the complaint, its findings and any observations.

Following on from the BSC's findings, if the ITC decides to take supplementary action as a result of those findings a report of the action taken must be submitted to the BSC.

The BSC is not usually allowed to consider fairness complaints made more than 5 years after the death of a person affected.

The BSC does have discretion in determining whether to consider a fairness complaint where it has not been made within approximately 3 months of the broadcast and a similar discretion if the complainant's interest in the subject matter of the complaint is not direct.

Hearings

When considering fairness complaints, on certain occasions the BSC will hold a formal hearing in private, although the complainant, broadcaster and ITC can attend the hearing and present their respective arguments.

Standards complaints must be made within 2 months of the broadcast of a programme. These complaints may be considered with or without a hearing.

However, in the instance that a hearing is held, it is usually held in private in similar circumstances to the hearing of a fairness complaint.

Standards Panel

The BSC's Standards Panel monitors programmes about which it has received complaints and determines whether to uphold the complaints or not.

The findings of the Standards Panel, following an investigation regarding the complaint, are published in a monthly bulletin.

The ambit of the panel overlaps to a degree with the functions of the ITC which also has a team responsible for watching programmes to monitor breaches of ITC licence conditions.

If a complaint about fairness or standards is upheld, the BSC has the power to require broadcasters to publish a summary of the complaint and its findings on the complaint. The broadcaster may be required to publish the finding in the Press as well as on the air. The BSC normally requires publication for upheld 'fairness' complaints but it is very unusual for it to require publication for an upheld 'standards' complaint.

THE BBC PRODUCERS' GUIDELINES (2001)

Background

The Producers' Guidelines are a public statement of the values and standards expected from the BBC and also set out a blueprint of how BBC programme makers are expected to achieve them. The guidelines apply to producers and editors whether working in radio, TV or on-line. With respect to the latter, the BBC undertakes never to put anything on the Internet which it would not be prepared to broadcast.

The current (fourth edition) contains Guidelines on the following:

- Values, Standards and Principles
- Issues in Programmes
- Programme Funding and External Relationships
- Politics and broadcasting during elections
- Matters of Law
- Accountability of the BBC

A full copy of the Producers' Guidelines is available from the BBC Corporate Press Office and those Guidelines that have or are likely to have an impact on marketers are reproduced and discussed in detail below.

BBC Statement of Editorial Values

We aim to be the world's most creative and trusted broadcaster and programme maker, seeking to satisfy all our audiences with services that inform, educate and entertain and enrich their lives in ways that the market alone will not.

We aim to be guided by our public purposes; to encourage the UK's most innovative talents; to act independently of all interests and to aspire to the highest ethical standards.

What this means for marketers is that the BBC can be held to account against any deviation of these guidelines where there is an issue of:

- Impartiality
- Accuracy
- Fairness
- Giving a full and fair view of people and cultures
- Editorial integrity and independence
- Respect for privacy
- Respect for standards of taste and decency
- Imitation of anti-social and criminal behaviour
- Safeguarding the welfare of children

▩ Fairness to interviewees

▩ Respect for diverse audiences in the UK

▩ Independence from commercial interests

Impartiality

As a former producer of the BBC's leading consumer affairs programmes *Watchdog*, BBC1, *Sound Advice*, BBC Radio 5 and *You & Yours*, BBC Radio 4, I am perhaps well versed in the finer points of the need for impartiality that is a foundation stone of the Producers' Guidelines.

We regularly had to submit our radio and TV scripts to the Chief Legal Advisor of the BBC, a wonderful man by the name of Glen del Medico, who would scrutinise items with great attention to detail to ensure we had complied with the Producers' Guidelines in full and therefore would be able to fully defend the decision to broadcast the item in the face of a complaint to the Broadcasting Complaints Commission.

Understandably, there is not a queue of marketers waiting to appear on consumer affairs programmes such as *Watchdog* or *You & Yours* but marketers should be aware that if they do end up on such programmes that they do have the right of reply.

POINT OF LAW

Where a programme reveals evidence of inquiry or incompetence, or where a strong, damaging critique of an individual or institution is laid out, there is a presumption that those criticised be given a fair opportunity to respond.

There may be occasions when (the right of reply) is inappropriate (usually for legal or overriding ethical reasons) in which case the Head of Department should be consulted. It may then be appropriate to consider whether an alternative opportunity should be offered for reply at a subsequent date.

The right of reply is not automatic and I have personally been involved in setting up stories about marketers that have been involved in criminal practices and significant wrong doing where it was in the public interest to expose them.

For example, on *Watchdog* in the early 1990s I investigated the UK's largest self-build marketer (Homesmith plc) that had enticed hundreds of people into risking all that they owned into joining self-build schemes in and around the North West of England.

The schemes were so bad and hundreds of people had been conned into joining them that I spent about 6 months investigating the story and gathering substantial evidence against the company. All my letters, faxes and phone calls to the company went unanswered and all attempts to offer it an opportunity to respond to a dossier of extremely serious allegations was met with complete indifference.

Once we had finished filming the victims of the fraud as well as seeking comment from the National Self Build Scheme Association and lawyers acting for the claimants, I organised what is known in TV jargon as a 'doorstep' interview between our reporter Bill Hannahan and a director of Homesmith plc.

'The Doorstep' – this term is used in broadcasting to mean occasions on which a reporter confronts and records a potential interviewee without prior arrangement, either in public or sometimes on private property.

The story was broadcast and very soon afterwards Homesmith plc became the subject of a police investigation and was put out of business!

The doorstep interview was justifiable given the exceptional circumstances of the story and the decision was taken at the highest level within the BBC.

People who are currently in the news must expect to be questioned and recorded by the media. Questions asked by reporters as public figures come and go from buildings are usually part of legitimate newsgathering, even if the questions are sometimes unwelcome, and the rules on doorstepping are not intended to prevent this.

In all other cases doorstepping should generally be the last resort. It needs to be approved in advance by the Head of Department who should do so only if:

- The investigation involves crime or serious anti-social behaviour and

- The subject of the doorstep has failed to respond to a repeated request to be interviewed, refused an interview on unreasonable grounds, or if they have a history of such failure or refusal.

Doorstepping should not be used merely to add drama to a factual report.

Controller Editorial Policy (CEP) must approve in advance any proposal to doorstep where there has been no prior approach to the interviewee. CEP will usually grant permission only if there is clear evidence of crime or significant wrong-doing, and if there is a reason to suspect that a prior approach will result in the individual evading questioning altogether.

Fairness and straight dealing

Marketers can expect to be treated honestly and with respect. Where a marketer is invited to appear on any BBC programme, the researchers and producers must, from the start, be as clear as they can be about the nature of the programme and its purpose.

For example, programme makers cannot seek to pretend that the programme is about praising the road safety efforts of car manufacturers over the last 50 years when in fact the programme is taking a critical look at a catalogue of failures by car manufacturers to improve levels of road safety for passengers over the last 50 years.

The Producers' Guidelines clearly state that unless there are special and legitimate considerations of confidentiality, programme makers should be open about their plans and honest with anyone taking part in a programme.

Contributors should not feel misled, deceived or misrepresented before, during or after the programme, unless there is a clear public interest, when dealing with criminal or anti-social activity.

Marketers have a right to know:

- What a programme is about.

- What kind of contribution they are expected to make, e.g. an interview or a part in a discussion. If invited to take part in a debate or discussion they should be told in advance about the range of views being represented and (where possible) who the other participants will be.

- Whether the contribution will be live or recorded and whether it will be edited. Given the nature of broadcasting, there is never any guarantee that a contribution will be broadcast, but the BBC should not normally record a substantial contribution unless it expects to use it.

Interviews

The Producers' Guidelines state that interviews should be well mannered and courteous.

POINT OF LAW

They may be searching, sharp, sceptical, informed and to the point – but not partial, discourteous or emotionally attached to one side of an argument.
They may be challenging but not aggressive, hectoring or rude, whatever the provocation.
Interviewees should be given a fair chance to set out their full response to the questions. In a well-conducted interview, listeners and viewers regard the interviewer as working on their behalf.

Many people, especially politicians and large multi-national organisations can expect rigorous interviews but the BBC must avoid impressions of bias through tone or inflection or through careless wording and should be dispassionate to contentious issues.

Marketers have a right under the Producers' Guidelines to:

- Understand why they are being invited for interview
- What subjects they are going to be asked about
- Context of the programme
- Sort of part they will play in it

However, the Guidelines stop short of providing a right for details of **actual questions** to be made available in advance or give any undertaking about the precise form of questions.

For example, with a chat show like BBC1's **_Kilroy_**, marketers will not get a list of precise questions given the fluid nature of the show which relies heavily on what the studio audience says in order to prompt a line of enquiry from its presenter, Robert Kilroy-Silk.

However, in practice, producers and reporters are willing to discuss in _general terms_ the type of questions likely to be asked but _precise questions_ are not really decided until recording or transmission of the live broadcast in most cases.

If a marketer makes a condition of participating in a programme the need to see and agree questions in advance, then the BBC has the right to withdraw the offer of the interview or vary the invitation to participate.

Where a marketer is put under the spotlight and the programme is recorded for later editing, the BBC must advise the marketer that the interview will be edited. The producers must ensure that the points of substance made by the marketer in the full recording are reflected in the edited programme.

Choosing only the weaker responses of an interviewee in preference to effective rebuttal is unfair. Overall, a reasonable person, seeing or hearing an interview both in full and in edited form, should conclude that it has been edited fairly.

Marketers **do not** have the right to see a copy of the programme before it is broadcast, largely because the BBC has editorial independence over all material and does not require approval from contributors to broadcast a programme.

However, there may be circumstances under which it is appropriate to allow a preview, e.g. if the subject of the programme deals with some trauma or distress.

In addition, once an interview has been given, a marketer cannot demand that the BBC withdraw it from a programme, so any requests for an interview must be very carefully considered before a marketer agrees to appear on a programme.

Refusal to take part

Where a marketer has refused to appear on a programme (for whatever reason) the BBC can explain on air the reason for the absence.

The refusal of an organisation or an individual to take part in a programme should not be allowed to act as a veto. Anyone has the right to refuse, but when the audience might otherwise wonder why a contributor or organisation is missing the reasons for their absence should be explained. This should be done in terms that are fair to the

> absentee. The programme editor should consider whether it is possible to give a good idea of the views of the missing contributor based on what is already known. It is rarely acceptable to exclude the missing view altogether.

The marketer should weigh up the risk of not taking part and the perception of guilt that could be created by the programme and the damage that this could have on its reputation.

This is particularly the case in product liability cases where it may be in the best interests of the marketer to try and put its own case forward rather than have the programme attempt to put an argument forward on its behalf which will have no credibility with the listening or viewing audience (see also Chapter 3 and Chapter 4).

Surreptitious recordings

Despite that the BBC Producers' Guidelines state that surreptitious recording should not be used as a routine production tool or to add drama to a report, the fact is that this technique has become widespread amongst programme makers fond of dramatisation of a story given that it can get high viewer ratings.

For example, the **ITC Programme Code** has similar rules applying to consumer programmes on commercial TV and arguably it is more difficult to do a surreptitious recording under the ITC programme code rather than the BBC Producers' Guidelines as any such request needs to be referred to the Programme Director of the licensee (broadcaster).

The interest in 'real life' documentaries and the blurring of fact and fiction filled the schedules in 2001 with TV programmes such as *The Real Holiday Show* (Channel 4), *Big Brother* (Channel 4), *Survivor!* (ITV1), *Airport* (BBC1) and *Ibiza Uncovered* (Sky One). The programme schedules in 2002 will reflect this insatiable demand for 'real' TV. For example, Louis Theroux is currently filming another series for BBC2 of *The Weird World of Louis Theroux* to be broadcast later in 2002 and another series of *Big Brother* has begun.

The technique of surreptitious recording that *The Real Holiday Show* and *Ibiza Uncovered* exemplifies has therefore gained in popularity amongst programme makers and has crept into news and current affairs programmes such as *Love in Oldham*, a programme on Channel 4 that tackled the taboo subject of racism.

Marketers are definitely targets for investigative style journalism and film making particularly where they could be perceived as being the 'baddies' in order for the story to be told.

For example, those marketers in the travel, chemical, pharmaceutical, tobacco, cosmetic or financial services industries are particularly vulnerable to criticism from all corners and therefore ensure that customer complaint procedures and relationships with the public and the media are on a sound footing otherwise they could run the risk of being the next subject of a surreptitious recording!

However, the BBC runs the risk of a claim against it for trespass if it attempts to film on private property, such as a chemical plant or laboratory, without permission.

Programmes must be satisfied that, where permission has not been or could not be granted, it is appropriate in the circumstances for the BBC to proceed.

Under the Producers' Guidelines, any surreptitious recording must be approved in advance by the Head of Department, National Controller or Commissioning Executive, or in the World Service, the Head of Region. Where necessary, the Controller of Editorial Policy should also be consulted.

On each occasion of the secret recording being carried out, the BBC needs to keep detailed records including who and what was recorded and who authorised it.

This record must be made irrespective of whether or not the material is broadcast.

The BBC Producers' Guidelines also state that so called 'fishing expeditions' where a camera crew may turn up in the hope of recording something interesting is not permitted and this also applies to the 'bugging' of private or public premises *unless* it is for the purpose of gaining evidence of a serious crime.

The Controller of Editorial Policy must always agree in advance and it will require clear evidence that the crime has been committed by those who are the subject of the recording.

Recording telephone conversations

There is a fear shared by many marketers that a conversation on the telephone with a broadcast journalist could end up being broadcast.

However, this is extremely rare and it is illegal to record telephone conversations without the permission of at least one of the parties involved in the call.

A BBC journalist would need to seek permission to do so from their Head of Department who in turn will consult the Controller of Editorial Policy. A recording will be authorised only if:

■ There is prima facie evidence of crime or serious wrongdoing

■ The programme maker can show why an open approach would be unlikely to succeed

If during a phone conversation the marketer is taken by surprise by a journalist that says without warning that the conversation is being recorded for broadcasting purposes or that the marketer is 'live' on air (equivalent to 'doorstepping') then this can only be done if the Head of Department at the BBC has approved that this is to happen on the grounds that:

■ The investigation involves crime or serious anti-social behaviour and

■ The marketer has failed to respond to a repeated request to be interviewed, has refused an interview on unreasonable grounds or has a history of such failure or refusal

Marketing and promotional activities of BBC personalities

Famous BBC personalities such as Jonathan Ross, Julian Clary, Terry Wogan, Michael Buerk, John Humphries, Jenni Murray, Noel Edmonds, Gary Lineker and Louis Theroux may be offered a wide range of non-BBC promotional activity that could include:

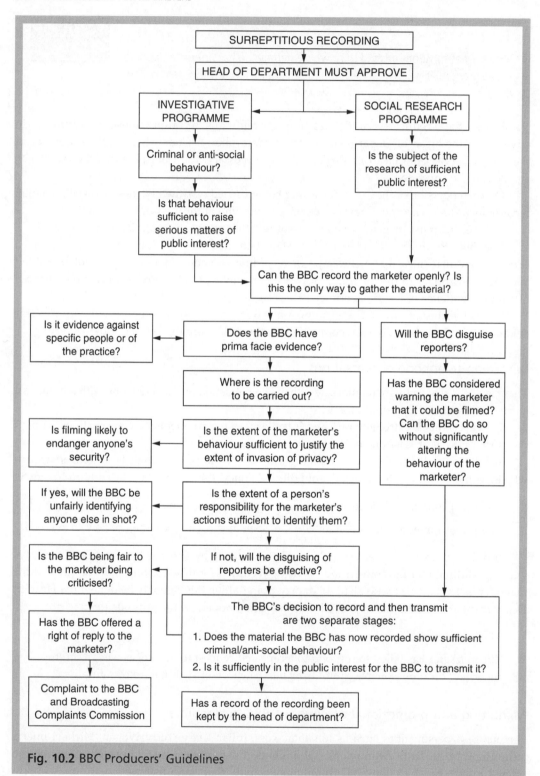

Fig. 10.2 BBC Producers' Guidelines

- Advertising products and services or organisations
- Making or appearing in corporate videos
- Attendance at commercial events
- Public relations work
- Charity work

Work of this kind which promotes non-BBC related activities is unacceptable for BBC editorial people (including presenters and freelances) when it might compromise public trust in the integrity of its programmes or of those who make and present them. Under no circumstances must this activity suggest BBC endorsement of a product, service or organisation. Heads of Department must determine the proper standards for the people working in their own areas.

POINT OF LAW

For example, **Gary Lineker**, presenter of BBC1's *Match of the Day* recently signed a £1.5m deal with **Walkers Crisps** to make at least five TV commercials a year plus personal appearances for the marketer.

However, Michael Buerk and John Humphries would not be permitted to appear endorsing road safety products or a range of organically grown foods given that they are front line BBC radio and TV news and current affairs presenters.

The BBC forbids presenters and editorial staff that regularly appear in news and current affairs, topical programmes, consumer programmes or associated on-line services from coaching marketers in how to be interviewed.

POINT OF LAW

We must not train potential interviewees to present themselves in the best light or to avoid robust questioning.

Artists that perform BBC owned characters, such as actor Todd Carty who plays Mark Fowler in BBC1's *EastEnders*, are not permitted to undertake any advertising or promotional activity for marketers which may suggest an association with the BBC and the programmes in which the artists appear.

The standard Equity contract stipulates that the artist should not appear in an advert or promotion which associates them with their character without the written permission of the BBC.

However, the BBC will permit actors and professional performers to appear in promotions or advertisements for marketers' products or services providing that they do not appear as 'their' BBC character and the advertisements or promotions do not replicate or reflect BBC programmes.

POINT OF
LAW

For example, actor **Neil Morrisey** played Tony in BBC1's hit comedy sitcom *Men Behaving Badly*. Actress **Lesley Ash** played Deborah and the nation followed the antics of Gary (played by Martin Clunes) and Dorothy (played by Caroline Quentin) with great interest.

After the show ended, Neil Morrisey and Lesley Ash landed lucrative TV advertising contracts promoting **Homebase** products and currently appear as a couple in the advertisements that are setting up home. Clearly leveraging the characteristics of the roles they played in the sitcom, the advert comes perilously close to looking like it is out of *Men Behaving Badly* but appears to have kept within the Producers' Guidelines that also stipulate that such work must not bring the BBC into disrepute and should not imply BBC endorsement.

Where the BBC does not own copyright in the character, e.g. the Chumley Warner character created by Harry Enfield, then it cannot stop advertisements that use the character to promote a marketer's products or services. In the case of Harry Enfield, he appeared in character for TV commercials for Mercury in the 1990s.

However, the Producers' Guidelines state that the BBC would like to be consulted about the use of such characters and formats, even to the point that it would seek to offer advice on scripts for TV commercials involving such characters as well as preventing TV commercials being broadcast at the same time of the related BBC programme.

POINT OF
LAW

In the unlikely event of the unwillingness of an artist or producer to co-operate, this may make it more difficult to contract them in the future.

Product prominence

Although marketers' products may appear on programmes that need to reflect the real world, such as soap operas and documentaries, the BBC must not give the impression that it is endorsing or promoting any marketer's product or service.

A product or service must never be included in sound or vision in return for cash, services or any consideration in kind. This is product placement and it is expressly forbidden in BBC programmes. It is illegal to make any such arrangements in the UK or anywhere else within the European Union.

The BBC will avoid references to trade and brand names and will only refer to a marketer's products or services where it can be editorially justified. No undue prominence should be given to any branded product or service and there must be no element of plugging.

When featuring branded products or services, we must take great care not to give an impression that the programme is being influenced in any way by a commercial concern. Television shots should not linger on a brand name or logo unless justified for strong editorial reasons.

The BBC has also issued Guidelines to producers for the naming of a company, product or service in the context of a news or factual report and warns of skilful public relations companies making approaches to more than one programme on the same news item for the same client.

The BBC's reputation for impartiality is not enhanced if the same commercially-orientated story appears on several programmes over a short period of time. Journalists and producers should think carefully about editorial justification, integrity and labelling before deciding whether to use material provided by a commercial company.

Consumer and lifestyle programmes

Such programmes that regularly review or feature a wide range of marketers' products may under certain circumstances accept such products for free or at considerably reduced costs.

However, detailed records must be kept of the product, when and how it was used and what information (if any) was included on support material. The producer must be able to demonstrate that no marketer is being favoured or discriminated against and products cannot be featured merely because they can be secured free or at a very reduced cost.

This is a sensitive area for the BBC and marketers can expect to receive a letter reminding them of BBC policy in this area and stating that:

- No question of the product being accepted in exchange for an assurance of an on-air reference

- No guarantee that the product will be reviewed in a favourable light or that it will feature in the programme at all

- Marketers will not be afforded an editorial say in the programme nor a preview of it

Programme makers should be wary of the promotional dangers posed by unsolicited offers of free or reduced cost products from manufacturers or suppliers. Any placement of products in exchange for reduced cost is prohibited.

Holiday and travel shows, such as BBC1's *Holiday* that regularly reviews a range of travel facilities and accommodation, cannot accept free trips and must pay a significant contribution towards these costs.

The programme never covers holidays offered by one company merely because they are offered at a particularly advantageous rate and a range of tour operators are covered in the course of the series.

Marketers offering media facilities and free trips

Marketers may be tempted to offer programme makers expenses paid trips to a facility within or outside the UK, for the purposes of gathering material for broadcast or as a background briefing for selected journalists.

The BBC will not accept these facility trips unless it is the only way to gather such material and that the trip is editorially necessary.

Such invitations will not be accepted if their acceptance might adversely affect the BBC's editorial integrity.

Any programme maker proposing to accept the offer of either a media facility or a fact finding trip must get advance approval from the Head of Department and the BBC is free to decide who (if anyone) accepts the invitation.

> **POINT OF LAW**
>
> For example, the story could be on private property (such as a hospital or nuclear reactor) and in such an instance an organised media visit may well be very appropriate.

Again, the fear of compromising editorial integrity is an issue and the marketer can expect a letter from the BBC producer pointing out that it is not normal policy to accept such trips and offering to make a realistic contribution to the costs (such as air fares) involved.

> **POINT OF LAW**
>
> On briefing and fact finding trips the BBC must take care that its editorial integrity would not be compromised by the acceptance of such a trip. Any acceptance needs to be able to pass the test of public reaction were the nature of the trip to be publicised. Again, the BBC should offer to make a realistic contribution (e.g. air fares) towards the costs involved. If such an offer is refused the presumption should be against acceptance.

Where a marketer makes such an offer to a named individual *only* rather than the programme, the Producers' Guidelines state that the presumption should be against acceptance of the invitation.

Video and audio news releases

Marketers are fond of providing video news releases (VNRs) to get their messages across and independent TV broadcasters have taken a more open minded approach to the use of such material provided that it has journalistic value and is of broadcast quality.

On the other hand, the BBC does *not* use such material if it is capable of gathering this for itself and largely for fear of being accused of compromising editorial integrity.

It may not always be possible for the BBC to send a cameraman to record an event given that resources are stretched to the limit and so if the difference is covering the story or not, the producer may decide to use external pictures.

If such material is used on sound editorial grounds, then this needs to be clearly labelled on-air (e.g. stating that the pictures have been supplied by the non-BBC source).

Marketers should be aware that only shots that do not promote its products or services may end up being used and may be added to other VT footage for illustrative purposes.

Coverage of sponsored events

The BBC will cover a range of public events, such as sports and cultural events, and will bear the costs for broadcasting from these events. Where the costs for mounting the event have been covered by sponsorship, e.g. the Volvo Challenge Round the World Yacht Race or the Mercury Music Awards, the BBC cannot accept any money from the sponsor or organiser for the coverage of the event.

POINT OF LAW

The BBC should not allow its coverage to be used as a vehicle for the sponsors' goods, services or opinions. Producers must never agree to display or mention the sponsor's goods or services.

Contractually, the BBC's contract for broadcasting all outside sponsored events is with the event organiser, not the event sponsor.

Titles of sponsored events

The incorporation of the marketer's name in the title of some sponsored sporting events, such as the Barclaycard Premier League, has become an established practice and the marketer's name can appear on the scorecard or results information that is broadcast for that event (see Chapter 12).

Although the BBC will honour this, it will not go as far as using the sponsor's name in the title of the programme or giving it a written credit at the end of the programme.

This compares with the practice on commercial TV which allows sponsored programming (see earlier in this chapter) and such programmes incorporate the title of the sponsor in the title of the programme broadcast.

Where there is signage and logos, slogans of the marketer clearly visible, then the BBC will broadcast these images as part of the coverage of the event being televised and will not black out commercial messages.

Where advertising is prominent, e.g. in Formula 1 or football, the BBC will follow the main action and will not dwell on any perimeter or billboard advertising in its coverage of the event.

> **POINT OF LAW**
>
> In covering an awards ceremony, some discrete signage for the sponsor may be acceptable, but all reasonable efforts must be taken to ensure that it is not to be included in the main shots.

When a presentation or an award is being given by a marketer at a sponsored event, the BBC will seek to limit the number of sponsor references during such presentations.

> **POINT OF LAW**
>
> Normally there should be only one mention of the sponsor in the introduction to the presentation and if possible the person presenting the award should be asked to restrict themselves to a single reference to the sponsor. If the design of the award or trophy itself prominently reflects the sponsor's name, slogans or logo care should be taken to ensure that it does not dominate main shots.

Marketers may wish to run promotions or advertising campaigns (see Chapters 9 and 13) to publicise an event which the BBC is covering. This must be done with extreme care as any attempt by the marketer to exploit the BBC's name in support of the event organiser or marketer may result in cancellation of the coverage for the event.

Complaints for breaches of the Producers' Guidelines

As discussed earlier, under the Broadcasting Act 1996, the BSC has a duty to publish a code relating to broadcasting standards, offering guidance on the portrayal of violence, sexual conduct and general standards of taste and decency. All broadcasters in the UK are required to 'reflect the general effect' of this code, and its provisions have been taken into account in the preparation of the Producers' Guidelines.

POWERS OF THE RADIO AUTHORITY

In the same way as the ITC licenses broadcasters in television, the Radio Authority licenses and regulates all commercial radio services, comprising national, local, cable, satellite and restricted services on both analogue and digital platforms. This includes the regulation of programming and advertising.

In performing its role as a regulator, the Radio Authority publishes **Codes of Practice** (similar to the ITC or BSC) which licensees must comply with, covering areas such as programmes, advertising and sponsorship.

Advertising and Sponsorship Code

The **Radio Authority's Advertising and Sponsorship Code** is relevant for:

- Product placement
- Undue prominence

The Code is based on the Radio Authority's legislative obligations in respect of advertising and programme sponsorship. All licensees are obliged to comply with the spirit and letter of its contents.

As with television, radio advertising should be legal, decent, honest and truthful. Product placement or undue prominence of commercial products or services in programming is prohibited. Any reference to products or services must be limited to what can clearly be justified by the editorial requirements of programming itself.

Unlike television, sponsors of programmes may buy spot advertising in and around the programmes they sponsor, provided that if the style is similar to the programme, an indent is inserted to separate the two.

Section 2 of the Code contains the **General Rules** relating, amongst other things, to transparency and clear separation of advertising, misleading listeners, superlative claims and fair comparisons. **Section 3** lays down rules for the advertising of specific categories of product.

Marketers must strictly observe the Code and only justifiable coverage of commercial products or services is acceptable.

The Radio Authority can apply sanctions against those broadcasters who breach the Codes of Practice as compliance with the Codes is a contractual obligation as it forms part of the radio licence.

Sanctions

Penalties include:

- Broadcast apologies
- Corrections
- Fines
- Shortened or revoked licences

LAW IN ACTION

Powergen Radio Commercial (September–December 2001)

A competitor marketer felt that Powergen's claim 'you get just one bill for gas, electricity and phone' was inaccurate, because Powergen's customers would continue to receive a bill from BT for the cost of renting their telephone line, as well as the one from Powergen for the cost of their calls. Powergen and the Radio Advertising Clearance Centre (RACC) argued that it was clear from the script that all the services purchased from Powergen were detailed on one bill.

Powergen argued that consumers were aware that it did not cover the line rental and therefore the three services it supplied were, taken literally, detailed on the bill.

The Radio Authority agreed with the competitor marketer that, within the context of the radio commercial, the claim 'one bill for . . . phone' was likely to mislead listeners and implied one bill for all phone services, regardless of whether Powergen supplied the line rental or not. The use of the word 'phone' was a generic term as opposed to 'phone calls', which was more specific. The Radio Authority asked the RACC to tell Powergen to amend the advertisement accordingly.

THE RADIO ADVERTISING CLEARANCE CENTRE (RACC)

The **RACC** is the radio equivalent of BACC. It is funded by commercial radio stations and is administered by the trade association of the industry. It provides a script clearance service in an attempt to ensure that commercial radio stations' obligations to act in accordance with the **Advertising and Sponsorship Code**.

All radio advertisements or sponsorship that fits into the 'special' categories of the Code requires clearance. These include, amongst other things, advertising aimed specifically at children, consumer credit, investment and complex financial advertising. Advertisements for national transmission also require clearance prior to broadcasting.

Scripts may be submitted by fax, by post or by e-mail (although the move is progressively towards an electronic submission and approval mechanism) accompanied by satisfactory substantiation of product claims.

Where evidence is insufficient to uphold a claim such as 'the leading' or 'the No 1' then the script may well be rejected.

Clearance is issued via Script Clearance Forms which will indicate whether clearance is absolute or conditional on amendment or subject to scheduling. An initial response should be provided within 24 hours. Emergency clearance is available out of hours or on weekends on advance notice for a small fee.

RACC also provides a telephone helpline for general queries on radio advertising and hypothetical radio advertising proposals. Information is available at www.crca.co.uk/racc.

Irrespective of the RACC's decision, the ultimate decision as to whether to accept any radio commercial for broadcast rests with the radio station concerned.

Radio copy guidelines

The **RACC's Guidelines** can be accessed on-line and are intended to be a quick-reference source for marketers who clear copy and are grouped by product. Their content is based on the RACC's clearance experience.

COMMUNICATIONS WHITE PAPER (2001)

Increasing convergence in the fields of broadcasting, telecommunications and spectrum usage led to calls for a single regulatory body.

In 2001, the **Department of Culture, Media and Sport (DCMS)** announced that the **Office of Communications (OFCOM)** will serve as such a regulatory body with a single strategic policy framework based on a core set of principles applied consistently across the areas of television, radio and telecommunications.

The Board of OFCOM will be collectively accountable, in contrast to the Office of Telecommunications (OFTEL) which is governed by a sole Director General.

OFCOM will incorporate the **Radiocommunications Agency's** responsibilities for managing radio spectrum, as well as be responsible for activities currently regulated by **OFTEL**, the **BSC**, the **ITC** and the **Radio Authority**.

An example of an area that OFCOM will address is the potential for electronic programme guides (EPGs) – a navigation screen that appears when a viewer turns on a TV set and wants to navigate to one of over 200 channels.

EPGs could be used by some broadcasters to limit competition and consumer choice because consumers may find it difficult to gain access to content or programmes not favoured by the electronic programme guide operator.

It is anticipated that Parliament will issue a bill as early as Spring 2002 which will establish OFCOM; however, the institution of the new regulatory regime to be administrated by OFCOM may not be fully effective until 2003.

DIGITAL ERA/INTERACTIVE SERVICES

When digital television technology was developed, further legislation in the form of the Broadcasting Act 1996 ('1996 Act') was needed to license and regulate digital terrestrial services and the Radio Authority to license digital audio broadcasting services.

The 1996 Act also changed the laws on who can own television and radio licences.

Digital television brings with it the potential for e-mail use and interactive programmes through the medium of television, thereby giving increased access to the Internet.

In this way the television becomes a haven for entertainment, information and two-way communication.

It is because of this convergence that strict protection is afforded to consumers who may engage in on-line shopping from the comfort of the living room.

THE FUTURE OF BROADCASTING

There has been a rapid evolution of broadcasting services and formats, as a result of which its regulation has not tracked its fast moving development.

Once OFCOM becomes fully effective as the single regulator for television, radio and telecommunications (it is still unclear whether the BBC will be subject to OFCOM rules or not) if successful then the current overlap between the regulatory functions will no longer exist.

This should be good news for marketers as it will hopefully make it less complicated to keep broadcast sponsorship and advertising within the law rather than having to apply a set of fragmented and out-dated legislation.

Hopefully, OFCOM will also be able to more easily keep up with any changes in technology and promptly adapt its regulations to that end.

CHECKLIST

- TV advertising must not be misleading, encourage or condone harmful behaviour and not cause widespread or exceptional offence, and marketers must take account of the 9 pm watershed

- Advertisements that are subject to investigation by the ITC will be off air and therefore marketing plans for new product launches will need to be revised

- Product placement, in its purest sense, is prohibited on both commercial TV and the BBC

- Sponsorship of programmes on commercial TV must not distort or call into question the editorial integrity of those programmes

- BBC will honour sponsorship of events but without undue prominence of the marketer in the broadcast

- Rules regarding product placement and undue prominence apply to radio broadcasts

- Sponsorship of news and current affairs is still off limits but the recent relaxation of the Code of Programme Sponsorship permits financial programmes sponsorship and a greater degree of branding within the credits

- Marketers can seek advice about TV advertising from the CAP

- Under the BBC Producers' Guidelines, marketers may not have an automatic right of reply

- Marketers should always ask:

  1. What the programme is about and the context for the programme

  2. Why they have been invited to give an interview

  3. What subjects they are likely to be asked questions about

  4. What contribution they are expected to make

  5. Whether the programme is 'live' or recorded to be broadcast at a later date

- Marketers should be extremely careful in refusing to appear on a programme and refusing to answer reasonable repeated requests to appear on a programme as a negative inference could be drawn by the programme and the audience

- When considering using celebrities, marketers should check the contractual obligations between the celebrities and the broadcasters

▧ Marketers should seek to build good relationships with broadcast media rather than seek to exploit broadcast journalists and misuse their economic position

▧ VNRs are appropriate for commercial TV and not used except in limited circumstances by the BBC

▧ Marketers should keep abreast of the changing regulatory framework surrounding broadcast and electronic media. The creation of a single unitary regulatory body – OFCOM – may have a profound effect on marketers by making it easier to comply with the complex regulations governing broadcasting in the UK

11
LICENSING AND MERCHANDISING

In this chapter:

- The licence agreement
- Legal protection for intellectual property rights – registered trademarks
- Guidelines on the use of trademarks
- The licensing process
- Penalties for illegal merchandise
- Parallel imports
- Combating counterfeiting
- Checklist

Other useful chapters:

- Chapter 2: Making agreements
- Chapter 4: Liability for defective products
- Chapter 5: Intellectual property rights
- Chapter 6: Copyright
- Chapter 12: Sponsorship and hospitality
- Chapter 13: Promotions and incentives
- Chapter 17: Ambush marketing

INTRODUCTION

The latest craze for Harry Potter™ merchandise has created a worldwide licensing phenomenon worth millions of pounds. However, it also creates one of the biggest headaches for those charged with protecting a global licensing and merchandising programme on this scale.

Likewise, the FIFA World Cup Japan/Korea 2002™ is set to become the biggest global licensing and merchandising programme in 2002, and will stimulate significant growth in southeast Asian markets for licensed merchandise not just for FIFA but for other rights holders in other sports as well.

However, FIFA is expected to face the largest assault on its licensing and merchandising rights in Asia, Europe and South America where football is extremely popular.

The tournament reflects a growing trend for rights holders to take their brands to consumers overseas wherever they may be in the world and the Olympic Games in China in 2008 will build on this momentum.

Licensing and merchandising – a brief description

Although these terms tend to be used interchangeably, in the industry licensing is understood to be the process and merchandising the product. With the benefit of the above chapters, we will look upon a licensing and merchandising campaign with a practical as well as legal application.

Management of expectations

One of the biggest obstacles is invariably unrealistic expectation on the part of the rights holder. Very few properties (the technical term used to refer to the subject of a licensing and merchandising campaign) are in the same league as *Pokémon*™, the Olympic Games™, FIFA World Cup™, *Star Wars*™ or *Bob the Builder*™.

Keeping licensing in perspective

Keeping a perspective on the reach of the licensing and merchandising campaign is an essential first step in understanding what legal and non-legal steps will need to be taken to fend off unwanted interest from the pirates of the licensing industry – the counterfeiters or 'rip-off merchants'.

Cost implications

A small fortune has already been invested by the rights holder of the intellectual property rights (IPRs) to negotiate with all the parties involved in a licensing programme – getting licensees to buy into the concept; convincing sceptical retailers to stock branded merchandise; persuading consumers to buy the stuff and deploying a protection policy that prevents those not licensing the property from unauthorised use of trademarks.

THE LICENCE AGREEMENT

It is useful to consider the actual nature of licensing, which in essence is a special type of marketing contract (see also Chapter 2).

Definition

The following is a commercially driven definition of licensing, as opposed to a strictly legal one:

INSIGHT
Licensing is the permission to allow well-known imagery from films, cartoon characters or sports events owned by licensors, to be used on consumer products or in promotions, created by manufacturers or retailers (licensees), to increase the appeal of that product or promotion and provide a unique selling point from other similar goods or services.

Licensing is therefore a contractually-based relationship between the rights holder and/or its agents – known as the licensor – and the 'renter' of those IPRs – known as the licensee.

In many examples of legal disputes, the prospective licensee is a manufacturer of clothing or consumer products.

There must be a valid licence, or contract, with each licensee. The formal permission to use the owner's IPRs is subject to certain terms and conditions, such as specific purpose, defined geographical area and a defined time period (usually measurable in months and years).

Each agreement will be subject to individual negotiation. This can be a time-consuming process but is one that cannot be shortcut if a long-term successful programme is to be put in place.

Contents of a licence agreement

- The company name of the licensee
- The name and/or description of the property being licensed
- The products licensed (together with a description of specifics such as sizes or weights of garments or maximum or minimum wholesale prices
- The territory in which the licensee is authorised to sell the items (distribution of licensed merchandise)
- The channels of distribution which the licensee is authorised to use (if applicable)
- The royalty rate and its method of calculation
- The minimum guarantee and when staged payments are to be made
- Royalty reporting and payment dates
- Conditions under which licensees may sub licence manufacture and/or distribution
- How and where artwork and product samples will be approved, and the time in which the licensor has to do this

- Grounds for termination of the agreement
- The law under which the agreement is governed

This is not an exhaustive list, but one that covers the basics. Even these points will result in a sizeable agreement that will need to be put together with specialist legal assistance. The licence agreement that could grant exclusive or non-exclusive rights to the licensee is just one aspect of the legal relationship between the licensor and licensee.

In many cases, the licensor or licensee hires a specialist licensing agency like Copyright Promotions Licensing Group (CPLG) to manage a range of functions which can include:

- Design
- Finance
- Legal

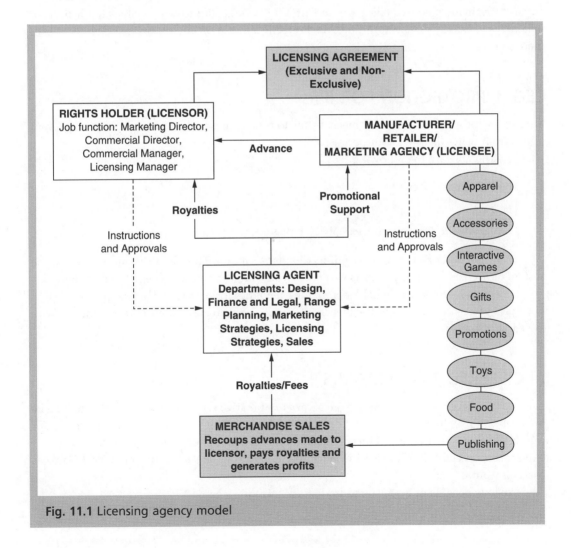

Fig. 11.1 Licensing agency model

- Range planning
- Marketing strategies
- Licensing strategies
- Sales

The manufacturer, retailer or marketing agency (or any combination of these parties) can be granted licences by the licensor in the context of the licensing programme.

An advance would normally be payable to the licensor who may pass instructions to the licensees through its licensing agent so, for example, designs for merchandise and the way in which the logo appears is managed by a specialist agency. It is also very common for the licensees to have their own agencies to deal with instructions and approvals, which can be a time-consuming process.

Once merchandise sales start then the manufacturer or retailer will start to earn back the advance originally paid to the licensor and after this would start to pay royalties to the licensor (again this is usually managed through the licensing agency) on any profits made on the sale of merchandise.

LEGAL PROTECTION FOR IPRs

English law provides a number of mechanisms to protect those who have rights and to prevent others from using them without permission.

Most notable are the following:

- The Trademarks Act 1994
- The Tort of Passing Off
- The Copyright, Designs and Patents Act 1988

These are described in more detail in Chapters 5 and 6. This chapter concentrates on the system of licensing and merchandising goods which are the subject of **registered trademarks**.

However, for those rights holders pursuing remedies for passing off or breach of copyright in respect of licensed merchandise, this chapter will also provide guidance in conjunction with the earlier chapters.

REGISTERED TRADEMARKS

An organisation or individual may have a variety of marks, which may or may not include its own name: it may have a single word or logo associated with its activities or separate marks for certain types of activities or products. These could also include nicknames, such as *The Gunners* (Arsenal soccer club), *The Red Devils* (Manchester United) or *The Yankees* (the New York Yankees baseball team).

Obvious benefits of a registered trademark include:

- Helping to boost brand recognition and awareness

- Assisting in the introduction of new products and services to the market
- Preventing other competitors from using similar marks for the same products and services
- Assumption of reputation in the trademark

Enforcing unregistered trademarks can be considerably harder and potentially more expensive than enforcing a registered trademark, requiring the marketer to rely on the complex tort of passing off (see Chapter 5).

From a practical perspective, brand owners need to be clear what rights they wish to grant to an organisation, what rights are being held back and the scope of any exclusivity.

Double counting of rights given away

The areas that most often go wrong are where brand owners end up giving away the same rights twice or where third parties think they have acquired rights and they have not.

Classes and territories

The classes and territories in which a mark is to be registered needs very careful consideration too.

INSIGHT

For example, too few classes and territories will leave the property under-protected, and too many classes will result in wasted time and money.

This is where the reality check is needed – what is likely to be licensed, and therefore requiring trademark registration, and in which territories?

Having made a decision, either based on experience, initial market research or with the guidance of a specialist rights exploitation agency, it is vital to register that which will be used in terms of name/image/logo and ensure these are the elements which will be licensed, not some derivation of them.

This will ensure adequate protection is available to licensees and licensors (rights owners) from the outset.

Transactions

Ownership of trademarks and trademark applications can be transferred by assignment, either in connection with the transfer of the business to which they relate or independently. Assignments must be in writing.

The assignment can cover all or part of the goods and services for which the mark is registered, and can be for use of the mark only in a particular location or a particular way.

Licensing of trademarks without actual transfer of ownership is possible, and this is very common within sports licensing and merchandising. However, the licensor must ensure that there are sufficient safeguards covering quality control in order to avoid the misuse of the mark's standing as a badge of origin or quality.

All transactions concerning registered trademarks must be recorded at the Trademarks Registry to ensure that the assignee and licensee's rights have priority over any later conflicting transactions which the original trademark owner may enter into.

Renewal

In the UK, renewal fees are due every 10 years after the mark is registered (see further below). If the mark ceases to be of value to the organisation or business, it is possible voluntarily to surrender it back to the Registry at any time, so that renewal fees are avoided and it becomes free for other businesses to use should they wish to do so.

A surrender of a trademark may be in respect of the whole or some of the classes for which the mark was originally registered.

'Proper use'

In terms of the protection of a registered trademark, proper use is extremely important either by a brand owner or a licensee. Failure to use a trademark for a period of 5 years will leave the registration open to an application for revocation by any third party that wishes to use the mark.

Clearly, it is important that the right form of the trademark is used and used in connection with the actual goods and services for which it is registered.

Guidelines to proper use of a trademark

The following guidelines should be borne in mind when marks, particularly word marks, are used in any form of advertising or packaging:

- When referring to a mark in text distinguish it from other words by putting it in capitals, italics or underlining it

- On any label or advertisement the trademark should appear in a prominent position

- Never hyphenate the trademark to another word or split a single word mark by punctuation, spaces or hyphenation

- Avoid using the mark as a generic term (if the mark passes into ordinary usage then the courts will be unlikely to stop competitors from using the same word and the trademark loses virtually all its value)

- Third parties should be discouraged from making use of the mark

- If the trademark is mentioned several times on a label or in advertising copy, combine it at least once with the product or service designation

- Ensure that the same typeface is used for all the letters of a word mark

- Where the trademark is a logo, ensure that the correct colours are used

- Have a standard black and white version to be used when colour printing is unavailable

- The fact that a mark is a trademark should be asserted at least once on any label and in any advertising

- Where a trademark is used in relation to goods for which it is registered, it may be accompanied by the sign ® – this is usually placed at the top or bottom right hand corner of the word or symbol

- Where a trademark is unregistered or is still at the application stage of registration or its status is unclear it should be accompanied by the sign^{TM}, with registration taking place as soon as possible

- Particular care should be taken only to use the symbol ® against marks which are actually registered

- Where space permits there should be a footnote to the advertisement/feature explaining the significance of the ® ,^{TM} and identifying the owner of the mark

National trademark registrations only give national protection: a UK registration will not assist in stopping someone using the same mark in France, for example. Therefore, brand owners operating internationally should consider whether a registration is needed outside the UK.

Where a mark should be registered in other countries

Where a mark is intended to be used in more than one country of the European Union (EU), it is possible either to apply for several national trademark registrations in the relevant countries or to obtain a Community Trademark (CTM) from the Community Trademark Office in Alicante, Spain.

The CTM

The CTM is a single mark applying in all countries of the EU, but because of this it can be refused on the basis of any prior conflicting mark in any Member State.

The costs of carrying out searches in every Member State before applying are very considerable, and it is therefore simpler to apply and leave it to the owner of any prior conflicting mark to notify the CTM office of its mark's existence. If a mark is refused as a CTM on the basis of such an opposition, it is possible (on payment of a fee) to convert the application into one or more national applications.

It should be noted that a CTM cannot be assigned for part of the EU only – as it is a unitary mark, it can only be assigned as a whole. The CTM also becomes vulnerable to revocation if not used over a 5-year period – but use in any single EU country is sufficient to protect it for the whole of the EU.

Madrid Agreement

The Madrid Agreement was an international treaty that aimed to establish an international filing system for trademarks, similar to the international patent system. However, several key countries failed to sign up to it and it was only a partial success.

World Intellectual Property Organisation (WIPO)

In 1989, the WIPO in Geneva negotiated a Protocol to the Madrid Agreement, which was aimed at removing the objections of the major industrial countries and bringing the Madrid system into wider use.

The Protocol, having been ratified by the necessary number of countries, including the UK, came into effect in April 1996. It is therefore possible once a UK trademark has been registered to apply for registration in any number of the countries which subscribe to the Madrid system.

Once the UK registration has been verified by WIPO, the Trademarks Registries of the nominated countries have up to 18 months in which to refuse the registration on national grounds. Once registered, the mark remains for 10 years and is renewable every 10 years *ad infinitum*.

Accurate use by licensees

Having registered, or at least made an application to register a trademark in the correct classes and territories, and issued a licence agreement which has been fully executed by all parties (and properly recorded at the Trademark Registry), the next stage in a licensing programme is to ensure that authorised licensees only use approved designs in their product development process and, ultimately, on the product itself.

To ensure licensees are equipped with correct artwork references, in terms of colour, size relationships and correct fonts, a style guide or graphics standard manual needs to be prepared.

Style guide 'bible'

Adherence to the style guide is an essential element of the contractual obligations entered into by the licensee.

Again, this can be a timely and costly process, but if a licensing programme is to succeed it is a process that must be completed.

It will need specialist design input in conjunction with legal advice to ensure the references, which will become a licensee's 'bible', are totally correct.

Compensation claims by licensees

Errors at this stage will not only be costly in terms of possibly having to compensate licensees for any breach of contract due to the supply of incorrect reference material but may delay the introduction of the product into the marketplace which could prove disastrous in a time-sensitive licensing programme, such as a sports event or film tie-in.

Approval process

As important as providing the reference material, to assist licensees in the accurate reproduction of the licensed property, is the ability of a rights owner, or their agent, to either approve the artwork, designs, samples or finished product or to disapprove the items submitted.

There needs to be a clear statement as to what must be done by the licensee to correct the errors. An efficient system of approvals needs to be put in place at the outset staffed with well-trained approvals staff who can quickly react to material sent by licensees and who can respond with clear statements as to the next action required.

Defining territories

Licensees themselves may be the cause, either deliberately or unwittingly, of causing a certain amount of confusion in the marketplace.

This can be especially true of licences granted in the EU. Under European Community law, any restrictions against the free movement of goods between Member States are prohibited.

Therefore, a licensee granted a licence to distribute certain products to an individual or group of EU member states will automatically have the rights to sell those goods throughout the EU.

A contract limiting them to individual member states is probably unenforceable.

The status of an exclusive licence is a moot point as competitors of the licensee would need to provide evidence of restraint of trade in order to bring an action and there is no guarantee that such an action would succeed in the courts.

How then can rights owners maximise the value of their rights through licensing but not cause confusion in the marketplace and a devaluing of the product offer at retail level?

There are a number of courses rights owners, or their agents, may wish to consider.

Distribution by EU territory

As previously discussed, this may well be contractually unenforceable but it may be possible to obtain the agreement of licensees that if each is awarded for separate territories they will not encroach on other licensees' territories.

However, care should be taken to ensure that such agreements do not fall foul of EU legislation prohibiting concerted practices, cartels, abuses of dominant positions and other anti-competitive behaviour.

Licence by product

This may seem an obvious category. It can though be a little more sophisticated than just individual product items or groups of product.

Licensees can be licensed to sell, for example, certain items but are limited by size, weight, cost, retail price, content of product or any other enforceable definition that can be agreed.

This then enables rights owners to put in place a programme which is not dependent on good will but accepts that, in the EU, licensees can and will trade as widely as they are able in the interests of generating business. The restriction put on them is through defining exactly what product they are being licensed to produce.

Licence by distribution

This allows for licensees to be granted as wide ranging a licence as they or the rights owners wish but limits them to either certain types of retail or defined retailers within the EU.

This enables a number of licensees to be appointed for the same or similar products each playing to their own particular distribution strengths, safe in the knowledge they will not have other licensees selling to their particular retailers.

INSIGHT

For example, some apparel licensees may be directed to supply exclusively to mass-market/'hyper-market' outlets, others to high street fashion multiples, while others only to dedicated, specialist sports or other unique outlets such as at airports or major railway stations.

This can have some negative side effects, not least individual licensees driving down price, and therefore royalty income, by, for example, demanding they are supplied product at a lower price or higher margin than their competitors supplied by other licensees.

The net result is that licensing becomes less attractive to the rights holder and it may therefore restrict licensing to a selected few products, thereby limiting the choice for consumers for branded merchandise.

Security devices

There are a number of ways in which rights owners can convey to both retailers and consumers the fact that a particular product is legitimately licensed.

Swing tags

At its most basic this might be a sewn-in label in a garment, for example, with the copyright (©) and/or trademark (® or ™) symbols with details of who owns the licensed material. It is an offence to claim a registered mark when this is not the case.

Licensors can go further and employ the use of, for example, hangtags with 'Official Licensed Product' as a statement that this is a legally licensed product.

Holograms

The use of holographic images and security numbering can make the counterfeiting of tags more difficult and the numbering can be used for both checking the licensee of origin as well as a useful source of double-checking tags ordered versus royalty reports.

There are a number of specialist companies who can design and ship security tags of an increasingly secure nature.

This is a very visible method of not only reinforcing the legitimacy of the licensee but of assisting with brand building and brand awareness.

Security devices not only provide a check of items ordered versus items declared on a royalty statement as an aid to double checking the accuracy of these returns but they can be used to assist rights owners and licensees in anti-counterfeit measures.

What happens when licensed goods are unlawfully exploited?

Counterfeit goods

Goods bearing without authority a mark that is identical or similar to that of a validly registered trademark are described as counterfeit. This also applies to packaging, labels, brochures and manuals.

Around 6–10% of world trade involves counterfeit products, so this is a major policing issue. The most heavily counterfeit industry sectors include:

- CDs
- Software
- Videos
- Clothing
- Spare parts
- Luxury goods

Both civil and criminal proceedings are open to the brand owner and enforcement in the UK can be carried out at the public's expense through trading standards officers' prosecution as well as assistance from HM Customs & Excise (see further below).

Civil proceedings

The registered proprietor of a trademark can bring infringement proceedings as can an exclusive licensee.

Non-exclusive licensees will also be able to sue if the brand owner fails to enforce the mark within 2 months. In such circumstances, a non-exclusive licensee is potentially subject to a 2-month delay before it will be able to take direct action against a counterfeiter, although the proprietor will hopefully be unlikely to acquiesce in such a serious situation.

In dealing with counterfeiters speed is of the essence as a key remedy is to remove the counterfeit goods off the market – particularly surrounding a major sporting event like the Olympic Games^{TM} or FIFA World Cup^{TM}.

Brand owners can seek wide-ranging interim relief pending a full trial before a judge (see Chapters 5 and 6 for further detail on infringement of trademarks and copyright, and passing off).

The claimant (be it the proprietor or licensee – see further below) must be able to show a good case of infringement, that damages will not be an adequate remedy and that the balance of convenience favours preventing the defendant from further transactions before the trial. To guard against the possibility of the claimant ultimately failing in its action, the court will often require a cross-undertaking in damages from the claimant, fortified by security in the form of a payment into court or bank guarantee. This will be used to compensate the defendant who is found to have been legitimately dealing in the allegedly unlawful goods.

As an injunction is an equitable remedy, it is important that the brand owner should have behaved appropriately, e.g. neither delayed in bringing proceedings nor acquiesced in the defendant's activities.

Search and Seizure Orders

A Search and Seizure Order can be a very effective means of recovering counterfeit goods and other evidence. This order empowers authorised representatives of, for example, the trademark owner to enter and search the premises of the counterfeiter for specified goods or information, and in certain circumstances to remove them.

It is obtained by the rights owner without notice to the suspected counterfeiter and the order is only executable during working hours and is usually supervised by an independent solicitor – which adds to the cost of the remedy for the brand owner.

To obtain such an order it is necessary to have a very strong case and to be able to show likelihood that the defendants will destroy the evidence if proceedings on the usual (slower) timetable are followed. It is especially useful against the fly-by-night operators.

As an alternative, a counterfeiter can be ordered to produce and hand over required items – this can be sought where there is less evidence available.

Delivery-up and destruction

Counterfeit goods that are seized will be delivered-up to the trademark owner and are usually destroyed, and this also applies to any articles adapted for producing counterfeit goods.

Damages/account of profits

Damages for infringement of an IPR are calculated to put the brand owner in the position it would have been in had the infringement not occurred. If in reality the brand owner would not have been in a position to make the sales that the counterfeiter made, then an alternative remedy is to ask for an account of profits which the counterfeiter in fact made from its activities.

Defences

These are dealt with in detail in Chapters 5 and 6.

Criminal infringement

It is a criminal offence (for profit or to cause loss to another) for a person without consent of the brand owner to use a *sign identical* or *likely to be mistaken* for a registered trademark on goods for which that mark is registered, or to sell/distribute the goods in the course of business.

Narrow protection

This is narrower than civil remedies for infringement since it only applies to goods which are the *same class* as the registration and it does *not* cover marks registered in respect of services.

However, much counterfeit merchandise are precise copies of goods and so are susceptible to both civil and criminal proceedings.

It is also an offence to use such a sign on packaging, labels, business papers or advertising, be in possession of goods *bearing the sign*, or have goods adapted for making *copies of the sign*. To be an offence, the unauthorised use must be in relation to the class(es) of goods for which the mark is registered, or must take unfair advantage of the distinctive character or repute of the mark.

The protection given is broad as any sign which is likely to be mistaken for a registered trademark can lead to prosecution and conviction. Purported disclaimers – 'these goods are fakes' or 'brand copies' – will not be a defence for a counterfeiter attempting to avoid prosecution.

Brand owners can also enlist the help of both the HM Customs & Excise (where illegal imports of counterfeit products are suspected) and the network of Trading Standards Offices that can serve notices on traders selling counterfeit merchandise to the public.

Counterfeiter's defence (criminal proceedings only)

'Reasonable grounds'

It is a defence for someone accused of counterfeiting to be able to show (beyond a reasonable doubt) that they believed on *reasonable grounds* that the use was not an infringement.

The best evidence for substantiating this would be that they had received professional advice that the sign or mark used did not infringe and thus their belief was reasonably held. However, such a defence cannot be raised in civil proceedings.

PENALTIES

The criminal penalties for counterfeiting are similar to those for theft, which can, in extreme cases, carry a 10 years prison sentence.

A Confiscation Order can be made in respect of the proceeds of the trademark infringement, but this can only be made after the counterfeiter has been found guilty of two or more offences.

In reality, because of the costs of such proceedings, it is unlikely that the Crown Prosecution Service (CPS) will bring applications for such orders before the Court unless it is understood that the defendant has at least £10 000 in realisable assets and it is for the defendant to prove that the assets have been lawfully obtained.

Powers of HM Customs & Excise

HM Customs & Excise are able to seize counterfeit products at the point of entry if these products are entering the UK from outside the EU for any reason (including transhipment) and to destroy the goods if proved to be unauthorised merchandise. This power is very effective against counterfeiters.

Time limits

HM Customs & Excise are free to act on their own initiative and to detain goods for up to 3 working days to enable them to contact the brand owner and for the latter to make an application for the goods to be impounded.

The time limit of 3 days is a very short time in which to act; it is advisable to have a specific application for detention ready prepared and someone specifically designated as a Customs & Excise contact that will be ready to take action as soon as they are notified.

However, the effectiveness of Customs & Excise acting on its own initiative is likely to be limited – it is unlikely to be aware of all registered marks and besides it has responsibility for many other matters apart from counterfeiters.

Keeping a watch for the brand owner

Alternatively, on the payment of a fee, a brand owner can request that Customs & Excise keep a watch for counterfeit goods in respect of any registered marks. In such cases, the Customs & Excise notify the brand owner if any suspected counterfeit goods are seized and the trademark owner then has 10 working days in which to inspect the goods and confirm their counterfeit or genuine status.

If the goods are counterfeit then they will be seized and destroyed unless the importer within 1 month contests the counterfeit status, in which case Customs & Excise will need to take legal proceedings seeking this remedy.

The information provided to Customs & Excise (and Trading Standards, see below) must be regularly updated to ensure its accuracy otherwise there is the risk of official licensed product entering the country with the consequent effects on the authorised licensee and its customers.

Trading Standards Offices

Trading Standards Offices of every local authority have the power to enforce the provisions of the Trademarks Act 1994. Trading standards officers have the power to make test purchases and enter premises and seize documents.

INSIGHT

The Football Association (FA) and Euro96

In the year before Euro96 there had been about 30 cases of counterfeit FA products being produced. These were usually quite poor imitations of the England replica strip and usually in quite small quantities.

The FA anticipated that because of the extensive TV coverage and sponsorship which coincided with Euro96 there would be an increased level of counterfeiting activity before, during and after the Championships.

The FA wanted to have a proactive, cost effective approach and in addition wanted to use the Euro96 anti-counterfeiting action as a springboard to raise the profile of the FA and its trademarks with the enforcement authorities. The FA produced its own anti-counterfeiting brochure, which provided:

- General background on the FA
- Details of all the FA marks and relevant graphical representations
- Details of the FA's licensees and the products they make
- Information on how to spot counterfeits and actual examples of counterfeit merchandise
- Contact details for inspection and the provision of witness statements

The brochure was sent to over 150 trading standards departments in England and Wales as well as to relevant HM Customs & Excise offices. Armed with this information, trading standards officers knew what was counterfeit merchandise on a first visit to a factory or trader and this avoided delays and further sales of counterfeit products.

The brochure also signalled the FA's intent to take the matter extremely seriously and was a good example of co-operation with trading standards officers and other authorities in order to secure convictions against counterfeiters.

In addition, the FA recruited over 200 experienced part-time investigators who actively searched for counterfeit products and who were able to bring their own criminal prosecutions.

As a result of all these highly proactive measures, trading standards officers successfully seized counterfeit merchandise on over 40 separate occasions including 800 England replica shirts intended for the market produced in one factory and numerous smaller quantities from a national chain of stores.

Trading Standards Offices of local authorities can greatly assist rights owners in ridding the market of unlicensed merchandise.

If trading standards officials are involved early on in a project they can proactively seek to remove unlicensed product from the market.

Meetings can be held with them to explain the nature of the property being licensed and when licensed product is likely to enter the market.

An outline checklist for use with Trading Standards:

- The name of the property

- The marks being licensed

- Any security devices used to donate Official Licensed Product

- A list of licensees and the products for which they have a licence

- List of manufacturers used by licensees

- Retail stores stocking the product

- Full contact details of the rights owner/agent

Best practice in the licensing industry is to give Trading Standards time, information and assistance. With careful planning, timely and accurate exchanges of information and a co-ordinated system of dealing, there are effective methods of dealing with the removal of unlicensed products from the marketplace without always having to resort to the courts.

PARALLEL IMPORTS – EU AND NON-EU IMPORTS

Trademarks, as the potential barriers of *free movement of goods between countries*, are viewed with suspicion by some EC Commissioners and the extent to which trademarks can be used to stop parallel imports has been fettered to minimise conflict with the principle of free movement of goods and services.

Free movement of goods and services

Individual countries' laws regarding the exhaustion of IPRs are central to the regulation of those rights. Parallel imports (so called **'grey market imports'**) are goods brought into a country without the authorisation of the trademark or copyright holder after those goods were placed legitimately into circulation elsewhere.

POINT OF LAW

For example, suppose that an authorised dealer of sports apparel in Thailand produced under licence to a brand owner sells it locally at wholesale prices below the retail price in, say, Japan. The dealer or third party parallel trader could ship the apparel to Japan and make a profit net of tariffs, shipping and distribution costs. These goods are legitimate copies, not pirated copies or 'knock offs' – parallel imports are identical to legitimate products except that they may be packaged differently and may not carry the original manufacturer's warranty.

National and international exhaustion of rights

1. Under national exhaustion, rights end upon the first sale within a nation but brand owners may prevent parallel trade with other countries

2. Under international exhaustion, rights are exhausted upon first sale anywhere and parallel imports are permitted

3. A third option is regional exhaustion, by which rights are completed within a group of countries thereby allowing parallel trade among them, but are not exhausted outside the region

In essence, once trademark rights have been exercised in the first marketing of a particular batch of goods by the brand owner (or with its consent), they are exhausted and cannot be used again against those particular samples.

POINT OF LAW

For example, if a brand owner based in the UK owns the same trademark in several EC countries and has licensed a local dealer to sell them under the local trademark in France or Italy, it will not be possible to stop the goods 'leaking' back into the UK by suing an importer for infringement of the UK trademark.

There are exceptions to this rule but these mainly concern potentially dangerous goods such as pharmaceuticals where the trademark owner may well have legitimate reasons for opposing resale of repackaged goods but these exceptions are unlikely to apply to sports licensing and merchandise.

Non-EU parallel imports

Less clear position

The position is less clear from the brand owner's perspective where imports originate from outside the EU.

EU law has less impact on a trademark holder's right to prevent the resale of such merchandise within the UK *unless* it has entered the UK after a sale has already taken place within another EU country – in which case the EU principle of free movement of goods applies exactly as for parallel imports originating within the EU.

Notice that the goods are not for circulation

In the situation where there has not yet been a sale within the EU, for example, legitimate merchandise comes into the UK direct from the Far East, then it may be possible to prevent resale of merchandise in the UK provided that efforts have been made to draw to the attention of the original and all subsequent purchasers (importers) that the goods are not for circulation in the UK.

POINT OF LAW

For example, a term to this effect must have been included in the contract of sale to the first purchaser (importer) and preferably the goods should be labelled to the same effect so that even resellers are aware of this limitation.

COMBATING THE COUNTERFEITER

There are several practical steps a rights owner or agent can take in order to combat the infiltration of pirate goods coming onto the market.

Trade fairs

If the brand being licensed is, say, an entertainment event such as a highly anticipated movie release or international sports events, it would be wise for the rights owner or its agent to attend some of the numerous licensing-related trade fairs which populate the licensing-marketer's calendar.

It might consider trawling the exhibition stands of various events such as the New York or Nuremberg Toy Fairs in February each year, the Munich ISPO Summer and Winter sports goods shows each February and July, the MAGIC apparel show in the US or Frankfurt Bookfair, or perhaps direct its lawyers to do so on its behalf.

At these events, it is possible to come across manufacturers quite brazenly promoting branded goods they have created without official sanction.

Should such a trader be encountered, the rights owner has a number of different options available to it:

'Friend not foe' approaches

It may wish to take a conciliatory approach and overlook the transgression, and invite the trader to apply for an official license, and thus legitimise the trader's merchandise.

Cease and desist approach

Alternatively, the rights owner could take a more aggressive approach and immediately serve the trader with a legal 'cease and desist' notice, requesting it to stop producing such goods.

Communicate regularly with retailers

A rights holder or its agent should take all possible steps to communicate directly with retailers. This has the effect of adding credibility to the licensee and establishes a direct point of contact with the rights holder/its agent. It is also important to try to communicate across the retail structure, from the high street to wholesale to discount. Advertising and public relations in the trade press are also useful tools.

Exclusion zones

If the brand in question is again a high-profile movie or sports event property, the rights owner may consider taking steps to protect legitimate merchandise right up to the 'opening curtain' of the event.

> **POINT OF LAW**
>
> For example, for sports events such as the **FIFA World Cup**, rights owners would do well to consider putting in place an exclusion zone around stadia, policed by staff, to ensure that no unauthorised vendors are selling pirate merchandise in the stadia's immediate vicinity, thereby usurping legitimate on-site trade. Such 'clean stadia' are increasingly an integral part of any anti-counterfeit campaign.

International Licensing Industries Merchandisers' Association (LIMA)

Another useful measure for rights holders and their agents to take is to become members of LIMA – the worldwide trade body for the licensing and merchandising industry which represents the interests of:

- Manufacturers
- Retailers
- Rights holders
- Licensing agents
- Support services such as lawyers

LIMA provides the following services to its members:

- Set up seminars and education
- Networking
- Free directory to members
- Web site
- Free legal advice for members

LIMA sees counterfeiting as a massive issue and has set up an initiative where a large number of rights holders are getting together to combat counterfeiting through the pooling of resources in order to set up a network of private investigators that will gather evidence that can then be used in prosecutions brought against counterfeiters.

LIMA recommends that rights holders have a contractual right to go into factories and warehouses at very short notice to check that the goods for which the licensee has a licence to make are in fact the only goods being produced.

However, in LIMA's experience problems occur when other parties are involved, where IPRs have been passed on and with parallel imports.

One of the most effective ways to combat the increase in counterfeiting on other territories is for the rights holder to ensure that it has a local presence – its own agents – in a local territory.

UK-based rights holders who do not have a local agent can contact the British Embassy or local Consulate in that territory for information and advice.

CHECKLIST

As discussed in this chapter, there are a number of ways in which rights owners can protect a licensing programme:

- Any licensing programme relies on the awareness of the brand/property with enough inherent goodwill to create a demand from consumers for licensed merchandise.
- One of the core principles of the EU is the right to free trade between member states. This can have advantages as well as disadvantages. Each must be considered and rights owners musty decide in advance of embarking on a licensing programme how multi-territory deals will be treated.
- An effective licensing programme relies on investment from the rights owner in a number of essential areas:
  - A clear strategy on what will be licensed in terms of logo/characters/brand name or other identity
  - A coherent, comprehensive and effective trademark registration programme
  - A graphics guide to ensure licensees are accurately reproducing the licensed elements
  - An effective approval mechanism to ensure consistent use by licensees, safeguard brand identity and ensure product development timetable is adhered to

- A licensing programme which is defined in terms of licensee/territory/products/distribution

- The benefits of a licensing programme can be numerous – if the programme is a success.

- For a licensee, the added attraction of a licensed tie-up increases demand for its products and promotions, enlarges its product and promotion's target group, offers the market a point of differentiation and can even create an emotional attachment to its product.

- For a licensor (rights owner), licensing can mean an increase in brand exposure, a strengthening of negotiating positions with third parties (with broadcasters, video, theatrical distributors and the media) and of course increased revenue.

- Where there are unregistered trademarks, the rights holder could resort to using the tort of passing off. However, as the Arsenal case (see Chapter 5) demonstrates, success in the courts is not guaranteed and therefore legal action should only be used as a last resort.

12

SPONSORSHIP AND HOSPITALITY

In this chapter:

- Definition of sponsorship
- Key legal issues in sponsorship
- Definition of hospitality
- Key legal issues with providing corporate hospitality to clients and staff
- Checklists

Other useful chapters:

- Chapter 5: Intellectual property rights
- Chapter 6: Copyright
- Chapter 10: Broadcasting
- Chapter 14: Lobbying
- Chapter 16: Niche marketing
- Chapter 17: Ambush marketing

INTRODUCTION

The legal jungle can be treacherous, even for experienced marketers. Thus, it is always prudent to seek specialist professional advice, particularly when negotiating complex sponsorship and hospitality agreements.

SPONSORSHIP

Sponsorship advisors may be asked to perform a variety of tasks that could include:

- Seeking appropriate sponsors for an event, team, club, cause or community programme
- Identifying suitable events, teams, clubs or activities that require a sponsorship partner or creating a bespoke sponsorship event
- Drafting a sponsorship agreement
- Negotiating 'personality rights' with a famous personality for use in a marketing campaign
- Drafting a licensing and merchandising contract
- Negotiating domestic and international broadcast and web rights for a major sports event
- Organising corporate hospitality at a major event
- Financial, tax and insurance planning

In each of these tasks, early management decisions concerning control, size and objectives of the event or the subject of the sponsorship programme (that could be a team, arts exhibition, major international athletics meeting or a local school – known in sponsorship jargon as the 'property') and the potential legal and commercial exposures for the sponsor or sponsors all have to be balanced.

This will typically determine the number of negotiations conducted and contracts drafted and executed by the respective parties.

Strictly speaking, there are no intellectual property rights in any type of sponsored event.

However, it is likely that the event title will be a trademark, e.g. FIFA World Cup Korea/ Japan 2002™ and the Ryder Cup™ are both registered trademarks.

Of course, there are other protections for the brand owner and the property (see Chapters 5 and 6).

Careful thought should be given to the territories in which the sponsorship will be promoted and whether appropriate trademark protection is in place for both the property owner as well as the sponsor's brand (see Chapters 5 and 6).

Successful sponsorship is all about leveraging the power of the brand combined with the sponsored event or property that creates impact with the brand owners' target audience in an experiential and measurable way.

It is arguable that modern day sponsorship, as a marketing and communications tool, has overtaken advertising in its ability to pinpoint and deliver brand messages with an extremely high degree of accuracy and control.

Sports Rights Holder	Areas of Activity	Revenue Streams	Key Revenue Drivers
Athlete/sports body representation	Creation, evaluation and negotiation of business opportunities including employment contracts, sponsorship sales, licensing and merchandising endorsements. Work with sports federations also includes event management and is increasingly focused on the negotiation of media rights deals.	➤ Commissions ➤ Licensing fees ➤ Royalties ➤ Fixed retainer fees	➤ Prize money ➤ Salaries ➤ Sponsorship ➤ Rights values ➤ Deal volumes ➤ Appearance fees
Event Management (This includes key players such as IMG, Octagon, SFX and CSS Stellar)	Promotion and management of major sporting events. Activities include event promotion, sale of media rights, sponsorship rights, naming rights, advertising, pricing, stadia presentation, and staging and logistics management. Event management includes the creation of new events, designing new tournaments that meet objectives of rights holders and sponsors.	➤ Profits ➤ Commissions ➤ Retainer fees ➤ Percentage of profits (depending on the relationship with other rights holders) ➤ Fees (work and materials)	➤ Sponsorship ➤ Rights values ➤ Advertising rates ➤ Attendance ➤ Space ➤ Number of events ➤ Utilisation rates
Club/Team	Clubs/teams generally possess the rights to events that take place within their venues. With respect to naming rights, the landlord of the stadium will hold these unless these rights have been specifically reserved for the tenant (club/team). The role of the rights holder is to exploit these rights to derive gate, advertising, sponsorship, media and licensing rights revenues.	➤ Gate ➤ Sponsorship ➤ Advertising ➤ Naming rights ➤ Merchandising ➤ Corporate hospitality	➤ Success ➤ Number of matches ➤ Attendance ➤ Ticket prices ➤ Rights values ➤ Advertising rates

Fig. 12.1 Sponsorship and exploitation of IPRs

According to the latest research by *Screen Digest*, the value of sponsorship rights expenditure in 2001 was estimated to be worth US$24.8 billion. This represents a 31% increase over the previous 10 years and although sport continues to account for the majority of the market, sponsorship has become one of the major sources of funding for both local and international events involving the arts, the environment, media, humanitarian and community projects and education.

Definition of sponsorship

> **POINT OF LAW**
>
> The **International Chamber of Commerce's (ICC)** code on sponsorship defines sponsorship as:
>
> *... any communication by which a sponsor, for the mutual benefit of sponsor and sponsored party, contractually provides financing or other support in order to establish a positive association between the sponsor's image, brands, products or services and a sponsored event, activity, organisation or individual.*

Through sponsorship, brand owners are able to convey key brand communication messages in association with an event, product, service or broadcast, in a manner that can create impact, excitement, interest and passion than many other forms of marketing activity, e.g. advertising.

It was such thinking that propelled Bulgari, the high fashion Italian jeweller, to enter into one of the most controversial forms of literary sponsorship seen in the last 10 years.

> **POINT OF LAW**
>
> In August 2001, a mixture of shock and hilarity greeted news that the best selling author Fay Weldon had been sponsored by the Italian jewellery maker **Bulgari** to write a novel featuring numerous references to Bulgari jewellery.
>
> Had the same novel been turned into a film for television, then Weldon would not have been able to do the same given the Independent Television Commission code on broadcast sponsorship (see Chapter 10) forbids such blatant product placement practice.

Whether Weldon has started something of a trend for novelists remains to be seen – it is a far cry from the involvement of beer brand Guinness and the *Guinness Book of Records* which seems to have been around a very long time and has severed almost all its commercial links from the brand that gave it its name in the first place.

However, if the US experience is anything to go by, this may not be the first or the last time that commercialisation will start to creep into areas that were considered 'off limits' in the past.

For example, in the US, there is an increasing predominance on terrestrial and digital television of US-made programming and movies, in which paid-for product placement frequently occurs.

Given that there is no US equivalent to the paid-for placement ban in the UK and many other EU states, this puts cash-strapped European programme makers at a commercial disadvantage.

Types of sponsorship

Almost anything can be the subject of sponsorship agreement provided it is for a legal and not an illegal purpose.

Type of sponsorship activity	Examples of sponsorship
Team/personality sponsorship	Vodafone and Manchester United
	Coca-Cola and Pele
Event sponsorship	Flora London Marathon
	BOC Covent Garden Festival
	Brit Awards sponsored by MasterCard
Championship sponsorships	Volvo/Mercedes Benz Masters
	Embassy Snooker
	Barclaycard Premier League
	Booker Prize
	Whitbread Prize
	BP Portrait Awards
Social and cause related sponsorship	Sainsbury's Wing at the National Gallery
	Barclays/Granada Civic Channel (Manchester)
	Ford sponsoring the National Trust leaflet
	Tesco and Computers for Schools
Arts and literary sponsorship	Fay Weldon and Bulgari
Broadcast sponsorship	Cadbury's and *Coronation Street*
	Mini and *Cold Feet*
	Domino's Pizza and *The Simpsons*
Educational sponsorship	Weetabix and Food File on Line
	Halifax and innumeracy
	Royal & Sun Alliance and National Fire Safety Education Pack
Web site sponsorship	EggCard and Freeserve
Naming rights	BT Cellnet Riverside and Bolton Wanderers FC

Fig. 12.2 Types of sponsorship

Motivation	Examples
Increase sales	Vodafone and Manchester United
Launch of new product	Sony Play Station National Skateboarding Championships
Associating name with more than making profits	Most banks sponsor local events to show they care about the community
Positioning of brand in order to establish associations	Benson and Hedges and the PGA European Tour
Media exposure	Brand owners receive a relatively high degree of media exposure for less expenditure than it may cost to buy the equivalent advertising space. Also, at its most successful, sponsorship results in the name of the sponsor becoming inextricably associated with the marketing opportunity, for example Barclaycard Premier League, the Booker Prize, Tate Gallery and Nobel Prizes
Employee motivation	John Hancock Insurance and the Olympic Games

Fig. 12.3 The main motivations for sponsorship by a brand owner

Categories of sponsorship

Exclusive sponsorship

An exclusive or sole sponsor is usually the title sponsor and has the exclusive right to use its name and logo in conjunction with the property.

For example, the Oval cricket ground in London is now known as the AMP Oval. By achieving this, the sponsor seeks to make its name synonymous with the event or venue. Such an arrangement provides the maximum possible assurance that the sponsor and the property are not referred to separately by the media and can give the sponsor a relatively high degree of control over the sponsored property.

Primary sponsor

A primary sponsor often shares exposure with other sponsors in different product categories, e.g. VISA, McDonald's, Coca-Cola and Kodak are all long-standing sponsors of the Olympic Games.

POINT OF LAW

Primary or event or title sponsorship – a marketer may acquire exclusive rights, or at least rights to be the main sponsor of the event, usually including its name in the title, such as the **Barclaycard Premier League**.

Primary sponsors always seek to obtain exclusivity within their particular product category.

Secondary sponsor

Secondary sponsors tend to provide goods or services and are often known as 'official suppliers'. Their products and/or services are used by the property to reduce its budgeted costs.

For this reason, many international events try to obtain an 'official' airline, hotel and information technology (IT) providers as secondary sponsors.

Secondary sponsorship – this will be non-exclusive and may be conferred as 'partner' status, joint sponsorship or sponsorship of an element of the event such as an individual race at a National Hunt race meeting.

In order to maximise the benefit from this type of sponsorship it is critical to obtain exclusivity within the marketer's product category (see also Chapter 17).

In return, a marketer is usually expected to give a warranty to the sponsored party that the products supplied will be of a required standard.

POINT OF LAW

Official supplier status – another non-exclusive arrangement as far as the event goes, but it could be exclusive to the aspect of the event such as **Slazenger** – the official ball of the Wimbledon Championships, or **Tag Heuer** – the official time-keeper of Formula 1.

Although it is not always possible, multiple secondary sponsors should try to avoid conflicts with rival brand owners.

POINT OF LAW

For example, if **Nike** is the title sponsor of a one-off charity tournament, it may be able to ensure that participants wear Nike clothing rather than the kit normally prescribed by the teams' sponsors. However, if Nike is the title sponsor of a league, it cannot reasonably expect to prevent rival sports apparel manufacturers from sponsoring clubs playing in that league.

However, in the US, where the major league sports are controlled centrally, **Reebok** recently signed a 10-year $250 million exclusive licensing agreement to supply 32 National Football League (NFL) teams with all their sports clothing from the beginning of the 2002 season.

In order to ensure that there is no conflict with competing brand owners in the same product category – which can cause confusion in the minds of the supporters and the public – a co-sponsor should enquire as to the identity of other potential co-sponsors before committing to a sponsorship agreement.

KEY LEGAL ISSUES IN SPONSORSHIP

Although sponsorship takes many forms, each of which will be uniquely affected by particular legislation, there are many legal issues that are common to all forms of sponsorship.

Capacity of sponsored party

Sponsored parties may be associations, charitable bodies, unincorporated members' clubs, organising bodies or trade associations and may not have the power to bind their members. If such organisations are to be bound, it is critical that all the required persons from each relevant entity are signatories to the sponsorship agreement.

Logos/trademarks

Trademark registrations (see Chapter 5) should be checked if the right to use a logo and other intellectual property rights are included in the sponsorship deal.

As the following case illustrates, carelessness and lack of protection of intellectual property rights can potentially damage a highly successful sponsorship programme.

LAW IN ACTION

BBC-v-Christopher Palmer-Jeffery (2000)

Before the BBC took over the sponsorship of the promenade concerts in 1927, a Dr George Cathcart had that responsibility, which he had discharged since the summer concerts began in 1895.

In 1996, after discussions with descendants of Dr Cathcart, a Christopher Palmer-Jeffery launched the 'Cathcart Spring Proms'. These were primarily aimed at the corporate market as part of clients' corporate hospitality activities and were staged at the Royal Albert Hall.

Palmer-Jeffery was amazed to find that the BBC had failed in 70 years to register the 'Proms' or 'Henry Wood Proms' as a trademark, and so he applied to register 'Cathcart Proms'. The BBC argued that this amounted to passing off (see Chapter 5) as 'the Proms' mark had become synonymous with the BBC and its annual summer concerts and to allow the registration by Palmer-Jeffery would be innately deceptive.

The Trademarks Registry disagreed with the BBC and held that the word 'prom' signified promenade concerts where the audience was not necessarily all seated and therefore could not be in any way unique to the BBC. In addition, the BBC had failed to show any evidence of confusion between the Cathcart and BBC Proms and in the BBC's promotional material the 'BBC' references were given ever greater prominence than 'the Proms,' with 'BBC Proms' hardly appearing at all.

Sponsor's rights

The provision of sponsorship funds does not automatically entitle a sponsor to any proprietary rights or control over a marketing opportunity.

In order to maximise the marketing and brand building opportunities, a licence to use proprietary rights for certain purposes must therefore be acquired.

The intellectual property rights (IPRs) to be licensed are diverse. These include the name of the sponsored subject (e.g. the team, event or venue) and logo for promotional and merchandising activities, plus in some cases the image or personality rights of participants may also be licensed to the sponsor brand owner (see Chapter 5).

Exclusivity

Sponsors may expect different levels of exclusivity dependent upon the level of sponsorship they have chosen (as discussed above).

Duration of the agreement

The agreement may or may not have a defined duration. In the case of a specified term, the circumstances and terms upon which the period can be extended should be defined.

> **INSIGHT**
>
> For example, in sports sponsorship, the average length of a football shirt sponsorship deal is 3 years. In contrast, a naming rights deal on a new football stadium could be as long as 5–10 years.

With respect to an event or TV broadcast, a sponsor will want to ensure there are timetables specified for the occurrence of the relevant event or broadcast of the sponsored programme.

Termination

The sponsor should retain the right to terminate the contract prematurely if the sponsored party goes into liquidation or fails to fulfil some or all of its obligations, such as failing to spend the sponsorship income on specified items, not obtaining additional sponsorship, not staging the event within a specific timescale or if one event in a long-term campaign does not meet specified criteria.

Any compensation payable in such case must be stated expressly in the agreement.

The consequences of termination or post termination restrictions must also be specified carefully.

A sponsor may also wish to include a provision to terminate if the sponsored property has changed its image, e.g. if a famous athlete has tested positive for the use of banned drugs and a full investigation corroborates this finding.

Where certain elements of a sponsorship agreement are of the 'essence' of the sponsorship, e.g. the appearance of certain sports personalities at an event on specified TV coverage, the sponsor should reserve the right to terminate the sponsorship agreement if these elements are not delivered.

'Essential conditions'

The fundamental matters giving rise to the sponsor's right to terminate should be cited as essential conditions within the body of the sponsorship agreement. If these fundamental matters are not fulfilled, the right to terminate should be stated to be automatic and immediate.

The alternative is to allow a sponsored party a specified time to remedy the breach. If a condition is not phrased in this way, damages may be held to be a sufficient remedy.

Any notice required to be given should allow both parties time to put alternative arrangements in place.

In the event of termination there should be provisions preventing the parties from continuing to promote their connection with each other and other provisions dealing with the handover of materials, logistics and any forward commitments made by the incumbent sponsor that may bind the new sponsor.

Payment structures

The sponsorship agreement may structure the payment method in a number of ways depending on various factors such as cash flow, risk assessment and tax effectiveness.

Different methods of funding sponsorship include:

- **A fixed amount.** The fee may be payable up-front or at fixed intervals (as in the case of Formula 1 sponsorship where payments are made for each of the individual grand prix races held). Repeat fees are normally subject to an annual increment calculated according to a specific formula or are re-negotiable following an agreed period. Sponsors should avoid payment of the whole sponsorship fee in advance if a marketing opportunity is new and there is no guarantee that it will deliver as agreed, or at all. In such a case, the sponsor should obtain an agreement to retain a proportion of the fee until the agreed criteria have been fulfilled.

- **Conditional.** This arrangement is often appropriate where the sponsor wishes to be satisfied that certain participants will attend, certain performance targets are met or that specified television coverage is obtained. The agreement must therefore cater for failure of one or more of the sponsored party's obligations. A specified consideration should be attached to each of the key rights to be received by the sponsor so that if one or more is not received, the sponsorship fee is reduced accordingly, or a refund given.

- **Variable.** The sponsor may wish to provide additional funds to the sponsored party if certain events occur, e.g. bonuses for improvements in league position. A cap on the maximum liability of the sponsor should be considered if this arrangement is chosen.

- **Payment for particular products and/or services.** If the sponsor is registered for value added tax (VAT), or its equivalent, but the sponsored property is not, it may be more tax efficient for the sponsor to enter into a direct contractual relationship with the relevant supplier. If so, the sponsor should check the supplier's terms of business to ensure there are no hidden liabilities. A sponsor should ensure that it agrees a method whereby it is satisfied that any costs it has contracted to pay are reasonable and that its maximum liability is specified.

■ **Provision of products and/or services.** The sponsor may provide its own products and/or services by way of payment to the sponsored party free of charge or at a nominal cost. For example, IBM supplies all the IT for the Wimbledon Championships as part of its sponsorship of the tennis tournament. The sponsorship agreement should specify any maintenance or insurance requirements as well as what will happen to any products or equipment after the event.

Event sponsorship

Given the huge choice of potential events available, the first decision a brand owner must take is whether to sponsor a single event, a seasonal or annual event or a one-off long-term project.

In some cases, the decision will already have been made by cash constraints, provided the brand owner has been realistic about its cash-flow requirements in each year of the event.

Subject to cash restrictions, the choice will depend on whether the target benefits are to be achieved within a short period or the intention is to make a long-lasting impression. If the latter is the target, the event must be capable of sustaining a prolonged marketing campaign.

Key considerations

Sponsor's rights

In order to take full advantage of the sponsorship of an event, it will often be necessary to obtain licences from more than one party.

In particular, regarding sports events, the relevant international or national federations may hold certain rights separately from the league organising the event, the participating clubs and individuals and the venue owner.

In addition to the exclusive or non-exclusive right to associate itself with the event and use the sponsored party's trademarks in connection with its promotional activities, the sponsor may seek to gain added value from additional activities.

Such additional benefits may include any of the following:

■ Rights to the appointment of a sponsor's representative on the Board of the event

■ Rights to be involved with the organisation and management of the event

■ Rights to supply and to insist that participants wear particular clothing

■ Additional advertisements in the event programme, on boards and banners in and around the venue, preferably within view of the television cameras, and product display facilities

■ Rights to take and publish its own photographs of the event having obtained the consent of any individuals prominently featured

■ Rights to use and publish official photographs of the event in marketing campaigns. In such a case a licence of the copyright in the photographs will need to be acquired (along with the consent of the individuals)

■ Personal endorsement (personality rights) agreements with participating individuals

■ The right to award prizes and trophies at major events

- Guaranteed television exposure
- Sponsorship of television and/or radio broadcasts
- Free tickets, hospitality rights and free parking
- Marketing and merchandising rights in respect of the event name and logo

Postponement

Unless the date of the event is expressed in the agreement as essential, the sponsored property may be entitled to postpone the event.

If, as a consequence of postponement, it is necessary to amend the material contract terms, the sponsor should be allowed a reasonable period of time to review its position and if necessary withdraw from its sponsorship. Third party contracts may also need to be extended or renegotiated.

Sponsors should consider insurance to cover any costs incurred due to the postponement of an event due to bad weather or act of war (*force majeure*).

Duration of the agreement

In the case of one-off events, the sponsorship agreement will usually cover the event and any postponement, plus any post event period during which the sponsor may continue its association with the event.

Periodic events may be treated in the same way or as a series of events with the sponsorship agreement also covering any period of inactivity in between events.

Cancellation

Whether cancellation of the event constitutes a breach of contract depends on the wording of the sponsorship agreement.

A breach may entitle the marketer to recover damages for wasted expenses incurred as a result of a campaign to promote its products/services connected to the event, the whole or part of any sponsorship fees paid (depending on whether the brand owner can be shown to have received some benefit from these already) and damages for lost opportunity if that can be clearly demonstrated.

Renewal

If an event is seasonal or annual, the parties may wish to maximise the return on their investment in the relationship by agreeing to maintain their relationship for a minimum number of years or seasons, e.g. Vodafone's 10-year sponsorship deal with Manchester United.

It is therefore important to specify this up-front and if relevant include a provision in the agreement such that at the end of the initial period there is a recalculation of the sponsorship fees on renewal by reference to a specified formula.

Matching option rights

If the sponsor may wish to have an ongoing relationship with a particular event but either the sponsor or the sponsored property is unwilling to commit up-front then the sponsor should consider including an option to renew the sponsorship agreement either on payment of an increased fee or through a matching rights option which is designed to establish the market value of the event.

In simple terms, the sponsor is granted an option to match the highest offer obtained by the sponsored party from any other bona fide potential sponsor.

Such options need safeguards to ensure that event owners cannot simply obtain a false offer from a third party in a bid to force the sponsor to pay more.

Where the sponsor has effectively helped create and fund a new event, and build it into something prestigious, matching option rights are a particularly effective method of achieving a return on investment and a marketing advantage over its competitors.

Clauses giving the sponsor a first right of refusal to renew the sponsorship contract must be carefully drafted to prevent a sponsored party circumventing its terms.

In order to protect the sponsor, the option must include the following key clauses:

- A clear statement of precisely what it is the sponsor has the first option to accept
- The time frame for negotiations. These should begin before the expiry of the existing agreement to enable a new agreement to be made
- A deadline for the acceptance of the new package

Broadcast sponsorship

There are numerous restrictions that apply to the televised broadcast of events that must be borne in mind by the sponsor of a TV programme. For a detailed discussion on broadcasting regulations, see Chapter 10.

The ITC Code of Programme Sponsorship (CPS)

In the UK these include the **ITC CPS** (revised in the autumn of 2000) and the **ITC Code of Advertising Standards and Practice (CASP)**.

The **ITC CPS** states that if any of the costs of a television programme's production or transmission are met by anyone *other than* the broadcaster or television producer, that programme is deemed to be sponsored, and is therefore subject to the ITC Codes.

Ordinary airtime barter does not itself make an advertiser a sponsor.

The CPS states that sponsored programmes cannot be advertised within or near to their own broadcast and that sponsorship must adhere to the ITC CASP.

Under the provisions of the ITC CPS, political bodies, tobacco manufacturers or suppliers, pharmaceutical manufacturers or suppliers and any other advertiser prohibited under the **ITC Code of Advertising** may not sponsor programmes (see also Chapter 9).

Betting and gambling sponsorship

Brand owners whose business is betting and gambling services may sponsor programmes but only subject to certain restrictions. In addition, news, business and financial reports and current affairs programmes *cannot* be sponsored.

This does not prevent items of specialist news, such as sports, traffic or weather news being sponsored, provided that these segments are clearly separated from the news programme.

The **ITC Programme Code** also states that news presenters may not be used in sponsorship credits and presenters of programmes which cannot be sponsored must not be used in any sponsored programmes shown next to the sponsor-free programme in which they have appeared.

Likewise, consumer advice programmes may not be sponsored by advertisers' products featured in the programme, although 'how to do' programmes may be sponsored by advertisers that supply featured products.

If a sponsor is paying for international exposure from TV broadcasts around the world, the domestic regulations of each country must be complied with.

LAW IN ACTION

An illustration of the problems caused by the lack of harmonisation of TV sponsorship rules across Europe is a recent motor racing grand prix where a French judge banned a broadcast of the event in France because tobacco companies were sponsoring some of the teams taking part in the event.

The contract should also address the possibility of future restrictions which could arise from a change in the law affecting the sponsor's product sector.

INSIGHT

For example, if implemented in its current form, the **draft EC Directive on tobacco advertising** and sponsorship would prohibit **Embassy**, the cigarette manufacturer, from continuing its sponsorship of the **Snooker World Championship**. Sponsors should thus ensure that appropriate termination and compensation provisions are included in their sponsorship agreements (see also Chapter 9).

HOSPITALITY

Traditionally, hospitality was considered a soft benefit of sponsorship, but today brand owners are getting smarter at demanding bottom line impact from their hospitality expenditure and tracking how well hospitality works and translates into new and incremental business.

Hospitality and corporate entertainment are now firmly established as effective tools of creating and nurturing business relationships and a useful element of a customer relationship marketing programme.

Major sporting events, such as the Wimbledon Championships (tennis), British Grand Prix (motor racing) and Ryder Cup (golf) are extremely popular with marketers.

Marketing tool and technique	Percentage of promotional budget in support of sponsorship
Public relations	15–30%
Promotions and incentives	10–20%
Hospitality	5–30%
Measurement/evaluation	1–10%
Licensing and merchandising	5–15%
Legal, accounting and consultancy fees	5–40%
Design/print	2–8%
Signage	5–10%
Special events	2–8%
Insurance	1–5%

Fig. 12.4 Percentage of promotional budget in support of sponsorship

However, the £700 million hospitality industry in the UK is very fragmented and a relatively unregulated sector of the economy, which means that marketers must be on guard for the 'cowboys' hospitality operators (particularly concerning the provision of tickets for major events).

Hospitality is not sponsorship

There is a good deal of confusion about the difference between sponsorship and hospitality. Contrary to the views of some marketers, the fact that they have a box at the Oval cricket ground does not make them sponsors of the venue or the Test series. Hospitality is an important and high profile element of many sponsorship programmes but not all sponsorship packages.

UK legislation

The critical question in relation to hospitality and legislation is when does hospitality amount to bribery? The use of hospitality is open to abuse as it can create an obligation and at the same time exposes the recipient to the marketer's influence.

The **Law Commission report (number 248)** issued in March 1998 called for simplification of the statutory framework concerning corruption.

Currently corruption in sponsorship is regulated by a mixture of common law and archaic statutes designed to prevent bribery in respect of wartime contracts.

The most important UK statutes, the **Public Bodies Corrupt Practices Act 1889** and the **Prevention of Corruption Act 1906**, provide different definitions of corruption and distinguish between the public and private sector.

Although public servants are more likely to be sanctioned by this legislation, because all employees owe a duty of trust and confidence to their employer, private sector employees cannot consider themselves immune to this legislation.

The **Law Commission's report** proposes to replace the existing law of bribery with a modern statute creating four offences. These are:

■ Corruptly conferring, or offering, or agreeing to confer an advantage

■ Corruptly obtaining, soliciting or agreeing to obtain an advantage

■ Corrupt performance by an agent of his or her functions as an agent

■ Receipt by an agent of a benefit which consists of, or is derived from, an advantage which the agent knows or believes to have been corruptly obtained

The view of most lawyers is that the Law Commission's proposal is unlikely to be adopted because it is simply a restatement of existing law.

Establishing corruption

The intention of the parties and their relationship will be crucial to establishing corruption. In addition, the Law Commission suggested that the disparity between bribery in the public and private domain was no longer relevant today and should also be abolished.

However, some practical difficulties remain. It is not always obvious to identify corrupt motives. The most straightforward example would be when money changes hands.

POINT OF LAW

For example, it would be hard for recipients to argue that in accepting any sum from a business contact, their commercial impartiality had not been compromised, an inference that former Treasury Minister Neil Hamilton found difficult to displace in respect of payments allegedly made to him by Harrods' owner Mohamed Al Fayed.

If gifts of money raise inferences of corruption, where does this leave 'freebies', hospitality or 'jollies' with tangible or perceived cash value?

The interesting thing about corporate hospitality is that it has a rather different look and feel to other straightforward aspects of corruption.

POINT OF LAW

For example, if a client was invited to a Formula 1 corporate hospitality day at Silverstone, then this is acceptable. However, if the client was offered £2000 by the marketer (the cost of the hospitality) and was encouraged to buy its products then this would be more sinister and probably would amount to bribery.

What the above example illustrates is that the cost of the gesture must be examined in the context of any existing commercial relationship. For example, receiving a 'thank you' to express appreciation is allowable, but only within certain limits usually set by the recipient's own organisation. The key is to declare the offer of hospitality or gift to the employer.

Many employers include provisions in their terms and conditions for their directors and all employees that *any* gift has to be declared and notified to the relevant manager. This may include the bottle of Chilean Riesling right up to the hospitality at the Olympic Games.

One reason for this is that company directors do not want to be seen to accept anything that could appear to compromise their business judgment.

POINT OF LAW

For example, financial services company **Zurich** applies very strict rules in particular parts of its business with respect to sales incentives. For example, the life side of its business (life, pensions, health insurance) is very heavily regulated by the Financial Services Authority and Zurich has to declare how much money it spends entertaining brokers and independent financial advisors, which is subject to a very low (£80) upper limit.

However there is more scope for hospitality and incentives on the general insurance (motor, car, home) side of the business, which is not so tightly regulated. For example, brokers can receive incentives to sell more of its products than a competitor's products and in the past Zurich has run a competition for brokers where the first prize is an all expenses paid trip to watch the Lions Tour in Australia.

It is very important for employers to have a formal process for the acceptance of such gifts or hospitality.

IBM provides strict guidelines to employees on what is acceptable. The company offering the hospitality must be an existing supplier, so that it is clear that IBM is accepting the invitation to develop the relationship. Accepting an invitation from a new supplier or one trying to forge a relationship with IBM is not allowable.

The Law Commission commented that the approach must not be too puritanical, although recognising that what is proffered as hospitality can far exceed the boundaries of acceptable graciousness, leading to the conclusion that bribery can 'simply be dressed up as hospitality'.

INSIGHT

However, if a company invited a client to the Monaco Grand Prix, some clients would refuse to go as a matter of principle because it is a step too far – an airfare to an expensive place, with a hotel and a weekend of activities smacks of corruption.

Alternatively, if the client made its own way on a Saturday afternoon to a football match that is no more than 100 miles away, and accepted a ticket and some hospitality at the stadium – then that would be perfectly reasonable corporate hospitality.

There are certainly different levels of client entertainment or hospitality. A number of key pointers may help to determine when the advantage offered is no longer above board. One of the most important features will be the business context on which the hospitality is offered.

INSIGHT

For example, something that might be appropriate for entertaining the managing director of a company might be inappropriate for a purchasing manager.

Company directors lunching clients is unlikely to be construed as imposing an obligation on guests to reciprocate with work, although there is an old saying that 'there's no such thing as a free lunch'. Wining and dining is part of negotiation rituals and will not raise eyebrows unless extravagant and even then, it is unlikely that it will become the subject of any legal sanction.

At the next level, there are specific events like hiring pods at the London Eye or flying guests to the Olympic Games in China in 2008.

While it will be hard to demonstrate continuous business discussion, provided that an element of business exists, these 'jollies' continue to have a fig leaf of respectability.

It may be completely appropriate to entertain, for example, the managing director of a leading plc in this way because she or he may expect that this is usual rather than unusual.

Some marketers find it impossible to regulate the offer and acceptance of corporate hospitality and are prepared to leave it to common sense of the individual giving or receiving the invitation.

It is when invitations extend to partners or where the hosts are absent at the hospitality event that acceptance becomes more difficult to condone.

INSIGHT

For example, if during an all expenses weekend to the Ryder Cup 2002 at The Belfry, England the guest never once meets the corporate host then it is questionable that this is hospitality.

Equally suspect would be an all expenses trip to the Olympics in 2008 as it could be misconstrued – and the company providing may need to disclose the trip to the Inland Revenue as a benefit in kind.

When it is necessary to declare hospitality to the Inland Revenue

Under **Section 154 Income and Corporation Taxes Act 1988**, benefits provided for employees or their families 'by reason of their employment' are taxable in the same way as if provided by their employer.

This applies irrespective of whether, for example, the ticket to Men's Finals Day at Wimbledon is received from the employer or from a third party.

POINT OF
LAW

For example, if an employee would not have received the gift but for the
fact that she is in employment, the implication is that she has received the
benefit by reason of her employment and the benefit must be declared for tax.

The first thing a recipient must do is look at the face value of the ticket, not its re-sale black market value. Even though the advantage of attending the Men's Finals Day is greater than the face value of the ticket, the value of the ticket will give rise to a taxable situation.

However, why it tends *not* to be taxable is that hospitality and entertainment is not a deductible expense in a company's accounts and the Inland Revenue will probably take the view in most cases that it's too much trouble to assess the benefit on the employee.

In some extreme cases, employees who have been rewarded by their employers and have been sent on a weekend away have faced a tax demand on their return.

POINT OF
LAW

For example, where a financial services company is offering hospitality, it
should calculate the gross value of the hospitality and send a cheque to the
employer of the guest so that it can declare the value of that benefit to the Inland Revenue and
pay the tax on it.

CHECKLIST

Sponsorship

Required licences/consents

- International and national governing bodies
- To use the name and logo of the governing body
- To use the name and official logo of the event
- To grant sub-licences to the organisers of the event

Event organiser

- To use the name of the organiser and the venue
- To use the annual logo of the event in a specific year
- To require participants to wear certain clothing or use specified equipment and take part in promotional campaigns
- For advertising space at the venue
- For photographic and broadcasting rights to the event
- For merchandising and hospitality rights at the event

Participants

- To take part in promotional campaigns
- To use the team logo
- To use any nicknames
- To use the image of individuals

Hospitality

- Establish the limitations and liability
- Ensure that the hospitality provider adheres to the agreed advertised packages
- Ensure that all accounts or services and goods which are not covered by an exclusive package price are due for payment
- State that all packages are subject to availability and that all prices include VAT
- Include an entire agreement clause
- Ensure that a severability clause is included so that if any part of the terms and conditions prove ineffective or unenforceable the remaining terms and conditions are valid
- Ensure that by booking with the hospitality supplier the booking client is not deemed to have entered into any partnership, agency or joint venture with the parties to the sponsorship agreement

13

PROMOTIONS AND INCENTIVES

In this chapter:

- Committee of Advertising Practice (CAP) Sales Promotion Code
- Contractual considerations
- Consumer Protection (Distance Selling) Regulations 2000
- Coupons and vouchers – special rules
- Information requirements
- Other sources of liability:
  - Value, quantity and nature of prizes
  - Value-added tax
  - Illegal lotteries
  - Prize draws and other competitions based on chance
  - Price promotions
  - Extra value incentives
  - Bribery and corruption
- Data protection issues
- Intellectual property issues
- Checklist

Other useful chapters:

INTRODUCTION

There are many more ways to reach consumers than there were 10 years ago. Today, marketers' agencies rosters also look very different. In the past, a traditional mix of agencies will have comprised of advertising, direct marketing, sponsorship, public relations and sales promotion.

These days, agencies' rosters are much more diverse. They may include agencies that specialise in customer relationship management, hospitality, sponsorship, data houses, events management, and web design and interactive TV.

Consumer expectations have also grown. Promotional campaigns need to work harder to cut through the 'noise' made by competitor marketers, capture the imagination and ultimately deliver an improvement to the marketers' bottom line.

Sales promotion is no longer simply a short-term tactical exercise involving the production of a standalone competition, a scratch card or similar point-of-sale (POS) campaign. Reaching consumers requires a mix of disciplines and solutions; while most of the mechanics remain the same the process is now far more sophisticated and requires a multi-dimensional team.

For example, sales promotions agencies now combine the creativity of sales promotion with a highly sophisticated data and direct marketing approach.

It is against this changing background that promotions and incentives have become an increasingly important part of the marketing mix.

This chapter deals with 'promotions' which are marketing techniques involving a range of incentives designed to make goods or services more attractive to consumers. Typical promotions involve giving away free goods, selling goods at a discount or inviting consumers to participate in competitions and prize draws – all with the intention of boosting sales of product or services.

Traditional media and the Internet

Promotions can of course take place across any media, from national newspapers, radio and television through to mobile phones and the Internet.

The rules outlined in this chapter also apply to most promotions run on the Internet (see also Chapter 15).

Marketers should at least assume that English law applies to an Internet promotion if it targets residents of England and Wales. By the same token, if a promotion targets, or is available to, residents in other countries, then other national laws will also probably apply. This is a complex area and this chapter discusses promotions and incentives under English law.

The future – pan-European promotions

Currently there is no European Union (EU) legislation harmonising Member State laws on sales promotions and each regulates promotions differently. This often means that a pan-European promotion is impossible. Prior to launching any European sales promotion, a marketer is therefore obliged to take advice on its legality in each country.

In October 2001, the European Commission presented a proposal for a Regulation concerning sales promotions in the internal market. The aim of the initiative is to ease cross-border activity and commercial communication of sales promotions by removing internal market barriers, whilst ensuring a high level of consumer protection.

It is hoped that the new Regulation will end much of the legal uncertainty through a mixture of harmonisation, increased consumer protection (including improved rights of redress) and mutual recognition of the remaining national restrictions.

Harmonisation is expected to result in some restrictions on sales promotions currently in place in certain Member States (e.g. prior authorisation) being outlawed.

This chapter is intended to provide a route map for the marketer to avoid common pitfalls when framing a promotion or incentive as part of the marketing campaign.

Failure to comply with legal requirements may result not only in legal sanctions, but may also turn the promotion into a public relations disaster!

The complexity of the legal issues involved should not be underestimated. Many of the rules described in this chapter are very old and continue to be disputed. As outlined above, it is also likely that new rules will be introduced on a European-wide basis in the medium-term future and these will be discussed in future editions of this book.

If in any doubt about how these rules apply, marketers should seek advice from the relevant professional or industry body or from a lawyer who specialises in this area of marketing practice.

It is essential that *any* promotion is evaluated at an early stage by reference to a number of critical tests:

Is it legal?

▓ In particular, are there any specific legal rules which apply (e.g. lotteries law). Failure to comply with these rules can be a criminal offence.

What are the legal commitments it imposes?

▓ Most promotions create legally binding contracts, which cannot be avoided by small print.

Does it comply with all relevant codes of practice?

▓ Even if an activity is legal, there are many codes affecting promotions which may be breached if care is not taken. Failure to comply with these can lead to serious sanctions and public relations repercussions.

Does it make sense?

▓ The test of common sense is often forgotten in the enthusiasm generated by an idea for a new promotional campaign (e.g. hunting for Easter eggs led to many children digging up plots of land around the country!).

▓ A useful test is: can an uninformed consumer understand the promotion? Marketers should ask someone who has not been working on the promotion to check it for sense prior to roll out.

This chapter covers some of the key factors in making an assessment of a promotional campaign taking into account the above general criteria.

COMMITTEE OF ADVERTISING PRACTICE (CAP) SALES PROMOTION CODE

Most promotions run by marketers will be subject to the **CAP Sales Promotion Code** issued by the **Advertising Standards Association (ASA)**. This is the best known code.

While this chapter deals predominantly with the **CAP Sales Promotion Code**, marketers should also familiarise themselves and comply with other codes applicable to their particular circumstances.

Even if these are technically voluntary, care should be taken to consider them because non-compliance could lead to serious public relations problems and sanctions other than criminal prosecution.

INSIGHT

For example, trade associations require compliance with their own code, e.g. the Direct Marketing Association's Code of Practice or the Institute of Sales Promotion's Sales Promotion Code. These codes range from detailed legal review to 'good practice' guidelines.

Advertising and the scope of the CAP Sales Promotion Code

In practice, the **CAP Sales Promotion Code** should be treated as applying to *any* promotion on general release in the UK, with a few notable exceptions such as promotional material broadcast over television or radio or heard during premium rate telephone calls. If in doubt, marketers should consult the ASA.

Promotions will also usually involve some form of advertising. If a marketer advertises across the same media as covered by the CAP Sales Promotion Code, the **CAP Code of Advertising** will also apply. For further discussion on the regulation of advertising, see Chapter 9.

By contrast, if a marketer publicises a promotion on TV or over the radio, the advertisements must comply with the relevant **Independent Television Commission Code of Advertising Standards and Practice (the ITC Code)** or the **Radio Authority Code of Advertising Standards and Practice** (see also Chapter 10).

Promotions

The CAP Sales Promotion Code requires that all sales promotions be 'legal, decent, honest and truthful' and sets out detailed rules for mechanics and information requirements relating to promoters . Even if not all are legally mandatory, they should become second nature to all marketers as they underpin most successful promotions. They are not set out in detail in this chapter, but a number of core requirements are covered (see the web site for the full ASA Code) (see also Chapter 9).

Getting clearance for promotions and advertising

Prior to publication of the promotion, marketers can consult the CAP for free and confidential advice on whether the proposed sales promotion complies with the CAP Sales Promotion Code and/or the CAP Code of Advertising.

This is not clearance that the promotion is legal and such advice is not legally binding. Conformity with the advice does not prevent the ASA from later investigating and upholding any complaints about breaches of those codes. However, it does substantially reduce the risk of such an outcome.

If the promotion appears on television, the commercial will be subject to mandatory clearance by the **Broadcast Advertising Clearance Centre (BACC)** prior to being aired. Again, this is not legal clearance, but it reduces the risk of a marketer being in breach of the **ITC Code**. Once again, the ITC can investigate and uphold complaints despite such pre-clearance.

Breaches of the CAP Sales Promotion Code

The ASA investigates complaints under the CAP Sales Promotion Code. If it finds that a marketer has breached the CAP Sales Promotion Code, it will publicise the breach among media and consumer bodies and often this publicity finds its way into the national press.

Negative publicity and damage to a marketer's reputation is the principal consequence of being held to be in breach of the CAP Sales Promotion Code or failing to successfully challenge the decision. Because of the wide-ranging membership of the ASA, a breach can, amongst other things, result in the media refusing to publish further similar advertising. A promotion in TV advertising can also be reported by any interested party to the **Broadcasting Standards Commission (BSC)** if it is unfair or causes offence, or the **Office of Fair Trading (OFT)** for action under the **Control of Misleading Advertisements Regulations 1988**.

CONTRACTUAL ISSUES

Although the CAP Sales Promotion Code is important, most promotions also create legally binding contractual commitments. Failure first to appreciate these and then to honour them have caused some of the most notorious sales promotions problems. The key to this issue is the contractual relationship.

Broadly speaking, a contract is an agreement which creates obligations enforceable in law. There are key elements in this, e.g. an offer by one party that has been accepted by another, consideration (which will provide payment) on both sides, an intention to create legal relations and certainty in the terms of the agreement (see Chapter 2).

Some promotional techniques try to avoid legal commitment on the basis of one or other of these rules, but these attempts will often fail.

Has consideration been given?

Usually a marketer will be providing something of value to a participant – whether selling goods or services or offering the chance of winning a star prize. In return, the marketer may require some form of 'consideration' (see also Chapter 2) from the participant, such as requiring them to pay a purchase price or entry fee or to provide *some other form of benefit*.

The question of whether a participant has provided a marketer with consideration is critical because it will bind the marketer and the participant in a contractual relationship. This could also turn a lawful free prize draw into an illegal lottery and may make the marketer liable for value-added tax (VAT) on the promotion (see below).

What constitutes 'consideration'?

This is not limited to cash payment.

INSIGHT

For example, if a participant is required to complete a questionnaire in order to enter the promotion, this may constitute consideration, particularly if the information has significant marketing value to the marketer.

The way the consideration is made by the participant is immaterial.

INSIGHT

For example, consideration could be 'disguised' by the fact that the participant has to make a premium rate telephone call to enter.

Lack of consideration

Where goods or services are sold at their normal retail price, the price paid for the goods will still amount to a 'payment', where it is linked with a promotion, and (in most cases) a contract will be concluded.

The fact that a promotion states that **'no purchase is necessary'** does not mean that when a consumer actually does make a purchase, no consideration is given.

INSIGHT

Where a marketer offers to supply goods or services under a promotion and asks for *no* consideration in return, then the marketer is offering a gift to participants.

For example, free samples of a shower gel or the invitation to a free prize draw where no purchase is necessary could amount to a gift.

If a marketer does not comply with the terms of such a promotion it is possible to argue that the participants have no right of action against the marketer for breach of contract.

In such a situation, the winner of a free prize draw, if it could be shown that there was genuinely no consideration, probably could not sue the marketer for the prize if the marketer refused to send it to them.

However, such an action would be likely to be in breach of the CAP Sales Promotion Code and/or other codes of practice, and may amount to criminal offence (e.g. under the **Trade Description Act 1968**).

In addition, in all circumstances if the free sample causes damage to the consumer the marketer will probably be liable in negligence or under product liability rules.

Terms of the promotion

Since the promotion is likely to create a legally enforceable commitment, it is important that the terms of the promotion are clear, and that any restrictions are fair and obvious to the consumer (making them legally effective).

Whilst it is possible to exclude or restrict liability for failure, it is much easier to 'get it right first time'. This means not running promotions which from the outset are clearly going to be incapable of fulfilment, and making any restrictions clear.

It is not possible to get it right all the time and as a promoter, a marketer will naturally be concerned to protect its position against unexpected liabilities.

Marketers also prefer to avoid onerous obligations and to have flexibility in relation to those obligations.

However, care must be taken in drafting the terms and conditions of a promotion because certain terms may breach codes of practice or be prohibited or made unenforceable by legislation, which is increasingly onerous (e.g. see the **Distance Selling Regulations**, Chapter 9). Breach of certain provisions may even be a criminal offence. It is, therefore, necessary to take care in drafting.

The following case illustrates how easy it is for a promoter to be challenged and the difference a term of a contract can make.

LAW IN ACTION

O'Brien-v-MGN Ltd 2001

In 1995, Lee O'Brien and 1471 other participants entered MGN's 'Mystery Bonus Cash Hotline' prize game and thought they had won £50 000. But not a penny in prize money was awarded after a printing error meant that scratch cards issued with *The People* appeared to be eligible as well as those issued with *The Mirror*.

This led to the 1472 winning cards being declared void by MGN, a decision which O'Brien and the other participants claimed was a breach of contract.

The legally aided case came to court in July 2000, with MGN defending a potential aggregate £100 million damages payout on the basis that the game rules allowed it to declare any scratch cards void.

O'Brien argued that on the day he entered the game by making a premium rate telephone call, no rules were published in the newspaper, so they could not apply.

However, through the course of the trial he admitted that he must have seen the rules at some stage during the promotion and the court accepted the argument put forward by MGN that although the rules were not published in every newspaper issue that promoted the game, the rules did appear eight times in *The Mirror*, once in *The Sunday Mirror* and on two occasions in *The People*.

As this case illustrates, a marketer should, in addition to taking all steps to ensure that the promotion is run without error, take steps to deal as fully as possible with unexpected problems and bring the terms of the promotion to the attention of consumers.

Other situations which a marketer might consider catering for include system failures with on-line prize events, bounced cheques for pay-to-enter skill competitions and prize winners of cars being disqualified from driving.

All such provisions must be tested against legal restrictions such as the **Unfair Contract Terms Act 1977** and the **Unfair Terms in Consumer Contracts Regulations 1999** (below), and in this regard specialist advice should always be taken. Carefully drafted terms of this kind can both be fair and save considerable aggravation later. Examples include:

1. **Unfair terms.** If a marketer's standard terms include terms that cause a significant imbalance in the parties' relationship to the participants' detriment then it may be prevented from enforcing those terms under the **Unfair Terms in Consumer Contracts Regulations 1999**. Those regulations also require that the marketer's terms be expressed in plain and intelligible language.

2. **Restriction of liability.** The **Unfair Contract Terms Act 1977** prevents a marketer from using certain terms excluding or restricting its liability to participants as consumers. For example, a marketer can never restrict its liability for negligently causing participants' injury or death; or exclude the implied terms that the goods it supplies to consumers are of satisfactory quality and match the description in promotional material. Indeed, if the goods that a marketer supplies do *not* comply with the description given then the marketer could also be committing a criminal offence under the **Trade Descriptions Act 1968**.

3. **Promotional services.** If a marketer supplies a service under a promotion, then under the **Supply of Goods and Services Act 1982** the marketer must provide the service with reasonable care and skill. In addition, if the marketer supplies that service without having agreed a price or a time for performance, then it must charge a reasonable price and perform the service within a reasonable time.

It is essential to apply the same quality standards to these goods and services provided under a promotion as provided normally, as they all give rise to liability and all affect the reputation of the marketer if they are defective.

In the end, if it goes wrong, the marketer could pay heavily in cash and public relations.

Incorporation of terms

For a marketer to make a set of terms binding on participants it must 'fairly and reasonably' bring those terms to participants' attention.

INSIGHT

In order to comply with the CAP Sales Promotion Code, it may be sufficient to refer participants to an easily accessible source from which 'full applicable terms and conditions may be obtained'. However, marketers must take greater steps to bring more onerous or unusual terms to the attention of participants.

For example, in the MGN case, the limited number of times that the terms of the scratch card promotion were published was held to be sufficient to bring those terms to the attention of O'Brien.

Care should be taken to avoid printing relevant terms and conditions on a section of marketing material which is not retained by the entrant (e.g. on an entry form which is returned by the participant).

INSIGHT

Marketing best practice in this area is to set out the full terms in all promotional materials independently coming to the attention of participants and inviting their parti-
cipation. However, where marketers cannot do this, the CAP Sales Promotion Code still requires a minimum set of information and terms to be brought to the attention of participants before they make a purchase under, or enter into, a promotion.

Civil proceedings for non-compliance and breach

If marketers do not honour the terms of the promotion, then they are likely be in breach of contract as well as the CAP Sales Promotion Code and/or other codes of practice, and they could well be negligent or committing a criminal offence (e.g. under the **Trade Descriptions Act 1968**).

INSIGHT

Notwithstanding what was said above, as a matter of best marketing prac-
tice, marketers should generally assume that promotional terms are legally binding where the consumer has to take significant active steps to enter even if the promotion appears to be free.

This is important, because if marketers breach any of the terms of the promotion, the participant may have the right to seek damages for any loss suffered as a result of the marketer's breach. Put simply, this could give legal rights to the value of a significant reward, such as a holiday, even if the original purchase was very low in value.

Indemnity and insurance for the marketer

Although this is an obvious point, marketers must not over-expose themselves to a floodgate of redemption which they have not counted on and which they are bound to honour: only promise what can be delivered!

For example, in the notorious **Hoover** free flights case in 1992 the marketer offered free flights to European and US destinations to UK purchasers of Hoover products worth more than £100. The promotion became heavily over-subscribed with about 600 000 participants taking up the promotion and Hoover had to spend nearly £50 million sorting out the problem.

In particular it may be advisable for the marketer in large volume promotions to guard against such over-exposure by taking out insurance. In addition, working with reputable and solvent parties who can underwrite the redemption or (if necessary) pay for their mistakes, is critical.

Although the marketer is likely to be directly liable to a consumer for any claims brought by participants, its marketing or advertising agency may also in certain circumstances be liable to its client under its terms of engagement, e.g. where the promotion goes wrong. Care needs to be taken to draft a binding contract to cover all circumstances.

'Subject to availability'

The **CAP Sales Promotion Code** states that the use of a promotional term to the effect that gifts, products or prizes are 'subject to availability' will not save the marketer from the liability to take all reasonable steps to meet consumer demand. As a matter of contract law, the term is of uncertain meaning, and so should not be relied upon to avoid over-subscription.

CONTRACTS WITH SUPPLIERS

Where a promotion involves the distribution of free items/prizes, the marketer should ensure that a contract is entered into with the suppliers of such goods. This contract should include, amongst other things, provisions confirming the quality of the product, numbers required, any date by which such goods are to be provided and use of intellectual property rights.

CONSUMER PROTECTION (DISTANCE SELLING) REGULATIONS 2000

A promotion may involve selling goods or services to participants without them being in face to face with the marketer, e.g. it may invite orders through the press, radio, TV or a web site; or by contacting participants directly by mail, phone, text message or e-mail.

In such cases, the promotion will probably fall within the **Consumer Protection (Distance Selling) Regulations 2000 ('the Regulations').** There are exceptions to the application of the Regulations (as a whole and its parts) in respect of particular types of contracts. Legal advice should be sought on the operation of these.

The key features of the Regulations are:

- The consumer must be given certain information (in a 'clear and comprehensible' manner) before a purchase of goods and/or services is made. This includes:
  - general information relating to the goods and services;
  - where applicable, the existence of a right of cancellation; and
  - acknowledgment that, if required, the supplier reserves the right to provide substitute goods/services of an equivalent value in the event that the original goods/services are not available.

- The consumer, after making a purchase, must be sent confirmation in writing or another durable medium. The information to be included in the written confirmation is prescribed by the Regulations.

- The consumer (subject to certain exceptions) has a cooling-off period of 7 working days in which the contract can be cancelled at no cost to the consumer.

- Where a consumer cancels a contract all money paid must be returned within 30 days of the date notice of cancellation is given and related credit agreements are also cancelled.

- The provisions of goods/services must be made within 30 days (beginning with the day after the order was placed).

This is not an exhaustive list of the features and effect of the Regulations. The DTI have produced a 'Guide for Business'; however, marketers are recommended to seek legal advice on the application of this relatively new piece of legislation.

For more discussion on these Regulations, see Chapter 9.

COUPONS AND VOUCHERS – SPECIAL RULES

Coupons are common. There are detailed guidelines issued by a number of organisations for the mechanics of redemption and form of voucher.

Whilst most coupons specifically restrict redemption to limited circumstances, technically the **Trading Stamps Act 1964** gives participants the right to redeem, *for cash*, any coupons with an aggregate 'cash value' of 25p or more.

A consumer might be able to argue that the 'cash value' of the coupon is its declared face value (e.g. '30p off'). Consequently coupons usually state a 'cash redemption value' of a fraction of a penny ('0.001p') in an attempt to limit the number of consumers seeking to exchange money-off coupons for cash. This wording is not guaranteed to succeed if challenged. This is an arcane and difficult area of marketing law.

Marketers should also bear in mind that under the 1964 Act, other information should also be included on coupons, e.g. the details of the promoter.

INSIGHT

Subject to the Parliamentary timetable in 2002, the Government is likely to repeal the **Trading Stamps Act 1964**. The 1964 Act was originally brought in to deal with what was then a national craze of collecting stamps in return for purchases which could be redeemed for a wide range of goods (e.g. Co-Op and Green Shield Stamps were very popular in the 1960s and 1970s).

The Trading Stamps Act 1964 placed a raft of legal obligations on retailers and promoters and applied to promotions offering vouchers, in return for a purchase.

Retailers selling products which included these vouchers had to display details of these offers worded in certain ways and promoters had to put a cash value on each voucher and allow participants to redeem those vouchers for cash if their total face value was 25p or more.

> Despite the virtual demise of 'trading stamp' schemes as a form of customer loyalty device, the 1964 Act is still in force.
>
> If the 1964 Act is swept away and the cash value/redemption rights and obligations with it, other parts of the 1964 Act will probably remain, such as the provisions ensuring that participants who receive products as a loyalty reward enjoy the same rights, e.g. as to the quality and performance of the product, as if they had paid cash for them.

INFORMATION REQUIREMENTS

The promoter is required to include detailed information for consumers as part of a promotion, and the extent of the information required will depend on the type of promotion. The requirements are legal, e.g. the contractual points above and the usual **Companies Act 1985** requirements (such as registered company number), or code based or deal with specific issues (such as VAT requirements).

These requirements include the following:

▨ Under the **CAP Sales Promotion Code**, the marketer is responsible for all aspects of the promotion. Its full and proper name and business address should be given on all promotional material.

▨ The **Trading Stamps Act 1964** similarly requires that the name of the marketer (or its business name) be stated in clear and legible characters on the face of coupons and vouchers. Where a promoter invites participants to order goods or services as part of the promotion, the order forms must legibly state the marketer's registered company number and the address of its registered office.

Although the CAP Sales Promotion Code requires marketers to state a number of terms on any materials inviting participation in the promotion, all such promotional materials (not just the terms) should clearly state factors likely to influence participants' understanding of, or entry into, the promotion.

Marketers must also ensure that the promotional mechanics are clear to all participants and this includes the promotional terms and copy. This broadly reflects the legal requirements referred to above.

For example, marketers should state prominently:

▨ The closing date for the promotion (e.g. 'entries must be received by 31 December 2002')

▨ Any proof of purchase requirements (e.g. 'four special pack tokens and the cut off entry form')

▨ Any limitations on availability of prizes (e.g. 'the first 100 correct entries received by the closing date') – this is a difficult issue to enforce and police

▨ Any entry restrictions (e.g. 'not open to employees, families or friends of employees')

▨ Age restrictions (e.g. 'over 18 years only')

▨ Geographical restrictions on entry (e.g. 'excluding the ROI')

If marketers want children to participate, then they should carefully consider whether the prizes being awarded are suitable and also consider requiring them to obtain adult permission (see also Chapter 16).

Marketers should refer to the CAP Sales Promotion Code and to the other sources applicable to the promotion in question for full information on its requirements in respect of promotional terms, especially where the promotion involves prizes.

OTHER SOURCES OF LIABILITY

In addition to issues of the CAP Sales Promotion Code and civil liability (contract and negligence), most promotions leave the promoter open to criminal prosecution if strict rules are not followed. There are many areas of concern, some of which (e.g. **Trade Descriptions**) are common to most marketers and others (e.g. lotteries) specific to sales promotion. This following section covers some of the key areas of concern.

Value, quantity and nature of prizes, gifts and other products

Value and quantity

▨ There is no general limit on the value or numbers of promotional gifts, products or prizes (note that discounts on goods can constitute gifts or prizes) that a marketer can offer.

INSIGHT

However, under the CAP Sales Promotion Code, a marketer must take all reasonable steps to ensure the availability of all the promotional products, gifts or prizes on offer.

▨ While lotteries are generally illegal, certain types of lotteries and amusements with prizes are lawful under the **Lotteries and Amusements Act 1976**. However, even in legal lotteries there tends to be restrictions on the amount, size and/or nature of prizes that can be awarded.

Nature

▨ As a general rule, the products offered under a promotion should comply with any relevant safety and other regulatory requirements and should be legal.

INSIGHT

For example, promotions of cigarettes or alcohol should not be made available to under 16s or under 18s respectively (see also Chapter 9).

▨ Where the promotion offers goods or services manufactured or provided by a third party, the marketer must ensure that the third party is also bound by the CAP Sales Promotion Code and by any contractual obligations that the marketer owes to the participants.

▪ It is also important, when running a trade incentive scheme, to avoid offering gifts or prizes to employees of another business if they may cause those employees to act against the interests of their employer (see Chapter 12).

VAT

If the marketer receives any consideration (see above) under the promotion, as a general rule it must account for VAT on that consideration.

Discounts (sometimes in the form of money-off coupons) or gifts for which participants genuinely do not pay any form of consideration *do not* generally give rise to a VAT liability.

However, this rule is subject to certain exceptions, e.g. marketers must account for VAT in respect of a series of gifts or if the cost to the marketer of a gift exceeds a certain amount (see also Chapter 12).

In addition, what are apparently gifts may sometimes involve a form of indirect consideration, such as requiring participants to contribute to the cost of postage and packing of gifts, in which case VAT is also payable on that contribution.

Given the stiff financial penalties for failing to pay VAT in full, it is advisable that promoters seek professional advice to determine the VAT liability under a promotion.

Prize draws and other promotions based on chance

Prize promotions are subject to statutory restrictions and promoting a lottery is *illegal* in the UK except in limited circumstances (e.g. private not-for-profit lotteries or the National Lottery).

Therefore, when devising a format for a promotion that involves the awarding of prizes, marketers must ensure that they comply with the following rules.

INSIGHT

This is probably the most difficult area of law in sales promotions and professional advice should be sought.

Legal definition of a 'lottery'?

There is no statutory definition of the term 'lottery' but case law indicates that this is a promotion whereby:

▪ Participants provide some form of consideration (e.g. purchase a product)

▪ Prizes can be won

▪ The awarding of such prizes is determined solely by luck (e.g. a random draw)

When is a prize draw an illegal lottery?

Difficulties arise when participants purchase a product or give some other form of consideration (e.g. call a premium rate telephone number) to enter the promotion.

POINT OF
LAW

For example, a marketer may be considering holding a promotion inviting
participants to call a premium rate telephone number to register their name
and address in a prize draw.

   If a marketer requires such direct or indirect consideration from participants for the chance
to participate in the prize draw, it risks holding a lottery that is illegal under the **Lotteries and
Amusements Act 1976**.

Criminal prosecution under the Lotteries and Amusements Act 1976

- Marketers and 'consenting and conniving' directors or managers may be prosecuted
  (usually by the **Gaming Board**) for running an illegal lottery under the **Lotteries and
  Amusements Act 1976**. Under the 1976 Act, 'conniving' can include turning a blind eye
  to or being reckless as to whether an offence is being committed.

- The penalties can theoretically be high with the Crown Court having the power to levy an
  unlimited fine or commit convicted individuals for up to 5 years in prison.

What constitutes 'payment'?

- The 1976 Act does not give guidance on what constitutes payment although this issue has
  been dealt with by the courts. This does, however, remain a highly contentious area.

LAW IN
ACTION

For example, in the case of **Imperial Tobacco-v-Attorney-General (1981)**
the tobacco company ran a promotion for one of its brands, offering
scratch cards (some of which awarded prizes) in packets of cigarettes. The cigarettes containing the scratch cards were sold at the normal retail price, hence there was no direct additional
payment involved in the promotion.

   Despite this, the House of Lords decided that because participants had to purchase a packet
of cigarettes to acquire a scratch card, participants were providing consideration in return for a
chance to win a prize and therefore the promotion constituted an illegal lottery.

Had the scratch card promotion not been publicised, meaning that consumers were not
induced into buying cigarettes in order to obtain a scratch card, it might have been possible to
argue that this promotion was not a lottery. In practice, however, promotions including prize
draws are likely to be publicised and participants will be aware of entry requirements.

   As promotional activity develops, it might be the case that other forms of 'consideration'
will be deemed to be payment.

INSIGHT

For example, consumers are increasingly asked to provide personal data (usually by means of questionnaire) in return for being entered in a prize draw. Where data requests become more detailed, providing marketers with increasingly valuable marketing information, there is the possibility that the provision of such information will be regarded as 'consideration', meaning that the subsequent prize draw will be illegal.

The attitude of the regulatory authorities towards this type of promotional activity must be monitored carefully.

Circumstances where entry into a promotion is likely to be considered free from payment

A promotion could avoid constituting a lottery if all entry cards (be they scratch cards or whatever) are distributed freely in retail outlets or in the street, as the following case illustrates.

LAW IN ACTION

Express Newspapers-v-*Liverpool Daily Post* (1985)

A newspaper randomly posted free scratch cards to participants who had then to read the newspaper to determine whether they had won a prize. Because participants had received the cards freely in the post, and could read the newspaper without buying it (e.g. at a public library), it was held that participants were not providing consideration. As a result, the promotion was deemed to be a valid (and legal) prize draw.

As a result of this case, some marketers have argued that it might be *legal* to run lotteries in which participants would typically provide consideration but were given the option of a free entry route. This is common practice, but care must be taken on a case by case basis, as the courts will assess the facts objectively. For example:

- In the Imperial Tobacco case, a small proportion of the scratch cards were, in fact, made available from free public dispensers.

- The existence of a 'free' entry route, e.g. via a postcard, may not be sufficient to prevent the promotion being an illegal lottery.

- Any 'free' entry route must be 'genuine and unlimited'. As such, the route must not impose restrictions nor should the entry requirements be so demanding as to discourage participation by this means. The courts have recently confirmed that the UK authorities will consider the extent to which a free entry route has been used when determining whether it is, indeed, 'genuine and unlimited' (see below).

- If a substantial number of participants make a contribution or payment of whatever kind, the promotion is likely to be challenged as a lottery. It is unclear, however, whether this means that a substantial number of entrants are required to pay, or whether a substantial number, in fact, do pay, as the following two cases illustrate.

LAW IN
ACTION

R-v-Interactive Telephone Services Ltd 1995 (unreported)

In the Telemillions case a 'free entry' postal route was included, although most participants called a premium rate phone number to enter the prize draw. The court found that the postal route was used by such a minority of entrants (some 0.2% entered free by means of a postal entry route) that it was to be disregarded, and the marketers of the scheme were prosecuted.

Russell-v-Fulling (1999)

Here, the court held that although payment was not a pre-requisite for entering the competition (i.e. due to the inclusion of a 'free entry route'), the facts showed that the vast majority of participants had made a purchase, meaning that the promotion amounted to an illegal lottery.

In all the cases mentioned the fact that participants could take part in the promotion without making payment was ignored because *in practice* the vast majority (or at least a substantial number) of participants had provided consideration to take part. The courts consequently held the promotions to be **illegal lotteries**.

Marketers can increase the likelihood of participants taking advantage of a 'free entry route' by using easy and/or completely free mechanisms (e.g. by freepost mail or a toll-free phone number) and referring to such a route prominently in all marketing material.

Marketers should always look at the facts closely and keep the authorities' attitudes under review.

When will a prize draw probably not be a lottery?
Participants' costs incurred in entering a prize draw which are equivalent to the cost of a first class stamp, for example mailing the entry by standard first or second class post or phoning a local or national standard rate telephone hotline, may not constitute consideration for the purposes of a lottery if they simply cover the administrative cost of entry.

In addition, standard Internet charges incurred by going on-line to register for a prize draw have also not been regarded as payment to date. In all these cases, the authorities' attitudes must be kept under review.

Any requirement that participants incur any additional cost, for example calling a premium telephone number to enter the prize draw or to find out whether they have won a prize could constitute payment because of the relatively high costs that would necessarily have to be incurred.

'Everyone's a winner'
Promotions where participants are given the chance to 'win a prize', but in fact all participants win prizes of equal value, are not lotteries because the prizes are not distributed by means of chance. Contrast this with promotions whereby all participants receive a prize, but the nature or value of the prize is determined by luck.

The CAP Sales Promotion Code requires that where all or most participants will win 'prizes', they should not be described as prizes, but as gifts or (if direct payment is involved) purchases.

A promotion guaranteeing all participants a minimum prize, combined with the chance of winning a further prize, is likely to be construed as a gift or purchase followed by a prize draw.

Criminal offences

Most forms of direct or indirect involvement in an illegal lottery are criminal offences.

A marketer can be prosecuted for the following acts or where it is procuring or attempting to procure a third party to commit the following acts:

▪ Selling, printing, publishing or distributing lottery tickets, advertisements or other lottery-related materials

or

▪ Using, causing, or knowingly permitting to be used, any premises for purposes connected with the promotion or conduct of the lottery

In addition, it is illegal to sell or distribute tickets and advertisements for a foreign lottery, e.g. the Spanish national lottery or the Italian national lottery.

Those marketers involved in promoting an unlawful lottery or prize competition risk criminal prosecution. If found guilty, a fine of up to £5000 and/or 2 years' imprisonment can be imposed. If a company is found to have committed any of these offences, its directors can also be held personally liable.

Gaming

Gaming is defined in the **Gaming Act 1968** as playing a game of chance or chance and skill combined to win money or prizes, irrespective of whether or not participants must pay to play.

Gaming or lottery?

Marketers will notice that there is a potential overlap between the definitions of gaming and lotteries.

The general rule in the **Lotteries and Amusements Act 1976** is that lotteries also capable of constituting gaming are treated exclusively under gaming law.

However, while marketers should be aware that unlicensed gaming is usually *illegal*, the types of contests typically held under a promotion are more likely to constitute lotteries or competitions than gaming.

Criminal proceedings under the Betting and Gaming Duties Act 1981

If the prize event is structured in such a way as to amount to gaming or betting, HM Customs & Excise may initiate a prosecution.

For example, this occurred in the case of **Customs & Excise Commissioners-v-News International Newspapers (1998)** in connection with 'Fantasy Fund' prize promotions where participants had to choose a portfolio of shares and the most successful won. All the ingredients of betting were said to be present, rendering the promoters liable to criminal prosecution unless they had a betting licence and were paying betting duty of 37.5% on the aggregate of the stake money paid by participants and the expenses and profits of the promotion.

Prize competitions

A promotion will be classified as a competition if:

▨ Participants stand a chance of winning prizes

▨ Such prizes are awarded on the basis of the exercise of a degree of skill by entrants

▨ Payment can be required prior to entry, although it is not necessary

Under the **Lotteries and Amusements Act 1976** a competition may be deemed *unlawful* if:

▨ Ultimate success in the competition *does not* depend to a substantial degree on the exercise of skill

or

▨ Prizes are offered for forecasts of the outcome of an unascertained event

The degree of skill to be exercised in a lawful competition can be small but must not be trivial and must require more than observation.

It is arguable that the common device of asking participants questions with very obvious answers or questions whose answers can easily be found in publicity material next to the questions is a 'competition' because a degree of skill is involved in locating the correct answers.

However, it must be remembered that such a competition is likely to result in a number of correct entries, meaning that the ultimate awarding of prizes will need to be determined by a second stage.

There is a risk that the promotion will be deemed an unlawful competition should prize winners be selected at random from all correct entries (see the section on 'Two-stage schemes' below).

The advantage of lawful competitions is that marketers can require payment or some other form of consideration from participants. It should be remembered, however, that such a requirement must be prominently brought to the attention of the participants prior to entering the promotion.

Two-stage schemes: does success depend to a substantial degree on the exercise of skill?
Promotions often involve two-stage schemes:

- Stage 1: requires skill (e.g. correctly answering multiple choice trivia questions)
- Stage 2: involves pure chance (e.g. a prize draw for all correct entries)

LAW IN ACTION

For example, in the **Bradfute case** (1967) the participants received bingo cards on tins of cat food. Those lucky enough to have winning bingo cards then had to solve a puzzle to win a money prize. It was contended that this promotion was a lawful competition involving skill and was not a lottery.

The court in fact held that the promotion was not composed of a single, united scheme but of a first-stage lottery, in which the 'prizes' were the randomly distributed winning bingo cards, followed by a second-stage puzzle competition.

The winning bingo cards were considered to constitute 'valuable' prizes because, although they did not entitle the holders to money prizes, they gave them the opportunity to win money if they answered the puzzle correctly.

The stage at which the skill is exercised is also important. If participants are asked to answer a question correctly in order to be placed in a prize draw, the courts will normally analyse the competition in stages.

LAW IN ACTION

For example, in the **Telemillions case** (above) participants phoned a premium rate telephone number and were required to answer a trivia question. Sixty percent of the participants answered the question correctly and were entered into a prize draw. However, the court took a unitary approach to the promotion, viewing it overall as a *lottery* where the skill element merely reduced the number of participants in the prize draw.

The court disregarded the defendant marketer's claim that participants paid exclusively to participate in the trivia competition for which the prize was entry into the prize draw, and held that participants had paid for a chance in the prize draw which was therefore an illegal lottery.

In addition, because the promotion involved the 'exercise of some degree of skill', but the distribution of prizes 'did not depend to a substantial degree on the exercise of skill', the promotion was also held to be an unlawful competition.

It can be concluded that if a marketer is considering running a pay-to-enter promotion involving a skill stage and a chance stage, there is a risk that such a promotion will be deemed to involve two distinct stages, a lawful competition followed by an illegal lottery. Legal opinion should be sought by the marketer prior to running a two-stage promotion.

Reducing the risks

Marketers have two alternative mechanisms that can be used to reduce the risks associated with two-stage promotions. It must be remembered, however, that using either option will not preclude regulatory challenge on the facts of the promotion, merely reduce the risk of such action:

1. **Limitation of the number of winners.** For example, 'the first 100 correct entries received', in which case marketers should prominently advertise the promotional opening date. This route may not be effective if participants have paid to enter the competition, as there is still an element of chance which may make the competition an illegal lottery.

2. **Competition followed by a tiebreak.** The tiebreaker is used instead of a random prize draw and introduces a further skill element, by which the awarding of prizes will be determined.

INSIGHT

For example: 'Complete the sentence "My favourite washing powder is Product X because ..." in no more than 20 words. The 50 most apt and original answers will win a year's supply of Product X.'

In terms of a tiebreak stage, it is important to ensure that any criteria being relied on to determine winners (e.g. completion of slogans in the *most apt and original* way) are made clear to participants. This information should also be sufficiently detailed to allow entrants to exercise the required degree of skill.

Competition judging – issues to consider

A marketer may run a competition in which judges are required to determine who are the winners, such as the completion of a tiebreaker (see above) where the judges will decide which 50 entrants have completed the slogan in the most apt and original way. It is important that promotional material makes it clear on what basis winners will be selected and that all entries are actually judged in accordance with such instructions.

INSIGHT

A marketer should therefore ensure that the judges' role is to decide who has correctly solved the competition or best completed the tiebreaker against a set of objective measurable criteria. In the tiebreaker example (above), the objective criteria are 'the most apt and original' answers.

In terms of answering questions, participants should not be required to guess answers, due to the question being so difficult or random. Where guess work is involved, it is likely that the promotion will not involve a sufficient degree of skill, making it an unlawful competition.

According to the **CAP Sales Promotion Code**, at least one of the judges reviewing entries against such a set of criteria should be independent and all judges should be competent to adjudicate on the subject matter of the competition (e.g. artists in respect of a painting competition).

To avoid disputes as to the winners, the marketer should state in promotional terms that the judges' decision is final, although if the judges decide the winners without proper reference to the relevant criteria, participants could still have an action for breach of contract.

For any promotions with prizes – whether they involve competitions, prize draws or gaming – marketers should make the names of winners available on request. Where the promotion has involved an element of judging, the judges' details should also be available.

Price promotions

The **Consumer Protection Act 1987** makes it a criminal offence to give a misleading indication of the price that participants must pay for promotional goods or services.

A price indication is typically 'misleading' if it suggests that the price is lower than it in fact is, or that the indicated price covers matters for which an additional charge will in fact be made.

Be aware that in certain circumstances a marketer may give an accurate price indication that later becomes misleading. If participants might reasonably be expected to continue to rely on the now misleading price indication, a marketer would be committing a criminal offence if it did not take reasonable steps to prevent participants from relying on that indication.

A marketer should also comply with the **Code of Practice for Traders on Price Indications**, as any breaches of that code can also form the basis for a prosecution under the **Consumer Protection Act 1987**.

Free and extra value incentives

If a marketer wishes to offer goods or services as 'free' or as 'gifts', the **CAP Sales Promotion Code** requires that participants pay no charges other than the actual cost of postage, delivery or collection of the gifts. There should be no additional charges for packing or handling.

'Buy one, get one free'
Some incentive offers require participants to make a purchase in order to qualify for a free offer – 'buy one get one free' offers are a common example. In all such promotions, a marketer should clearly separate the sale and gift elements in order to avoid confusing participants.

The CAP Sales Promotion Code also prohibits promoters from attempting to recover the cost of the promotion by reducing the quality or composition, or by inflating the price, of any product a participant must buy to qualify for a gift. In addition, a marketer must have maintained the product price at the same level both for at least 28 consecutive days in the previous 6 months before introducing the special offer and afterwards.

Labelling restrictions

Alternatively, a marketer may wish make a free offer along the lines of '25% extra free on this pack'. In such cases the usual rules on free offers apply. However, there are additional considerations to take into account.

By law, some foodstuffs and other products have to be packaged in fixed quantities (see also Chapter 9) restricting the type of 'extra free' offers that can be made.

INSIGHT

For example, a marketer can sell a 500 g box of cereal but not a 550 g box – making a '10% extra free' promotion on a 500 g box of cereal unlawful. However, a marketer can sell cereal in 750 g boxes, allowing it to run a '50% extra free' promotion on 500 g boxes. By increasing a pack size a marketer will also have to comply with labelling requirements relating to description of quantity (see Chapter 9).

A marketer should always be extremely careful with free offers clearly and unambiguously to set out in any promotional material the incidental costs, prior purchases and other conditions that participants must meet to qualify under the promotion.

It is also very important to avoid any form of misleading price statements that may be unlawful under the **Consumer Protection Act 1987** (see above).

Bribery and corruption

As discussed in Chapter 12, the **Prevention of Corruption Act 1906** makes it a criminal offence to corruptly give, promise or offer an inducement for a public servant to carry out his/her work in a certain way.

A marketer should therefore take great care to avoid running trade promotions and other forms of incentive schemes aimed at public servants working in central or local government.

There are similar statutory requirements in respect of employees in the private sector.

INSIGHT

For example, under the **CAP Sales Promotion Code** an incentive scheme should not compromise the obligation of sales people to give honest advice to consumers.

In addition, if a company intends to run a trade promotion scheme aimed at employees in another business, e.g. trade buyers for a retailer, it should first obtain that retailer's permission before inviting its employees' participation.

Where the marketer's promotional scheme individually targets those employees, it should ask that they themselves obtain their employer's permission to participate or run the risk of accusations that their judgment has been unduly influenced by a third party.

Furthermore, a marketer should always comply with internal procedures of its clients when aiming incentive schemes at its client's employees and it should highlight to those employees that they may be liable for tax on the incentives being offered (for further discussion, see Chapter 12).

In the light of these requirements, where feasible a marketer should aim promotions at participants in their private as opposed to working capacity.

DATA PROTECTION

This section highlights some of the areas where data protection may be relevant in a promotion. For a full discussion of data protection issues, see Chapter 7.

Collecting personal information

Many promotions invite participants to order something, complete a short questionnaire or send in a prize draw or competition entry.

In addition, participants may be required to supply their name, address and perhaps other personal information, such as purchasing preferences and household income.

INSIGHT

If a marketer has not already got permission to use such personal information for direct marketing purposes and wishes to use it going forward it will need to procure consent which can be done by including a suitable data protection statement on the order form, questionnaire or entry form.

As discussed in Chapter 7, the marketer will then have to comply with the **Data Protection Act 1998** in order to process, store and later use that information or face civil and even criminal sanctions for non-compliance.

Direct mail

Where a marketer wants to send a promotion as a piece of direct mail, it may want to use a database containing personal information (including but not restricted to names and addresses) of the recipients where marketers have obtained the database from a third party, they must ensure that the individuals they mail have consented to the use of their data in this manner.

INSIGHT

The most practical way to meet these requirements is to obtain such consents at the time marketers first collect the recipients' personal information, notifying them and having their agreement that the marketer may use their personal data for general marketing purposes.

Where marketers have obtained personal information directly from the individual in question, it is a breach of the Data Protection Act 1998 for a marketer to send unsolicited promotional material to that person if that individual has previously indicated that they do not wish to receive such materials. However, a marketer can randomly send promotional material and unsolicited incentives to unidentified persons, although it is an offence to require payment for them.

Cold calling

A marketer cannot call or fax unidentified persons at random numbers to tell them about a promotion or to ask to send them promotional material where the person in question has previously notified the caller that such unsolicited calls or faxes should not be made on that number or if the number has been listed on the Telephone or Fax Preference Services. Unsolicited calling or faxing cannot be made by automated calling system apart from to people who have made known that they consent to receive such calls.

INTELLECTUAL PROPERTY ISSUES

Sometimes in a promotion a marketer may refer to third party businesses and their products or services. If so care must be taken to avoid infringing their intellectual property rights (IPRs).

Some intellectual property issues of particular importance relating to promotions are discussed below. For a full discussion of IPRs, see Chapters 5 and 6.

Copyright

A marketer should not copy or deal with unlawful copies of another party's copyright material without a licence to do so.

POINT OF LAW

For example, if a marketer offers holidays as prizes and uses copies of a tour operator's publicity photographs in its promotional material without the tour operator's consent, it is likely to constitute an infringement of the tour operator's copyright in those photographs.

When a marketer or third parties commissioned by the marketer create original brochures, vouchers or any other promotional materials (all of which may include photographs), copyright will usually subsist in those materials as literary or artistic works because this will normally have involved a sufficient degree of creativity or effort.

Copyright in works created by the marketer's employees in the course of their employment will be owned by the marketer.

If materials are created outside the marketer, the marketer should always ensure that copyright in materials created by third parties on its behalf are assigned to it before the promotion or competition is launched.

In this regard, a careful review of third parties' terms and conditions before commissioning any work is essential.

Copyright can subsist in more than just printed materials. Therefore, if a marketer's promotion involves audio-visual materials then the marketer should also ensure that it also owns (or has a sufficient licence to exploit) the copyright in any films or sound recordings used in the promotion. If the promotion is broadcast on TV or radio, depending on the contractual terms agreed with the relevant broadcaster the marketer may also be able to obtain ownership of the copyright in the broadcast itself.

As discussed in Chapter 6, copyright arises from the *expression* or recording of the ideas and concepts behind the promotion and *not* in those ideas and concepts themselves.

Consequently, if a marketer formulates a new type of competition or marketing campaign it cannot use copyright to prevent competitor marketers from using that campaign or competition concept in their own promotions.

However, the marketer can prevent competitors from using elements or all of its promotion or competition if it can show that a substantial part of the copyright work(s) it owns have been copied and/or that copies of its works have been issued to the public without its authority.

Patents and confidential information

In order to protect the intellectual property of a promotion or competition, the marketer may (in very limited circumstances) be able to obtain patent protection in respect of the promotional scheme or a key part of it if it is a patentable invention.

INSIGHT

As discussed in Chapter 5, obtaining patent protection involves considerable time, cost and effort and is unlikely to be a viable option in this context.

More effective in protecting the integrity of the promotion or competition is confidentiality *prior* to its publication – making sure that people with access to it know that it is confidential and have entered into confidentiality agreements that the marketer can rely on. This applies equally to the marketer's own employees as well as sales promotion agencies and other third parties it has a business relationship with.

Trademarks and passing off

As discussed in Chapter 5, a marketer should avoid trademark infringement by seeking permission to use third party trademarks in any promotional material. This approach applies whether those trademarks are well-known and highly recognisable brands or less well-known marks; infringement is infringement and will be restrained by the courts whether or not the mark infringed is the brand of a global marketer or a small company only trading locally. Accordingly, the marketer should carry out registered trademark clearance searches at an early stage in the promotion project.

Conversely, consideration should also be given to applying for registered trademarks in respect of key elements of the promotion such as logos, images of any characters associated with the promotion or distinctive jingles.

A marketer must also ensure that its promotion is not so similar in look and feel to the promotion or branding of a third party such that it causes confusion in the minds of potential participants who are led to mistakenly think that both marketers are associated with one another.

If such misconception can be shown to have influenced those persons to participate in the promotion or competition, it may lead to a claim for passing off.

INSIGHT

For example, a passing off action could arise if a retailer is running a special promotional offer on a range of products made by another company and the marketer's promotion leads participants into incorrectly believing that that company has officially endorsed the marketer's promotional campaign.

CHECKLIST

▪ Confirm that the promotional activity is legal (i.e. not an illegal lottery or an unlawful competition)

▪ Ensure that the promotion does not mislead participants in any way (e.g. as to the chance of winning a prize, or the nature of the prizes)

▪ Be satisfied that the promotion complies with relevant legislation and Codes of Practice, depending on the type of media, together with any specific rules relating to certain activity (e.g. promotions aimed at children)

▪ Confirm that contracts are in place with relevant third parties (e.g. suppliers of prizes, confirming number and quality of goods and/or owners of any intellectual property rights featured in material, confirming the use of such rights)

▪ Ensure that all instructions, restrictions on entry and terms and conditions are brought prominently to the attention of participants

▪ Obtain final approval for promotional mechanics/copy from in-house compliance officers and/or legal support before any costs are incurred producing material

▪ Make sure that the copy makes sense and will be easily understood by participants

14

LOBBYING

In this chapter:

- Introduction
- Definition of lobbying
- Impact of the Data Protection Act 1994 on lobbying
- Impact of the laws of defamation on lobbying
- Political Parties, Elections and Referendums Act 2000
- Association of Professional Political Consultants (APPC) Code of Conduct
- Institute of Public Relations (IPR) Code of Conduct
- Checklist

Other useful chapters:

INTRODUCTION

The right to lobby or to 'petition for redress of grievance' (to use the language of **Magna Carta**) has long been established in Anglo-Saxon democracies.

Lobbying is as old as Britain's Parliamentary democracy and in fact the House of Commons was itself established as a lobby aimed at influencing the King. As power shifted to elected representatives of the people, Westminster and Whitehall became the target for those with grievances and this has eventually evolved into the modern day process of lobbying.

The freedom to lobby those with power is a defining feature that distinguishes between democracies and totalitarian societies. In a free society, just as people can pay for a lawyer, a doctor or a marketer, so they are free to pay for professional advice on how best to make a case to government.

Bona fide lobbyists earn their living by explaining to clients how the public policy process works and how they can best ensure that their concerns and interests are appropriately considered by politicians and officials.

Just as a lawyer owes a duty to his client and to the court, so a professional lobbyist has duties to his client and to the political system.

The key to lobbying is to understand the legislative process and how those of the UK and the different national assemblies operate within the European Union.

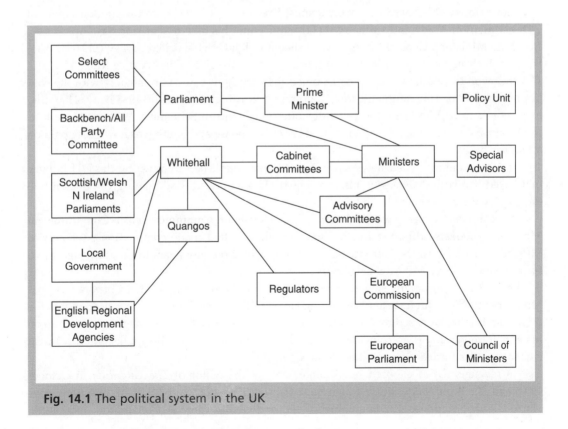

Fig. 14.1 The political system in the UK

Companies and organisations have the right to take advice on how best to put a case forward to government and statutory bodies.

Concerns have arisen not over the right to lobby itself but rather over *how that lobbying is done*, and in particular over the issue of financial connections between businesses and MPs and officials of public bodies.

As discussed in Chapter 12, the **Public Bodies Corrupt Practices Act 1889** and the **Prevention of Corruption Act 1906** provide different definitions of corruption and distinguish between the public and private sector.

The 'Cash for Questions' Affair (1989)

Much of the public perception of lobbying can be traced to the 'cash for questions' affair in 1989 that claimed the careers of two Government Ministers and led to the spectacular fall from grace of one of the most respected lobbyists in the industry.

Egyptian-born owner of Harrods, **Al Fayed**, was caught up in a bitter feud with the chief executive of Lonhro, **Tiny Rowland**, after the latter had failed to secure the purchase of the world famous department store. Al Fayed turned to lobbyist **Ian Greer** who in turn enlisted the support of a number of Conservative backbenchers, including **Tim Smith MP** and **Neil Hamilton MP**. They agreed to help and Hamilton was soon tabling Parliamentary questions designed to discredit Rowland.

However, events moved decisively against Fayed in April 1987 with the announcement of a **Department of Trade and Industry (DTI)** inquiry into his takeover of Harrods.

A month later a General Election was called and Ian Greer solicited money (£12 000) from Fayed, which he used to support constituency campaigns of 26 Conservative MPs. Margaret Thatcher won the election and Fayed resumed his Commons campaign, notably with the continuing support of Tim Smith and Neil Hamilton. According to Fayed, by 1988 he was handing over money in cash to Hamilton ('cash for questions') and in September 1988 the Hamiltons stayed at Fayed owned Ritz Hotel in Paris at Fayed's expense and Smith was now being paid on a retainer by Fayed.

In 1989, Lonhro owned newspaper *The Observer* published findings by the DTI inquiry that Fayed had both dishonestly misrepresented his origins and wealth and given evidence to the inquiry which he knew to be false.

A year later, Greer gave evidence to the **House of Commons Select Committee on Members' Interests** admitting for the first time that he had made commission payments to MPs in return for business introductions. He spoke of three payments to the (now deceased) **former Conservative MP Michael Grylls**.

In 1992 the Conservatives were re-elected and Hamilton was appointed Corporate Affairs Minister at the DTI. But instead of providing Fayed with a direct line of communication into the DTI, Hamilton was advised by DTI officials not to reply to Fayed's letter congratulating him on his appointment. It was no coincidence that shortly afterwards Fayed's application for British citizenship was turned down by the Home Office.

In revenge, Fayed exposed his arrangements to the editor of *The Guardian* in October 1994 and the front page story which ran: 'Tory MPs were paid to plant questions says Harrods chief' signalled the beginning of the end of the careers of Hamilton and Smith.

Fayed was reported as having said of Greer 'He told me you need to rent an MP like you rent a London taxi'.

Smith immediately resigned as Minister for Northern Ireland admitting he had taken cash for questions from Fayed.

The next day, *The Guardian* published a copy of the Hamiltons' £3600 hotel bill for their stay at the Ritz.

Greer issued a writ against *The Guardian* for defamation and within days Hamilton had resigned from Government and Prime Minister John Major announced the establishment of the **Nolan Committee on Standards in Public Life** (for further discussion on the laws of defamation, see Chapter 8).

In 1996, just before the defamation trial was about to commence in the **High Court**, Greer was advised by his lawyers to drop the action on the basis that there was evidence of six payments by him to Grylls and not three he had mentioned to the House of Commons Select Committee in 1990.

Although this was not central to his action against *The Guardian* it would have been evidence that Greer had misled the House of Commons Select Committee and this would have had the effect of discrediting his version of events in his defamation action.

Released from the legal constraints of the case (*The Guardian* was under a court order not to discuss the matter before trial or face contempt of court proceedings) the newspaper published further damaging material against Greer.

Greer's clients were concerned at the allegations of sleaze and not wanting to be tainted with the same brush left Greer to salvage what he could of his own reputation by himself. A mass exodus of clients and staff inevitably led to Ian Greer Associates seeking voluntary liquidation in 1996.

To this day, Hamilton continues to assert his innocence and to dispute the finding of **Sir Gordon Downey**, the former **Parliamentary Commissioner for Standards**, that there was compelling evidence that Hamilton had received cash payments from Fayed.

The critical edge to this is that Hamilton sued Fayed for libel and lost, culminating in his bankruptcy, although the funders of his action have been held not liable to contribute to Fayed's legal fees. It has the bizarre twist of a jury finding that Fayed had given cash for questions, thereby defeating his opponent!

This 'cash for questions' affair put a harsh spotlight on the nascent lobbying industry and in particular on the issue of financial relationships between consultancies and MPs. This forced the industry to confront issues it had previously avoided and take action to safeguard its own future.

The most tangible outcome was the establishment of the self-regulatory body – the **Association of Professional Political Consultants (APPC)** in 1994 by five of the largest lobbying consultancies in the UK (see below). However, 4 years later the APPC faced its first major test in the 'Drapergate' affair.

The 'Drapergate' affair (1998)

The Observer newspaper carried out an investigative 'sting' with journalists posing as representatives of a US energy company seeking influence in government (which is spooky given that the Enron crash happened 4 years later).

The Observer accused three lobbyists (two of them APPC members) of unethical behaviour. This 'Drapergate' affair was less serious than 'cash for questions' in the sense that this time there were no allegations of inappropriate financial links but rather of inappropriate bragging about the closeness of links with politicians and what could therefore be achieved.

Derek Draper, former aide to **Peter Mandelson**, boasted there were only 17 people who counted in the Government and he had access to all of them. His ill-advised comments attracted so much criticism that he was forced to resign immediately from his position.

Prime Minister Tony Blair asked **Sir Robin Butler**, then Cabinet Secretary, to draw up rules for government dealings with lobbyists and the **APPC** met to decide what, if anything, to do about its member consultancies.

The APPC decided to set up its own inquiry to be conducted by **Lord Armstrong**, former head of the Home Civil Service, and **Nicholas Purnell QC**, a highly respected barrister.

The findings of the inquiry were

... that there is nothing intrinsically improper about the role of political consultants. On the contrary, they have a valuable role to perform in assisting their clients to make proposals and cases to agencies of government in the most effective way.

Some cynics argue that this was an inevitable outcome of the inquiry given that the APPC members had paid for the inquiry out of their own pockets and were desperate to repair any damage to the reputation of lobbyists that had been tarnished by 'cash for questions' or inappropriate and unprofessional conduct by other members.

Nevertheless the inquiry did recommend that it was critically important that:

... political consultants should conduct themselves so as not to impair the integrity of their clients and the integrity of government and those in government positions with whom they have dealings.

This led to the creation of a 'culture of compliance' with the APPC rules within member consultancies (see **APPC Code of Conduct** below).

However, as the next two recent examples illustrate, lobbying still attracts its critics particularly wherever the heady mix of power, influence and money are involved.

The 'Mittalgate' affair (2002)

In February 2002 the Labour Party was left smeared by the 'Mittalgate' row where **Richard Ralph**, the Ambassador to Romania, gave assistance to billionaire **Lakshmi Mittal** in respect of Mittal's £300m bid for a privatised steel mill in that country.

Mittal had made donations to the Labour Party and it was also reported that **Prime Minister Tony Blair** wrote to the Romanian Prime Minister in support of the deal. Leaving aside the furore that followed, this illustrates how governments themselves will seek to lobby in given circumstances.

Enron crash (2002)

At the beginning of the 2002, the business news headlines were gripped by the 'cash for access' scandal as multi-billion dollar **Enron Corporation** filed for Chapter 11 protection from bankruptcy in the US after the banks refused to support re-financing of the energy multi-national after it had accumulated massive losses within its trading operations.

It was revealed that the board directors of Enron Corporation had made substantial political donations in return for access to government officials ('cash for access') on both sides of the Atlantic.

Understandably, given the enormous amount of negative publicity that the Enron crash generated, the public do not always make distinctions between an organisation's legitimate lobbying, fund raising or sponsorship activities of political parties and something much more sinister that smacks of abuse of power and corruption (see also Chapter 12).

Organisations and politicians run the risk of being accused of cronyism and bribery should they indulge in such practices to excess.

However, as discussed below, the **Political Parties, Elections and Referendums Act 2000** has led to some confusion as to the ground rules that must be observed by lobbyists and their clients.

According to the **APPC**, given that the requirements of clients have changed dramatically in recent years, so too has the role of lobbyists.

For example, in the past there was often pressure on consultancies to trade inappropriately on their political contacts.

It is still there to some extent but clients today are generally more concerned to ensure that lobbyists do not risk damaging their reputation by behaving unethically and as a result there has been an increase in frequency with which clients insist that lobbyists belong to the **APPC** or the **Institute of Public Relations (IPR)**.

According to the APPC and the IPR, self-regulation is working because consultancies are keen to stamp out misbehaviour by individuals that can damage the business prospects for the whole sector. This has helped to create an atmosphere where all consultants feel an obligation not to let each other down and, conversely, they are more inclined to be mutually supportive where unsubstantiated allegations are made.

DEFINITION OF LOBBYING

There is no standard definition of lobbying (sometimes referred to as public affairs although some commentators feel this is not an accurate description) but two useful definitions are:

POINT OF LAW

Any action designed to influence the actions of the institutions of government.

Alternatively:

... the management skill that internalises the effects of the environment in which an organisation operates and externalises actions to influence that environment.

Government, both centrally and locally and through a large number of agencies and other public bodies in the UK and in Brussels, makes thousands of decisions every day on policy, legislation and regulation. The Government is the largest purchaser of goods and services in

Europe (as well as being the biggest advertiser in the UK) and it dispenses billions of pounds in grants and aid.

Government depends on a constant flow of information and views from those who may be affected by its actions; and those affected also need, and have a right, to know what is going on inside the system.

Organisations need to deal with the system either because they have a specific concern – a need to make representations on a policy, Bill or commercial decision, or because they want to inform legislators and officials before the need to lobby may arise. Lobbyists exist to facilitate this process.

Professional lobbying firms fall into five categories:

1. **Political consultancies** – who specialise in dealing with government; most APPC members fall into this group

2. **Regulatory consultants** – who specialise in issues such as pharmaceutical and foodstuffs clearances, and technical aspects of utility regulation

3. **Parliamentary agents** – who used to specialise in promoting Private Bills, but who now increasingly provide broader monitoring and lobbying services

4. **Public relations firms** – some of whom have dedicated lobbying divisions

5. **Law and accountancy firms** – who advise on issues such as Budget or competition representations; a number have specialist policy units.

Lobbying is not about tapping officials on the shoulder and urging them to follow a particular course of action. Not only will this not work but also politicians and civil servants expect to hear directly from those who are affected by their actions and are generally impatient with intermediaries.

The role of the above consultant or agent is one of advisor to the organisation in how best to put its case across: who to contact, when, how, at what length and in what tone of voice.

All of the above generally offer most or all of the following services:

- **Monitoring** – parliamentary, Whitehall, political party, local government, public body, think tank, pressure group and European Union (EU) institution activity, debates, committee inquiries, statements, reports, legislation and regulation and database management

- **Case assembly** – involving advice on or handling research and drafting of submissions

- **Strategic advice** – on whom to lobby, how and when

- **Campaign management** – involving either administrative support for the client's own representations or handling briefing and debriefing

- **Media management** – and other PR support for lobbying programmes

- **Auditing** – the effectiveness of in-house resources and drafting programmes for implementation by clients

DATA PROTECTION ACT 1994

The **Data Protection Act 1994** can apply to lobbyists that keep records on MPs, civil servants, pressure groups and organisations as part of their intelligence gathering services.

Lobbyists that may have kept biographies of MPs on a database need to take care to remove anything that could be interpreted as being potentially **libellous** as anyone that appears on such a database has the right to see the biography on themselves! (see Chapter 7 and Chapter 8).

POLITICAL PARTIES, ELECTIONS AND REFERENDUMS ACT 2000 (PPERA)

The 2000 Act exists primarily to control donations to political parties and the funding of referendum campaigns. It also imposes controls on expenditure by political parties.

PPERA seeks to ensure that all donations above a certain value are recorded by companies and political parties, registered by companies and parties, and in certain cases made public by companies and parties. PPERA also effectively bans foreign donations.

The **Electoral Commission** is the statutory body responsible for implementation of the 2000 Act. Companies can turn to the Electoral Commission for guidance on tricky points of detail. Nevertheless, the final interpretation of any clause will remain, of course, with the courts.

The following guidance has been provided by the **APPC** and provides advice on how PPERA is likely to affect the work of political consultancies. However, it is advisable that clients as well as lobbyists seek legal advice on the interpretation of PPERA if in any doubt about its applicability.

How the PPERA affects companies

There are four ways in which PPERA affects companies making political donations.

1. **Companies have to be a 'permissible donor'.** The only donations that can legally be accepted are those from 'permissible donors' which, broadly speaking, *excludes* foreign companies and foreign nationals (see the note below on 'permissible donors'). It is an offence for anyone to facilitate the making of a donation by anyone other than a 'permissible donor'.

2. **The company must pass a resolution allowing donations to be made.** It is unlawful for any company to make a political donation unless it (or in certain circumstances any holding company) has passed a resolution allowing the company to make political donations. This cannot be retrospective. Donations made in breach of this restriction may result in directors being personally liable to pay the company the amount of the unlawful donation, plus damages and interest. These liabilities may be enforced by shareholders.

3. **Some donations must be reported to the Electoral Commission.** PPERA requires donors to make annual reports to the Electoral Commission of certain political donations, and makes failure to comply a criminal offence.

4. **All political 'donations' must be reported in the directors' annual report.** PPERA extends the obligations to include details of political donations in the directors' annual report.

What counts as a 'donation'?

Under PPERA a 'donation' is one or all of the following:

▨ Money

▨ Property

▨ Provisions of sponsorship, which includes expenses of any party events, research or study

▨ Preparation or dissemination of publications

▨ Subscription and affiliation fees

▨ Payment of expenses

▨ Loans, property, services or facilities provided to a party on other than commercial terms

Any of the above are 'donations' whether given directly to a party or indirectly through a third person (this latter point can trap an unsuspecting lobbyist unfamiliar with the provisions contained in PPERA – see below).

What is *not* classified as a 'donation'

▨ A gift valued at £200 or under – unless gifts in any one calendar year add up in total to more than £1000 to an individual or more than £5000 to a political organisation

▨ The provision by an individual of his own services, but *only* if provided voluntarily in his own time and free of charge (see below)

▨ Admission charges to any party event, which includes party conference passes

▨ The hire of a stand at a party conference (subject to a maximum hire charge rate to be set by the Electoral Commission)

▨ The purchase price of any publication and payment at the full commercial rate for advertising in a publication

▨ Party political broadcasts provided free of charge

▨ A candidate's election expenses (which come instead under the **Representation of the People Act 1983**)

With respect to passes bought to attend party political conferences, the Electoral Commission takes the view that any charge made for a conference pass will normally be a commercial arrangement.

However, if the cost of the pass exceeds the true commercial value, this excess will be a donation for the purpose of the PPERA.

As regards other events, the initial Electoral Commission view is that any amount of the entrance fee/ticket price over and above what is needed to cover the costs of the event is sponsorship and therefore a donation. It is not clear how this would be valued.

A 'donation' is covered by PPERA if it is made to one of the following:

- UK registered political parties
- Individual party members
- Members' associations
- Permitted participants in referendums
- Election candidates
- EU political organisations

Acceptance of a 'political donation'

A party or a candidate may only accept a donation from a 'permissible donor' and where the identity of the donor is known. Non-compliance is a criminal offence.

'Permissible donors'

A permissible donor includes:

- Individuals registered in an electoral register
- Companies registered in the UK and incorporated in a member state of the EU and which carry on business in the UK
- Any unincorporated associations which have their main offices in the UK
- Trades unions
- Registered parties
- Building societies, friendly societies or limited liability partnerships

Position as to foreign companies

A foreign company that does not satisfy the above criteria is *not* a permissible donor.

It is therefore **unlawful** for political parties or candidates to accept donations over £200 in total from any such company. This means, of course, that foreign companies can still make small contributions (£199 and under); attend conferences (subject to the Electoral Commission's view); and hire conference stands and advertise. But they cannot, for example, pay for attending fund-raising dinners.

Foreign-owned subsidiaries operating in the UK *can* make donations if they are registered under the **Companies Act 1985** and incorporated in the UK or EU.

All other controls apply however (see above). In particular, a foreign holding company must pass a resolution authorising political donations by a UK subsidiary.

Current practice

There are signs that the tradition of companies giving donations to political parties may be consigned to the past as BP announced in March 2002 that it would cease making contributions to political parties in order to 'safeguard the legitimacy of the political process' (which begs the question whether this was compromised whilst BP made substantial political donations for many years!).

This recent *volte-face* came in the wake of concern over the contributions made by Enron to the Republican Party in the US and payments to the Labour Party by Mittal.

What is the position for employees who take time off to work for a political candidate?

If a company gives its employees time off to work to canvass for a candidate or political party at any time (whether or not during an election), it will *potentially* be making a political donation.

In order to avoid this arising, the employee *must* take the time either as holiday within his normal holiday entitlement or as unpaid leave. Work done by an employee outside his normal working hours, e.g. weekends, early mornings or evenings, will *not* count, as the employee will be working in his or her own time.

The legislation cannot be circumvented by, say, granting additional holiday. However, the Electoral Commission takes the view that an employer who gives special paid leave to an employee to stand as a parliamentary candidate does *not* make a political donation.

How is the value of a donation calculated?

Donations other than money are valued in commercial terms at market value. This would include, for example, property lent for campaign purposes.

Where any payment is made by (or on behalf of) the party but is less than full market value, the value of the donation is the difference between the two.

PPERA treats an employer's provision of employees to work for a political party or candidate as the provision of services by the employer. It says that the value of this as a donation is the value of those services if they had been provided on commercial terms, less any payment actually made for the employees' services.

The Electoral Commission interprets this as meaning that the commercial value of the services is valued on the basis of each employee's commercial charge-out rate.

In the context of calculating campaign expenditure, the commercial rate for an employee's services is taken to be the amount of remuneration payable by his employer for the period during which the employee's services are made available.

It would be strange if the amount of notional expenditure were different from the notional donation. This matter is being taken up by the APPC with the Electoral Commission at the time of writing.

What other sort of day-to-day political activity does PPERA cover?

While some significant day-to-day activities fall outside PPERA, e.g. hiring exhibition stands (provided they are paid for at commercial rates), there are many activities that will still be caught by the 2000 Act.

For example, the annual Labour fund-raising dinner is an event where at least part of the purchase price of the ticket is a donation.

Donations to bodies whose existence is intended to benefit a political party or to influence the outcome of a referendum would also be caught.

The Government has indicated in a recent parliamentary written answer that this definition does *not* cover think tanks or campaigning charities, but companies should be aware that this is an interpretation, not settled law.

Companies may wish to seek reassurance from the think tanks or campaigning charities about their own legal advice on the 2000 Act.

Lobbyists should be aware they themselves will become donors if, for example, the consultancy acts as a third party and buys a ticket to an event for a client without re-charging it to the client (but see further below).

When do donations have to be reported?

Political parties themselves must record all donations above £200 and make detailed quarterly (or weekly in a general election period) reports to the Electoral Commission when a donation from a company is more than £1000 for an individual or more than £5000 for a company.

Additionally, the election expenses return, which is to be made by election candidates, must give details of the sources and amount of donations of more than £50. There are separate detailed provisions governing the control of election expenses otherwise than by a candidate and also governing the control of campaign expenditure under PPERA.

The reporting provisions in the 2000 Act are detailed. Although certain small donations are not required to be reported, all large donations and a great many small ones will be reported to the Electoral Commission by the recipient and so companies' donations are likely to be in the public domain.

Political expenditure other than donations, which a company may be required to authorise and report

EU political expenditure may also require authorisation. This includes any activity by the company that is intended to affect public support for any EU political organisation (including both parties and independent candidates) or to influence voters in any regional or national referendum in any EU state.

What action must companies take?

According to the APPC, any company that may want to do anything amounting to a political donation *must* take the following action:

1. Pass a company resolution which authorises the company to (a) make donations to EU political organisations not exceeding in total a sum specified in the resolution and/or (b) incur EU political expenditure not exceeding a specified total sum.

■ The resolution must specify the period for which it operates. This can be a maximum of 4 years beginning with the date of the resolution. The resolution *must* be in the general terms set out above. It must *not* authorise any specific donation or political expenditure.

Example of Special Resolution

Resolved as follows:

The company may

(a) make donations to any EU political organisation not exceeding in total the sum of **[£ in each financial year that this resolution is in force] [£ throughout the period that this resolution is in force]** *or*

(b) incur any EU political expenditure not exceeding in total the sum of **[£ in each financial year that this resolution is in force] [£ throughout the period that this resolution is in force]**.

This resolution has effect for a period of **[specify – maximum 4 years]** from the date on which it is passed.

It is recommended that companies should also pass an ancillary resolution along the following lines:

The making of any political donation or the incurring of any political expenditure authorised by **[specify the approval resolution above]** shall be at the sole discretion of the directors, in particular as to timing, recipients and amount.

■ The resolution must be passed by the company at a general meeting, not necessarily an AGM. It can be an ordinary resolution (unless the directors determine – or the company's articles require – that the resolution should be a special resolution or a resolution requiring a larger majority than is needed for an ordinary resolution).

■ The resolution must be passed *before* any donation or expenditure is made or incurred. Retrospective authorisation is not allowed.

■ Where the company making the donation or incurring the expenditure is a subsidiary company, the appropriate resolution must be passed by the holding company. The subsidiary must pass a resolution of its own only if it is *not* a wholly owned subsidiary.

2. Record all donations and be prepared to report them to the Electoral Commission as follows:

■ The reporting requirements relate to the calendar years. The first period runs from 16 February 2001 to 31 December 2001.

■ The requirement is to report where several small (e.g. less than £200 each) donations made to a particular registered party in the period total more than £5000. The report must contain specified details about the donations, the donor and the party to which the donations were made. It must be verified by a declaration that it is correct and that no other small donations were made to that party in the year.

◼ The requirement is to report as regards each party to whom small donations have been made totalling more than £5000. If a company has made such donations to more than one party, e.g. £12 000 of small donations to two parties totalling £6000 for each party, separate reports are required.

◼ The report must be delivered to the Electoral Commission. *It must reach the Commission by 31 January* in the year following the year in which the reported donations were made. Companies therefore have only 1 month to get their report to the Electoral Commission. Bearing in mind the public holidays in January, it is a short working month, so companies should be well prepared before the year end.

◼ It is a **criminal offence** for any person to:
    (a) Deliver a report which does not give all the requisite details
    (b) Fail to deliver a report on time, or deliver it without a declaration
    (c) Knowingly or recklessly make a false declaration.

3. If the *total of all* a company's political donations or political expenditure in any financial year exceeds £200, then it must include details in its annual report. Companies should also note that:

◼ This reporting requirement relates to the company's first full financial year after February 2001, so that recording details may need to accommodate two reporting periods (because the reporting period for the Electoral Commission is the calendar year – see 2 above).

◼ The requirement covers the total of *all* donations, where that total exceeds £200 (unlike the reporting requirement for the Electoral Commission which totals donations to specific parties).

◼ Holding companies must include in their report details of political donations and expenditure by any subsidiary company.

◼ *Wholly owned* subsidiaries are not obliged to report themselves but can rely on the parent company's report.

What must lobbyists clear with a client?

As a matter of best practice, lobbyists are well advised to get advance clearance from a client for anything that amounts to a political donation on behalf of that client.

INSIGHT

For example, buying a ticket to a party function and re-charging it to a client will be a donation to the party *by the client*, and therefore lobbyists should clear such expenditure with the client *in advance*.

APPC

Background

The **APPC** was set up in 1994 and currently has 25 member companies, who together account for about three-quarters of fee income earned by political consultants.

APPC members act for a wide spectrum of clients, including major global companies, small businesses, trade associations, charities, local campaign groups, professional bodies, trades unions, professional firms and academic and public sector organisations.

APPC member companies and their employees are required to sign a **Code of Conduct** (below) which provides detailed guidance on how lobbying should be carried out, based on core principles of honesty and openness.

The Code, for example, bans any financial relationship between member companies and members of either House of Parliament.

Twice yearly publication of company client lists ensures that everyone can see on whose behalf member companies are operating.

The Code of Conduct has been used against APPC members following newspaper allegations of improper conduct and two companies were subject to a period of suspension from APPC membership and their internal arrangements were inspected by Lord Armstrong and Nicholas Purnell QC before they could be readmitted.

The APPC argues that the Code should extend to those lobbyists that have traditionally been outside the APPC and include in-house practitioners (working for companies, trades unions and non-governmental organisations) as well as lawyers, management consultants and accountancy firms who may, from time to time, engage in lobbying.

APPC Code of Conduct

The **Code of Conduct** covers the activities of political consultants in relation to all UK, English, Welsh, Scottish and Northern Ireland central and local government institutions.

It is a condition of membership of the APPC that the member firm, its staff and non-executive consultants should accept and agree to abide by the Code for itself, and that members will be jointly and severally liable for the actions of their staff in relation to the Code.

Political consultants are required to endorse the Code and to adopt and observe the principles and duties set out in it in relation to their business dealings with clients and with institutions of government.

POINT OF LAW

Professional political consultants stand upon the bridge between their client and departments and agencies of government. If they are to retain the confidence of their clients and of the institutions of government with whom they have dealings, they must conduct, and be seen to conduct, their activities with the highest standards of integrity towards both, and in such a manner as to respect and not to impair, or to give the appearance of impairing, the integrity of his company, of his clients, or of the institutions concerned (hereinafter 'institutions of government' should be taken to include 'public body').

According to the Code, the duty of political consultants is to monitor the activities of the institutions of government and to enable their clients to present a proposal or a case in the most effective way to the relevant institution.

This involves consultants providing factual and other information to their client, analysing both the client's proposal and case and the political and policy environment in which it is to be put forward, assisting clients in preparing and advocating their case and to direct it efficiently and appropriately.

The Code applies equally to all clients, whether or not fee paying.

1. In pursuance of the principles in this Code, political consultants are required not to act or engage in any practice or conduct in any manner detrimental to the reputation of the Association or the profession of political consultancy in general.

2. Political consultants must act with honesty towards clients and the institutions of government.

3. Political consultants must use reasonable endeavours to satisfy themselves of the truth and accuracy of all statements made or information provided to clients or by or on behalf of clients to institutions of government.

4. In making representations to the institutions of government, political consultants should be open in disclosing the identity of their clients and other information, subject always to the requirements of commercial confidentiality.

5. Political consultants must advise clients where their objectives may be unlawful, unethical or contrary to professional practice, and to refuse to act for a client in pursuance of any such objective.

6. Political consultants should not make misleading, exaggerated or extravagant claims to clients about, or otherwise misrepresent, the nature or extent of their access to institutions of government or to persons in those institutions.

7. Save for entertainment and token business mementoes, political consultants should not offer or give to a client any financial inducement to secure or retain that client's business; not to offer or give, or cause a client to offer or give, any financial or other incentive to a Member of either House of Parliament, the Scottish Parliament, Welsh Assembly or Northern Ireland Assembly or Greater London Assembly, to any aide or assistant of any such Member, to any member of the staff of either House of Parliament, the Scottish Parliament, Welsh Assembly or Northern Ireland Assembly or Greater London Assembly, or to any Minister or official in any institution of government; not to accept any financial or other incentive, from whatever source, that could be construed in any way as a bribe or solicitation of favour.

8. Political consultants should not place themselves in a position of potential conflict of interest, for example by acting for any client ('Client A') where, in the view of another client ('Client B') to do so would conflict with duties to Client B; appointing to their main or subsidiary board, or to the board of any body corporate in which they have a majority interest, or causing to be appointed to any parent or associated company board, any MP, MEP, sitting Peer or any member of the Scottish Parliament or the Welsh Assembly or the

Northern Ireland Assembly or the Greater London Assembly; making any award of, or allowing the holding of equity in, any Member firm; or payment in money or in kind to any MP, MEP, sitting Peer or to any member of the Scottish Parliament or the Welsh Assembly or the Northern Ireland Assembly or the Greater London Assembly, or to connected persons or persons acting on their account directly or through third parties; failing to comply with any statute, Westminster or Scottish parliamentary or Welsh or Northern Ireland Assembly or Greater London Assembly resolution and adopted recommendation of the Committee on Standards in Public Life in relation to payments to a political party in any part of the UK.

9. Political consultants who are also local authority councillors are prohibited from working on a client assignment of which the objective is to influence a decision of the local authority on which they serve.

10. Political consultants must keep strictly separate from their duties and activities as political consultants any personal activity or involvement on behalf of a political party. Where any conflict may arise between consultants' professional duties and their personal political activity, the former must have precedence.

11. Political consultants must abide by the rules and conventions for the obtaining, distribution and release of parliamentary and governmental documents.

12. Political consultants must not hold, or permit any staff member to hold, any pass conferring entitlement to access to the Palace of Westminster, to the premises of the Scottish Parliament or the Welsh Assembly or the Northern Ireland Assembly or any department or agency of government.

13. Political consultants must conduct themselves in accordance with the rules of the Palace of Westminster, Scottish Parliament, Welsh Assembly, Northern Ireland Assembly or Greater London Assembly or any department or agency of government while within their precincts, and with the rules, conventions and procedures of all institutions of government.

14. Political consultants must always abide by the internal rules on declaration and handling of interests laid down by any public body on which they serve.

15. Political consultants must not exploit public servants or abuse the facilities or institutions of central or local government within the UK.

POINT OF LAW

In all their activities and dealings, political consultants should be at all times aware of the importance of his observance of the principles and duties set out in this Code for the protection and maintenance of their own reputation, the good name and success of their company, and the standing of the profession as a whole.

Compliance with the APPC's Code of Conduct

The APPC is responsible for taking appropriate disciplinary action should its Code of Conduct be breached and details of its Complaints, Arbitration and Disciplinary Rules and Procedures can be obtained from its secretary.

Lobbyists may also belong to the Institute of Public Relations ('IPR') Government Affairs Group and may also be bound by the IPR's Code of Conduct.

Institute of Public Relations (IPR) CODE OF CONDUCT

Background

The **IPR** was founded in 1948 and has over 7100 members involved in all aspects of the public relations industry. It is the largest professional body of its type in Europe, with rigorous qualifications for membership (based on educational qualifications and/or multi-disciplinary experience) ensuring that standards are high and maintained.

In March 2000, the **IPR Professional Practices Committee ('PPC')** issued a member consultation on the review of the **IPR Code of Professional Conduct**.

The IPR, which counts some 300 professional lobbyists among its members, gave evidence to the **Committee on Standards in Public Life** and modified its own Code of Conduct in light of **The Funding of Political Parties in the United Kingdom (1988)** and **Reinforcing Standards: Review of the First Report of the Committee on Standards in Public Life (1999).**

A new **IPR Code of Conduct** was ratified and adopted in 2000. All complaints against IPR members are, and remain, confidential and breach of confidentiality may arise in a separate complaint being made.

Members of the IPR agree to:

1. Maintain the highest standards of professional endeavour, integrity, confidentiality, financial propriety and personal conduct

2. Deal honestly and fairly in business with employers, employees, clients, fellow professionals, other professions and the public

3. Respect the customs, practices and codes of clients, employers, colleagues, fellow professionals and other professions in all countries where they practise

4. Take all reasonable care to ensure employment best practice including giving no cause for complaint of unfair discrimination on any grounds

5. Work within the legal and regulatory frameworks affecting the practice of public relations in all countries where they practise

6. Encourage professional training and development among members of the profession

7. Respect and abide by this Code and related Notes of Guidance issued by the Institute of Public Relations and encourage others to do the same

Principles of good practice

Fundamental to good public relations practice (and lobbying) are:

Integrity

■ Honest and responsible regard for the public interest

■ Checking the reliability and accuracy of information before dissemination

■ Never knowingly misleading clients, employers, employees, colleagues and fellow professionals about the nature of representation or what can be competently delivered and achieved

■ Supporting the IPR Principles by bringing to the attention of the IPR examples of malpractice and unprofessional conduct

Competence

■ Being aware of the limitations of professional competence: without limiting realistic scope for development, being willing to accept or delegate only that work for which practitioners are suitably skilled and experienced

■ Where appropriate, collaborating on projects to ensure the necessary skill base

■ Transparency and conflicts of interest

■ Disclosing to employers, clients or potential clients any financial interest in a supplier being recommended or engaged

■ Declaring conflicts of interest (or circumstances which may give rise to them) in writing to clients, potential clients and employers as soon as they arise

■ Ensuring that services provided are costed and accounted for in a manner that conforms to accepted business practice and ethics

Confidentiality

■ Safeguarding the confidences of present and former clients and employers

■ Being careful to avoid using confidential and 'insider' information to the disadvantage or prejudice of clients and employers, or to self-advantage of any kind

■ Not disclosing confidential information unless specific permission has been granted or the public interest is at stake or if required by law

Maintaining professional standards. IPR members are encouraged to spread awareness and pride in the public relations profession where practicable by, for example:

■ Identifying and closing professional skills gaps through the Institute's Continuous Professional Development programme

■ Offering work experience to students interested in pursuing a career in public relations

■ Participating in the work of the Institute through the committee structure, special interest and vocational groups, training and networking events

- Encouraging employees and colleagues to join and support the IPR
- Displaying the IPR designatory letters on business stationery
- Specifying a preference for IPR applicants for staff positions advertised
- Evaluating the practice of public relations through use of the IPR Research & Evaluation Toolkit and other quality management and quality assurance systems (e.g. ISO standards) and constantly striving to improve the quality of business performance
- Sharing information on good practice with members and, equally, referring perceived examples of poor practice to the Institute

CHECKLIST

- A lobbyist's contacts are no use unless a company has a sound case
- No amount of entertaining can substitute for a well-researched case
- Clients should think Government, not Parliament; it is also important to talk to MPs' advisors
- Think political system and take account of the network of institutions
- Do not act unless it is known how Government will react to the client's case
- Ensure that appropriate resolutions have been passed in order to make a 'political donation'
- Observe strict reporting deadlines to the Electoral Commission
- Comply with the provisions of the Data Protection Act 1994
- Beware law of defamation (see Chapter 8)

15

CYBER MARKETING

In this chapter:

- Domain names – ownership and disputes
- 'Webvertising'
- Defamation
- Direct marketing
- Directive 31/00/EC (E-Commerce Directive) 2000
- Checklist

Other useful chapters:

- Chapter 3: Making statements
- Chapter 5: Intellectual property rights
- Chapter 7: Data protection
- Chapter 8: Defamation
- Chapter 9: Advertising and labelling
- Chapter 10: Broadcasting
- Chapter 13: Promotions and incentives

INTRODUCTION

'Cyber marketing' is one of the fastest growing economic activities within the European Union.

The term 'cyber marketing' includes the following activities:

- Marketing on-line
- Fax direct marketing
- Call centre direct marketing or canvassing
- Short Message Service (SMS) mobile phone direct marketing

Given the level of consumer nervousness about using the Internet as a medium for business transactions this chapter will concentrate on marketing on-line.

Over the last few years there have been various attempts made to make the on-line transaction process more secure and to communicate this to the public.

The **Telecommunications (Data Protection and Privacy) Regulations 1999** and the **TrustUK** 'web safe' standard are two recent examples of attempts made to protect consumers from unwelcome interest as well as attempting to signal to consumers that parting with their credit card details on a particular web site is both safe and secure.

The latest European Union (EU)-wide effort to raise public confidence levels is the imaginatively titled **Directive 31/00/EC (E-Commerce Directive) 2000**. This is an attempt by the European Commission to clarify legal aspects of electronic commerce and harmonise the application of regulations throughout the EU.

In the UK, the E-Commerce Directive is unlikely to be implemented within existing laws until well into the second half of 2002 (see at the end of this chapter).

This chapter is a summary of the essential laws regulating the practice of cyber marketing as it relates to the Internet and over the next 2 years marketers can expect to comply with additional UK and EU regulations.

DOMAIN NAMES – OWNERSHIP AND DISPUTES

Ownership of domain names

Domain names used by a marketer are likely to have a significant impact on the success of any 'cyber marketing' campaign because customers and prospects need to be able to navigate to the marketer's on-line site or store and will need its IP address in order to do so successfully.

Given that domain names are generally registered on a **'first-come, first-served'** basis, a marketer may simply find that the name it wants to use is unavailable because another competitor marketer has registered that name for itself.

Sometimes there is a more sinister reason for the unavailability of a domain name and the practice of 'cyber squatting' has presented some challenges for marketers.

Cyber squatting

'Cyber squatting', or known by its less glamorous description 'domain name piracy' can present a problem when setting up a web site if the marketer discovers that the domain name it wishes to use has already been registered to a third party.

Worse still, customers and prospects of the marketer could be diverted away from being able to communicate with it and could end up transacting with its competitor marketer!

Ownership and registration of the company name at **Companies House** or even the registration of a particular trademark is *not* automatic entitlement to registration of the same name as an Internet domain name.

INSIGHT

For example, a few years ago the **Inland Revenue** paid £194 to a third party for the Internet domain name www.inlandrevenue.org.uk. By comparison, Globalvision.com, a small multimedia company, reportedly paid $2 million for the names *Britain.com*, *London.com* and *England.com*, a UK record at the time. Case law has since, however, moved on, and there is now more protection afforded to trademark owners through the Courts and the **ICANN/Nominet** dispute resolution procedures (see below and Chapter 5).

Marketers can avoid these problems by purchasing a range of services that have sprung up as a result of 'cyber squatting'. For example, **NetBenefit**, one of the Internet name registrars, offers an on-line 'I-Watch' service to check internationally for notification of any domain name registrations that may impact on a marketer's corporate or brand names.

INSIGHT

However, there is no substitute for registering the right domain name(s) as soon as possible in order to protect the integrity of any marketing or trading activities.

Trade names

As domain names are generally registered on a 'first-come, first-served' basis, disputes can, and often do, arise when the owner of a trademark is denied use of that mark as a domain name because another party has already registered it as a domain name.

The potential for conflict is exacerbated by the fact that trademark laws allow the *same* mark to be used by sellers of *different* types of goods and services provided there is no confusion in the marketplace regarding the origin of those goods and services.

INSIGHT

By contrast, Internet technology allows only one entity to utilise a particular domain name.

Although trademark laws may be relied upon to protect trademark owners, such laws are of little assistance in resolving disputes between owners of *identical marks* used in conjunction with *different* products or services.

In this regard, the technical nature of the Internet makes it difficult or impossible for multiple users of the same mark to distinguish their own use of the mark.

INSIGHT

For example, whilst a marketer may use capitalisation, special fonts or designs to distinguish its mark, such distinctions are technically precluded as a means of distinguishing different domain names.

Clearly, a domain name that consists of a business' trademark or trade name, or which is related to its mark or name, can make it easier for a marketer's customers and third parties to locate its business on the Internet.

The use of related domain names can also be a means of enhancing the goodwill associated with its particular service or product.

However, where a domain name is registered which does incorporate a UK registered trademark of a competitor marketer, the domain name holder could be in breach of the **Trademarks Act 1994**, but *only* if it relates to identical or similar class of goods or services.

An action under the tort of **passing off** may also arise if a competitor marketer wrongly represents, in the course of its trade or profession, that there is a connection between itself and the trademark owner (see Chapter 5).

Before registering any domain name, it would be prudent and advisable for the marketer to undertake a trademark search, and, if necessary, to obtain the trademark owner's consent to the use of the name in order to avoid a potential passing off action or trademark infringement.

LAW IN ACTION

For example, a company called **One in a Million** registered a number of well-known names and trademarks as domain names *without* the consent of BT and others (the owners), and then sought to sell them to the respective owners.

The owners took legal action for passing off and trademark infringement. The Court held that registration of a distinctive name falsely represented that One in a Million was associated with the name registered, devalued the goodwill associated with that name, causing damage to the owners and amounted to passing off.

Disputes

If a marketer discovers that a third party has registered its trade name, brand name or trademark, then there are a number of steps it can take:

Step 1: Commercial agreement with the third party

The marketer could enter into negotiations directly or through an agent to see if it can purchase the domain name and have it transferred to it.

A marketer may be able to agree a set fee plus incidental costs of transfer. It can then gauge whether the seller has a business of substance and wishes to protect its rights, or whether it is simply an opportunist 'cyber squatter' looking for easy money in order to hand over the domain name. This makes a considerable difference in the event that it proves necessary to bring legal proceedings.

Step 2: Direct approach to the Internet Corporation for Assigned Names and Numbers (ICANN) or Nominet

If during such negotiations the marketer is getting nowhere or the third party is insisting on an exorbitant or unrealistic amount of money in order to transfer the domain name, the next step for the marketer is to get in touch with **ICANN** if the domain name is US registered, or **Nominet** if the domain name is UK registered.

Both organisations have similar domain name disputes resolution policies, e.g. the **Uniform Dispute Resolution Procedure (UDRP)** that sets out the terms and conditions on which a dispute over domain name registration can be resolved. Most of the UDRP happens on-line and achieves a result within a couple of months.

Generally, a complaint submitted by a marketer must state that:

- The domain name is identical or confusingly similar to a trademark or service mark in which it has rights

- The third party has no rights or legitimate interests in respect of the domain name

- The domain name has been registered by the third party ('cyber squatter') and is being used in bad faith. Evidence of bad faith can be one of the following:

  - An offer to sell, rent or otherwise transfer the domain name to the owner of the trade or service mark, or to a competitor marketer of the owner of the trade or service mark, for valuable consideration

  - An attempt to attract, for financial gain, Internet users to the domain name holder's web site or other on-line location, by creating confusion with the trade or service mark of the complainant marketer

  - The registration of the domain name in order to prevent the owner of the trade or service mark from entering the market and corresponding domain name, provided that a pattern of such conduct has been established on the part of the domain name holders

  - The registration of the domain name in order to disrupt the business of the marketer

As the next case illustrates, if a 'cyber squatter' tries to sell the domain name of a marketer by inviting an offer through a letter, but adds the words 'without prejudice', then the marketer needs to be careful before immediately issuing proceedings and relying on the 'without prejudice' letter as evidence of bad faith.

WH Smith-v-Peter Colman (2000)
Court of Appeal

Newsagent and stationer WH Smith brought passing off and trademark infringement proceedings against Peter Colman who had registered WH Smith.com as a domain name.

During prior correspondence Colman wrote a letter marked 'without prejudice' to WH Smith's Chairman, referring to the possibility of settling the matter on the basis of a payment by WH Smith. WH Smith tried to put the letter in as evidence of bad faith on the part of Colman, who opposed this on grounds that as it was marked 'without prejudice' the letter should not be placed before the court.

The letter was certainly 'disingenuous, rambling, repetitious and unrealistic' said the Court of Appeal, but it seemed to indicate that Colman was seeking a settlement in order to avoid litigation and fell short of showing the 'unambiguous impropriety' which was required before the 'without prejudice' protection fell away.

WH Smith were held not entitled to produce the letter in evidence.

As seen from the One in a Million case (above) courts in the UK do take the view that any attempts to sell the domain name is prima facie an act of bad faith.

What if a domain name registrant is not a cynical 'cyber squatter' and genuinely wants to explore the possibility of agreeing terms whereby the name can be transferred? If such a proposal cannot be made without it being thrown back in the face of the proposer as evidence of bad faith, then an out of court settlement of domain name dispute may become impossible *unless* the parties resort to UDRP.

The procedure is not intended to deprive the parties of their legal remedies and the parties to a dispute can at any time litigate the issue. However, once a panel decision has been made it will not be implemented for 10 days during which time either party may apply to a national court.

Registrars of domain names like Nominet are still required to abide by the decisions of the courts and any decision reached by the arbitration panel would be superseded by a court judgment.

For example, in February 2001 'cyber squatter' **Anthony Stewart**, who called himself a trader in domain names, offered to sell comedian **Billy Connolly** the domain name www.billyconnolly.com in return for 5 years' supply of Connolly's Tickety-boo tea.

Connolly did not see the funny side to the proposed deal and was not much persuaded by Stewart's claim that he took out the domain name in order to offer the stud services of his pet Labrador *Rougemar Billyconnolly*.

Connolly offered Stewart £202.80, being the cost of the Tickety-boo tea in question, to hand over the e-moniker. This was rejected and Connolly increased his final offer to £750. Stewart felt he was not obliged to sell and held out for £7500.

Connolly was advised to initiate the **UDRP** introduced at the end of 1999 by ICANN. The adjudicating panel rejected Stewart's labrador story, especially as the Kennel Club had him down as *Rougemar Pindar*! As a result, the UDRP found Stewart had acted in bad faith and ordered him to transfer the domain name into the name of the 59-year-old comedian.

The case is a classic example of 'cyber squatting' that has plagued famous personalities as well as brands dealing with a .com (as opposed to a country suffix such as .co.uk), the only scenario where the UDRP can be used.

If the situation is not so clear cut and it is a .co.uk in play, there is for many no contest between paying an asking price of, say, £1000 and litigation. However, Nominet does now have its own dispute resolution procedure which can be used.

So far as personality domain names are concerned, commentators have expressed concern at some UDRP decisions.

In a report prepared by the **World Intellectual Property Organisation (WIPO)** and submitted to ICANN in 1999, which underpinned the creation of the UDRP, the report stated that the policy should be limited to bad faith domain names using brands that were already *registered* trademarks.

Limiting the procedure's ambit in this way should make its operation easier as international rules for the registration of trademarks are relatively homogeneous (see Chapter 5).

When it came to unregistered trademarks and personality rights, however, laws differed so much that a swift, written submissions-based procedure would not be appropriate.

Against this, it is perhaps surprising that the likes of Julia Roberts, Celine Dion and now Billy Connolly have achieved success using the UDRP, without having any trademark registrations to their name.

In contrast, the Elvis Presley estate was denied the right in the UK to prevent others registering Elvis Presley trademarks (see Chapter 5), despite the massive allure and value of the dead legend's name.

Step 3: Legal action

If the dispute cannot be resolved through ICANN or Nominet, then the marketer should consider whether legal action is appropriate if it can substantiate registered trademark infringement or passing off.

Just because a marketer may have a registered trademark in the UK or elsewhere may not give it precedence over other registered owners in different classes or different jurisdictions. It may also not be able to assert any rights against other parties who have a genuine right to the name.

Recent case law shows how important it is for a marketer to protect its company name, trade name and trademarks in every jurisdiction it intends to trade in, or run the risk of a competitor marketer obtaining rights to that name and preventing it from using it itself. For example, registration of .co.uk, .com, .net, .tv equivalents of the marketer's domain name, backed by usage in the relevant jurisdictions in which it wishes to trade, is likely to prove a relatively inexpensive alternative to the potential costs of negotiating the purchase of that name from another user (should they wish to sell) or of litigating to procure that result, with the inherent uncertainties that brings.

If a marketer is setting up a web site it should ensure that the name it wishes to use is not already registered, either as a domain name or as a registered trademark. It is also worth checking if the name is registered at **Companies House**. If it is a registered trademark, the marketer can probably still register the domain name but it should be aware that it may be potentially liable for trademark infringement and/or passing off actions.

Alternatively, if the marketer discovers that its trade name is registered by a third party as a domain name, it should consider whether there may have been any trademark infringement or passing off as well as whether to 'buy' the name from the third party.

New suffixes for domain names

Marketers should also consider, along with the established generic top level domain names suffixes (GTLDs), the new .aero, .biz, .coop, .info, .museum, .name and .pro where these may be relevant to its business – an up-to-date understanding of where these new GTLDs now are on accepting registrations can be found on the ICANN web site at **www.icann.org** and information on the proposed EU GTLD can be found on the EU web site at **www.europa.eu.int**

These new suffixes have led to a rash of 'pre-registration' deals being advertised claiming to ensure first place in the queue when .aero .biz .museum .web .coop .pro .info and .name become available.

Marketers should be very wary of dealers taking deposits or in some cases non-returnable administration fees, of say £35 per name to 'pre-register' domain names with the new suffixes. Some are even offering pre-registration of .eu, which does not yet seem to have appeared on ICANN's radar!

None of these pre-registration bodies has official ICANN sanction to offer this service, so there can be no guarantee that pre-registration with them will assure the marketer favourable treatment if and when the new GTLDs come on stream.

Hence the interest of **UK Trading Standards Officers** in what in some cases may be **Trade Descriptions Act 1968** offences at the very least.

'WEBVERTISING'

Legal issues relevant to advertising in traditional media are equally relevant to web advertising.

Web site advertisements are passively displayed and can be accessed from anywhere in the world and therefore may be subject to the laws of each country in which it is accessed by an Internet user. However, this can be problematic for the marketer.

Web site content

It is important for the marketer to consider the use of its web site and the target audience of visitors it wishes to attract to it.

Whether a marketer is using its web site for marketing, promotion, advertising, information or for transactional purposes, it is vital that the content of the web site is legally correct.

INSIGHT

Marketing best practice is to ensure that the marketer's web site complies with English law rather than the law of the country of visitors to the site.

There are also likely to be mandatory requirements, such as compliance with the **Companies Act 1985** (where applicable) and the **Business Names Act 1985**, where a marketer will be required to state its registered name, number and registered office on the web site.

Depending on the sector in which the marketer operates (see Chapter 16), there may also be additional regulations that will need to be complied with.

POINT OF LAW

For example, a member of the **Association of British Travel Agents (ABTA)** will need to comply with its **Code of Practice**.

Legal regulation

Advertising and sales promotion is subject to a variety of legislative and regulatory provisions which vary substantially from jurisdiction to jurisdiction.

UK web marketers have to comply with a plethora of domestic legislation including:

- Obscene Publications Acts 1959 and 1964
- Trade Descriptions Act 1968
- Lotteries and Amusements Act 1976
- Consumer Protection Act 1987
- Control of Misleading Advertisements Regulations 1988
- Copyright, Designs and Patents Act 1988
- Trademarks Act 1994
- Defamation Acts 1952 and 1996

- Data Protection Act 1998

- Consumer Protection (Distance Selling) Regulations 2000

There is also much non-English legislation that will be potentially breached as a result of a web advertisement.

LAW IN ACTION

For example, in the case of **United States-v-Thomas** (1996) the operators of a pornographic electronic bulletin board in California were convicted of criminal obscenity laws by a Federal Court in Tennessee based on Tennessee law. It was held that the material was 'sent' to Tennessee and subject to local law, despite the 'sending' being electronic and the bulletin board being essentially accessible worldwide.

In **Germany**, there are strict rules against comparative advertising and it can be illegal to give free gifts with purchases or to offer 'two for the price of one'.

In **Italy**, a permit must be obtained to run competitions and in **France,** by law, all advertising must be in the French language.

Chapter 16 provides further information on the regulations that apply to financial services products, tobacco and cigarettes, pharmaceuticals, children's products, alcoholic beverages and food marketing.

Conflict of laws

A key issue for the marketer is whether web site content is subject *only* to the law of the country of origin of the advertisement or to the law of each jurisdiction in which the advertisement is capable of being received.

There is no consensus on this issue at this time, although the **EU Directive on E-Commerce 2000** (when implemented) should assist, if not completely resolve, this issue. In respect of the applicable jurisdiction, see the section on the **Brussels I Regulation** (below).

Merely placing information on a web site is not generally considered evidence of directed activity provided it is clear that it is not targeted at consumers in a particular country.

The wording of the advertisement and the use of clear and unambiguous disclaimers will assist, as will technical methods of filtering web users.

Self-regulation

All advertising in the UK should comply with the **Advertising Standards Authority (ASA) Code of Advertising and Sales Promotion** and with other applicable codes of practice depending upon the sector of the marketer (see Chapter 9).

Direct Line Insurance and the ASA (2001)

A magazine advertisement promoted Direct Line's 'jamjar.com' car sales web site with the claim 'Huge savings on manufacturers' list prices'. At the foot of the advertisement readers were encouraged to 'buy on-line now' at the jamjar.com web site.

One consumer found that the price offered by jamjar.com for a Seat Arosa 1.4 Tdi was actually more than the manufacturer's UK list price and a complaint was made to the ASA.

Direct Line said there was actually a mistake on the web site and at most the list price should have been quoted. It also provided examples of huge savings on cars listed on the site but the ASA was not assuaged.

The ASA felt the likely inference drawn by consumers from the 'Huge savings on manufacturers' list prices' would be that jamjar.com would invariably offer huge savings on the list price of every single car manufacturer and the complaint was upheld.

Web marketers should consider informing their customers that they take their legal obligations seriously by becoming members of the **Direct Marketing Association (DMA)** as well as signing up to its **Charter** and complying with its **Codes of Conduct** in relation to all types of direct marketing.

Alongside its general Code, the DMA also has specific Codes in relation to direct marketing on-line and direct marketing to children. These can be accessed through the DMA web site at **www.dma.org.uk** and compliance with these Codes should go a long way to ensuring that e-marketing remains within the law.

Which? Web Traders Code of Practice

The *Which?* **Web Traders Code of Practice** provides that advertising must meet the standards of the **ASA Codes of Advertising and Sales Promotion**, and, in particular, must be legal, decent, honest and truthful. Unsolicited, untargeted mass-marketing e-mails are also prohibited under the Codes. Details of the Advertising Standards Authority can be found at **www.asa.org.uk.**

Comparative advertising

As discussed in more detail in Chapter 9, this is where an advertisement deliberately refers to a competitor marketer or to goods or services offered by a competitor marketer.

Such advertising can be risky as different countries have divergent views on such advertising (see, in particular, our comments regarding Germany above). The US and the UK encourage comparative advertising but most EU countries consider that it constitutes unfair competition.

The EU adopted a Directive on comparative advertising which was implemented in the UK by the **Control of Misleading Advertisements (Amendment) Regulations 2000** and allows comparative advertising on web sites provided it:

■ Is not misleading or confusing

■ Compares like with like

■ Objectively compares one or more material, relevant, verifiable and represented features of the relevant goods or service

■ Does not create confusion in the marketplace

■ Does not discredit or denigrate the competitor marketer and does not infringe a protected name or trademark

Controlling access

A marketer should place great importance on controlling the access to its web site.

For example, it may not wish to market to certain persons or deal with certain countries or jurisdictions for one or more of the following reasons:

■ Import or export embargoes/local sale restrictions

■ Consumer protection legislation

■ Illegal/regulated activity

■ Avoiding sales to certain persons, e.g. children

The Internet brings with it its own particular problems, e.g. the identity and location of customers are not necessarily apparent. However, web server checks and site disclaimers will help to avoid problems, and should be implemented.

A marketer needs to consider:

■ To whom its advertising is directed

■ Whether its advertising constitutes contractual offers or are merely invitations to treat (see Chapter 2)

■ Limitations of liability/warranties

■ Applicable law and jurisdiction

Data protection

The new **Data Protection Act 1998** came into full effect in October 2001 and marketers need to be aware of their obligations and the rights of data subjects.

This is discussed in more detail in Chapter 7, but in summary if the customer completes an on-line form providing personal details, e.g. financial details, issues over acquisition of data arise. These issues relate to the way in which data is acquired, the nature of that data and the control, storage and use of that data. The first data protection principle requires personal data to be obtained and processed fairly and lawfully.

Cookies can also cause data protection issues as they are files that track the users' preferences on a marketer's web site and even the pages visited so as to use the opportunity to market further products and services to the visitor based on their identified interests.

This clearly amounts to the collection of personal data and must therefore comply with the data processing principles of the **Data Protection Act 1998**.

In particular, a marketer will need to display a clear and unambiguous notice on its web site that it is using cookies and the reasons behind this.

Currently, a marketer must allow the visitor to its web site to opt-out of the collection of their data and if the marketer will be collecting any 'sensitive personal data'. In such cases, the data subject's express consent to collect this information must be obtained.

The above activities would also constitute direct marketing and the visitor to the web site could therefore request at any time that the collection and use of their data is ceased and so a marketer must ensure that it has processes in place in order to comply with such requests.

Web site disclaimers

A web site can potentially give rise to legal liability for the marketer in any country in which it can be accessed. It is therefore important to include appropriate disclaimers but there are limits on what liability can be excluded or restricted in each country and no disclaimer will be effective in all countries, or to the same degree in those countries in which it is effective.

> **POINT OF LAW**
>
> The wording of disclaimers are normally governed by the law of the country from which the web site is accessed.

As with on-line terms and conditions, in order for a disclaimer to be effective, it must be brought to the visitor's attention.

There are several ways in which a disclaimer can be included:

- On the entry page which requires the visitor to acknowledge the terms before gaining entry to the marketer's site or page

- On the word page containing the information or services

- To include a prominent link entitled 'disclaimer' placed at various points on the marketer's web site

- To include a prominent link above the acceptance icon where the contract is concluded

Ideally, from a legal perspective, a disclaimer should not be capable of being bypassed by the viewer as the marketer may not otherwise be able to rely upon it if the need arises.

The marketer will need to strike a balance in how it complies with the above requirements in order to keep its web site legal. On the one hand, it will want to bring its terms and conditions to the notice of the visitor but not in such a way that it is unfriendly or uninviting.

Marketing best practice is for any disclaimers to expressly *exclude* any representations or express or implied warranties to the fullest extent possible and require the visitor to accept the application of English law. Whether this will be enforceable in all jurisdictions (outside the UK) is, however, a moot point.

DEFAMATION

It is necessary to ensure that any statements made by a marketer on a web site (or elsewhere for that matter) do not amount to defamatory (libellous) statements.

Defamation is covered in detail in Chapter 8.

Marketers should take into consideration that due to the global nature of the Internet, defamation actions can be brought in any jurisdiction where publication of the defamatory statement occurs.

POINT OF LAW

For example, a US citizen or business who is defamed by a defamatory statement published on an English web site could bring defamation proceedings in either the UK or the US, or indeed any other country in which publication occurs and loss is suffered.

Law and jurisdiction

Due to the unique nature of the Internet, issues over jurisdiction are inevitable and the question as to which country will determine a dispute and enforce contractual terms is decided by the rules of jurisdiction.

For those marketers doing business on the web, the doomsday scenario has always been having to comply with the legal requirements of every state where the site can be accessed and many marketers have ignored the risks and largely escaped legal difficulties.

Jurisdictional complexities, enforcers' limited resources and lack of physical presence in problematic states had made the risks a commercially acceptable one for many marketers.

Now all of that has changed as a result of both the **Brussels I Regulation (BIR)**, which came into force on 1 March 2002, and the **Directive 31/00/EC (E-Commerce Directive) 2000** (see end of this chapter).

Jurisdictional issues as between EU member states are governed by the BIR, which is in similar terms to its predecessor, the Brussels Convention. The broad effect of the BIR is to implement, as between the present EU members, the provisions of the Brussels Convention by a directly effective community instrument.

Accordingly, if the defendant marketer is domiciled in an EU Member State, the BIR will apply (otherwise, English common law rules will apply).

If the BIR applies, and there is no jurisdiction clause in the contract, then as a basic rule jurisdiction will ordinarily lie in the defendant's domicile, as the policy of the BIR is that subject to exceptions, a defendant has the right to be sued in its own domicile.

The basic rule of the BIR will *not* apply:

1. In respect of contracts dealing with intellectual property rights (IPRs) – jurisdiction lies in the country of registration of those rights.

2. Where a defendant is sued in the place of performance of the obligation in question. This will mean the principal obligation forming the basis of the claim. In relation to a contract

for the provision of services, a defendant marketer could therefore be sued in the courts of the place where the services were provided or should have been provided.

3. Where a defendant marketer is sued in tort. Here, proceedings may be brought 'in the courts of the place in which the harmful event occurred'.

4. Where a contract relates to consumer contracts. The BIR provides that in certain circumstances, the consumer can elect to sue in either the defendant marketer's domicile or the consumer's own domicile. For example, if a French resident consumer buys goods advertised on a marketer's English web site, the defendant marketer could be sued in England or France. However, the consumer can only be sued in his own domicile.

If a marketer is dealing with consumers, it must therefore carefully consider the jurisdictions it is willing to trade in.

Relying on the BIR or, if the BIR is inapplicable, English common law to determine jurisdiction can create difficulties for e-commerce marketers.

INSIGHT

Marketing best practice in this area is to include a specific jurisdiction clause in the marketer's standard terms and conditions, whereby a particular jurisdiction will have either the exclusive (or, potentially, non-exclusive) right to hear disputes. This will usually override all other determinations and jurisdictions.

However, the BIR restricts the recognition of jurisdiction clauses to non-consumer contracts, and the jurisdiction agreed must be an EU member state.

Accordingly, consumer rights to be sued in their domicile and, potentially, to elect to sue outside their own domicile cannot be overridden by contractual terms. Therefore, ascertaining whether the marketer's web site is offering goods or services to businesses or consumers (or possibly both) will determine how the jurisdiction rules will apply.

The applicable law to govern the contract is distinct from the question of jurisdiction, and the **Rome Convention** allows almost total freedom of choice in selecting the applicable law of the contract.

This freedom even applies to consumer contracts, except where there are specific mandatory laws. A specific contractual term or standard terms and conditions can expressly select the law that governs the contract.

In the absence of an express choice the courts will infer the applicable law from the circumstances under which the contract was formed.

The most important application of mandatory laws in respect of the Rome Convention is where it grants consumer protection against choice of law clauses.

However, this consumer protection clause is *not* automatically applicable and to qualify for protection either:

- The customer contract must have been solicited by the marketer in the consumer's domicile and the consumer must have completed all contract formation steps there

▨   The consumer's order must have been received through an agent in the consumer's country

Law and jurisdiction are also important issues in determining the target audience for the marketer's web site.

It should be possible, by means of registration or some filtration process, to screen out potential customers in those countries with whom the marketer does not wish to trade.

POINT OF LAW

The marketer can expressly state that it will not trade with customers within or outside of certain geographical territories or will refer enquiries to a local distributor or agent or to some other party, or simply refuse to trade. For example, mail order marketers frequently restrict sales to UK mainland.

There are complications surrounding these issues and which are by no means yet resolved. However, the **Directive 31/00/EC (E-Commerce Directive) 2000** does address this issue and, once implemented, should go some way towards clarification.

Practicalities

If a marketer is selling products worldwide it is unlikely that it will have the resources to obtain clearances in each of the countries in which it intends to market its products.

However, it is prudent for the marketer to seek legal and trademark clearance in certain countries and particularly those in which it may have a physical presence or assets, and those territories with especially onerous laws and regulations or to which it wants to roll out a widespread direct marketing campaign.

The extent to which a marketer exercises control over material posted on or linked to its web site may also give rise to liability.

For example, allowing third parties to post material onto its web site could leave it responsible for any such material that contains defamatory or otherwise illegal material.

Clear terms and conditions of access and use, as well as appropriate disclaimers, should be displayed.

INSIGHT

If the marketer uses an advertising agency then, in view of the risk of liability for breach of foreign advertising regulations, it is essential that its contract with the advertising agency clarifies who is responsible for ensuring legal compliance of advertising material (see also Chapter 9).

DIRECT MARKETING

There are many forms direct marketing can take, including:

- E-mail and 'spam' marketing
- Cookies
- Fax marketing
- M-commerce (mobile phone marketing)

E-mail and 'spam' marketing

Spam (mass unsolicited commercial e-mails) is not currently prohibited under English law and the **EU Directive 31/00/EC (E-Commerce Directive) 2000** will also not outlaw this practice.

However, marketers need to be very careful, especially with consumers who are likely to have rights under the **Data Protection Act 1998** (see Chapter 7).

In all unsolicited commercial e-mails, the E-Commerce Directive 2000 provides that the Internet Service Provider (ISP) must be clearly and unambiguously identifiable and must consult regularly with opt-out registers.

INSIGHT

Marketing best practice is for the marketer only to use its own or reputable 'opt-in' lists for e-mail marketing so that it can be sure it has the individual's consent and it should also check its business' contract with its ISP.

Many ISPs prevent the use of 'spam marketing' and breach of such a contractual term in the service agreement is likely to result in the termination of the marketer's ISP contract which could cause serious problems to its business and cyber marketing activities.

The **Direct Marketing Association (DMA)** has also published a **Code of Practice for E-Commerce**, containing detailed rules on spamming, similar to **Directive 31/00/EC (E-Commerce Directive) 2000**.

Under the **DMA Code of Practice for E-Commerce**:

- Unsolicited e-mail must be clearly identifiable
- Members must not send random, untargeted commercial e-mail
- Members must consult opt-out registers
- The unsolicited e-mail must contain mechanism for the consumer to object to receiving further similar communications
- Unsolicited e-mail sent as a result of a 'member-get-member' scheme must make it clear to the recipient that the personal information has been obtained through such a scheme

Cookies

The data protection implications of the use of 'cookies' is discussed above but, with regard to direct marketing, marketers should be aware that, at the end of November 2001, an amendment was made to the **proposed EU Directive** concerning the processing of personal data and the protection of privacy in the electronic communications sector, to provide that users will have to 'opt-in' to the use of 'cookies'.

Consequently, marketers' web sites will not be entitled to automatically use 'cookies' unless the individual has given express prior consent to the collection of their data in this way and the marketer has provided an explanation of how 'cookies' are to be used.

The Directive is not finalised yet, but major changes get less likely the further down the legislative track the draft progresses. As the **Interactive Advertising Bureau (IAB)** has commented, the new suggested requirements are unclear as to precisely what information must be provided by the marketer before the opt-out opportunity is given.

However, the IAB is optimistic that the rule's spirit can be satisfied and is currently working to develop practical self-regulation for cyber marketers. This will enable users to opt-out of accepting cookies, but not so that marketers will need to make prohibitively costly alterations to their web sites.

Fax marketing

The **Telecommunications (Data Protection and Privacy) Regulations 1999** prohibit marketers sending unsolicited faxes to individuals without prior consent and allows individuals to opt-out from receiving unsolicited direct marketing telephone calls.

LAW IN ACTION

For example, in 2000, the **Data Protection Commission** started legal proceedings against two cyber marketers – **Second Telcom** and **Top 20** – in respect of the sending of unsolicited marketing faxes.

In order to resolve the matter without going to court, both marketers agreed to accept service of formal notices, ratified by the Data Protection Tribunal, requiring them to abide by **Regulation 23 of the Telecommunications (Data Protection and Privacy) Regulations 1999** which makes it a criminal offence to send unsolicited marketing faxes to any number, individual or corporate, listed on the **Fax Preference Service (FPS)** register. **Regulation 24** makes it an offence to send such faxes to an individual's number without prior consent. This also applies to numbers of individuals who are sole traders or partners in a business partnership.

There is no charge for individuals who wish to register with the **FPS** as not wanting unsolicited marketing faxes, but cyber marketers must pay to search the register and 'clean' their lists.

Even if individuals' numbers have not been registered with the FPS, it is still illegal to send unsolicited marketing faxes to numbers of individuals as opposed to companies, unless the individual has given prior written consent ('opted-in').

Commercial conference marketers sending unsolicited faxes about forthcoming events to individuals' direct fax numbers within organisations could easily fall foul of these provisions.

Further legislation has been introduced into this area and the **Consumer Protection (Distance Selling) Regulations 2000** requires that cyber marketers obtain the express prior consent of consumers to use of faxes or automated calling machines because individuals must have expressly opted-in to receive this material.

Other means of distance marketing communications, unsolicited or not, including e-mail, traditional mailshots and 'cold calls' may only be used where there is no clear objection from the consumer (that is where they have not opted-out).

Consumers have to be given the opportunity to register their objections to receiving such marketing communications and the identity of the marketer and the commercial aim of the communication must be stated at the outset of the communication.

This is an area that is being continually reviewed though and there are always discussions and campaigns by consumer groups for only opt-in, as opposed to opt-out, regimes for all unsolicited marketing, including e-mail and SMS messaging.

M-commerce marketing

SMS marketing is the latest form of direct marketing given the explosion in popularity of mobile phones amongst a young consumer age group worldwide.

According to the **Mobile Data Association**, British mobile phone users now send 40 million SMS text messages every day. A growing number of these messages (10%) are interactions between individuals and brand owners such as Carlsberg, McDonald's, Pepsi, *Men's Health* magazine, Channel 4 and Worldpop.com.

SMS marketing moved from being a fringe marketing activity into mainstream marketing practice when in 2001 Cadbury's promoted an SMS-based competition on 65 million chocolate bars and received a phenomenal response to the campaign that directly led to an uplift in overall sales.

Despite this success, there are fears in the marketing profession that SMS 'spamming' could have a negative impact on the take up of permission-based services.

For example, in some parts of the world such as Japan, the commercial damage done to brand owners offering permission-based 'pull' services has been immense as the quantity of 'spam' has even begun to dwarf the number of person-to-person messages and inevitably 'text fatigue' has set in, meaning that responsible marketers are making little impact.

INSIGHT

There has been growth in location-based 'spam' where users are sent uninvited SMS messages relating to whichever business they happen to be near and this could start to taint the medium. The prospect that a consumer could receive an SMS message from every store that she walks past in the high street is probably not in the best interests of brand owners as it is likely to turn into an irritant and damage rather than enhance brand owners' reputation in the process.

One reason why SMS is so powerful is because it provides brand owners with a way of breaking through the media clutter. However, brand owners need to exercise caution and restraint in the use of SMS marketing.

According to an NOP survey in 2001, consumers are only willing to receive about five commercial SMS messages a day and although very few consumers are receiving in excess of this amount at present, there is a very real threat of 'SMS overload'.

The effect of SMS message abuse will impact other forms of direct marketing. The danger is that subscription or 'pull' services will start to feel the knock-on effect as mobile phone owners start to think twice about subscribing to a service for fear of their mobile number being 'spammed' at a later date.

It was this fear that prompted the **DMA** to launch a consumer campaign called 'It's Your Choice' dealing specifically with SMS and e-mail marketing, in February 2002.

While the DMA was focusing its campaign on public awareness, the **Wireless Marketing Association (WMA)**, Europe's first wireless-focused marketing body, announced details of its **Code of Practice** to encourage responsible use of SMS in the industry and to provide consumers with confidence that when they sign up to a service provided by a member of the WMA, all communications will be permission based and consumers will have complete control over receipt of wireless marketing.

Formulated by key industry players that include Orange, BT Cellnet (now O_2) and Vodafone, the 19-point Code covers 'spamming' and attempts to offer safeguards to user privacy.

The Code of Practice is a collective move by the wireless industry in the UK to ensure both operators and consumers benefit from the explosion in wire-free services.

At its core, the Code of Practice provides consumers with the right to define if, what kind, when and how often they want to receive commercial messages on their mobile phones.

Key points of the Code of Practice include:

- A ban on all spamming; wireless marketing must be permission based

- Simple opt-out clauses offered to all mobile users who do not want to receive messages or promotions

- A fast and effective customer complaints system

- The establishment of a Consumer Protection Committee

- Promoters' names clearly displayed on every communication

- All information held on individuals to be held in a secure, protected environment and made available to individuals on request

Protocols and regulations regarding SMS marketing are still in development and on an international level, US-based **Wireless Advertising Association (WAA)** published its first set of **Guidelines on Privacy and Spam** in 2000 as well as creating a number of **definitions** that will become familiar within M-commerce.

Term	Definition
'PII'	Data which can be used to identify or contact a person uniquely and reliably.
'Push advertising/messaging'	Content sent other than at a time when the recipient requests it.
'Pull advertising/messaging'	Content is requested by the recipient.
'Standard opt-in'	Requires active choice on the part of the individual to express permission.
'Confirmed opt-in'	Involves verifying any permission given by, for example, sending a message to an individual who has given permission, asking that individual to positively reply to confirm that permission has been given.
'Wireless spam'	Push messaging sent without confirmed opt-in.
'Opt-out'	Taking action to withdraw permission.

Fig. 15.1 WAA definitions

The WAA is the leading global industry body representing hand-held device makers, carriers and operators, software developers, agencies, retailers, advertisers and service providers. Having set these definitions, the **WAA Guidelines on Privacy and Spam** establishes some general principles.

These require WAA members to adopt privacy policies regarding PII that are readily available to consumers at the time the PII is collected and encourage business partners to do the same.

Explicit consent must also be obtained before using data for purposes other than those disclosed at the time of collection.

Other aspects to be dealt with in privacy policies are set out in detail. When it comes to sending marketing messages, the WAA states quite clearly that although in e-mail marketing 'Confirmed opt-in' might be regarded as the highest level of subscriber permission, in the wireless marketing sector it should be the baseline.

All the indications are that 'opt-in' will be regarded as the baseline permission requirement in m-commerce, but it is still unclear what 'opt-in' or for that matter 'opt-out' actually means in practice.

The WAA's definitions help but are still not sufficiently granular to inform marketers whether, for example, having the opportunity to un-tick a ready-ticked 'opt-in' box is in fact 'opt-in'.

On a more positive note, proponents of permission-based marketing hope that the more consumers get used to signing up for rewarding campaigns, the less likely it is that 'spammers' will tarnish the future potential of this powerful marketing medium.

Marketers can expect more developments in m-commerce marketing through the course of 2002/2003.

PROPOSED EU DIRECTIVE CONCERNING THE PROCESSING OF PERSONAL DATA AND THE PROTECTION OF PRIVACY IN THE ELECTRONIC COMMUNICATIONS SECTOR

This **proposed new EU Directive** applies to cookies (as discussed above), but it is also intended to prevent any unsolicited direct marketing by fax, SMS or automated calling systems unless the individual has opted-in.

This is currently the case for fax marketing in the UK, but the legislation envisages taking this further by only allowing direct marketing to those who have expressly requested this by opting-in the marketer's own mailing lists or the mailing lists of reputable organisations for this purpose.

Whether there will be a requirement for individuals to opt-in, as opposed to opt-out, of e-mail marketing is yet to be determined but the current position is that this is likely to be left to the individual Member States to decide when they implement the Directive.

The Directive is still in its formative stages but it indicates the current thinking of the EU for the future and marketers should ensure they keep up to date with developments to keep on the right side of the law.

DIRECTIVE 31/00/EC (E-COMMERCE DIRECTIVE) 2000

This Directive was adopted in the EU on 8 June 2000 and should have been implemented in all Member States by 16 January 2002.

Marketers are still waiting for UK draft legislation and which, at the time of writing, is now not expected until later in 2002.

The Directive covers all information society services (ISS), both business to business and business to consumer, and aims to ensure that such services benefit from the internal market principles of free movement of services and freedom of establishment.

The Directive also ensures that ISS can be provided throughout the EU as long as they comply with the law in their home Member State. Issues over jurisdiction as discussed earlier in this chapter could therefore be lessened.

However, the 'place of establishment' of a service provider (marketer) for the purposes of the Directive is not where the service provider's equipment is located, where its web site is accessible or where its services are targeted, but is the 'centre of its activities'. What this means in practice is unclear and likely to be a point of contention in legal actions taken against marketers once the Directive has been implemented in all Member States.

The sectors and activities covered by the Directive include:

- On-line newspapers
- On-line databases
- On-line financial services
- On-line professional services
- On-line entertainment services

- On-line direct marketing
- On-line advertising
- Other on-line services

Marketers are therefore prime targets for compliance as the Directive requires transparency in web advertising. The Directive only applies to service providers established in the EU, but endeavours to avoid incompatibility and inconsistency with legal developments in other parts of the world in order to minimise obstacles to global e-commerce.

It is, however, only a 'framework' Directive and is intended to be followed by others.

It establishes common principles on several issues that the **European Commission** believes are sufficient to guarantee the free circulation of on-line services, including rights of establishment, transparency requirements for commercial communications, requirements relating to on-line conclusion of contracts and liability for illegal transmissions that violate rules on copyright, protection of minors or involve criminal activity.

The Directive aims to ensure high levels of protection for consumers by giving them the right to opt-out of unsolicited e-mail messages or 'spam marketing' by signing up with the opt-out registers in their home country. ISPs will be obliged to consult these registers regularly.

The Directive exempts service providers from liability for the transmission of illegal material if, upon receiving facts about the illegal nature of a transmission, they act quickly to remove the transmission from the network or disable it.

However, as the next well-publicised case demonstrates, ISPs must be careful not to confuse free speech with illegal activities otherwise they will face legal action and the possible punishment of fines by Member States' law enforcement authorities.

LAW IN ACTION

In 2000, a judge in France gave judgment against ISP **Yahoo!.com** in proceedings brought against the marketer by three Jewish/anti-racist organisations. It was alleged that Yahoo! had breached **R645-1 of the French Penal Code**. The law criminalises any dealing in Nazi memorabilia, which was being auctioned off on a site hosted by Yahoo! Inc. The site was in English and could not be accessed direct through Yahoo!.fr.

Yahoo! Inc. challenged the jurisdiction of the French court and also ran a first amendment/ free speech argument based on US law.

The French judge said that the court did have jurisdiction to hear the matter as the alleged offence in question was being committed in France every time a French resident accessed the offending site.

Having been satisfied by an independent tribunal that it was technically possible for Yahoo! Inc. to take measures to sift out 90% of French surfers who might otherwise have accessed the site, the judge ordered Yahoo! Inc. to take these measures within 3 months or face up to £9000 a day fines.

The French court did refuse to levy fines against Yahoo! until it had been given a fair amount of time to incorporate the technology apparently capable of stopping most French people accessing the offensive auction site.

As a result of the negative publicity, Yahoo! Inc. removed the offending site and issued a policy statement that it would not carry such sites in the future.

Just as the UK's commercial TV networks are a soft target when a marketer wants to take a competitor marketer's hard-hitting comparative advertising off air (see Chapter 9), in the same way ISPs may now offer an 'easy win' for state regulators who might otherwise have not considered it worthwhile to devote resources to hunting down an obscure web site operator on the other side of the world.

Where a service consists of the storage of information, service providers will not be held liable for illegal material if they do not have factual information about the illegal nature of the information.

The Directive is also likely to impact marketing practice in the UK in the following ways:

- Web sites must give the business' name, address, e-mail address, details of whether they are registered, e.g. a limited company number, and details of any relevant regulatory scheme, or professional body, to which they are subject and VAT details.

- Certain minimum information must be given for 'commercial communications'; this includes details of the person, such as the employer, on whose behalf the e-mail is sent, details of discounts and offers and must state if something is a promotional competition.

- Unsolicited e-mails should be clearly identifiable as such as soon as they are received. Member States have to make sure that service providers sending unsolicited commercial e-mails, consult opt-out registers; the DMA in the UK has already set up an e-mail preference service (see above).

- Service providers are not liable for content, e.g. libellous messages on a bulletin board, if they do not select or modify the information and if they remove the information quickly when told it infringes someone's rights; however, a court can still order an ISP to remove an infringing message. There is no general obligation to monitor content.

The Directive will lead to new national laws in due course and marketers would be well advised to keep up to date.

Impact for web sites and marketing

A large number of different legal areas are covered by the Directive and marketers should ensure that their e-mails and web sites contain the business address, telephone, fax and e-mail contact numbers and details of the organisation.

Although the legislation has not yet been implemented in the UK, the Directive gives marketers a good indication of what will be covered and what their obligations will be. Marketers would be well advised to at least review their current practices now to ensure that they are able to comply with the legislation in due course.

CHECKLIST

▦ Marketers should be quick to register a domain name before a competitor marketer decides to do the same thing

▦ Ownership of a domain name is not an automatic simply because the marketer has got other legal registrations for the company name or trademarks

▦ Marketers should consider buying a net watch name service as an early warning system for competitive activity on the Internet

▦ Protections for the marketer may be available through trademarks and passing off, but certain conditions that are pertinent to the Internet will apply

▦ Faced with a 'cyber squatter' a marketer can negotiate, approach Nominet or take legal action as a last resort, although should be careful not to rely on 'without prejudice' correspondence as central to its legal action

▦ Marketers should consider registering new domain name address with a new breed of suffixes: .biz, .coop, .info, .museum, .name and .pro

▦ Marketers will need to take account of other national laws where material on their web sites can be accessed from other territories

▦ Marketers may be affected by some of the following UK legislation:

 ● Obscene Publications Acts 1959 and 1964

 ● Trade Descriptions Act 1968

 ● Lotteries and Amusements Act 1976

 ● Consumer Protection Act 1987

 ● Control of Misleading Advertisements Regulations 1988

 ● Copyright, Designs and Patents Act 1988

 ● Trademarks Act 1994

 ● Defamation Acts 1952 and 1996

 ● Data Protection Act 1998

 ● Consumer Protection (Distance Selling) Regulations 2000

▦ 'Webvertising 'is also subject to the ASA's Code of Advertising and Sales Promotion

▦ A marketer should consider becoming a member of the DMA and signing up to its Code of Conduct as well as signing up to the *Which?* Web Traders Code of Practice

▦ Marketers should consider limiting access to their web sites in order to avoid potential legal problems with consumers outside their home territory and should also take advice on the use of disclaimers against liabilities

▦ In order to avoid costly jurisdictional issues, UK marketers should include a clause in their standard terms and conditions that English law applies to the contract

- Although 'spam marketing' is not unlawful, marketers may still fall foul of the Data Protection regulations and the DMA Code of Practice

- As a matter of best marketing practice, marketers ought to provide 'opt-in' boxes on their web sites, for example, where they wish to plant 'cookies' on visitors' computers to assist in navigating the site on subsequent visits

- Sending unsolicited faxes is an offence under the Telecommunications (Data Protection and Privacy) Regulations 1999 and marketers are under a duty to check the Fax Preference Service register on a regular basis; permission is also required under the Consumer Protection (Distance Selling) Regulations 2000

- Marketers using m-commerce marketing tactics should consider adopting the Wireless Advertising Association Guidelines on Privacy and Spam

- Marketers should ensure that they are up-to-date with European-wide regulations on e-commerce and comply with the Electronic Commerce Directive 2000 when it comes into force later in 2002

16

NICHE MARKETING

In this chapter:

- The regulatory landscape
- How the self-regulatory system works
- Alcoholic drinks
- Organic foods
- Genetically modified foods
- Medicines
- Cigarettes and tobacco products
- Financial services products
- Products aimed at children

Other useful chapters:

- Chapter 3: Making statements
- Chapter 4: Liability for defective products
- Chapter 5: Intellectual property rights
- Chapter 6: Copyright
- Chapter 9: Advertising and labelling
- Chapter 10: Broadcasting
- Chapter 13: Promotions and incentives

INTRODUCTION

Niche marketing is the term commonly used to refer to commercial activities linked to a particular service or product of a sensitive or controversial nature such as tobacco and cigarettes, alcoholic drinks, toys, pharmaceuticals, and personal financial services products.

When developing a marketing campaign to promote these so called 'niche' products or to reach a 'niche' audience (e.g. children), marketers will have to comply with a range of specific legislation and regulatory rules developed mainly to control the manner in which such marketing is carried out.

Marketing is a fast moving industry which covers a wide spectrum of activities, the most traditional of which is advertising. The emergence of new media platforms and the development of marketing practices such as sponsorship have meant that everyone involved in the business has had to keep pace with a rapidly evolving environment.

Paradoxically, legal and regulatory controls relating to these new practices or new types of marketing are scarce. The lack of official regulations in these areas means that the rules governing advertising and the approach adopted by the advertising industry in relation to 'niche' products are to date the primary source of guidance available.

This chapter provides marketers with a 'user-friendly' introductory guide to those areas of law and regulations that are relevant to the advertising of 'niche' products and to identify the various steps marketers will have to go through when mounting an advertising campaign in relation to one of these products.

From the outset, marketers will need to identify the media through which they plan to launch their niche marketing campaigns. There are two reasons for this:

- Advertising is media driven, not product driven
- Different restrictions will apply to different methods and types of advertising

For example, requirements for television and radio advertising may differ from those imposed for all other non-broadcast media (see Chapter 10).

Once the media has been chosen, marketers will need to refer and consult the relevant texts for guidance as to what can or cannot be done. In addition to the various legal controls that will determine whether advertising a particular type of product is lawful or not, marketers will also need to deal with a comprehensive system of self-regulation.

Different sets of rules and regulations will be applicable depending on whether the product or service is being marketed through broadcast media, non-broadcast media or a combination of both.

Everyone in the marketing industry will be familiar with the main regulatory bodies. These are the **Independent Television Commission (ITC)**, the **Radio Authority** and the **Committee of Advertising Practice (CAP)**.

Each has drawn up a non-legal regulatory code establishing standards of practice in their respective area, i.e. television, radio and non-broadcast media, and each contains specific sections or provisions which provide guidelines on the advertising of alcoholic drinks, cigarette and/or tobacco products, medicines, financial services, and advertising aimed at children.

For a general discussion on self-regulatory bodies and their impact on advertising and sponsorship, see Chapter 9.

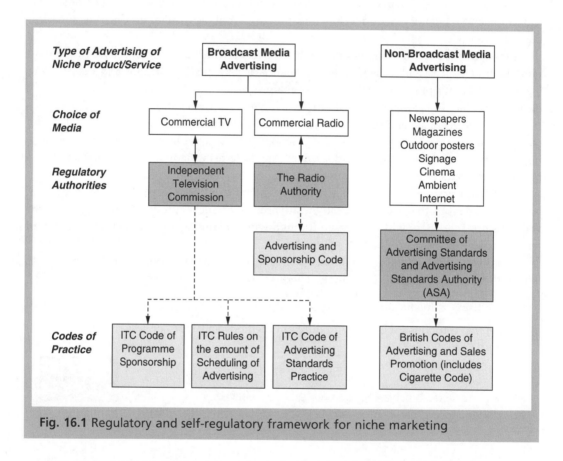

Fig. 16.1 Regulatory and self-regulatory framework for niche marketing

In addition to the above, several other professional regulatory bodies have developed over the years to regulate particular types of products or a particular industry.

POINT OF LAW

For example, within the alcoholic drinks industry, the **Portman Group** plays a leading role in the control and monitoring of the advertising of alcoholic drinks as well as advising its members on how to promote sensible drinking and reduce the incidence of misuse of alcohol. The **Association of the British Pharmaceuticals Industry** plays a similar role in relation to the advertising of pharmaceutical products.

HOW THE SELF-REGULATORY SYSTEM WORKS

It is essential for anyone involved in the development of a campaign to understand how the self-regulatory system works in order to ensure that their proposed campaign complies with all requirements.

In the initial planning stages of a campaign for a niche product or service, marketers must ensure that the advertising concept complies with the letter as well as the spirit of the provisions contained in the relevant regulatory codes.

These include all restrictions and provisions specific to a particular product but also those of a general application such as taste and decency. In so doing, marketers must bear the following in mind:

Regulatory provisions are not an alternative to legal controls

The self-regulatory system simply co-exists and complements the laws applicable to advertising (and other related activities) as well as those specific to the advertisement of a 'niche' product or service.

Compliance in every respect with the law, whether it is common law (judge made laws) or statutory laws (made by Parliament), is essential. This fundamental principle is reiterated in the respective regulatory codes of practice (see Chapter 9), i.e. all advertising should be 'legal, decent, honest and truthful'.

Non-compliance with the regulatory codes may have costly consequences

If for one reason or another, a marketer has not adhered to the provisions of the relevant code, it will run one or all of the following risks:

The advertisement may not pass the clearance process

As discussed in Chapter 10, the **ITC** and the **Radio Authority** both require that all television and radio advertisements be formally approved or cleared prior to transmission. A script of the proposed advertisement must therefore be submitted either to the **Broadcast Advertising Clearance Centre (BACC)** or to the **Radio Advertising Clearance Centre (RACC)**, the bodies responsible for clearance of television and radio advertisements, respectively.

The purpose of the pre-clearance process is to reassure the radio and television broadcasters that the proposed advertisement complies with the provisions of the applicable codes.

However, whilst the clearance process provides an adequate safeguard against potential breaches of the Code, it does not necessarily protect the advertisement from being the subject of a subsequent complaint.

The broadcaster may refuse to broadcast the advertisement

The ultimate decision to broadcast an advertisement rests with the broadcaster. A television or radio broadcaster may refuse to transmit a particular advertisement but in doing so the broadcaster must ensure that it does not discriminate unreasonably either against or in favour of a particular advertiser. This requirement is imposed by the Broadcasting Act 1990.

The publisher may refuse to publish an advertisement

As there is no self-regulatory clearance system in place for non-broadcast advertising, media owners can refuse space for advertisements that are in breach of the provisions of the **British Code of Advertising and Sales Promotions (BCASP)** and are under no obligation to publish advertising offered to them.

A complaint may be lodged against the advertisement

Any individual or organisation can lodge a complaint against a particular advertisement if it is felt that the substance, wording or portrayal of such advertisement contravene one or more of the principles or provisions set out in a particular code.

A detailed examination of the respective complaint procedures adopted by regulatory bodies can be found in Chapter 10 (broadcast) and Chapter 9 (non-broadcast). After careful examination, each regulatory body decides whether to uphold or dismiss the complaint. If a complaint is upheld, the offending advertisement will have to be amended or withdrawn immediately.

Other statutory requirements must be taken into account

One of the fundamental principles set out in the various codes is that advertising in general should not contain anything that is likely to cause serious or widespread offence to the viewers or readers.

Marketers should take particular care to avoid causing offence or discrimination on the grounds of race, sex, religion or disability and must comply with the provisions of the:

- **Race Relations Act 1976**
- **Sex Discrimination Acts 1975 and 1986**
- **Disability Discrimination Act 1995**

Marketers should ensure that their advertisements do not include any material which might reasonably be construed by the public to be discriminatory, hurtful or tasteless.

Seeking a second opinion on the proposed campaign is always advisable

'Niche' marketing presents a number of pitfalls and falling foul of any of the legal or regulatory requirements referred to in this chapter can have disastrous consequences.

As a result, it is vital that marketers ensure that the marketing concept adopted for the campaign fulfils and meets all requirements imposed by the legislation and the appropriate regulatory bodies.

If in doubt about the interpretation of the provisions of the Codes or their respective procedures, marketers should consult the **Committee of Advertising Practice (CAP)**.

The CAP

The CAP runs an information hotline in relation to any issues relating to the interpretation of its Codes and provides guidance on a wide range of topics on its website (see **www.cap.org.uk**).

The RACC

The RACC regularly publishes materials on its clearance procedures, interpretation of the **Radio Authority Code** and other issues which have a bearing on radio advertisements.

The BACC

The BACC offers advice to advertisers on the interpretation of the **ITC Codes** and regularly publishes guidance notes on a wide range of topics affecting television advertising.

The ITC

The ITC also publishes a number of guidance notes on its website (**www.itc.org.uk**).

For advice in relation to the likely acceptability of a particular advertising proposal, marketers should either consult a lawyer or the particular broadcaster who will transmit the proposed advertisement.

ALCOHOLIC DRINKS

Background

There is a general feeling amongst marketers that self-regulation of the alcoholic beverages industry may not be enough to ward off tough advertising legislation in the next couple of years.

A key reason is the concern over the health risks in consuming alcoholic products.

> **INSIGHT**
>
> For example, a Department of Health survey in 2001 found a worrying increase in the number of young people, and particularly young women, suffering from alcohol-related liver problems and said that 'binge drinking' was to blame.

The report prompted a new round of cries for tighter restrictions on alcohol sales, packaging and advertising and chief medical officer Professor Liam Donaldson initially appeared to have confirmed marketers' worst fears that the government was considering placing health warnings on packaging and labelling of alcoholic products.

Many in the industry agreed with the view expressed at the time by the **Incorporated Society of British Advertisers (ISBA)** and the **Institute of Practitioners in Advertising (IPA)** that such warnings would be 'pointless' and 'unlikely to work'.

Marketers in the drinks industry argued that warning labels only make a product more attractive to a younger consumer and if a product has a warning on it, it can become a 'cool' thing to do.

The Portman Group (see below) has repeatedly called for more government action to help promote the message of *responsible* drinking and despite running advertising campaigns to tackle drink-driving, the government has not to date actively discouraged binge drinking.

Some in the drinks industry are nervous that if brand owners abandon a policy of restraint
in advertising and adopt a more aggressive stance it could signal the beginning of the end of
self-regulation and more government intervention in the sector. Previous attempts by marketers
to create cut-through advertising campaigns have been met by criticisms from within the drinks
industry.

Drinks marketers are also nervous that alcohol marketing could be moving into the same
murky waters as tobacco. In 2000, the European Commission called for tighter controls on
alcohol advertising to combat under-age drinking.

Nothing came of it, but it was enough to put marketers on notice. In the UK, pressure
group Alcohol Concern has called for warnings to be placed on packaging and for a levy on
advertising to fund awareness and health campaigns.

Of more concern for marketers is the emerging and profitable 'alcopops' niche sector.
Consumed by and marketed to a younger audience, 'alcopops' are very popular amongst
women and under-18s, but have been the source of negative publicity for the past several
years as their appearance and taste has belied their strong alcoholic content.

For example, a lemonade type product called **Hooch** was forced to change its packaging as it relied on cartoon images which showed that it appealed to under-age drinkers.

In its Code of Practice, the Portman Group further requires marketers not to promote their products as lending to a person's physical, social or mental prowess, effectively banning the term, 'energy drink'.

As illustrated by the next two cases, 'energy' could be interpreted as meaning 'revitalising' and this would be unacceptable. In addition, 'glamorising' a brand deliberately to appeal to a younger audience by a play on a swear word would also be unacceptable.

For example, the rules forced Beverage Brands to rename its VRB, or Vodka Revitalising Beverage, as VR – and the marketer blames the name change in part for the poor sales that forced it to scrap the brand.

Matthew Clark Brands' decision to market an FCUK-branded 'alcopop' also attracted criticism from the industry claiming that it is still possible to launch a brand in a responsible way that does not encourage alcohol misuse.

While television and radio regulators have the power to jettison advertising and levy fines, the industry remains largely self-policing but the government's first national alcohol strategy report is due to be released later in 2002 and some European Union member states are pressing for more stringent regulation of the sector throughout the EU.

The **ITC Codes**, the **Radio Authority's Advertising and Sponsorship Code** and the **BCASP** all contain specific rules on the advertising of alcoholic drinks on television, radio and non-broadcast media respectively.

Television advertising

Restrictions on content

All television advertising for alcoholic drinks must comply with the provisions set down in **Rule 40 of the ITC Code of Advertising Standards and Practice**. These rules impose a number of restrictions on the style in which the advertisement is portrayed, its content and on the context the advertisement is set in.

POINT OF LAW

For example, advertisements of alcoholic drinks must not:

- Be directed at people under 18 years
- Show anyone under the age of 25 years or anyone who looks like they may be under the age of 25 years
- Portray children or use pop stars or professional athletes with a particular appeal to youngsters
- Do anything that condones or encourages alcohol misuse

In addition the substance or the wording of the advertisement cannot imply that drinking is essential to social or sexual success or that the consumption of alcohol enhances performance or mental prowess. Drinking cannot be associated with driving or any other situations or activities where drinking would be potentially dangerous. Neither should the advertisement encourage the excessive consumption of alcohol, nor foster, depict or imply immoderate drinking or encourage consumers to make multiple purchases.

Restrictions on scheduling

According to **Rule 4.2.1(a) and (d) of the ITC Rules on the Amount of Scheduling and Advertising** alcoholic drinks containing 1.2% alcohol or more by volume may not be advertised in or adjacent to children's programmes or programmes commissioned for, or likely to appeal particularly to, audiences below the age of 18 years.

Alcoholic products containing less than 1.2% alcohol by volume when presented as low or non-alcohol versions of an alcoholic drink may not be advertised in or adjacent to children's programmes.

Clearance

At pre-production stage, a script of all television advertising for alcoholic drinks must be submitted to the **BACC** for approval prior to being broadcast on television.

Radio advertising

Restrictions on content

The Radio Authority requires all alcoholic drink advertisements to comply with the minimum standards set out in **Rule 11, Section 3 of the Radio Authority Advertising and Sponsorship Code**.

Rule 11 imposes similar restrictions as the ITC and covers issues such as the protection of young listeners, safety, and treatments that are considered unacceptable.

Restrictions on scheduling

According to **Rule 11.1 of the Radio Authority Advertising and Sponsorship Code** advertisements for alcoholic drinks must not be broadcast in or around religious programming or programming aimed particularly at those below 18 years.

Clearance

At pre-production stage, a copy of the script of the advertisement must be submitted to the **RACC** for central copy clearance.

Non-broadcast advertising

All other media advertising for alcoholic drinks must comply with **Rule 46 of the BCASP** as laid down by the **CAP**.

Rule 46 provides that the drinks industry and the marketing profession accept responsibility for ensuring that advertising does not contain anything that is likely to lead people to adopt styles of drinking that are unwise. Whilst advertising for alcoholic drinks can use humour, they must still comply within the spirit of the rules. The rules of the CAP mirror those of the ITC.

The Portman Group

As mentioned earlier in this chapter, specific regulatory bodies governing a particular industry or product have also drawn up their own code of practices.

The Portman Group is a pan-industry organisation established in 1989 by the UK's leading drinks' marketers. Its main role is to ensure that alcohol marketing is carried out in a sensible and responsible manner.

The Portman Group has drawn up and published a **Code of Practice** which defines and formalises best practice on issues such as naming, packaging and merchandising of alcoholic drinks (having an alcoholic strength above 0.5% alcohol by volume) as well as point of sale materials.

The Code is currently undergoing a second review and a revised code is expected later in 2002.

The provisions of the Code are consistent with those contained in the regulatory codes referred to above and apply to all those companies who are signatories to it.

In the same manner as the other regulatory codes, the Portman Group handles complaints submitted to it. Whilst it does not have any enforcement powers to punish or prevent breaches of its Code, it is highly regarded by members of the industry and recommendations issued by it are generally followed.

Sponsorship

Programme sponsorship

According to **Rule 5.7 of the ITC Code of Programme Sponsorship**, an alcoholic brand may sponsor a television or radio programme only if advertisement of alcoholic drinks is permitted in connection with such programme.

For example, a children's programme such as *SM:TV* could not be sponsored by an alcohol brand, but **Baileys** sponsorship of *Sex and the City* is permissible.

Sports sponsorship

Sports sponsorship by alcoholic brand owners has become increasingly popular over the years and has grown especially in football and motor racing.

Some have expressed concerns over the association of alcohol and sport and alcohol and driving. More often than not, however, alcohol producers involved in the sport sponsorship try as much as possible to take a responsible attitude either by running 'don't drink and drive' campaigns around their sponsorship or by not getting involved with the younger market.

Specific legislation

Marketers must also avoid falling foul of any legal provisions which are relevant to the advertising of alcoholic products.

LAW IN ACTION

Particular care should be taken when using the designation 'spirits' in advertising to describe an alcoholic drink. The use of the designation is strictly regulated by the **Alcoholic Liquor Duties Act 1979 (Section 71)**. Unlawful use of the designation could result in a fine being imposed on the marketer or advertising agency responsible for the development of the advertisement.

Similarly, the use of terms such as 'non-alcoholic wine', 'low alcohol', 'liquor' and 'tonic wine' in an advertisement are subject to certain specific restrictions under the **Food Labelling Regulations 1996**.

In accordance with **Section 168 of the Licensing Act 1964**, any advertisement seeking to encourage under-age children into a bar is unlawful. Any person guilty of this offence is liable to payment of a fine.

ORGANIC FOODS

In July 2001, the **CAP**, which draws up the **BCASP**, the UK's self-regulatory code for non-broadcast advertising, published a **'Help Note' (Code)** on claims made of organic food.

The idea is that as these foods' popularity increases, consumers should be able to make accurately informed purchasing decisions and the Code is an attempt to reduce the number of complaints received about the advertising of organic products.

The Code states that food can only be described as 'organic' if it comes from farms, processors or importers that follow the minimum standards laid down in the **EU Regulation (EEC) 2092/91** and are registered with and regularly inspected by an approved certification body.

In the UK, that body is the **UK Register of Organic Food Standards (UKROFS)**.

UKROFS' standards do allow organic farms to use certain 'approved' substances such as paraffin oil, so the Code states that if such substances are being used, it *cannot* be claimed that no chemicals, composts, fertilisers, plant protection products or similar substances are used in production. Claims that *fewer* such substances are used should, however, be acceptable.

Similarly, if such approved substances are used, 'natural' or 'no artificial aids used' *cannot* be claimed but 'more natural' or 'fewer artificial substances' should be acceptable.

Given that all managed food production systems have some form of environmental impact, marketers should be wary about claiming that their products are 'environmentally friendly', but could claim 'environmentally friendlier' instead.

INSIGHT

For example, if the organic equivalent of a locally produced product, such as soap or face cleanser, has had to be flown in from Peru, the environmental impact of that process should be taken into consideration in the preparation of the advertising copy.

Broad-based claims made without supporting evidence are likely to offend the Code and includes the following words:

- 'Safer'
- 'Healthier'
- 'Tastes better'

The Code can be found at **www.cap.org.uk**.

GENETICALLY MODIFIED (GM) FOODS

Marketers can expect new regulations controlling the advertising of genetically modified (GM) products to be in place in 2004/2005 if the findings of a major government-backed research project give the green light to food producers to put GM foods back on the shelves of the supermarkets in the UK.

In 2003, scientists will publish some of the most explosive and eagerly awaited test results ever published in the UK, and the research findings will help to set the direction of the UK food industry over the next decade.

These will be the results of over 250 government-sponsored crop trials – on genetically modified sugar and fodder beet, rape seed and forage maize – which have been running in locations around the British Isles since 1999.

In spring 2002, the government commenced the next round of Farm Scale Evaluations (FSE), which will be the last of the 3-year FSE programme, with the final trials planted in autumn 2002.

The trials are intended to go some way towards settling one of the most controversial issues to confront the food industry: whether growing genetically modified crops is harmful to the environment.

The results will fall far short of conclusive, as the trials are only designed to find out whether herbicide-resistant GM crops are more harmful to the diversity and abundance of farmland wildlife than are non-GM.

But if the tests show that there is little difference between the two – and a number of scientists privately think this will be the outcome – many marketers in the food industry will jump on the results as justification of what they have been saying for the best part of a decade – that GM crops are harmless and possibly even beneficial (requiring lower quantities of herbicides) – to the environment.

Unilever may be in the vanguard of attempting to change public opinion and perceptions of what has been labelled 'Frankenstein food' as it recently went on record publicly extolling the benefits and choice that GM foods can bring to the consumer.

The food industry axed GM food in the spring of 1999 after a successful campaign by environmentalists amid consumer fears about the long-term effects of GM foods on health and the environment.

Unilever itself was forced into an embarrassing withdrawal of its GM-based Bachelors' 'Beanfeast' brand and has axed GM ingredients from its Vesta ready meals range.

However, most food producers are watching and waiting to see if results of the government's research support Unilever's position before declaring an interest in GM foods.

Indeed, the government's own Agriculture and Environment Biology Committee concluded in autumn 2001 that the trials would fail to address the wider safety implications of GM foods and so the scope of the results will be limited.

However, Cropgen, a group of scientists which promotes the benefits of genetic engineering in agriculture, is confident that public acceptance of GM will come about through products that offer real benefits to consumers.

INSIGHT

For example, these could take the form of fruit which has some major advantage such as medicinal use, is much cheaper than the non-GM equivalent or that merely tastes better than the non-GM variety.

The total area of cultivatable land used for GM crops worldwide increased by 20% in 2001 to 130 million hectares, an area twice the size of the UK, and the number of countries permitting GM cultivation could increase as a result of acceptance of GM products by consumers.

At present, only the US, Canada, Argentina and China have dedicated significant areas to GM plantations.

Should public opinion be influenced by new research on GM foods, UK marketers can expect all advertising and labelling to be strictly regulated in relation to GM food products.

PHARMACEUTICAL PRODUCTS

Background

At the time of writing, a major row has broken out over whether the UK and EU proposed liberalisation of drugs marketing will lead pharmaceutical marketers to cross the thin dividing line between information and advertising in the pursuit of boosted sales.

The row centres around the launch in 2001 of Schering's morning after pill Levonelle® which is freely available over the counter (OTC) at a cost of £19.99. The pill is taken in two doses, 12 hours apart and claims to be 95% effective if taken within 24 hours of unprotected sex.

INSIGHT

The following advertising for Levonelle® has appeared in poster formats in pharmacies and in women's toilets in bars, clubs and cafes:

Split condom.
   Oooops.
   Emergency contraception!!!
Quick.
   Pharmacy.
   Buy Levonelle . . . phew

Not surprisingly this advertising has been challenged by 'pro-life' pressure groups. For example, Life rejects the argument that the advertising is information based and have slammed the campaign as irresponsible and likely to encourage the use of the pill as a 'lifestyle' drug.

The Society for the Protection of Unborn Children (SPUC) has gone one step further and has mounted a High Court challenge to Levonelle®'s status as an emergency contraceptive (and therefore an OTC drug) rather than an aid to abortion drug (that would make it prescription only drug). The SPUC has also gone on a major public relations offensive by arguing that Levonelle® induces miscarriages and does not prevent sexually transmitted diseases.

Schering maintains with some justification that the drug has widened choice for women and that is to be welcomed given that only 40% of all women are aware of such products being available through pharmacies.

The government, on the other hand, wants to declassify drugs like Levonelle® in order to take unnecessary burdens off the NHS by reducing the demands made on GPs' time.

Although the Consumer's Association (CA) has campaigned against the European Commission's proposals to relax the ban on advertising prescription only medicines directly to the consumer, it accepts that consumers are entitled to more information on pharmaceuticals although draws the line that this should be provided by pharmaceutical marketers themselves.

Curiously, it has welcomed the move to make Levonelle® an OTC drug, which appears to contradict its position on pharmaceutical advertising.

The European Commission is proposing to allow consumer advertising for three specific medical conditions initially.

Medical Condition	Brand Name	Description	Pharmaceutical Marketer
AIDS	Retrovir	Anti-AIDS drug	GlaxoSmithKline (GSK)
Diabetes	Starlyx	Diabetes drug	Novartis
Respiratory illness	Oxix	Asthma	AstraZeneca

Fig. 16.2 Specific medical conditions and OTC products

What is indisputable is that the purpose of advertising for any marketer is to increase its market share and the **Medicines Control Agency (MCA)**, the regulatory body of the pharmaceutical industry in the UK, has been exploring ways since December 2001 into declassifying more prescription drugs and within a shorter time span.

The time taken to de-classify a drug from prescription only to OTC has already reduced from 18 to 12 months and the MCA is proposing to introduce a wider range of OTC medicines by the end of 2002 which could spark off an advertising war amongst competitor marketers.

This could result in US style advertising coming to the UK. For example, some commentators have expressed concern that Pfizer's recent sponsorship of a radio programme on an independent radio station is nothing less than a thinly disguised advertisement for Viagra.

The **National Pharmaceutical Association (NPA)** is also concerned about whether marketers of pharmaceutical drugs will draw a clear distinction between advertising and providing information. The issue needs to be handled sensitively given that consumer expectations will be altered by advertising and therefore misuse of OTC drugs could well increase.

However, there is unlikely to be a rush by pharmaceutical marketers to apply for prescription drugs to be declassified and switched to OTC as an excuse to advertise because the prescription-only market continues to be much more lucrative.

For example, Zantac used to make a lot of profit for GlaxoSmithKline as a prescription drug, but since it went OTC and off-patient its profits have fallen.

The **Proprietary Association of Great Britain (PAGB)** accepts that although marketers in the pharmaceutical industry have a clear advantage being able to advertise their drugs once they have the OTC pharmacy licence, they do need to sell a lot more drugs through OTC to make a profit than they would have done had the drug remained as prescription only.

It adds that it is not in favour of the US system where consumers favour brands that receive advertising support and prefers that the pharmaceutical industry in the UK focuses its efforts on providing information to promote awareness of availability of OTC remedies.

What is clear is that marketers in the pharmaceutical industry will be under increasing pressure in the next few years to market their products directly to consumers using the whole panoply of marketing tools and techniques.

Although the PAGB stops short of saying that pressure to make a profit will lead some pharmaceutical marketers to make false or misleading claims in their advertising (see Chapter 9), nonetheless the risks of this occurring within the industry will undoubtedly increase.

Should such abuses occur, then marketers can expect more self-regulation and even tougher statutory controls over pharmaceutical advertising and marketing.

Current controls over pharmaceutical advertising and promotions

As discussed in Chapter 16, the **Medicines Act 1968** and the **Medicines (Advertising) Regulations 1994** which implements the **EC Directive 92/28/EEC** governs the advertising and promotion of pharmaceutical products.

Advertising of medicinal products to the general public

Prohibited advertising

The Medicines Act 1968 and its regulations prohibit the advertising to the general public of prescription-only products, of medicinal products containing certain substances (e.g. narcotics) or referring to specified diseases (e.g. diabetes, genetic disorders, serious infectious diseases and serious skin disorders).

The marketing authorisation (licence)

The marketing authorisation, issued by the Medicines Control Agency, sets the framework for the advertising of medicinal products and specifies the conditions under which the products can be sold to the public.

If the marketing authorisation contains any restrictions on the manner in which the advertising of the product must be conducted, such restrictions must be observed.

Comply with the Act/Regulations

Under the 1968 Act, it is an offence to:

■ Make false representations about the descriptions of a medicinal product or mislead the public when describing its nature, quality, use or effect

■ Make recommendations for the use of a medicinal product for purposes other than those specified in the product's licence

Advertising on television, radio and non-broadcast media

The advertising of medicines and treatments on television and radio is confined to OTC products only.

The **ITC**, **Radio Authority** and **CAP** have all imposed specific requirements aimed at controlling the content and form of such advertisements in their respective codes, namely:

■ Appendix 3 of the ITC Code of Advertising and Practice in relation to television advertising

■ Rule 4, Section 3 of the Radio Authority Advertising and Sponsorship Code in relation to radio advertising

■ Rule 50 of the Advertising Code of the Committee of Advertising Practice for all other non-broadcast media

Common restrictions on content

Each of the above-mentioned sections imposes common content restrictions. For example, advertisements promoting medicines:

- Must not be directed at people under 16 years

- Must not use health professionals or celebrities to endorse the products

- Must not use fear or anxiety

- Must not claim that the effects of one product are as good as or better than those of another identifiable product

- Must not suggest that medicines are either a food or a cosmetic

- Must always include the name of the product, an indication of what it is for, text such as 'always read the label' and the name of the active ingredient if there is only one

- Must not contain any reference to sales promotions

Clearance process

All television and radio advertisements must be submitted to the **BACC** or the **RACC** respectively for clearance prior to broadcast.

Restrictions on scheduling

The **ITC Rules on the Amount and Scheduling of Advertising** provides that medicines, vitamins and food supplements cannot be advertised in or adjacent to children's programmes.

Advertising in which children are shown having medicines, vitamins or other dietary supplements administered to them or advertising which uses techniques that are likely to affect children (e.g. cartoons) cannot be advertised before 9 pm without the prior consent of the ITC.

Trade Association	Remit	Code
The Association of the British Pharmaceuticals Industry (**ABPI**)	Regulates the promotion of prescription-only medicines to members of the health professions and the information made available to the general public.	Code of Practice for the Pharmaceuticals Industry (1996), administered by the Prescription Medicines Code of Practice.
The Proprietary Association of Great Britain (**PAGB**)	Regulates the advertising of over-the-counter medicines and food supplements to the general public only.	Code of Standards for the Advertising Practice for over-the-counter medicines (1994).
The British Herbal Medicine Association (**BHMA**)	Regulates the advertising of herbal products, herbal medicines and herbal remedies.	The Advertising Code of the British Herbal Medicine Association (1997).

Fig. 16.3 Other trade associations

The provisions of the codes published by the trade associations are consistent with and mirror those contained in the Medicines Act 1968 (and its Regulations) as well as those contained in the ITC, the Radio Authority and the Codes of the CPA.

The **PAGB** and the **BHMA** both impose a pre-publication process on all types of advertising issued by their respective members, including all packaging, labels, leaflets and point of sale materials. The **ABPI** requests that strict internal procedures must be put in place by their member companies for the review of all promotional materials and activities.

CIGARETTE AND OTHER TOBACCO PRODUCTS

Background

According to statistics recently published by the Department of Health, UK tobacco marketers spend £130m a year on tobacco advertising and promotions. Of this, £50m is spent on press and poster advertising, £70m on sponsorship of Formula 1, £8m on other sports sponsorship and £7m on direct marketing.

Tobacco advertising and tobacco sponsorship has always been the subject of much debate and controversy and the stance taken by the Labour government in the last two years with a pledge to ban all tobacco advertising and sponsorship from the UK has continued to fan the flames of this debate.

There have even been calls that tobacco advertising should be banned because it legitimises smoking in the eyes of addicts, according to the evidence given to a Parliamentary health select committee by Chris Powell, chairman of advertising agency BMP DDB.

However, all legal attempts to ban advertising and promotion of what is a legitimate and legal product have been met with resistance from tobacco marketers.

In November 2001, plans for a Europe-wide ban on tobacco advertising suffered another set back after the European Parliament's legal affairs committee questioned the legal basis for the **Directive on Tobacco Control 2001/37/EC** which proposed to ban terms such as 'light' and 'mild' on cigarettes.

The Committee argued that the Directive did not fall under the remit of the European Parliament because it concerned public health rather than European harmonisation.

The legal basis for the previous directive to ban tobacco advertising from Europe had also been questioned by the European Parliament's public health committee and was annulled in 2001 by the **European Court of Justice** following a successful legal challenge by tobacco marketers, largely on the same grounds.

In the UK (January 2002) the House of Lords vetoed a proposed amendment to the **Tobacco Advertising and Promotion Private Members Bill** which if left in could have led to the Bill being scrapped 6 years after its introduction.

The amendment, proposed by three members of the Lords, stated that if the ban on tobacco advertising failed to reduce the number of smokers within 6 years it should be scrapped. The same clause delayed progress of a government bill to ban tobacco advertising in 2001 following the Conservative Party's insistence that it should be included.

Proposals to allow all sports to continue using tobacco sponsorship until 2006 rather than 2003 has also been rejected and at present only Formula 1 will have special dispensation.

The **Tobacco Advertising and Promotion Private Members Bill** is currently before the House of Lords and subject to Parliamentary time is due for a second reading in the House of Commons in 2002. The government has already indicated that it will back the Bill, a carbon copy of its own, providing none of the amendments are too radical.

The European tobacco advertising directive is due to be debated again and so marketers can expect further political discussions at curbing tobacco advertising and promotions throughout the European Union throughout the course of 2002.

Control of tobacco advertising and promotions in the UK

According to **Rule 18(a)(v) of the ITC Code of Advertising Standards and Practice** the advertising of all tobacco products on television is prohibited.

Similarly, advertising for cigarettes, cigarette tobacco and papers (but not cigars and pipe tobacco) are prohibited on the radio (**Rule 10, Section 3 of the Radio Authority Advertising and Sponsorship Code**).

Non-broadcast advertising

All other forms of advertising are permitted but are subject to very stringent restrictions and controls contained in the **Cigarette Code**.

The Cigarette Code

The Cigarette Code forms part of a 'voluntary agreement' entered into by the tobacco industry and the government, which covers issues such as advertising expenditure, media selection, health warnings and promotions.

The Cigarette Code sets out a number of provisions and restrictions by which tobacco marketers agree to abide in relation to the advertising of:

- Cigarettes
- Hand-rolling tobacco
- Cigarette papers
- Filters
- Wrappings
- Special offers
- Competitions
- Other sales promotions
- Products displaying the colours, livery, insignia or name of a cigarette brand in a way that promotes smoking rather than these other related products

As a general principle, advertisements for the above-mentioned tobacco products must not glamorise smoking, make smoking appealing to children, nor suggest that smoking is safe, healthy, natural or popular.

Clearance

All advertisements falling under the scope of the Cigarette Code must be submitted to the **CAP** for clearance prior to publication. The issue of a signed, dated and numbered certificate of clearance from CAP is mandatory in relation to all advertisements for cigarettes and hand-rolling tobacco.

Sponsorship

Following the ban of cigarette advertising on television, cigarette marketers found a loophole in the legislation and started to sponsor sports events in order to achieve the television exposure lost through television advertising.

Over the years tobacco marketers targeted a handful of sports and/or events and success-fully developed carefully planned marketing strategies around them.

INSIGHT

For example, cigarette brand **Embassy** became the title sponsor of both the World Snooker Championship and a version of the darts World Championships.

Silk Cut associated itself with rugby league and all major cigarette brands were fighting to get pole position on a Formula 1 grid.

Guidelines for the manner in which sponsorship by tobacco brands can be carried out are set out in the second part of the voluntary agreement between the tobacco industry and the government.

FINANCIAL SERVICE PRODUCTS

Background

This is an extremely complex and strictly regulated area of niche marketing and marketers planning a campaign to promote financial service products will need to comply strictly with the laws and regulations in this area or face severe penalties from the regulator.

The strict legal controls imposed on the advertising and promotion of financial products are designed for the protection of clients and to help them make informed decisions in relation to the type of products they would like to purchase.

The Financial Services and Markets Act 2000

The 2000 Act has overhauled the regulatory system for financial services in the UK.

Businesses to be authorised and regulated under the 2000 Act include banks, building societies, insurance companies, credit unions, investment and pension advisers.

The main purpose of the 2000 Act is to modernise the regulatory framework by appointing a single regulator, the **Financial Services Authority (FSA)**, to co-ordinate and supervise all activities in the financial services industry.

When fully implemented, the 2000 Act will have to have a major impact on the marketing of financial services products.

Content of advertising

At the time of writing, the **ITC**, **Radio Authority** and **CAP** have not yet reviewed their respective guidelines to bring them in line with the 2000 Act.

Each Code makes it clear that it is the responsibility of every marketer, its advertising agency and media owner to comply with the laws governing financial products and services.

The provisions set out in all three Codes aim to ensure that the advertising (irrespective of the nature of the product being advertised) does not take advantage of the audience's inexperience or gullibility.

Special safeguards are contained in the **Radio Authority Code** and the **ITC Code** in relation to the advertisement of particular types of financial services products:

- Investment
- Deposit
- Saving
- Interest on savings
- Insurance
- Lending
- Credit

The ITC and the Radio Authority both require that all financial services advertising be submitted to the **BACC** or the **RACC** respectively for central copy clearance prior to transmission.

Consumer Credit Regulations

Under **Section 46(1) of the Consumer Credit Act 1974** and the **Consumer Credit (Advertisements) Regulations 1989 (CCAR)** credit advertisements must not be false or misleading in any material respect.

The above provisions *do not* apply to advertising which either expressly or by implication indicates clearly that a person is willing to provide credit for the purposes of a person's business and does not indicate (expressly or by implication) that a person is willing to provide credit otherwise than for the purposes of such a business.

In other words, if the marketer wants to avoid the rules affecting consumer credit advertising, it must ensure that the advertising refers *exclusively* to credit deals available to businesses.

CCAR

Only three types of consumer credit advertising is allowed:

- Simple credit
- Intermediate credit

▦ Full credit

In each category certain information must be given to the customer and other information is discretionary.

Under the **CCAR**, any consumer credit advertising that fails to fall into any of the above three categories will, regardless of the intention of the marketer, be illegal. It will also be illegal even if it falls within these categories if it is misleading.

All advertising for consumer credit must comply with the following criteria:

▦ Must be clear and legible

▦ Must contain the name, address and telephone number of the marketer offering credit

▦ Logo of the marketer or its trade association

▦ The information about the credit must be shown together as a whole

Any comparative advertising claim can only appear in a 'full' credit advertisement, and this must be alongside, with no less particularity or prominence, the details of the other competitor marketers concerned and the comparable terms offered.

Although this is a requirement of the 1989 Regulations it is rarely observed in practice (see Chapter 9 for further discussion on comparative advertising regulations).

Other blanket rules are that 'interest free' can only be used if the credit price does not exceed the cash price and 'no deposit' can only be used when no advance payments whatsoever are to be made.

In addition, the annual percentage rate (APR) must be given greater prominence than any reference to any other interest rates and no less prominence than statements relating to:

▦ Any period of time

▦ The amount of any advance payments or a statement that none is required

▦ The amount, number or frequency of any other payments or charges except the cash price

Under the 1989 Regulations, marketers can provide credit deal information to be conveyed by means of a worked example provided it is reasonably representative.

For example, a national advertising campaign for a new car model along with the offer of finance terms available will need to comply with the following requirements under the 1989 Regulations:

▦ The name of the advertiser and a postal address or telephone number unless in the case of a manufacturer's advertisement the name and address of a particular dealer is included

▦ A statement that written quotations are available on request

▦ Where a cash price is given in the advertisement in relation to a specified car, either the APR or a statement that the total amount payable is not greater than the total cash price of the product

▦ Where the advertisement specifies a particular car which can be bought on credit from an identified dealer, the cash price of the car

- If credit is available only to people falling within any particular class or group, a statement of that fact, identifying the class or group

- A statement of the frequency and number of advance payments required and the amount expressed as a sum of money or percentage

- A statement indicating any respect in which cash purchasers are treated differently from those acquiring the product on credit

- A statement of the frequency, number and amount of repayments of the credit on condition that no expressions such as 'weekly equivalent' will be used unless weekly payments are actually required under the agreement

- A statement of the total amount payable by the debtor

- In the case of an advertisement specifying a particular vehicle which can be bought on credit, the cash price of that car (which would apply in this example)

Within the same advertisement the following *discretionary* information can also be provided by the marketer:

- A logo of the marketer and/or its trade association

- A statement of the marketer's occupation, e.g. 'second-hand car dealer'

- A statement that credit facilities are available and where applicable a statement indicating how long the facilities are available for

- A statement indicating that credit is only available to persons falling within a particular identified class or group

- The maximum or minimum amount of credit that is on offer

- Where the APR is specified, a statement as to whether any advance payment is required and if so the amount specified as a sum of money or as a percentage, e.g. 50% deposit

- A statement indicating any respect in which cash purchasers are treated differently from those acquiring by credit

PRODUCTS AIMED AT CHILDREN

Background

Marketers face two challenges when marketing products to children or for use by children.

The first challenge is to ensure the success of the marketing campaign while the second challenge is to maintain credibility and responsibility for the campaign with a wide range of stakeholder groups.

The ethics of marketing to children has become one of the hottest issues in the marketing profession and within the media and arguments for and against bounce from parents, to schools, to national governments and beyond the European Union.

Marketers sometimes get a bad press for campaigns that encourage children in unhealthy eating habits and as a result the charge laid at marketers is that they are turning a nation of children into the next generation of unfit and obese adults.

What is clear is that a marketing campaign aimed at children must win the trust and respect of the public if it is going to have any chance of commercial success.

The **ITC**, **Radio Authority** and **CAP** all have a specific section related to advertising aimed at children and provide a number of guidelines on what marketers are allowed to do and safeguards to protect children in general.

Children are defined by the Codes as those below the age of 16 years and are generally considered to be vulnerable and lacking experience. As a result, the ITC, the Radio Authority and the CAP all have adopted similar general principles in relation to broadcast and non-broadcast advertising aimed at children.

General principles

Advertising to children must not:

- Contain material which might result in harm to children, whether mentally, physically or morally
- Take advantage of the immaturity or natural credulity of children
- Directly urge children to buy products or ask adults to buy products for them
- Show children using or handling anything which would be unsafe or otherwise unsuitable for children's use
- Encourage bad eating habits, such as eating or drinking at bedtime
- Show children entering strange places or talking to strangers or in situations where they may be at risk

Specific restrictions are also imposed on the manner in which certain type of advertising must be carried out:

- Advertising for competitions or games with prizes must include a clear reminder of the need to obtain parental permission before entering
- Advertising for toys and games must at all times be accurate with regards to their size, quality and capacity
- The use of special effects or other filming techniques is also strictly monitored and must take into account the age category of the children at whom the advertisement is aimed

All television and radio advertising aimed at children must be submitted to the **BACC** or the **RACC** respectively for copy clearance prior to broadcast.

If there is a reference to a competition for children in an advertisement, the published rules must be submitted in advance to the relevant broadcaster.

Restrictions on scheduling

As already discussed in this chapter, the **ITC Code** provides that advertising relating to alcoholic drinks, medicines, vitamins and other food supplements cannot be shown in or adjacent to children's programmes or programmes principally directed at or likely to appeal particularly to audiences below 16 or 18 years (depending on the nature of the product).

In addition, the ITC imposes a gap of a *minimum of 2 hours* between the broadcast of a programme and that of any advertisement for merchandise based on that programme.

17

AMBUSH MARKETING

INTRODUCTION

'Ambush marketing' or as it is sometimes known 'vigilante' or 'parasitic marketing' is a phrase that describes the actions of a brand owner who seeks to associate itself with a sponsored event or property without paying any rights fee for the privilege.

'Ambush' or 'parasitic marketing' is not a term of art, although the following represents a reasonable definition:

POINT OF LAW

> *The unauthorised association by a business of its name, brand, products or services with a sports or other event, team or individual through deliberate marketing activity.*

This kind of activity creates the impression that the ambush marketer is actually a sponsor or is somehow affiliated with the event or property.

Rights holders are therefore faced with the problem of trying to protect what they have sold to the legitimate sponsor.

Increasingly, the rights holder is being asked to guarantee that it can deliver sponsorship and licensing rights within certain territories and that these rights can be protected both from a legal as well as business perspective.

Concern for the sports sponsorship industry

Ambush marketing is of huge concern for the sports sponsorship industry and the total amount of revenues lost each year by counterfeit merchandise has been estimated by the SportBusiness Group to be around $1 billion worldwide.

The net effect is that brand owners will no longer pay huge sums for rights if they have no confidence in the ability of the rights holder to deliver those rights or that those rights will be protected.

At the top end of the sponsorship market, brand owners will always be vulnerable to ambush marketing and therefore will need procedures in place to ensure that they are protected.

Brand owners pay vast amounts of money to rights holders for an exclusive association, whether in relation to brand sector or title sponsorship, with a competition, team or individual. That much is obvious. What is less obvious are the ways in which this exclusivity can be preserved.

Clearly, if a rights holder attempts to resell rights to one brand owner which it has already allocated to another, the legitimate sponsor can take action against the rights holder.

What is considerably more difficult is preventing a third party which has no official or contractual link with the rights holder from exploiting a much more ambiguous association with the sports property.

This is the ambush marketer, whose activities may involve one or more of the following:

- **Counterfeiting.** This is unauthorised activity at its most aggressive. Consumers are, in effect, conned into purchasing non-authorised goods in the belief that they are officially sanctioned or genuine licensed products (see also Chapter 11).

- **Opportunist ambush.** This is at the opposite end of the spectrum and occurs when circumstances conspire to throw up an opportunity for a marketer to take advantage of a photograph or film clip showing an individual inadvertently using that marketer's product. This technique is particularly effective where the athlete or celebrity officially endorses a competing product (see also Chapter 5).

- **Parasitic Marketing.** This involves a marketer with no officially sanctioned connection with an event staging a promotion that piggy-backs the media hype around such an event and is by far the most common type of ambush marketing.

COUNTERFEITING

Not only is this association unauthorised, as discussed in Chapter 11, it can also be illegal. Broadly speaking, counterfeiting involves the intentional infringement of another party's intellectual property rights (IPRs) at a commercial level.

Counterfeiters may be subject to both civil liability and criminal sanction as a result of their activities, but there are a number of steps rights holders would be well-advised to take before considering invoking such penalties.

The prerequisite to taking action against counterfeiters is holding IPRs. Therefore, rights holders should take the necessary measures to identify, maintain and enforce their trademark, copyright and design rights so that they are ready to act if the need arises.

Rights holders would also benefit from having systems in place to record details of instances of complaints from, and confusion among, consumers arising from infringing products.

In addition to safeguarding their IPRs, rights holders could also deter prospective counterfeiters by publicising those rights and the fact that they are prepared to enforce such rights.

Of course, one of the best ways to achieve such publicity is to take action against counterfeiters. Rights holders have a number of options at their disposal.

They can take action themselves by sending what are known as 'cease and desist' letters (which warn the counterfeiter that legal action will follow if products are not withdrawn) and seeking undertakings from counterfeiters, backed up by the threat of civil court proceedings for **copyright, trademark** or **design right infringement**, as applicable, or **passing off**.

Rights holders should, however, be aware of the remedies available for making groundless threats of trademark infringement (see Chapter 5).

Rights holders are also entitled to **seize** counterfeit goods from non-permanent places of business, which is a particularly useful weapon against itinerant stall holders.

Alternatively, rights holders may enlist the assistance of the **Trading Standards Department (TSD)** local to the counterfeiter.

TSDs have a statutory duty to enforce fair trading, trade descriptions and trademark legislation, and the power to enforce copyright and design right legislation.

Pursuant to such legislation, TSDs are able to seize infringing product and to instigate criminal proceedings against counterfeiters, and sanctions include imprisonment and fines. It is well-worth fostering good relations with TSDs.

Rights holders may also apply to **HM Customs & Excise** to intercept and suspend suspected counterfeit or pirate products on arrival in the UK.

Rights holders should, however, be aware that, unlike TSDs, HM Customs & Excise requires an indemnity before it will take action and the rights holder may be required to provide detailed information about the expected arrival of the counterfeit product.

As far as the other forms of ambush marketing are concerned, there is no single statute which deals specifically with the concept, largely because this is a relatively recent phenomenon which can take many forms. Instead, brand owners looking to prevent ambush marketing are obliged to draw on various other legal protections and attempt to apply them to the relevant circumstances.

OPPORTUNIST AMBUSH

Circumstances can conspire to give brand owners an opportunity to promote their products in connection with an individual or an event completely by chance. The technique relies on the opportunist marketer managing the materials that have fallen into his lap. The following series of examples illustrates how different brand owners have profited from these opportunities.

INSIGHT

Britney Spears and Pepsi

Britney Spears enjoys a $75 million exclusive soft-drink sponsorship with Pepsi, though was recently photographed with a bottle of Sunkist, a soft drink produced by rival manufacturer Cadbury-Schweppes.

This was not the first time that Spears had offended, having earlier been captured on film in Australia drinking Coca-Cola (thereby prompting several 'Oops . . . I did it again' headlines).

A Pepsi spokesman is reported to have confirmed that the pop-star had been spoken to in the 'strongest possible terms'. Britney Spears does, however, continue to front the Pepsi campaign.

Jamie Oliver and Sainsbury's

Celebrity TV chef Jamie Oliver earns £250 000 a year advertising the products of Sainsbury's. Marketers at Sainsbury's were no doubt less than happy to see photographs that appeared in *Heat* magazine of Oliver's wife Jules apparently leaving a branch of Waitrose laden with Waitrose-branded shopping bags.

The endorsement deal survived, with a Sainsbury's spokesman reported as claiming that (somewhat unconvincingly) Mrs Oliver had indeed been shopping at Sainsbury's but was simply recycling Waitrose carrier bags.

David Beckham and Adidas

David Beckham is the high profile face of Adidas, earning millions of pounds in relation to a boot endorsement deal. He was, however, recently photographed while on holiday wearing Nike trainers. Whilst Nike were quick to capitalise on this, explaining how it was delighted that the star found its shoes so comfortable, Adidas remained tight-lipped in public.

Beckham does nevertheless continue to be handsomely rewarded for promoting Adidas.

A pattern can be seen to emerge in relation to this type of opportunist ambush marketing. More often than not, it is the carelessness of an individual rights holder that creates the opportunity rather than any deliberate mischief on the part of the ambush marketer that is making capital out of the error.

It is particularly difficult to guard against this kind of activity, since the opportunity tends to arise as a result of a mistake rather than deliberate action, as the following example illustrates.

INSIGHT

Blackburn Rovers and McEwan's Lager

When Blackburn Rovers won the FA Carling Premiership in 1995, the football club's shirts featured the McEwan's Lager sponsorship logo.

Shortly after the final match at Anfield, Liverpool, a photograph appeared in various football magazines of Blackburn Rovers' goalkeeper Tim Flowers sitting in the dressing room still in his kit enjoying a well-deserved lager straight from the can.

This was, however, provided not by shirt sponsor McEwan's but by competition sponsor Carling. It was an opportunity that could not be missed and the following day's press advertising campaign carried the strapline 'Actually, I bet he drinks Carling Black Label'.

PARASITIC MARKETING

In contrast with opportunist marketing, parasitic marketing involves some form of deliberate action on the part of the ambush marketer relating to the event involved.

Whether this involves close physical exposure in the vicinity of the venue, or taking advantage of the wave of media publicity to create an association in the public eye that does not exist, this form of marketing keeps many creative professionals very busy.

Some of the forms of parasitic marketing include:

■ Becoming a TV broadcast sponsor and using in-broadcast promotions to gain association

■ 'Owning' former champions and using these personalities in advertising campaigns and product endorsements

■ Advertising in associated publications including fan guides and event programmes

■ Offering individual sponsorship to a team member for use in advertising campaigns

■ Advertising outside the venue using billboards, including mobile signage (which can also attract PR coverage)

INSIGHT

1994 Olympic Games, Lillehammer, Norway

There are many marketers who will recall the build-up to the 1994 Winter Olympics in Lillehammer, Norway.

Credit card marketer VISA, one of the official sponsors, broadcast TV advertisements that, in addition to prominently featuring the Olympic logo, highlighted the message that American Express cards were not accepted in the Olympic Village.

American Express was not a sponsor. Nevertheless, in response to VISA, it broadcast TV advertisements explaining that American Express cards were accepted throughout Norway and featured a tagline stating that American travellers did not need a 'visa' to go to Norway. This also happened to be the case (literally) so the campaign message was well targeted.

However, this double entendre left unanswered the question of whether viewers of the American Express advertisements mistakenly believed that American Express was a sponsor of the Olympic Games or was somehow affiliated with the Games.

The Olympic Games in 1996 probably attracted the most parasitic marketing activity of any modern Olympic Games and led to an urgent review by the International Olympic Committee (IOC) in the measures needed to combat ambush marketing.

Today, the IOC advises major rights holders in how to combat ambush marketing as it now enjoys some of the best anti-counterfeiting and counter-ambush marketing strategies in the world.

But it was not always that way ...

INSIGHT

1996 Olympic Games, Atlanta, US

The IOC has strict regulations relating to the use of the five Olympic rings on sports equipment and merchandise.

At the Olympic Games in Atlanta 1996, Nike set up its 'alternative' Olympic village near to the official sponsors' village where it paraded athletes with Nike endorsement deals, including one of the star athletes of the Olympic Games, basketball legend Michael Johnson.

Nike embarked on a high-profile poster campaign all over the city that was the talk of the Games. In fact many people believed that it was an integral, if not official part of the Olympics.

A similar style TV and poster campaign at football tournament Euro96 led to one in four people questioned to believe that Nike was an official sponsor.

Nike were not alone in adopting this technique. Sports brand Puma provided Jamaica's Merlene Ottey with Puma-branded earrings and Britain's Linford Christie with Puma-branded contact lenses. Ottey wore her earring on the track, whilst Christie's contact lenses attracted a huge amount of publicity at Olympic press conferences. These gimmicks side-stepped regulations as they involved a form of brand exposure that fell outside the regulations on equipment.

Nike is estimated to have spent £20 million on marketing and advertising in the run-up to the 1998 FIFA World Cup in France – a figure that is roughly equivalent to what official sponsor and supplier, Adidas, committed to over the same period.

Adidas has been involved with the World Cup finals since the 1970s as well as supplying the football officials' kit and the match ball, whilst Nike's interest in football is comparatively recent. In fact, it is best known for its involvement with basketball and athletics.

Nike showcased its sponsored teams and personalities at the 1998 World Cup in France at its football village on the outskirts of Paris. These 'personality' sponsorships were supported as before by poster and TV campaigns.

Surveys of these and other activities showed that Nike once again came away with higher awareness levels than many of the official sponsors of the FIFA World Cup which led some sponsors to question the perceived value of being an official sponsor in light of poor public prompted and unprompted awareness.

As the above case demonstrates, in the absence of any intellectual property infringement, the rights holder in a sports event can only police the geographical areas which it controls.

Opportunities for branding around venues at which events are being held can, therefore, legitimately be bought up by competitor marketers of official sponsors, with the rights holder being able to do little or nothing to prevent this.

INSIGHT

For example, at the time of the **All England Tennis Championships at Wimbledon**, Nike 'branded' Southfields tube station with Nike tennis regalia including giant posters of Nike-sponsored Pete Sampras and Carlos Moya. Given that tennis spectators alight at the tube station, Nike enjoyed substantial awareness and association with the tournament and yet was not a partner. The All England Tennis Club did not receive anything in connection with the campaign because it does not own or control the tube station.

At the opening match of the **1999 Rugby World Cup at the Millennium Stadium in Cardiff**, Nike unfurled a giant poster of Laurence Dallaglio (a Nike-sponsored player) which covered one side of a nearby NCP car park. Again, because the poster site was not controlled by the event organiser, no action could be taken against Nike.

And at the **1999 Heineken Cup Final at Lansdowne Road**, a large Guinness blimp was spotted floating in the vicinity of the stadium. The rope holding the blimp in position was traced to the stump of a tree in an enterprising local resident's garden, beyond the rights holder's control.

Advertising ambush

This is a common form of parasitic ambush marketing within the sports world. Any major sporting event generates massive media coverage and during this time all manner of marketers can purchase advertising which takes advantage of this media coverage *without* necessarily claiming any formal association with the event.

INSIGHT

For example, beer brand **Becks** wanted to trade off the heroic efforts of **David Beckham** whose last minute free kick for England against Greece ensured England's qualification for the FIFA World Cup Korea/Japan 2002™. The following day, and capturing the euphoria that surrounded Beckham, Becks took out advertisements in national newspapers featuring a Becks bottle with the number 7 etched into the foil top, captioned with the word 'Saviour'. Beckham is of course nicknamed 'Becks' and he wears the number 7 jersey.

Examples of this type of advertising ambush have also arisen in rugby union.

INSIGHT

For example, the **Bombardier** beer brand regularly runs advertisements in newspapers on the day of **England's Rugby Union internationals** which feature the national flag (in which there are no protectable IPRs to infringe) with some oblique reference to rugby, even though Carlsberg-Tetley is the official beer of England Rugby.

MINIMISING THE RISKS OF AMBUSH

Any sponsor who believes that the sponsorship fee payable under its contract should be the limit of its investment will see a fraction of the potential benefit from the sponsorship it has undertaken. As a rule of thumb, a similar amount to the sponsorship fee is normally required by way of marketing spend to invigorate the rights purchased.

At least some of this additional investment would be well spent on buying up advertising sites or broadcast airtime around the event in order to squeeze out potential ambush marketers by limiting opportunities to achieve non-authorised exposure.

In certain circumstances, a sponsor can achieve such an intimate association with the event that ambush marketing campaigns will be still-born. One such way is through the development of a composite logo which combines the event logo with that of the sponsor.

Whilst this normally only protects title sponsors of events, a composite logo may attract intellectual property protection through trademarking and/or copyright, and can come to represent the essential identity of the event.

Certain sponsors pre-empt ambush marketing by a blanket purchasing strategy.

INSIGHT

For example, Brazilian footballer **Ronaldo** has three commercial capacities – as an individual, a club player and as an international player. Nike has successfully managed to buy up these rights (see Chapter 5).

Not only does Nike supply the player's footwear, it also supplies kit to both Ronaldo's club, Inter Milan, and the Brazilian national team. In this way, any time Ronaldo is photographed playing football, he is branded head-to-toe in Nike footwear and apparel.

DEFENCES AGAINST AMBUSH MARKETING

Though a brand owner can adopt an anti-ambushing strategy, the majority of commercial partners will, however, reinforce this with a number of obligations on rights holders and their commercial representatives requiring them to take steps to prevent ambush marketing and, should such ambush marketing occur, put a stop to it with the minimum of fuss and expense.

Even though it is the official sponsor whose brand will be prejudiced by non-authorised activity, unless there is unlawful denigration of the sponsor's brand, the marketer in question is unlikely to have a direct legal remedy against the competitor marketer and will need to rely on the rights holder to police non-authorised commercial activity which trades off the reputation and good will of the event.

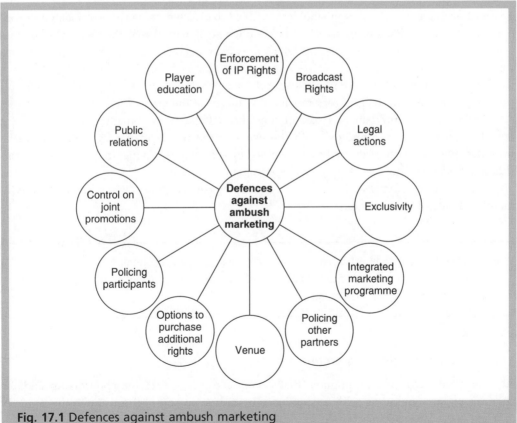

Fig. 17.1 Defences against ambush marketing

Some sponsorship contracts will contain a general obligation on the rights holder to 'prevent ambush marketing'.

However, this by itself is unlikely to be sufficient. Definitions of what constitutes ambush marketing can vary dramatically, and marketing best practice is to establish specific requirements in the contract to ensure that both rights holder and official sponsor know exactly where the obligations lie.

Anticipating and pre-empting all ambush marketing is practically impossible, though rights holders and brand owners can adopt several practices that will improve their chances of minimising the effects of ambush and vigilante marketing.

Trademarks and other IPRs

Primary among the steps necessary to protect against ambush marketing is to ensure that the rights holder has effectively protected, usually via trademark registration, the principal visual identifiers of the event, including logos and mascots (see Chapter 5). This alone may not, however, deliver full protection, and a wider strategy is necessary.

Broadcast Rights

The relationship between the rights holder and the broadcaster can vary enormously in sport. For example, the holders of football rights are often so powerful that they may well be in a position to negotiate numerous clauses which are advantageous to marketer sponsors in their contracts with broadcasters.

At the other end of the scale, smaller sports, such as darts, will be simply glad for the air time and exposure, and will be very much at the mercy of the broadcaster.

Although not a fundamental part of the fabric of the event, broadcast sponsorship is, nevertheless, intimately connected with the event in the minds of the viewers and official marketer sponsors of an event can be undermined by a third party taking up broadcast sponsorship at a fraction of the cost of an official sponsorship package.

Conversely, an official sponsor can reinforce its own event sponsorship with further investment in broadcast sponsorship.

INSIGHT

For example, beer brand **Carlsberg** registered very high sponsor recognition figures for soccer tournament **Euro 2000** – Carlsberg was both an event sponsor and also the broadcast sponsor of ITV's coverage.

Integrated marketing programme

An integrated marketing programme that covers every aspect of the sponsorship and the channels of communication with the audience both directly and indirectly with the property or event is the latest approach used to combat ambush marketing.

If properly negotiated with the rights holder, the sponsor can eliminate the risk of competitive advertising (see also Chapter 9).

Essentially, an integrated marketing programme is the association of sport or event sponsorship and broadcast coverage, normally through a third party or a joint venture.

An integrated marketing programme secures the TV rights and broadcast time, the signage, the sponsorship property or event and promotional opportunities in a single integrated package. For example, most PGA golf tournaments use this system of packaging sponsorships.

Exclusivity

One of the most important issues in contracts between the brand owner and the rights holder is exclusivity in relation to the sponsor's products or services.

All multi-sponsor commercial programmes depend on the definition of 'brand sector'.

Briefly, each commercial partner will be allocated a brand sector definition in its contract. That partner will have *exclusive rights of association* with the event in relation to the products and/or services covered by that definition.

It is important that the definition is clear, to prevent misunderstandings whereby a rights holder may engage a brand owner whose business somehow impinges on that of existing sponsors and partners.

One approach involves the sponsor scheduling a list of all competitive brand owners to the agreement itself.

Whilst this has a certain appeal, it is unwieldy; other businesses may break into the market during the period of the contract, businesses may merge to form competitors and conglomerates may extend into the protected area.

Instead, the brand sector should be defined by reference to products and/or services.

Ideally, a sponsor should look for as wide a brand sector definition as is reasonable (taking care not to cut across principles of competition law by closing off too large a market), and allow for the addition of any other related areas which the marketer reasonably believes may prejudice its core business.

INSIGHT

For example, a fizzy cola brand may seek to exclude related categories such as squashes, cordials, juices and mineral waters which are all viable alternative products to the sponsor brand.

Once this brand sector definition is clear, both rights holder and official sponsor will be aware of the extent to which the rights holder will be obliged to prevent unauthorised association with the event by businesses acting in this sector.

Exclusivity Action Plan:

- The rights holder should undertake a rights audit to check what is available for exploitation
- The rights holder should then determine how rights may be bundled into sponsor packages, and how many of such packages the event can support

▪ Standard form contracts should be developed, each offering exclusivity to the relevant sponsor in a particular brand sector

▪ If necessary, a trademark registration programme to protect the event logos and other intellectual property in the classes covering the sponsor's products and/or services should be undertaken

Venue

As indicated above, a lot of ambush marketing activity focuses on the venue and the area around it. Measures to counter ambush marketing activity can, however, be taken even before the event venue has been chosen.

INSIGHT

For example, stung by successful ambush marketing campaigns mounted in connection with, amongst other events, the Euro96 European Football Championships in England, UEFA's then commercial agents ISL introduced conditions into the tendering process for future events. These conditions required host cities to secure control of advertising sites located near stadia and in high profile areas of the city, and to make these available to official partners of the event.

An increasingly difficult issue when selecting venues for major events is stadium naming rights.

If the owner of a stadium (more often than not a club or team) grants its own official sponsor the rights to include a brand name in the stadium's title, the organisers of international events face a problem.

Do those event organisers risk holding matches in a stadium that at worst may be named after a competitor of an official event sponsor, or at best may provide the party enjoying naming rights with an association with the event for which it has not paid? Indeed, certain stadium naming rights deals in Germany have been postponed or suspended until after the 2006 World Cup to allow FIFA to present its commercial partners with a 'clean' stadium (free of branding) as demanded by the tournament rules.

The most important tool in protecting the official sponsor is the sponsorship contract with the event organiser. While a rights holder will try and resist obligations which are owed to owners in respect of brand protection, an official marketer sponsor would argue that the rights holder provides the only means of defence against an ambush marketing campaign.

Certain key clauses in a contract will establish the extent to which ambush marketing protection can be procured for a sponsor from the rights holder.

Legal remedies

A prudent official sponsor will also require the rights holder to enforce those legal remedies available to combat unauthorised association with events.

All major events have at the centre of their commercial programme some sort of event logo or emblem.

The official sponsor will need contractual assurances that the logo is properly registered as a trademark in the relevant classes for that sponsor's products and/or services, and in those territories in which the sponsor is active (see Chapter 5).

Once assurances to this effect have been given, the marketer will require the rights holder diligently to pursue any infringement and use the full might of trademark law against unauthorised use. However, as discussed in Chapter 11, the **Arsenal-v-Reid case** has put a question mark across the enforceability of registered trademarks.

A further legal remedy which has been employed in the past to protect parties enjoying official status has been the tort of passing off. The law of passing off is intended (amongst other things) to prevent consumers being misled into believing that goods or businesses are those of someone else. For further discussion on passing off, see Chapter 5.

Options to purchase 'extra' rights

The rights holder will offer a precise inventory of rights to the official sponsor and will be expected to control and deliver those rights. There are, however, certain peripheral rights connected with the event or property which may or may not be within the gift of the rights holder.

Obviously, the more that the rights holder can offer the official sponsor, the better the official sponsor will be protected should it choose to take up the full complement of rights.

These additional rights can include any of the following:

1. Option to purchase external billboard space – the rights holder may be in a position to secure preferential rates for official sponsors with the owners of billboards outside the stadia. Purchase of these may well be a useful defensive move to combat ambush marketing around the venue.

2. The option to engage players on individual endorsement deals – any marketer sponsor buying into an event or a team will have only limited rights relating to the participants. This is because participants on the whole jealously guard their individual image rights and their ability to do commercial deals on their own behalf. If, however, a team has written into a player contract provisions regarding support of official sponsors, the team sponsor may wish to take advantage of initial rights of negotiation with players to secure individual endorsement deals to complement and reinforce the team sponsorship (as seen in the Nike/Ronaldo arrangements, above).

3. Broadcast sponsorship (see above). The 'break bumpers' – short promotional trailers which top and tail each advertising break – are normally the preserve of the broadcaster and are sold almost as premium rate advertising. The rights holder should, however, strive to control those break bumpers and secure at least a first option of negotiation for its event sponsor to purchase such broadcast sponsorship.

Policing other commercial partners

Events can be ambushed from the inside, e.g. one brand owner who is part of a multi-sponsor structure claims and exploits rights beyond those which it has been granted.

Any official partner in this type of structure should look to the rights holder to ensure that all co-sponsors operate strictly within the ambit of the rights that they have been granted, and that all commercial partners of the event will enjoy similar rights and owe similar obligations in respect of the event.

INSIGHT

Snickers and Euro96

Food giant Mars enjoyed official sponsor status of the European Football Championships in England in 1996 under its Snickers brand.

However, not content with achieving the media exposure guaranteed in its official sponsorship package, the company also arranged for Mars-branded novelty bowler hats to be handed out to fans attending matches. The extra exposure this achieved in close-ups of the crowd on TV saw Mars 'ambushing' an event with which Snickers had already had an official association, thereby cannibalising any media value for the Snickers brand!

Policing participants

As mentioned above unless a side-deal has been done, an event or team marketer sponsor will not enjoy any rights to players as individuals. It is therefore important that the rights holder (be it an event organiser or team) passes contractual obligations regarding anti-ambush marketing down to its players.

Similarly, in relation to sponsorship of an event, the event organiser will be expected to police the commercial messages displayed by the participating team. In practice, a compromise is reached.

POINT OF LAW

For example, Liverpool FC's club sponsor is **Carlsberg**, who enjoy shirt branding and perimeter board advertising at domestic matches. When the club plays in the UEFA Champions League, it is obliged by the competition regulations to provide a 'clean stadium' to allow the Champions League sponsors (which include alcohol brand Amstel) exclusive rights of branding within the stadium. The club is, however, permitted by those regulations to retain Carlsberg branding on its shirts, that area of exclusivity being carved out of UEFA's contracts with its sponsors.

One area which can create difficulties involves players with a boot sponsor which is different to that of the team's kit supplier. Normally, an uneasy peace is brokered with neither technical marketer over-using the player.

Occasionally, however, incidents can flare up, as this very early example of ambush marketing illustrates.

> **POINT OF LAW**
>
> During the 1974 World Cup, Dutch players **Johan Cruyff** and **Johan Neeskens** were contracted to boot supplier **Puma**. The KNVB (The Dutch FA) had a kit deal with Adidas, and on the eve of the 1974 World Cup final against West Germany, Cruyff and Neeskens approached Adidas and demanded extra money to appear in the Adidas strip, claiming that this compromised their Puma deal.
>
> When Adidas refused, explaining that its deal was with the Dutch team, Cruyff and Neeskens each tore off one of the three distinctive Adidas stripes from his shirt.

Since then kit brand owners have included in their sponsorship contracts an obligation on the rights holder to ensure that players do not damage, deface or obscure any of the branding on the kit.

Control on joint promotions

A joint promotion can allow a brand owner which has no formal association with an event to acquire one through a relationship with an official sponsor.

> **POINT OF LAW**
>
> For example, a snacks supplier acquires official status through a contract with an event organiser.
>
> This official partner strikes a distribution deal with a third party (supermarket), which has no official connection with the event.
>
> The point-of-sale materials used in the joint promotion suggest that the supermarket in question does, in fact, have an association with the event.
>
> This may be all the more embarrassing if the rights holder has done a separate deal with a different supermarket relating to official status within that brand sector.
>
> Even if this is not the case, other official sponsors may be dismayed that a third party seems to be acquiring rights for nothing, further cluttering the marketplace with association with the event brand.

To combat this, the sponsor should seek to *prevent* joint promotions proposed by other co-sponsors or at least have a right of approval over any that are contemplated.

Player education

Participants in a team or event must be made to understand that their activities can have a profound impact on the value of the rights which the rights holder is selling.

Player education programmes should be undertaken to remind participants of the importance of observing the requirements of club or event sponsorship agreements, not least to prevent the kind of accidental mistakes which allow for opportunist marketing initiatives as described above.

A 'good-boy' bonus may help cut down on instances whereby opportunist marketing occasions arise. If a sponsored player stands to receive an annual payment based on non-infringement of exclusivity, that player may well take more care to avoid embarrassing photographs with competitor products.

Psychologically, the culture of reward, rather than seeking a refund for a breach, is likely to be more effective.

As discussed in Chapter 5, sports clubs should consider separate image rights contracts for their players or at least include a section in the player contract which deals specifically with image rights.

Image rights contracts help to establish the extent to which the club may use the player's image in its own commercial activity, limiting the extent to which the player can promote products or services competitive with those of the club's official sponsor, and requiring the player to provide a specified amount of support for the central commercial programme.

Public relations

With the best will in the world, even the most vigilant rights holder will not be able to prevent all instances of ambush marketing.

Mistakes will be made and competitors will find other new ways of associating their product or service with a high profile event or property.

Once the horse has bolted, however, rather than seeking to lock the stable door, the aggrieved official sponsor may be better organising strategy for recapturing the horse.

Public relations management at a time of ambush marketing is crucial. It is highly likely that the sponsor's marketing team will be more experienced in brand management than those of the event organiser, and the marketer should look to establish the fact in the contract that any ambush marketing issues will be handled by its own department.

CHECKLIST

■   Have you alerted the appropriate anti-counterfeiting authorities?

■   Do you have a rapid response PR strategy in respect of instances of opportunist marketing?

■   Do you have full control of signage, pitch branding, concessions, sampling space and other branding sites within the venue?

■   What kind of control can you exercise outside the venue, through the purchase of billboard and related advertising?

■   Have you developed and protected a composite logo?

■   Do your sponsorship contracts clearly define your obligations concerning prevention of ambush marketing?

- Are you clear on brand sector definitions?

- Have you protected your event logo properly?

- What extra rights can you offer your sponsor by way of broadcast advertising and sponsorship opportunities?

- To what extent can you control the commercial activity of participants in your event?

- Do you properly police the activities of all your commercial partners?

A rights holder who follows most of these check points will have substantially reduced the risk to ambush or vigilante marketing.

USEFUL SOURCES OF INFORMATION

Regulatory authorities

Advertising Standards Authority	www.asa.org.uk
Broadcast Advertising Clearance Centre	www.bacc.org.uk
Committee of Advertising Practice	www.cap.org.uk
Independent Television Commission	www.itc.org.uk
Press Complaints Commission	www.pcc.org.uk
Radio Authority	www.radioauthority.org.uk
Radio Advertising Bureau	www.rab.co.uk

Legal sites

Marketing law	www.marketinglaw.co.uk
Lawyers	www.adlaw.com
Department for Culture, Media and Sport	www.culture.gov.uk
Recent Acts of Parliament	www.hmso.gov.uk/acts
Patent Office and Trade Marks Registry	www.patent.gov.uk
Data Protection Information	www.dataprotection.gov.uk
Fair Trading Magazine	www.oft.gov.uk
European law portal	www.europa.eu.int
Berwin Leighton Paisner	www.berwinleightonpaisner.com
Simkins Partnership	www.simkins.com
The European Commission	www.cec.org.uk
Couchman Harrington & Associates	www.chass.co.uk
Hammond Suddards Edge	www.hammondse.com
Rawlison Butler	www.rawlisonbutler.com

Trade organisations

Advertising Association	www.adassoc.org.uk
Direct Marketing Association	www.dma.org.uk
Direct Selling Association	www.dsa.org.uk
Incorporated Society of British Advertisers	www.isba.org.uk
Institute of Practitioners in Advertising	www.ipa.co.uk
Institute of Sales Promotion	www.isp.org.uk
International Advertising Association	www.iaaglobal.org
Promotion Marketing Association	www.pmalink.org
Institute of Public Relations	www.ipr.org.uk
Chartered Institute of Marketing	www.cim.co.uk
Newspaper Society	www.newspapersoc.org.uk
World Intellectual Property Organisation	www.wipo.org
Marketing Society	www.marketing-society.org.uk
Association of Professional Political Consultants	www.appc.org.uk
European Advertising Lawyers Association	www.eala.net
Promotion Marketing Association	www.pmalink.org

Marketing news

Campaign	www.campaignlive.com
Marketing Week	www.marketingweek.co.uk
Revolution	www.revolution.haynet.com
Marketing magazines	www.mad.co.uk
Connected in Marketing	www.connectedinmarketing.com
Brand Republic	www.brandrepublic.com
SportBusiness	www.sportbusiness.com

Other sites

Account Planning Group	www.apg.org.uk
Advertising Information Group	www.aig.org
Food Advertising Unit	www.fau.org.uk
gamesbiz.net	www.gamesbiz.net
Copyright Promotions Licensing Group	www.cplg.com

Essential Law for Marketers Matrix

Cross Reference Chapters (rows) × Chapter Heading (columns, 2–17)

Cross Reference Chapter	2	3	4	5	6	7	8	9	10	11	12	13	14	15	16	17
2: Making Agreements		×	×	×						×						
3: Making Statements	×		×		×	×	×			×				×	×	
4: Liability for Defective Products	×	×				×				×					×	
5: Intellectual Property Rights	×	×					×			×	×	×		×	×	×
6: Copyright				×						×	×	×			×	×
7: Data Protection													×	×	×	
8: Defamation		×			×	×		×						×	×	
9: Advertising & Labelling	×	×	×	×	×	×	×		×					×	×	×
10: Broadcasting						×	×	×				×			×	×
11: Licensing & Merchandising	×			×	×											
12: Sponsorship & Hospitality						×			×	×			×			×
13: Promotions & Incentives			×	×	×	×				×					×	×
14: Lobbying							×		×			×				
15: Cyber Marketing				×		×	×					×				
16: Niche Marketing			×	×				×	×	×		×		×		
17: Ambush Marketing	×			×	×			×		×	×					

INDEX

Marketing titles from BH

Student list

Creating Powerful Brands (second edition), Leslie de Chernatony and Malcolm McDonald
Direct Marketing in Practice, Brian Thomas and Matthew Housden
eMarketing eXcellence, PR Smith and Dave Chaffey
Fashion Marketing, Margaret Bruce and Tony Hines
Innovation in Marketing, Peter Doyle and Susan Bridgewater
Internal Marketing, Pervaiz Ahmed and Mohammed Rafiq
International Marketing (third edition), Stanley J Paliwoda and Michael J Thomas
Integrated Marketing Communications, Tony Yeshin
Key Customers, Malcolm McDonald, Beth Rogers, Diana Woodburn
Marketing Briefs, Sally Dibb and Lyndon Simkin
Marketing in Travel and Tourism (third edition), Victor TC Middleton with Jackie R Clarke
Marketing Plans (fifth edition), Malcolm McDonald
Marketing: the One Semester Introduction, Geoff Lancaster and Paul Reynolds
Market-Led Strategic Change (third edition), Nigel Piercy
Relationship Marketing for Competitive Advantage, Adrian Payne, Martin Christopher, Moria Clark and Helen Peck
Relationship Marketing: Strategy & Implementation, Helen Peck, Adrian Payne, Martin Christopher and Moira Clark
Strategic Marketing Management (second edition), Richard MS Wilson and Colin Gilligan
Strategic Marketing: Planning and Control (second edition), Graeme Drummond and John Ensor
Successful Marketing Communications, Cathy Ace
Tales from the Market Place, Nigel Piercy
The CIM Handbook of Export Marketing, Chris Noonan
The Fundamentals of Advertising (second edition), John Wilmshurst, Adrian Mackay

Forthcoming

Marketing Logistics (second edition), Martin Christopher, Helen Peck
Marketing Research for Managers (third edition), Sunny Crouch and Matthew Housden
Marketing Strategy (third edition), Paul Fifield
New Marketing, Malcolm McDonald and Hugh Wilson
Political Marketing, Phil Harris and Dominic Wring
Relationship Marketing (second edition), Martin Christopher, Adrian Payne and David Ballantyne
The Fundamentals and Practice of Marketing (fourth edition), John Wilmshurst and Adrian Mackay
The Marketing Book (fifth edition), Michael J Baker (ed.)
Total Relationship Marketing (second edition), Evert Gummesson

Professional list

Cause Related Marketing, Sue Adkins
Creating Value, Shiv S Mathur, Alfred Kenyon
Cybermarketing (second edition), Pauline Bickerton and Matthew Bickerton
Cyberstrategy, Pauline Bickerton, Matthew Bickerton and Kate Simpson-Holley
Direct Marketing in Practice, Brian Thomas and Matthew Housden
e-Business, James Matthewson
Effective Promotional Practice for eBusiness, Cathy Ace
Essential Law for Marketers, Ardi Kolah
Excellence in Advertising (second edition), Leslie Butterfield
Fashion Marketing, Margaret Bruce and Tony Hines
Financial Services and the Multimedia Revolution, Paul Lucas, Rachel Kinniburgh, Donna Terp
From Brand Vision to Brand Evaluation, Leslie de Chernatony
Internal Marketing, Pervaiz Ahmed and Mohammed Rafiq
Marketing Made Simple, Geoff Lancaster and Paul Reynolds
Marketing Professional Services, Michael Roe
Marketing Strategy (second edition), Paul Fifield
Market-Led Strategic Change (third edition), Nigel Piercy
The Channel Advantage, Lawrence Friedman, Tim Furey
The CIM Handbook of Export Marketing, Chris Noonan
The Committed Enterprise, Hugh Davidson
The Fundamentals of Corporate Communications, Richard Dolphin
The Marketing Plan in Colour, Malcolm McDonald, Peter Morris

Forthcoming

Go to Market Strategy, Lawrence Friedman
Marketing Logistics (second edition), Martin Christopher, Helen Peck
Marketing Research for Managers (third edition), Sunny Crouch and Matthew Housden
Marketing Strategy (third edition), Paul Fifield
New Marketing, Malcolm McDonald and Hugh Wilson
Political Marketing, Phil Harris and Dominic Wring

For more information on all these titles, as well as the ability to buy online, please visit **www.bh.com/marketing**.